OUT OF THE SKY
A History of Airborne Warfare

OUT OF THE SKY

A History of Airborne Warfare

Michael Hickey

Charles Scribner's Sons
New York

1 3 5 7 9 11 13 15 17 19   I/C   20 18 16 14 12 10 8 6 4 2

Printed in Great Britain
Library of Congress Catalog Card Number 79–84860
SBN 0–684–16062–5

Contents

	Acknowledgments	6–7
	List of Maps	8
	Introduction	9
ONE	Airborne	13
TWO	The Observer Aloft	24
THREE	The Eyes of the Army	36
FOUR	First Blood	43
FIVE	The German High Tide: Crete	57
SIX	The Allied Answer: 1940–42	74
SEVEN	The Break-in: Sicily and Normandy	98
EIGHT	Casting the Net: Airborne Operations Worldwide, 1942–43	126
NINE	The Final Throw: Arnhem, the Ardennes and the Rhine	150
TEN	Slack Water: the Post-War Years	183
ELEVEN	The Third Dimension	192
TWELVE	Air Cavalry	206
THIRTEEN	Vietnam 1: The Proving Ground	218
FOURTEEN	Vietnam 2: Into Battle	232
FIFTEEN	Vietnam 3: Climax	245
SIXTEEN	The State of the Game	260
	Appendix: Table of Equivalent Ranks	273
	Select Bibliography	274
	Miscellaneous Sources	276
	Index	278

Acknowledgments

I owe much to veterans of the campaigns depicted within. Brigadier George Chatterton, Major-General Tony Dyball, Major John Howard and Colonel John Waddy have all patiently answered my questions and allowed me to make use of their personal accounts; Lieutenant-Colonel Tony FitzGerald's impeccably researched annals of the Joint Experimental Helicopter Unit not only refreshed but corrected my own defective memories; the late Lieutenant-Colonel Len Williams gave me the run of the archives at the Museum of Army Flying, Middle Wallop, and unearthed much original material; Major Mike McRitchie introduced me to the Airborne Forces' Museum at Aldershot and to its wealth of unpublished archives; Major Gordon Murray produced much information on the aerial delivery of equipment from aircraft and on Air Despatch; Major Peter Verney kindly allowed me access to the papers of his father, the late Major-General G. L. Verney DSO, MVO. A number of officers of the Israeli Defence Forces personally described their parts in the wars of 1967 and 1973 and Andrew and Mary-Jane Duncan conducted me on a lightning battlefield tour of the Golan Heights, regaling me with a memorable *al fresco* meal at Nimrod, in the shadow of Mount Hermon. Mr Richard Tierney, editor of the *US Army Aviation Digest*, not only sent me a mass of historical material but also a generous selection of photographs, some of which appear in this book; this invaluable contribution is largely due to the enthusiastic co-operation of Lieutenant-Colonel Richard Eccles, A.A.C., the British Liaison Officer at Fort Rucker. Major Adriaan Van Vliet of the Netherlands Army Historical Section provided much information on operations in Holland in 1940 and kindly allowed me to study the unpublished papers of the late Colonel Theodor Boeree who devoted many years' study to an examination of the fight at Arnhem. I gratefully acknowledge the encouragement received, over many years, from Dr Noble Frankland, Director General of the Imperial War Museum, and the help of his staff – particularly that of the museum's photographic department. The staffs of the Public Record Office at Chancery Lane (and latterly at Kew) have never failed to meet my requests for outlandish source material. Brigadier Shelford Bidwell, sometime editor of the Journal of the Royal United Services Institute, and his assistant Jenny Shaw have endured my frequent visits for five years and have given much help. Eversley Belfield of the University of Southampton – himself a Second World War Air OP pilot and co-author with the late Major-General Parham of the Air OP history – allowed me to read the draft of a major article on this subject with highly beneficial effect to Chapters 2 and 3. My friends in the Department of War Studies at King's College London have listened to my expositions of much of the material used in this book, which incorporates many of their suggestions; Professors Laurence Martin, Bryan Ranft, Dr Wolf Mendl, Mr Brian Bond and my fellow post-graduate students have all shown much tolerance and good will. Warrant Officer Keith Teasdale and Flight Sergeant Peter Keane saw to it that I gained personal experience of parachuting with minimal distress by twice supervising my descents into the English Channel. Michael Stephenson, at Mills & Boon, presided calmly over the gestation of the work; Inge Richards not only typed the script but provided invaluable information on the operations in Holland, where she resided throughout the Second World War. Mary Lewis proved more than equal to the job of coping with my eccentric indexing. It would have been impossible to research and write this book without the constant encouragement of my wife, to whom it is dedicated with much love.

Brize Norton – Winchester – 1979.

List of Maps

1   Norway: 'Weserübung' Airmobile Operations   44
2   'Fall Gelb': Airmobile Operations against Holland   49
3   'Fall Gelb': Airmobile Operations against Belgium   54
4   The Assault on Crete   64
5   'Overlord' – The Airborne Plan   111
6   'Overlord' – 6th Airborne Divisional Area   117
7   US Airborne Operations in 'Overlord'   122
8   Vyazma, 1942 – The First Major Soviet Airmobile Operation   128
9   Russian Airborne Operations in the Dnieper Loop, September 1943   130
10   Burma and the 1944 Chindit Expedition   137
11   Airborne Assault at Tagaytay, 1945   142
12   'The Airborne Carpet' Market Garden   157
13   Operation 'Varsity' – The Rhine Crossing   179
14   The Assault on Port Said, 1956   190
15   South Vietnam – The Seat of War   224
16   Bong Son – 1st Cavalry in Vertical Envelopment   237
17   Khe Sanh – The Battlefield   250

Introduction

On 21 November 1783 François Pilâtre de Rozier and the Marquis d'Arlandes became the first men to ascend in free flight. They achieved this with a hot-air balloon, in which they drifted to and fro over Paris for 25 minutes. Less than a fortnight later two more intrepid Frenchmen, Jacques Charles and Ainé Robert, used a hydrogen balloon for a longer flight, cheered on by a delirious crowd of nearly half a million Parisians as they rose from the Tuileries gardens to land 27 miles away at Nesles.

Amidst the excitement attending these early flights, their military significance passed almost unnoticed; but one spectator, the American scholar-scientist and statesman Benjamin Franklin, had the vision and wit to put it down on paper. 'Five thousand balloons, capable of raising two men each, could not cost more than five ships of the line,' he wrote in January 1784. 'And where is the Prince who can so afford to cover his country with troops for its defense, as that ten thousand men descending from the clouds might not in many places do an infinite deal of mischief before a force could be brought together to repel them?'

It would be a century and a half before this dream became a practicable operation of war but the military possibilities of using a tethered balloon as an observation post were quickly recognized. Within ten years Revolutionary France was fighting for survival against the ancient monarchies of Europe. On 25 June 1794 the Duke of Coburg and 50,000 Austrians confidently attacked the French General Jourdan at Fleurus, in Flanders. The French repulsed their opponents and drove them off the field. Over the French lines Capitaine Jean-Marie-Joseph Coutelle observed the enemy from his tethered balloon. Military aviation had embarked on its eventful career.

Coutelle in his perilous basket and the US Air Cavalry in Vietnam seem worlds apart, but they are connected by a thread which constitutes the subject of this book – the use of the air to provide battlefield mobility for armies. This includes not only the deployment of formed bodies of fighting men but also of individuals: artillery observers, liaison officers, commanders and their staffs. It includes the carriage of weapons – whether in the form of underslung artillery pieces or as an integral part of the aerial vehicle carrying them – and of ammunition, fuel and supplies. Battle casualties, whose chances of survival would otherwise be poor, can now be carried rapidly to the rear areas for life-saving surgical attention. All this movement, if carried out in aerial vehicles, can be achieved regardless of the nature of the terrain, undetected by the enemy, and in a fraction of the time required by ground vehicles.

The invention and development of the helicopter in the last 30 years has made it possible for armies to be truly air-mobile. A reconnaissance pilot, briefed for his mission by a combat commander in the thick of the battle, can be airborne in his helicopter within minutes and will be able to report by radio throughout his flight. The passage of tactical information is thus far speedier than it was, say, in 1945. The same pilot can perform a wide range of other roles during the same sortie. He can gather information specifically required by the ground commander; he can also maintain continuous observation, or surveillance, on areas in which the enemy is known or thought to be. If necessary he can use cameras and other sensors to confirm visual evidence. Artillery fire can be controlled, or airstrikes by friendly ground attack aircraft directed accurately to their targets. When radio communications are bad the helicopter can be used as an elevated radio aerial to improve transmission. Sections and platoons of infantry can be moved around the battle area in larger helicopters; their heavy support weapons such as light artillery pieces and mortars, and their combat transport, can be slung underneath helicopters and redeployed across any natural obstacle. It is now practicable to install complete guided-weapons systems onto helicopters, endowing them with tremendous fire power and posing a mortal threat to the badly handled tank.

Until practical helicopters capable of meeting these requirements were developed, battlefield airmobility had to be achieved with the means available at the time. From Fleurus to Mons this meant lighter-than-air vehicles for observers. Between 1914 and 1918 huge strides were made in the development of fixed wing powered aircraft which displaced the balloon and airship as observation, air combat and bombardment vehicles, and led to the construction of large bomber aircraft suited for eventual modification into passenger transports. In pace with the development of the warplane came that of the parachute, soon recognized as a feasible (if hazardous) way of deploying infantry to the point on the ground where a tactical decision was to be sought.

The Second World War was to see the development of full-scale airborne warfare in which the techniques of parachuting men and equipment and of landing them by glider were brought to a high degree of achievement. By 1945, progress made in the field of anti-aircraft weaponry was on the point of driving transport aircraft and gliders from the skies. The final operation of classical airborne warfare was that of the Rhine crossing.

The helicopter, still in its infancy when Japan surrendered in August 1945, underwent a process of development during the next 25 years as remarkable as that of the fixed-wing aeroplane during the preceding quarter-century. Whereas the parachute and glider had provided only a one-way journey, the helicopter could re-deploy troops having once carried them to the battle. Total air mobility was now a reality.

The planning and execution of airborne and airmobile operations, conducted as they are in three dimensions, poses the same sort of demands as those faced by the composer, conductor and performers of an opera of Wagnerian proportions. The composer, like the operational planner, can only visualize his monster work; sitting at his piano and desk he must transfer his vision to sheets of blank music staves. Until the huge resources necessary for performance are brought together for the dress rehearsal – when it is far too late for major alterations – he will not know exactly how the work will look and sound; from there on to the first performance it is in the hands of the musical director, stage manager, chorus-master, conductor and the actual performers. The audience will be unaware of the elaborate administrative effort required to stage an opera on the scale, say, of 'Gotterdämmerung'. They will only see and hear what takes place on the great stage. The conductor must rely on the professional competence of singers, orchestral players and a host of backstage technicians. After the curtain rises he alone can guarantee success, which he achieves through his own skill, intuition and total identification with the performance. As for the conductor, so it is for the commander of an airmobile force; unless his interpretation and execution are in accord with the concept of the high command, the training of the performers adequate for their demanding task, or the logistics capable of sustaining the operation, it will falter and fail.

CHAPTER ONE

Airborne

In the summer of 1917 Gen. 'Black Jack' Pershing and his staff crossed to Europe as the vanguard of the United States expeditionary force which was still frantically mobilizing and training for the European war into which President Wilson had at last been drawn. It was more than a year before Pershing's First Army fought its first independent major battle, playing a key role in the Franco-American victory of St Mihiel in September 1918; the intervening months were to be spent in careful and progressive familiarization with a type of warfare totally new to the US Army. At times this initiation was full-blooded, as when some of the First Army's divisions were flung in piecemeal to stem the great German offensives of the spring and early summer of 1918. Although after St Mihiel Pershing's eyes were fixed on the glittering prizes of Metz, Belfort and Luneville, they were not to be his; the bloody battle of the Argonne was to be the final great test for his troops.

On the staff of the First Army, however, was an officer who believed that Metz could, and should, be taken by American troops, and in a most unusual way. Col. William 'Billy' Mitchell, the 39-year-old head of air operations, was a man destined to be a major prophet of aerial warfare in the years following the Armistice. His plan for the capture of Metz was startling in its originality: no less than the delivery of 12,000 men by parachute behind the German lines. The airlift was to be provided by 60 squadrons of Handley Page bombers, already entering service with Trenchard's Independent Air Force; each aircraft would carry ten paratroops and two medium machine guns. A whole infantry division was to form the striking force. The monstrous burden of converting this vision into a workable plan fell on Mitchell's assistant, Maj. Lewis Brereton. After making his appreciation of the situation he felt obliged to tell Mitchell that his brainwave was, to say the least, impracticable. Neither aircraft nor parachutes were available in the quantities demanded, nor had it occurred to Mitchell that even the cream of Pershing's army might not enthuse at the prospects of glory held out to them. The proposed operation would make impossible demands on the army communications system; no organization existed capable of controlling the assembly and transit of such a force of aircraft; nobody had given thought to the provision of rations and ammunition to the assault troops or to their assembly and tactical handling once delivered onto the objective.

Pershing took one look at the plan and rejected it. Mitchell went on, after the war, to become a brigadier-general, assistant chief of the US Army Air Corps, and a ceaseless advocate of air power wielded by an independent air force. Waging his campaign with energy and considerable venom he eventually overstepped the mark and accused the US Navy and War Departments of 'incompetence, criminal negligence and almost treasonable administration of the national defence'. Following the inevitable court martial he resigned in 1926 to continue his crusade outside the service and died a bitter and frustrated man in 1936.

Mitchell had, however, seen the same vision as fellow countryman Benjamin Franklin. The trouble was that the technology necessary to make it work was simply not available; and even if it had been, the military world – which had received a number of nasty shocks during the war years through such innovations as the submarine and the tank – was not mentally prepared for the idea of airborne warfare. To bring off such radical changes in military science it is essential that new ideas fall on fertile ground and that the requisite military technology is available to carry them through.

The years following the 1918 Armistice brought a world-wide revulsion against the follies and horrors of war and a waning of intellectual vigour in military circles. This was not an auspicious period for the innovator, especially in the field of aerial or airborne warfare. Mitchell had, however, planted a few seeds. Modest trials were carried out in the early 1920s by the US Army at Wright Field in which infantrymen and their weapons were dropped by parachute; the Italians actually led the world in this direction by 1930, having perfected the 'Salvatore' static-line parachute with which a unit of paratroops was successfully dropped on exercises in November 1927. There was a set-back in 1928 when Gen. Guidoni, the head of the new force, plunged to his death after a parachute malfunction, but by the late 1930s the Italians had formed several parachute battalions. They had also studied the techniques of using parachutes for logistic re-supply and used them in 1928 to re-victual the stranded crew of the airship *Italia* in the Arctic.

The third technique of airborne warfare, that of air-landing men and equipment, was under tentative development in a number of countries during the 1920s. The RAF used Vickers Vernon transports in Iraq to carry whole companies of infantry, 11 men to an aircraft, in order to subdue dissident tribesmen. The commanding officer of one of the air-transport units, No. 45 Squadron RAF, was Squadron Leader Arthur Harris. In the Second World War, as the autocratic and single-minded chief of Bomber Command, his insistence on absolute priority of aircraft production for the strategic bomber offensive would exercise a markedly adverse effect on the formation and operation of British airborne forces.

As will be seen in this narrative, strongminded individuals were to make their mark for good and ill in the evolution of airmobile warfare. One, destined to make an outstanding contribution, came to the fore during the US Army manoeuvres of 1932; Capt. George C. Kenney of the US Army Air Corps turned a blind eye to his exercise instructions and airlanded a unit of infantry at a critical moment, to inflict an impartially decisive defeat on 'enemy' and umpires alike.

The real cradle of airborne warfare, however, was Russia. Seeking any method of welding the huge population into a disciplined and conformal whole, the Soviet leaders instituted a vast scheme of nation-wide sporting activities. One of these was parachuting. All over the USSR associations were formed as part of the Voluntary Society for Aid to the Air Force and Chemical Defence, or *Osoaviakhim*. Parachute training towers sprouted in every major town and civilians of both sexes were enrolled in thousands. Parachute units appeared on Red Army manoeuvres as early as 1930 when small 'intruder' parties were dropped behind enemy lines, and wide publicity was given to the 'capture' of a corps commander by one such group.

In 1935 cinema audiences world-wide were treated to the spectacle of a battalion-sized Red Army parachute descent, and during the 1936 autumn manoeuvres of the Moscow Military District a distinguished invited audience of military observers and attachés watched a complete brigade drop from ANT6 transport aircraft to seize river crossings in order to deny them to a retiring 'enemy' formation. The troops were equipped with a Russian copy of the American Irving aircrew parachute. As no static line was incorporated, the jumper opened the canopy by pulling the ripcord himself. Reserve parachutes were carried, and photographs of these early Russian massed drops show that many of the men prudently deployed both their canopies. Ciné film of the actual departure from the four-engined Antonov monoplane shows the parachutists swarming out of a hatch onto the upper surface of the wing at the bidding of a jump-master standing in the open forward gun turret, then sliding off into space. The descents observed by the Western attachés were from about 3000 feet. Maj.-Gen. Archibald Wavell, one of the British observers, was impressed by the spectacle but noted that it was $1\frac{1}{2}$ hours before the brigade was formed up and ready to fight, and that the troops were only lightly armed, with no motor transport. (During the 1935 Soviet exercises near Kiev a small tank had actually been dropped; it landed intact but declined to start.)

Another British observer of the 1936 exercise, Lt-Col. Giffard Martel, was equally impressed by the spectacle, and especially by the mode of descent favoured by the parachute brigade commander, who '... did a delayed drop. That is to say, that he did not pull the rip cord till he was about half way down. The battalion commanders did a semi-delayed drop and the remainder of the brigade dropped in the ordinary way, from a height of about 2000 feet ... the bulk of the men ... just slid off the wings and pulled their rip cords. They jumped into the air just as sea bathers might jump into the sea at a crowded seaside resort.'

The Russians had developed an alternative method of deploying small parties of men. A film clip of 1935–36 vintage shows a low-flying aircraft releasing a wheeled trolley from a height of no more than five feet; it careers across the ground, and, when it comes to rest, four men with sheepish grins crawl out of tubes placed athwartships, doubling smartly off to where motor cycles have been conveniently parked for their use. Although the whole sequence bears the hallmarks of an elaborate spoof (there is a significant cut between the trolley's actual landing and a close-up of the emergence of the men) there is one documented case of this technique actually being used against the Germans in the winter of 1941/42. On this occasion the trolley arrived in the midst of an alert German unit which promptly shot down the aircraft and despatched the Russians as they struggled out of their tubes.

Although the Russians were the first publicly to display a military parachute force, discreet work had been going on in Germany, where military aviation was banned under the terms of the Treaty of Versailles. Numerous flying schools disguised as sports flying and gliding clubs, staffed by ex-service pilots, were formed all over Germany in the 1920s. In addition, German pilots were trained to combat standard in Russia, whither 'liaison officers' had been posted to assist in the formation and training of the Soviet Air Force. In Berlin a government department called the Central Flying Office (*Fliegerzentrale*) was set up ostensibly to develop civil and commercial aviation. Into this office was drafted, in 1920, an ex-fighter pilot who was to be the founder of the German airborne forces.

Kurt Student was born in 1890, the son of a Junker family in

Brandenburg. His family was typical of the dedicated, loyal and patriotic men who had emerged as a professional military caste under Frederick the Great and whose single-minded application to their profession had brought a poor and undistinguished German kingdom to pre-eminence in the wars of the 1860s and '70s. Young Student underwent a conventional Junker education: military school at 11, thence to the Lichterfelde cadet school from which he emerged in 1909 as a potential officer and was posted on two years' probation to a *Jäger* regiment. Having satisfied this requirement he was fully commissioned into the first battalion of the Graf Yorck von Wartenburg Regiment in 1911. Two years later he volunteered for flying training and reported to the aviation school at Johannistal, near Berlin. Throughout the war he served in staff and aircrew appointments, fought on the Eastern and Western fronts and emerged unscathed in 1918 as a *Hauptmann** with five 'kills' to his credit. He elected to remain in the post-Versailles *Reichswehr* even though no military flying was available and was duly posted to the *Fliegerzentrale* where his professional ability was soon evident. His task was no less than to create the framework of a combat air force which could be brought to life at some time in the future, and he flung himself into it with the gusto that was to characterize his whole career.

Like any man with flying in his blood he could not be kept behind a desk and quickly became involved in the sports gliding movement. In 1921 he was lucky to survive a major crash with a broken skull. Two years later he paid his first visit to the secret German flying school at Lipetsk, near Voronezh in the Soviet Union. After eight years in the *Fliegerzentrale*, with the foundations of the *Luftwaffe* well laid, Student was recalled to the infantry in 1929 to receive, as a major, the command of a battalion in the 2nd Infantry Regiment. Three years later he was back in the aviation business as Director of the Air Technical Training Schools which would provide the yet unborn *Luftwaffe* with its supply of highly trained technicians.

Although Hitler, who became Chancellor of the Reich in 1933, did not formally abrogate the Treaty of Versailles until 1935, it was apparent to the world from 1933 that a powerful German air arm was being formed. Student, now an *Obersleutnant*, continued to preside over its technical training; by now he enjoyed the confidence of Hermann Göring whose vanity and personal ambition were ulti-

* Throughout this book, national ranks will be used, as transposition to a standard 'British' structure (e.g. Major-General for General-Major) often does not reflect the true status of the foreign rank. A comparative table is given at Appendix 1 to assist readers unfamiliar with German ranks.

mately to result in the decision to allot all *Wehrmacht* airborne activities to the *Luftwaffe*.

Göring was already a prestigious figure in Germany, being one of the most notable surviving fighter aces of the 1914–18 war and a holder of the coveted *Pour le Mérite* or 'Blue Max'. In February 1933 as Prussian Minister of the Interior he had ordered the formation of a special police parachute unit to act as a spearhead against Communist organizations. 'Police Department Weche', as this force was called, was absorbed into Göring's *Luftwaffe* in 1935 and its personnel became, in April 1938, the cadre of the 1st Battalion, 1st Parachute Regiment (*I Bataillon, Fallschirmjägerregiment I*), the resident depot battalion at the Stendahl parachute school. Its first commanding officer, *Major* Brauer, came under command of the depot commander *Oberstleutnant* Bassenge, a sound staff officer whose views on the employment of paratroops proved to be less dramatic than Student's though, as time would reveal, more thoroughly reasoned. Brauer would also play an important part in the subsequent history of German airborne forces.

Although an Army parachute unit joined the 1st Regiment at Stendahl in 1936, Göring's influence enabled the *Luftwaffe* to retain control of airborne warfare. In 1937, *Luftwaffe* demolition units were dropped at the autumn Army manoeuvres to demonstrate to Hitler that certain targets which could not readily be attacked by bombers (such as heavily defended airfields or key bridges) were vulnerable to parties of well-trained parachutists expert in demolition techniques. It is clear that Bassenge was in urgent need of a clear directive at this time on the proposed employment of parachutists; Göring's police squads had been an intervention force for internal security; the *Luftwaffe*'s demolition squads were considered to have been a success in the 1937 manoeuvres; and now a parachute infantry company was dropped in front of the *Führer* himself – which clearly impressed him but provided nothing of military value.

Apart from the *Luftwaffe* and the Army, other elements were interested in parachuting. Himmler's private army, the SS, sent a platoon to Stendahl for training, and in May 1938 Bassenge was ordered by Jeschonnek, the *Luftwaffe* Chief of Staff, to train a unit of the *Sturmabteilung* (SA). The SA, the original Brownshirts of the Nazi movement's early days, had been recruited from the beery bullyboys of the Munich and Nuremberg back streets; they were initially a political strong-arm movement for use at Nazi meetings and had also proved adept at running protection rackets. They had been put firmly in their place in 1934 when Hitler purged them bloodily in the 'Night of the Long Knives' in which Röhm their leader and many others had died. Now, as the result of lobbying by their new leader, Reimann, they were bent on regaining their former status and increasing it if possible by becoming a para-military force. The SA parachutists were to be provided by a battalion of the élite *Feldherrnhalle* regiment. Reimann continued to pester Göring; he was jealous that SS airborne troops had upstaged the SA, as had the *Luftwaffe*'s airborne demolition experts from the Hermann Göring Regiment.

Bassenge was baffled and angry. Charged with training a parachute force, he had been given no clear instructions as to its war roles, and was now having to accept trainees from the Army, the *Luftwaffe*, the SS and the SA. He felt that the whole confused situation was being orchestrated by Göring for his own personal and political ends, and he was quite correct. The situation was now taken out of his hands by further developments. In June 1938 Göring ordered Student to form all existing airborne and parachute units, together with the requisite air transport force, into the 7th *Fliegerdivision*, and to be prepared to command it in impending operations to annex the Sudetenland, the ethnically German north-west province of Czechoslovakia.

Student's preparatory work had paid off. Creation of the 'Air Division' was relatively straightfoward. The trained parachute units had been raised, and the aircraft to carry them into battle were also available. The workhorse of the German airborne forces was the Junkers Ju52 transport, which rightly deserves its acknowledged place in the ranks of the world's outstanding aircraft. A three-engined low-wing monoplane with a robust fixed undercarriage, it had first appeared in 1932 as a passenger aircraft operated by Lufthansa, the German flag-carrying airline. Although conceived during the years when military aircraft were forbidden to Germany under the terms of Versailles, the Ju52 was designed with two covert roles – those of troop transport and medium bomber. In the latter role it duly appeared, in 1934, in *Luftwaffe* squadrons, equipped with an open dorsal gun position and a retractable 'dustbin' gun turret on its underside. It received its baptism of fire during the Spanish Civil War in both roles, most spectacularly when Hitler sanctioned an airlift by the *Luftwaffe* of something like 9000 Moorish infantry and their artillery from Morocco to Seville in 1936 – a badly needed reinforcement for Franco which probably tipped the scales in his favour.

From the start, the Germans rejected the ripcord-operated parachute used by the Russians and chose static line equipment. Their first model, the RZ1, gave its passenger an unstable ride and was discarded in 1940 for the RZ16 and RZ20, the latter remaining in service throughout the war. All these German parachutes used a harness with a single suspension point between the parachutist's shoulder blades, causing him to hang forwards whilst descending. No directional control was possible and a somewhat violent downwind landing was inevitable. To minimize injuries, German paratroops were issued with composite-rubber knee pads. The great advantage of the RZ series was their rapid opening, which permitted descents from very low altitude; normally 400 feet, but frequently as low as 250 feet, as was observed in Crete in 1941.

7 *Fliegerdivision* was established with 250 Ju52s, a close air support group with fighters, liaison aircraft and dive bombers, and with gliders. Student's years of involvement with the sports gliding movement had led to a belief that troops delivered soundlessly to their objective could achieve overwhelming surprise; arriving suddenly on target they required no time-consuming form-up period, like parachutists. Moreover, they could carry heavier weapons, explosives and even light vehicles and motor cycles with them. One of Student's most able gliding pupils, Herr Ingr. Stamer, designed an assault glider for him. The DFS230's design reflected its kinship to the sailplanes for which the Germans have been famed since the 1920s. Derived from an earlier Stamer design for a high-performance sailplane for meteorological work, its high-aspect ratio wing gave a shallow gliding angle coupled with a good lift-to-weight ratio. It carried, in addition to its two pilots, eight fully equipped men who sat astride a fore-and-aft bench inside the cramped fuselage, which consisted of a fabric-clad tubular steel box frame. A simple skid undercarriage enabled the pilot to bring the glider to a dead stop in a few yards. To its empty weight of three-quarters of a ton almost a ton in payload could be added.

As it transpired, there was no requirement for 7 *Fliegerdivision* to 'liberate' the Sudetenland, although it was ready to do so by 1 September 1938. Chamberlain's Government shrank from duty and honour and the abandoned Czechs were obliged to cede the Sudetenland without a struggle. Cheated of the chance to show the *Fliegerdivision*'s mettle in combat, Student – always aware of the value of good public relations – flew part of it into Moravia in Ju52s, and followed this with a set-piece airlanding demonstration for the benefit of Göring, who was so impressed by the operation that he agreed to a further expansion of the airborne forces – with Student in command.

This was easier said than done. On completion of the Sudeten operation the division returned to Germany where it was virtually dismembered as the parent services of its regiments claimed their own back. The SA gave up the struggle to become 'legitimate' soldiers and the Hermann Göring Battalion reverted to its *Luftwaffe* formation: the Army reclaimed its parachute battalion and the 16th Infantry

Regiment. Although stripped of his troops, Student would not concede defeat. He redoubled his backstage activities; as a result, he was appointed Inspector of Airborne Forces whilst retaining the command of the skeletal 7 *Fliegerdivision*, and secured the service of Bassenge as his chief of staff. Göring's influence was now in the ascendant, and his determination to acquire all airborne units for his *Luftwaffe* succeeded in January 1939 when the Army parachute battalion changed services. 7 *Fliegerdivision* was designated as a parachute division and 22 Infantry Division, whilst remaining under Army command, was placed under Student's operational control for use in the airlanding role as part of the airborne forces.

The *Führer* himself was now taking a keen personal interest in Student's corps. He was looking ahead to the execution of his plans for European domination, plans which depended on a mixture of cunning diplomacy, threats of violence, surprise strokes against victims lulled into gullibility and sheer treachery. In the aggressive, patriotic and well-trained units under Student's command he saw the means of seizing key points which, once secure, would allow the *Panzers* to pour through and overwhelm the enemy's main armies. The élitism of the parachute units had a special appeal for the ex-*Unteroffizier* of Bavarian infantry and his hand is evident in the drafting of the so-called 'Ten Commandments' committed to memory by every German paratrooper:

1. You are the chosen fighting men of the *Wehrmacht*. You will seek combat and train yourselves to endure all tests. To you the battle shall be fulfilment.
2. Cultivate true comradeship, for by the aid of your comrades you will conquer or die.
3. Beware of loose talk. Be incorruptible. Men act while women chatter. Chatter may bring you to the grave.
4. Be calm and thoughtful, strong and resolute. Valour and the offensive spirit will cause you to succeed in the attack.
5. The most precious thing when in contact with the enemy is ammunition. He who fires uselessly, merely to assure himself, is a man of straw. He is a weakling who merits not the title of *Fallschirmjäger* (Paratrooper).
6. Never surrender. To you, death or victory must be a point of honour.
7. You can win only if your weapons are in good order. Ensure that you abide by this rule – first my weapons, and then myself.
8. You must grasp the full intention of every operation, so that if your leader is killed you can fulfil it yourself.

9. Against an open foe fight with chivalry, but to a guerrilla extend no quarter.

10. Keep your eyes wide open. Tune yourself to top condition. Be as agile as a greyhound, as tough as leather, as hard as Krupp steel: and so you shall be the German Warrior incarnate.

In his public acclamation of the new fighting arm, Hitler displayed an intuitive knowledge of the German character, especially its tendency to admire a *corps d'élite*. Parachutists were given, on completion of their training, a bronze gilt uniform badge depicting a plunging eagle which brought with it a similar *cachet* to that later associated with the British airborne forces' red beret. The German parachutists lived up to their Ten Commandments even in the post-1941 period when they mainly fought as infantry whose calibre drew admiration from friend and foe alike. They invariably fought hard and clean; their commanders saw to that. After the fighting in Crete, one German parachute battalion commander, Baron von der Heydte, buried his own dead and those of the New Zealanders, British and Greeks who had fought against them in adjacent graves, sharing a common memorial. From every front came similar reports of these incredibly tough yet chivalrous soldiers.

The jump training inflicted on German paratroops was dramatic and well-publicized. Supreme physical fitness was a prerequisite, coupled with agility, for the exit from a Ju52 consisted of an athletic dive for which considerable 'synthetic' training was necessary. Emphasis was also placed on the acrobatic skill needed to ensure a good landing when using the RZ parachute. All this made for excellent cinematic material, and German audiences were frequently treated to dramatic sequences featuring the tough training of their bronzed and muscular *Herrenvolk* at the parachute school.

The motive force behind the German parachutist's professionalism and code of conduct can be identified as that of the austere Junker tradition in which Student himself had been schooled. The hidden staffwork which enabled his dream to take wing was that of *Oberst* Bassenge; a pragmatic officer of the old school who had actually declined Göring's offer of the command of 7 Air Division, he instinctively baulked at Student's more extravagant ideas, favouring airlanding operations rather than massed parachute descents, and army rather than *Luftwaffe* control of the airborne corps. His methods were more pedestrian, but he made a perfect foil for Student's dynamic ideas and was able to project them in a way which partly disarmed the hostility of senior Army officers whose distrust of Student as a relatively junior officer – and an airman at that – was further piqued by their knowledge of his special relationship with the *Führer* and Göring. For his part, Hitler may have derived amusement by flaunting his approval of Student before the General Staff, for whom he had a deep-seated mistrust and contempt.

Following the German march into what was left of Czechoslovakia in March 1939 the stage was set for general war. The *Führer* could sense the mood of the German nation, eager to show its mettle and to erase the humiliations of the post-1918 period. This mood was taken up by the *Wehrmacht*; the paratroops' chorus caught the spirit of the time:

'Fly on this day, against the enemy!
Into the planes, into the planes!
Comrades, there is no going back! . . .'

– and indeed the war machine was now irreversibly in motion.

An airborne force such as that created by Student and Bassenge could only be used offensively; its organization and equipment were clearly unsuited for a defensive slogging match. This was evident to the French and British governments, but neither had seen fit to take serious notice of the original Russian experiment. Wavell's 1936 report to the War Office had been luke-warm; the French had toyed with airborne warfare by forming two or three trial units but had allowed these to lapse. As the war-clouds gathered and Germany's frightening offensive power was recognized, her future enemies continued to think only in terms of defensive land warfare behind the concrete walls of the Maginot line. Even after the outbreak of war in September 1939 the Western allies were content to sit tight.

The Germans, however, were not yet sated; at the *Führer*'s direction the High Command were at work on plans for the next two stages – the seizure of Denmark and Norway ('*Weserübung*') and the grand design itself, *Fall Gelb*, the overthrow of France and her British ally.

CHAPTER TWO

The Observer Aloft

The appearance of Coutelle's balloon at the battle of Fleurus proved to be an isolated incident, and one has to wait until the American Civil war for the first systematic use of military balloons; on 1 October 1861 the splendidly named Thaddeus Sobieski Coulincourt Lowe was given the resounding title of 'Chief Aeronaut of the Army of the Potomac', entrusted with five captive balloons, and directed to employ them for observation and artillery control. Two enthusiastic British officers, Capt. Beaumont and Lt Grover, both of the Royal Engineers, attached themselves to Lowe's unit whilst on extended leave. They attempted, on their return to England, to interest the War Office in the use of observation balloons but failed to raise any support. This is hardly surprising; the post of Commander-in-Chief at the Horse Guards was filled by Field Marshal His Royal Highness George William Frederick Charles, Duke of Cambridge, a grandson of King George III; he had assumed this post in 1856 at the age of 37 and succeeded in retaining his seat for an incredible 39 years, a pillar of conservatism against which successive waves of innovation and reform crashed in vain.

Beaumont was undeterred. He was a member of a corps which throughout the 19th century displayed tremendous intellectual and physical vigour. Self-sufficiency, supreme self-confidence and frequent personal eccentricity characterized the Victorian sapper officer. Whilst most pursued fairly conventional professional activities, some became obsessed with esoteric causes; Gen. Gordon, of Khartoum fame, advanced strange theories on biblical topography, claiming not only to have located the true Golgotha just outside the Damascus gate of old Jerusalem (it now overlooks a bus station) but also the Garden of Eden (in the Seychelles). It is hardly surprising that the Royal Engineers espoused the cause of aeronautics on Beaumont's return from the United States, and eventually succeeded in gaining official recognition for military ballooning in the British Army. In 1863 a group of sapper officers constructed their own coal-gas balloon and flew it successfully at Aldershot and Woolwich. Although a Royal Engineers committee repeatedly recommended the construction of balloons to the War Office, no action took place until 1878, when the Treasury granted £150 towards the manufacture of experimental balloons at Woolwich Arsenal.

By 1880 systematic balloon training was under way at Aldershot, conducted by the Royal Engineers. Balloon detachments were included in military field forces despatched in 1885 to Bechuanaland and the Sudan, where it was reported that the continuous presence of a captive balloon floating above the marching square as it crawled dustily across the landscape 'gave great confidence to the troops'. It also had a salutary moral effect on the enemy, who promptly dispersed. The Bechuanaland campaign, unlike that in the Sudan, was a bloodless affair, but at Mafeking – 15 years later to gain immortality as the scene of Baden-Powell's beleaguerment – Gen. Sir Charles Warren personally went aloft to survey his operational area and thus became the first British general to make use of an aerial command post.

New uses were quickly found for the balloon. One attended the Royal Field Artillery practice camp in 1886 where it was found that a trained airborne observer could direct fire accurately at ranges well beyond the scope of the ground observation post. Maj. Elsdale – another sapper – pioneered aerial photography in 1883 with a remotely controlled camera fixed to a balloon moored over his barracks in Nova Scotia. At home, no annual manoeuvres at Aldershot were now considered complete without balloons and the aeronauts secured powerful support from Gen. Sir Evelyn Woods after their activities during his 1889 field exercises. His patronage ensured further expansion despite the continuing presence in Whitehall of the indomitable Duke of Cambridge. Aeronautics became fashionable and there was a queue of staff officers for places in the basket on manoeuvres, although many found difficulty in abandoning well-established habits. The dress for field training consisted at that time of a dark blue patrol jacket, breeches, jackboots and spurs, helmet, cross-belt, sword and sabretache. It was difficult, one report from 1890 says, to convince scandalized staff officers that these accoutrements had to be discarded before take-off, '. . . even though a visit from Princess Beatrice during the morning was expected'.

By 1906 the balloon was a proven instrument of war, having confirmed its value as an observation platform in the South African War of 1899–1902. The ground handling equipment and actual design of the balloons had been developed to a high degree of efficiency and excellent results were consistently achieved by well-trained observers. However, new developments were afoot.

In 1894, Maj. Baden-Powell, later of Mafeking and Boy Scout

fame, had designed and built a kite capable of lifting a man to a height of 100 feet. An equally picturesque figure arrived on the scene. Mr S. F. Cody arrived in England from America. Although not related to his colourful namesake 'Buffalo Bill', S. F. Cody was his equal as a showman and outshone him as a practical man. He persuaded the Royal Engineers in 1906 to take into service a man-lifting kite of his own design, on which an observer could be rapidly hoisted to a height of 1500 feet, from where he communicated with the ground by means of a telephone and message bags. Flying a Cody prototype in 1905, Lt Broke-Smith of the Royal Engineers had achieved a height of 3000 feet. Unlike the captive balloon, the kites thrived on high winds and were at their best in windspeeds of 20–50 mph. Cheaper, less vulnerable, requiring less than a third of the transport and personnel of a balloon unit, and capable of use from a moving platform such as one of the new-fangled motor lorries, the kite appeared to be a major breakthrough. Instead, it was stifled at birth by technological development when the Wright brothers became the first men to achieve controllable flight in a powered heavier-than-air machine.

For several years nobody successfully imitated the Wrights in Europe, though numerous powered devices hopped, floundered and collapsed ruinously in Britain and elsewhere. Success appeared imminent in 1908, however. In 1906 an officer of the Wiltshire Regiment, Lt J. W. Dunne, who had been invalided out of the army after the Boer War, had started to design model gliders of high inherent stability. He built a biplane glider at the Aldershot Balloon School, from where it was transported in great secrecy to Scotland. At Blair Atholl, the seat of the Duke of Atholl, it was subjected to flight trials. Elaborate steps were taken to exclude the press, the general public and any foreigners. The Duke's private army, the Atholl Highlanders, and a horde of stalkers, water-bailiffs and house servants patrolled the estate. After two seasons of trials, a petrol engine was fitted to the arrow-shaped biplane with which it staggered into the air for a longest flight of 40 yards. Dunne returned to his drawing board (and also to his other obsession, the analysis of dreams; his book *An Experiment with Time* brought him far more fame than his aeroplanes and still sells well).

Meanwhile, at Aldershot, Cody had also built an aeroplane, in which, on 10 May 1908, he made the first recorded powered flight in the United Kingdom; it was terminated abruptly when he flew into a horse-trough. Egged on by his Royal Engineer backers, he repaired his machine and in it, on 5 October, made the first officially observed flight in Britain, landing successfully after covering 496 yards. The

War Office commemorated the feat by forbidding further powered aircraft trials; the cost of the Dunne and Cody experiments was already £2500 and this was held to be excessive. The sappers had tasted success and pressed on at their own expense. Cody's machine was progressively refined and by 1912, when the first military aircraft competitive trials were held, a Cody aeroplane emerged as the easy winner and was immediately acquired by the newly-formed Royal Flying Corps which had been built around the cadre of the Air Battalion, Royal Engineers. Cody did not survive to enjoy the fruits of success; he was killed in the wreck of his new amphibian aircraft on 13 August.

Dunne had continued to work away on his monumentally stable designs. In 1914 the War Office tried out his latest biplane and rejected it because, once airborne, it proved almost impossible to dive, sideslip or even change direction. It was wisely decided that although these characteristics made for a high degree of safety, they were hardly conducive to survival in combat.

The lighter-than-air school was still active, and after several earlier experiments with airships, the British Army purchased two French dirigibles in 1910. The arrival of one of these, a Lebaudy, at its Farnborough shed, was the occasion of considerable ceremonial. A large crowd, including the aged Commander-in-Chief of the Army, Field Marshal Lord Roberts of Kandahar and seven other generals turned out to watch the initial docking. A landing party of 160 guardsmen and sappers stood by to pull the airship into its hangar. The Air Battalion officer in charge suddenly realized that the hangar was too small – by about 15 feet – to accept its new occupant, and called a halt to the operation. At this point, according to a contemporary press report, 'an enthusiastic spectator, believed to be an officer of high rank in uniform, shouted to the landing party to go on, which they did'. The punctured envelope thereupon collapsed ingloriously on crowd, landing party and senior officers alike. This event effectively ended the British Army's flirtation with the airship and apart from the observation balloons which were used with success on the Western Front throughout the 1914–18 War, with all lighter-than-air activity.

The Royal Flying Corps was still in its formative stage when it went to war with 63 assorted aeroplanes in 1914. Its primary roles were those of scouting for signs of enemy troops and observation – including the use of cameras and the control of artillery fire. At first all the combatant air arms used their aircraft for these purposes. Aerial combat developed as each side tried to prevent its opponents from using their scout and observation aircraft. Aeroplanes specifically designed for fighting were quickly evolved, their function being to provide escort for friendly observation planes and to drive hostile aircraft out of the sky. From this it was a logical step to carrying bombs with which to attack enemy airfields. The struggle for air supremacy had been launched; but despite the fame of the great fighter pilots on both sides, the glamour with which their hazardous war has been invested should not be allowed to obscure the fact that until the evolution of practicable heavy bombers in 1917, this was the aerial war of the *observer*.

The world's first independent air arm, the Royal Air Force, came into being on 1 April 1918 as the result of a series of daylight bombing raids on London and coastal towns, which led to a politico-military crisis. Prime Minister Lloyd George convened a powerful committee to study the air defence of Great Britain. As the result of its recommendations the Royal Naval Air Service and Royal Flying Corps were amalgamated as the Royal Air Force and a special Independent Air Force of heavy bombers was created in June 1918 for the express purpose of bombing German cities. Its commander was Maj.-Gen. Hugh Trenchard, lately in charge of the Royal Flying Corps.

Trenchard is a central figure in any study concerned with the usages of air power. Born in 1873 he had only qualified for a commission in the Army with difficulty, having failed to satisfy even the moderate academic requirements of the Sandhurst entrance examination. For 20 years he served obscurely with his regiment – the Royal Scots Fusiliers – and in overseas posts. In 1912, almost by chance, he had taken up flying ('. . . only a moderate flier', his instructor reported) and was almost a founder member of the Royal Flying Corps. By 1915 he was at its head in France. Although no pilot and a poor staff officer (his writing was a legend for its illegibility and he was an unimpressive speaker) he was gifted with powers of insight and character which drew the loyal support of a cabal of outstanding air-minded officers. Together they forged the RAF into a splendid instrument between the wars despite the hostility of the navy, the indifference of the army and the reluctance of the Treasury to allot funds for new aircraft.

Unlike the top soldiers of the British Army on the Western Front – especially Haig, who at first regarded the RFC as merely a supporting arm for infantry and artillery operations – Trenchard believed that the primary task of an air arm was to drive the opposing air force out of the sky. His arrival at HQ RFC was the signal for aggressive techniques; squadrons were encouraged to seek out the enemy in the air behind the German lines and to attack his airfields. Thus, for the first time, a doctrine of pure air power was being applied by a commander who had the vision to see the yet untapped offensive power of a new arm. Until Trenchard's arrival at HQ RFC the emphasis had been on reconnaissance. This was perhaps to be expected, for when the RFC had been formed in 1912, the Director of Military Training had been Brig.-Gen. Henderson, an acknowledged expert in ground reconnaissance who had written a well-reviewed book on this subject after the South African war. He had been quick to appreciate the value of the aircraft in this role and especially its advantages of three-dimensional mobility when compared to the vulnerable captive balloon. The first commander of the military wing of the RFC had been Maj. Sykes, whose whole military career had been devoted, as a light cavalryman, to scouting and reconnaissance.

Resistance to innovation has always been apparent in some military circles; the difficulties encountered by Trenchard in 1915–18 were later met with by the founders of airborne warfare in the 1940s, and the pioneers of airmobile warfare 20 years after that. Initially the RFC had experienced difficulty in persuading the British high command that their air reconnaissance reports were of any use. Now, when Trenchard proclaimed his doctrine of offensive air warfare, Haig's staff opposed it because it seemed that air reconnaissance support for the Army would fall off as a result.

In fact, although the RFC and, later, the RAF began to raid targets deep inside Germany from October 1917 with Stuttgart, Karlsruhe, Heidelberg and Strassbourg all coming under bombardment, there was no appreciable change in the pattern of air operations on the Western Front. Artillery observation, photo reconnaissance and general surveillance flights continued. Trenchard's earlier offensive operations bore fruit and by the end of the war in November 1918 the German Air Force had been overwhelmed.

During the war the air arm had undergone an enormous expansion. Sixty-three aircraft had been despatched with the BEF in 1914. By the Armistice the RAF had more than 3000 in front-line service and many thousands more in reserve and in the training organization. Now came the reversion to peace establishments. By the end of 1919 10,000 aircraft, 30,000 aero engines and thousands of tons of aircraft spares had been sold as scrap. The RAF's establishment was cut to a fraction of the wartime organization. Trenchard, appointed Chief of the Air Staff (CAS), now began his greatest battle – for the very survival of the Royal Air Force. It was to last throughout the inter-war period and would come near to setting in concrete an unhappy relationship between the three British armed services stemming from their fight for funds. This mutual suspicion cast a dark shadow over all early attempts to create Airborne Forces in the Second World War and on the efforts of a small group of Royal Artillery officers in the 1930s to create an entirely new system of artillery observation.

Immediately after the Armistice of 1918 Trenchard deployed his few remaining squadrons to the furthest corners of the Empire, where they would be safe, he hoped, from the acquisitive hands of the Admiralty; to India, Egypt and Mesopotamia. A further squadron was split between a number of Far Eastern bases, including Singapore. Only two squadrons were allocated to the Army Co-operation role in the early 1920s.

In distant theatres such as the North-West Frontier of India and in the Middle East, the Army grew accustomed to close air support given by DH9A light bombers, and close inter-service rapport was achieved in the field. Army officers were attached to the RAF for pilot training and served as a proportion of the aircrew in Army Co-operation (A.C.) Squadrons. Other soldiers, trained at the RAF's school of Army Co-operation at Old Sarum, were posted to squadrons as Air Intelligence liaison officers. It seemed that due attention was in fact being paid to the principle of inter-service co-operation but this was not the case. In 1919 Trenchard had opened his career as CAS with a White Paper in which he declared that the RAF's primary role in any future war would be '. . . to paralyse from the very outset the enemy's productive centres of munitions of war of every sort' but that a part of the RAF would be '. . . specially trained to work with the Army . . . probably becoming, in time, an arm of the older Service'. In other words, he was bent on forming a strategic Air Force capable of taking the war to the enemy's heartland, whilst retaining an Army Air Force on the lines of the old Royal Flying Corps for direct involvement in the land battle. The types of aircraft allotted to this role in the 1920s and 1930s were accordingly designed to fulfil a variety of roles, of which artillery observation, reconnaissance and ground attack were the most important.

Although no attempt was ever made to unload the Army Co-operation task onto the Army as suggested in the 1919 White Paper, it was clear that the Air Ministry regarded the strategic mission as their *raison d'être*. The 'Bomber School' gathered momentum during the inter-war period. A strong strategic air force, it was argued, could make conventional maritime and land operations impossible. The only defence against widespread bombing of one's own homeland was a stronger aerial bombardment of the enemy's. The nation with the most effective bomber force would win the war by demoralization of the enemy's civilian population and disruption of his industrial base. The bomber, it was declared, would always get through.

By the mid-1930s several unpalatable facts were evident. Germany was re-arming apace; the RAF's front-line squadrons were inadequately equipped; and current arrangements for Army Co-operation were likely to be ineffective in the type of war now envisaged by such prophets as Capt. Basil Liddell Hart.

The secret measures by which Germany created the cadre of her *Luftwaffe* have already been mentioned. In 1935, when the RAF staged a great Review at Mildenhall in honour of King George V's Jubilee, the world's air attachés were treated to the spectacle of a fly past by a collection of what were supposed to be front-line aircraft. They were all biplanes; many of the heavy bomber squadrons, supposedly the instruments of Trenchard's strategic bombing doctrine, were equipped with the Vickers *Virginia* which was in first-line squadron service from 1924 to 1937. This machine cruised at less than 100 mph and was totally incapable of carrying an effective bombing campaign to the German heartland. Technology had fallen far behind.

Apart from the inadequacy and obsolescence of the RAF's fighters and bombers, there was growing disquiet over its capability to provide support for the field army with Army Co-operation squadrons whose aircraft were well-suited to colonial campaigning but, being derived from observation aircraft of the 1918 era, clearly unsuited for combat under full-scale war conditions in Europe.

The Hawker *Audax* entering squadron service in 1932, could cruise at 132 mph and had a claimed top speed of 170 mph. Its armament, however, was no better than that of the First World War Bristol fighter and its bombload actually less – presumably a concession to the dawning recognition that a slow biplane could not be expected to fulfil a mission spectrum ranging from artillery observation to low-level ground attack.

Whilst the RAF fought to retain credibility in the teeth of political apathy, outright naval hostility and almost total lack of interest on the part of the War Office, the Royal Artillery was actually moving towards modernization. By 1930 the decision to mechanize all field batteries had been made. The Gunners regretfully parted with their horses, realizing – unlike many diehard cavalryman – that mechanical traction was far more practicable in terms of mobile warfare; by 1933 most batteries were using a tracked vehicle called a *Dragon* to pull guns and limbers and the implications of this newly acquired mobility were not lost on a number of intelligent Gunner officers. In that year Capt. H. J. Parham wrote an article in the Journal of the Royal United Services Institution advocating the use of the autogyro as an observation platform. Flown by an artillery officer it could be based in the field, alongside the gun positions. The pilot would double as artillery observer, using modern radio with speech to control the fire of the guns with a streamlined fire orders procedure, relying on the agility of his unarmed aircraft to keep out of trouble. Parham's idea was greeted incredulously in the Air Ministry as a compound of two heresies: the RAF, as the flying service, could alone provide the pilots for service aircraft; and the idea of a flimsy unarmed autogyro surviving for more than a few minutes in the face of enemy fighters was laughable. Autogyros were in fact tried out by the RAF in 1933, carrying Army artillery observers, and again in 1935. The results were inconclusive and not entirely satisfactory – probably because the Air Ministry insisted that as flying was a full-time occupation, the artillery observation must be done by a specialist artillery officer in the rear cockpit. Parham insisted that both functions must be in one man's hands so that he could place his aircraft where he wanted so as to observe fall of shot, then dive to below the treeline to remain out of enemy observation until ready to zoom up again to observe the next ranging round. This 'tactical' approach to battlefield flying was a direct contradiction of all previous air observation methods and laid the foundations for the skills later acquired and practised by Army aviators worldwide. In 1933 it was iconoclastic.

Undeterred, Parham and his supporters got together in 1934 to form the Royal Artillery Flying Club at Larkhill on Salisbury Plain, where the School of Artillery was located. The proclaimed function of the club was to provide low-cost club flying for gunner officers. Its covert purpose was to conduct trials in Parham's techniques for air observation. The secretary of the club was Capt. H. C. Bazeley; after three years of trials he submitted a paper in the annual prize essay competition of the Royal Artillery Institution. By now it was clear to all that Germany was preparing for aggressive war based on a devastating combination of armoured assault backed by artillery and close air support. The age of static trench warfare had gone. In future, mobility and firepower would be paramount. Immediate response to the enemy's every move would be essential. Bazeley argued that the traditional 'Arty R' aircraft operating from a distant airfield, with its outdated tactical information would be worthless in the new type of war. On the other hand light aircraft based in the gun-lines and at immediate readiness, could do away with the delays endemic to the Army Co-operation system. If flown by officers who were already proven as good artillery forward observers, the fire of any number of batteries could be registered, adjusted and switched quickly around the battlefield. The use of two-way speech radio and slightly modified standard artillery fire-control procedures would be immeasurably faster than the 'clock' system of fire direction used since 1916 (and not finally discarded by the RAF until 1941). Further advantages accrued, in Bazeley's opinion, from the use of light aircraft flown by soldiers: the chief being that the RAF could be absolved from a significant part of its existing commitment to close reconnaissance and observation for the ground troops, thereby releasing the maximum air effort for close support of the land battle.

Although Bazeley's radical paper failed to gain the prize of the R.A. Institution it evoked widespread interest and in particular the support of the General Officer Commanding Southern Command who in April 1938 pointed out to the War Office that there were now over 100 Royal Artillery officers serving under him who had qualified as light aircraft pilots. He pressed for official 'Air Observation Post' (Air OP) trials to be carried out forthwith. One can detect the strong hand of the R.A. Flying Club behind the GOC's letter; in any case he, too, was a gunner. His suggestion, passed over to the Air Ministry, drew a lukewarm response. The RAF, anxious to provide up-to-date Army Co-operation support, aware of the shortcomings of the Hawker *Hector* which had entered service in 1937 to replace the *Audax* and determined at all costs to keep their hands firmly on all military aviation activities, were planning to introduce their first monoplane Army Co-op aircraft into service. This was the Westland *Lysander*. By any standards it was a remarkable aircraft. Ingenious design, including a fully flapped and slotted wing and a powerful engine, gave it a sensational short take-off and landing (STOL) performance. Its wide speed range – from 55 to over 200 mph – would enable it to operate in and out of confined landing grounds and also, it was hoped, to cope with the air combat conditions in which it was designed to operate. It was armed with two fixed forward-firing rifle-calibre machine guns, a third gun in the observer's position, and could carry six small bombs or supply containers on racks attached to its wheel spats. Like all its biplane predecessors, therefore, the *Lysander* was regarded as a multi-role aircraft.

When the RAF eventually agreed to hold Air OP trials early in 1939 it was stipulated that *Lysander* and *Audax* aircraft were to be used; as a concession these were to be flown by the ubiquitous Bazeley and a group of his disciples who had meanwhile qualified as RAF Army Co-operation pilots. Although the trials proved the efficacy of the new streamlined radio fire-control procedures, they also demonstrated that the aircraft used were too cumbrous and vulnerable to be used in the manner advocated by Parham and Bazeley, who continued to press for unarmed light aeroplanes with a one-man crew.

Bazeley now threw himself into the Air OP campaign with the fervour of Peter-the-Hermit preaching his crusade. By 1938 something near panic stalked the corridors of the Air Ministry. For 20 years the bomber school had reigned supreme, helped by the acceptance of successive governments that the prospect of war was remote and that strategic bombing was the panacea absolving them from serious defence policies. Now, war clouds were looming to the East; the *Luftwaffe*, tried and proven in the Spanish War and equipped with the most effective combat aircraft in the world, faced the Anglo-French alliance with its obsolescent front-line air forces. It was painfully clear that no bombers capable of waging a credible strategic offensive against Germany could be in service with the RAF before late 1940, and that urgent steps must be taken to prepare for the defence of the United Kingdom against enemy air attack on an unimaginable scale. Providentially, radio directing finding (RDF) – later known as radar – was being developed, and as the result of the RAF's outstanding performances in the Schneider Cup contests of the early 1930s, good monoplane fighter aircraft were under development.

The RAF faced the challenge with high resolution, temporarily ditched its bomber policy, and prepared for a defensive air war over Britain. The Air Ministry's hands were full of more pregnant business than Army Co-op, and this gave Bazeley the heaven-sent chance to persuade, wheedle and lobby his way to attain his aim. His personality matched the occasion. Described by one who knew him in those crucial months of the summer and autumn of 1939 as 'an amusing, lively man, sardonic, critical, observant, a good talker', he was also hyper-sensitive to criticism. He demanded much of his subordinates and was intolerant of superiors who expressed dissent with his views, often to the point of being disloyal to them. On occasion he could be impulsively outspoken. He had the Messianic qualities of Billy Mitchell or Orde Wingate who could almost hypnotize people with the intensity of their pleading. Like them, he had a dark face to his character; prone to depression and despair when thwarted, he was to die tragically years later by his own hand.

By dint of identifying and recruiting powerful allies such as the Director of Military Training (Maj.-Gen. Massy) and later the Commander-in-Chief Home Forces, Gen. Sir Alan Brooke (both gunner officers), Bazeley carried out further trials throughout the last six months of 1939 using light aircraft. The Air Ministry, with bigger fish to fry, hardly noticed that they were going on.

No public relations fanfares therefore sounded on 1 February 1940 to greet the formation of 'D' Flight RAF at Old Sarum. Commanded by Maj. Bazeley, it was the first Air OP unit. Its charter, jointly drawn up by the Deputy Chief of the Imperial General Staff and the

Deputy Chief of the Air Staff, directed Bazeley to '. . . determine the possibilities and limitations of the use of light aircraft as Air OPS, the most suitable aircraft for this purpose, and the most suitable organisation for the operation and maintenance of these aircraft'.

'D' Flight was manned by pilots and non-technical groundcrew drawn from the Royal Artillery, with an adjutant, supply officer and aircraft mechanics provided by the RAF. This mixture of the two services was quickly found to be highly satisfactory and continued to be the standard manning system for all such units in the British Services until the formation of a separate Army Air Corps in 1957. Having assembled his little unit and carried out a few weeks of intensive training at Old Sarum and Larkhill, Bazeley took it to France in April 1940 so that trials could be held under operational conditions on the Saar front. He had four light aircraft; one was an American Stinson 105, and three were Taylorcraft Ds, American designed machines built in England under licence.

The Saar trials were scheduled to begin on 9 May 1940, but never took place. Tension was rising in Europe as the result of the German invasion of Denmark and Norway in April, and the full might of the Nazi war machine was unleashed against the Low Countries on 10 May. Bazeley extricated 'D' Flight, intact but unproven, returned to Old Sarum and anxiously awaited further developments. For the time being, all that he had worked for seemed to be in ruins; it was a time for despair.

35

CHAPTER THREE

The Eyes of the Army

The Battle of Britain was about to break over southern England, and the RAF had more pressing affairs to attend to than those of 'D' Flight. A trickle of gunner pilots, however, started to arrive at Old Sarum, trained by civilian firms such as de Havillands at Hatfield and Marshalls of Cambridge. During the gloomy winter of 1940–41, with the immediate risk of invasion diminished as the result of the RAF's superb performance in beating off the *Luftwaffe*'s day offensive the Air OP again came under critical scrutiny.

Although Bazeley had rallied some support for his ideas in RAF circles, the Air Officer Commanding Army Co-operation Command was an active opponent. In his opinion the unarmed light aircraft was a sitting target for any enemy fighter. Bazeley turned to a powerful ally: Gen. Sir Alan Brooke, himself a gunner and now Commander-in-Chief Home Forces, who made it quite clear to War Office and Air Ministry alike that he considered the Air OP essential. The influence wielded by this great soldier – soon to become Chief of the Imperial General Staff – was quite sufficient to ensure that 'D' Flight not only survived, but started to spawn further Air OP units.

The search for a suitable spotter aircraft was an early problem. The RAF's *Lysanders* had been shot out of the sky over France and Flanders and the Taylorcraft 'D' used initially by 'D' Flight was under-powered and fragile. It also possessed a disadvantage potentially fatal to an aircraft reliant solely on its agility to get out of trouble if attacked by enemy fighters – there was virtually no field of vision for the pilot to his rear and below. Moreover, the design had been deliberately kept simple in order to commend the aircraft to flying clubs with limited funds and it therefore had no flaps. Without these it could not make a steep approach at low flying speed into the confined space of a small field surrounded by trees, or across high obstacles on its glide path. The search for a better aircraft was fruitless.

The British light aircraft industry was fully committed to mass-producing training aircraft, and it was decided to purchase a number of Stinson *Vigilants* from the USA. The *Vigilant* was much larger than the Taylorcraft; its powerful engine and an array of flaps and slats gave it a fine short take off and landing performance but it was almost as cumbersome as the ill-fated *Lysander*. That the *Vigilant* never entered Air OP Service was due to a stroke of fortune in which the hand of providence seems to have played a part, for while on their way by sea across the Atlantic, a consignment of cheese subsided onto the crated aircraft and flattened them. The Taylorcraft therefore had to carry the first Air OP pilots to war in Tunisia.

Before the north-African expedition was launched, an important development took place. During the summer of 1941 an American military mission saw a demonstration of Air OP techniques at Larkhill. The senior artilleryman in the party was Maj.-Gen. Robert M. Danford, Chief of Field Artillery in the US Army. He directed that a similar trial be carried out at Fort Sill, home of the US School of Artillery. The trials, conducted with Piper *Cub* aircraft, were a resounding success. From an initial group of 32 Army officers a huge aviation organization emerged, fired with the tremendous enthusiasm which characterizes the American approach to a new enterprise. By the time of the north-African landings, light aircraft were beginning to join all Field Artillery battalions in the US Army and were soon in action – although the first-ever Air OP shoot was conducted by one of Bazeley's pilots.

During 1941 and 1942 the Air OP organization steadily expanded. The unit establishments worked out in 1939 proved to be highly successful, welding soldiers and airmen into small, friendly, highly efficient units in which high morale was the natural product of professionalism and determination to do a good job with equipment which left much to be desired.

The first Air OP Squadron to form was given the RAF numeral of 651 and Bazeley formed it in the Autumn of 1941. Its constitution is of interest. There were 11 Royal Artillery officer pilots, 39 soldiers as non-technical ground crew (drivers, signallers, storemen), 25 RAF airmen as technical ground crew, a staff car, 3 radio trucks, 10 lorries, 10 motorcycles and 8 Auster Mk I (as the military version of the Taylorcraft was called).

On 12 November 1942, the squadron arrived by sea at Algiers, quickly uncrated and assembled its Austers, and by 16 November was ready for action. Flying and driving eastwards towards the combat zone, where the British 1st Army was making its bold but unsuccessful dash for Tunis, the Austers were in action for the first time on 24 November. Maps were non-existent or in desperately short supply; the military situation was extremely fluid, and there was an incessant demand for tactical information which the Air OP pilots found they could provide although reconnaissance – particularly in the face of the strong German air threat – was certainly not one of the jobs they had envisaged.

From the start, their life was adventurous. On 28 November Capts. Billingham and Newton were set upon by four Messerschmitt 109s as they were landing at a forward airstrip. Newton was shot down but escaped from the burning wreck of his Auster. Billingham, in his damaged aircraft, moved his section to another airstrip and continued to provide air observation for the guns, ignoring an order forbidding all Air OP missions because of the unfavourable air situation. On 30 November the landing ground came under direct fire from German tanks which had broken through the forward positions. Billingham and his drivers, signallers and fitters joined in the battle as infantry; the next day brought even fiercer fighting, with the airstrip under attack by tanks, artillery and bombers. Billingham took to the air to direct artillery fire, driving off the attackers. During the night the British infantry around the airstrip had to pull out, taking most of Billingham's men with them, but as his Auster could not be flown in the dark he lay low until dawn, then crept out to his aircraft and took off under heavy fire from the Germans who had unwittingly shared the farm with him all night.

Another pilot, caught over no-man's land by Messerschmitts, was watched by the infantry of both sides, who stopped shooting at each other in their fascination as he nimbly evaded a series of attacks – the Germans desisting only when they started to run out of fuel. Here, if any evidence was needed, was proof of Parham's old thesis that an unarmed light aircraft could survive even in a hostile air situation. Doubters began to be converted, and amongst the most generous supporters of the Air OP in north Africa were the RAF. They had discovered that the gunner pilots, serving in RAF units, could educate the rest of the Army in aviation matters, explaining the difficulties faced by the RAF in providing close air support and generally oiling the complex machinery of Army/Air operations.

After the successful outcome of the North African campaign, the Air OP squadrons moved across to Sicily with the invading Allied armies, and then on into Italy. Their operational efficiency was greatly increased when the Auster Mk I was replaced by the much improved Mk III. A 130 hp De Havilland Gipsy Major engine gave it a higher maximum speed and flaps permitted the steep landing approach lacking in the Mk I. Its cockpit was redesigned, with ample visibility to the rear for the pilot, and an observer could also be carried in a rear-facing seat to keep look-out for hostile aircraft. The Mk III was the mainstay of the Air OP squadrons which fought the Italian campaign and is remembered even today by the pilots who flew it with the affection accorded only to the most outstanding aircraft.

The Germans, too, were acquiring a knowledge of the potency of aerially-controlled artillery fire and prisoners increasingly expressed, under interrogation, a grudging respect for the pilots of the harmless-looking light aircraft whose appearance in the sky – even during periods of *Luftwaffe* domination – inevitably resulted in devastating artillery action. There was clearly a division of opinion as to how to deal with the 'Flying Flea' (the 'Lame Duck' or 'the Orderly Officer' were two more German nicknames for the Air OP) for any small-arms fire directed at the plane drew an immediate response from the Allied guns; but to let it fly up and down unmolested allowed the pilot to work without distraction. On 28 September 1943 the correspondent of the London *Times* singled out the Air OP as responsible for much of the flexibility and accuracy of the British artillery. It is therefore hardly surprising that before long the *Luftwaffe* made a concerted effort to drive the Austers from the sky.

The occasion was the battle for the Anzio beachhead, where an Anglo-American landing was made on 22 January 1944 with the aim of taking the main German defences in the rear, breaking the stalemate around Monte Cassino and opening the road to Rome. The attack was directed by the American Lt-Gen. Lucas, who dithered on the beaches, honourably reluctant to risk the lives of his troops on what was clearly a fearful gamble; this gave the Germans time to react, which they did with their accustomed speed and violence. The troops in the beach-head had no good raised observation points and were subjected to ferocious German counter attacks which could form up and approach along deep gorgelike wadis, invisible to Allied ground observers.

Providentially, a flight of 655 Air OP Squadron had flown into the beach-head on 22 January with the first wave of the attack, and continued to operate there until the final break-out in May. The pilots had huge artillery resources at their disposal, including the guns of the Allied fleet; over 90 per cent of all naval gunfire and 70 per cent of all other forms of artillery fire were directed by the intrepid Auster pilots, operating from crude airstrips, farm tracks and the beach itself.

German counter attacks were repeatedly broken up before they could be launched and in the end it proved extremly dangerous for them to move even a single tank or vehicle in daytime for fear of the terrible retribution such folly would invite. The *Luftwaffe* made repeated attacks on the Air OPs; the beach-head was beyond the reach of constant Allied air cover, and German fighters were quick to take advantage of any temporary absence of RAF or USAAF fighter protection. An Auster pilot attacked by one fighter stood an excellent chance of survival by using superior agility to lure his assailant into range of the Allied anti-aircraft guns, but when attacked by a swarm of Messerschmitts or Focke-Wulfs his chances were slim. An even greater risk was due to strikes from 'friendly' shells – the cause of more fatal casualties to Air OP pilots than any other throughout the war. It is quite easy for the Air OP to conduct a shoot under normal conditions from either behind the guns or from a fly-line in front of them and below the shells' trajectories. In the crowded Anzio beach-head, however, it was virtually impossible to stay clear of the danger zones of so much close-packed artillery and two of 655 Squadron's pilots died in this way, accidentally blown out of the sky by the guns whose fire they were directing.

As the Italian campaign entered its final phases in 1945 the opposing armies faced each other across the plain of Lombardy; instead of directing huge forces of guns, the pilots were now required to control single pieces, generally of large calibre, in 'destructive shoots' against individual tanks, self-propelled guns or infantry strong points. Although the mathematical odds against hitting an individual vehicle with fire from a single gun are extremely high, it was found possible to harass the German armour and prevent it from closing with the forward Allied infantry positions, and on a number of occasions direct hits – with highly spectacular results – were obtained with heavy guns on these difficult targets.

Before the Italian campaign had ended, the invasion of north-west Europe was well under way. By the summer of 1944 13 Air OP squadrons had been raised of which eight served in France, Belgium, Holland and Germany. Austers were flying from forward airstrips in Normandy by the evening of D + 2; one was only 120 yards long and all were well within German artillery and mortar range. In the early weeks of the Normandy campaign, as at Anzio, the Air OPs controlled the fire of the naval armada anchored off the beaches as well as a continually augmented amount of land-based artillery. On 7 July Bazeley, now promoted and in command of a light anti-aircraft regiment at the eastern extremity of the beach-head, was able to listen on his radio as an Air OP directed the guns of HMS *Rodney* on a target just north of Caen, '. . . as I listened to his orders over the wireless and the response from the Navy and the whine of *Rodney*'s big [16 in] shells as they passed overhead, I looked back on the years since the summer of 1938 when the Air OP had been only a dream. Safe in the security of its own A.A. defences it was controlling the biggest guns of His Majesty's Navy – that shoot seemed to me the epitome of all for which we had striven.'

As in North Africa and Italy, the Auster pilots earned the grudging admiration of their redoubtable enemies. The writer of the War Journal of the 10th *Panzer SS Division* describing the difficulties of conducting operations in the face of Allied air superiority, summed it up, '. . . But the greatest nuisance of all are the slow-flying artillery spotters which work with utter calmness, just out of reach, and direct artillery fire on our forward positions.'

With the collapse of German resistance in the Falaise pocket, the floodgates opened and the great Allied advance was unleashed – Patton and his armour careering like cavalry across France and through to the frontiers of the *Reich*, the British and Canadians to Brussels and beyond. By the end of August it seemed that victory was within sight; indeed, it was hard to see how the *Wehrmacht* could recover from such days as those described in the War Diaries of the Air OP Squadrons: '18 August – an epic day. The [Falaise] gap nearly closed and enormous slaughter of enemy tanks, motor transport and infantry . . . by evening the whole area littered with fires from burning vehicles, tanks and woods.' A few days earlier a single Air OP pilot had conducted a shoot which exemplified the effect of combined air mastery and artillery power; unmolested by enemy aircraft or ground fire, he engaged a group of 40 German tanks massed in preparation for an attack. He was allotted all the artillery of three corps and the heavy guns of the Army Groups, Royal Artillery. Nearly 600 guns of all calibres from field artillery to the heaviest weapons were under the control of one man in a light aircraft – something which would have been dismissed as sheer fantasy only a few years earlier.

By the Autumn of 1944 the Air OP organization was regularized, proven in war, versatile and confident. The years of struggle were over and the value of airborne artillery control now went unquestioned. At the same time, many other claims were now being made on the squadrons. The Auster was found to be an ideal staff car, spiriting senior officers across country, free from delays caused by congested main supply routes, time saving and prestigious (if extremely uncomfortable). More and more hours were now being spent on these 'liaison' tasks. In addition, the map-reading talents of the pilots were increasingly put to use for close reconnaissance; often it was found quicker and easier to put up an Auster for a quick look 'over the hill' than to call for RAF assistance. Air OP units were now equipped with reasonably good cameras and each squadron had its own photo-processing vehicle; this enabled commanders to call for air photographs of the ground over which they would be fighting, and to get good large prints within hours. Urgent stores, providing they were not too bulky, could be dropped to units out of reach of ground transport; telephone cables could be paid out across rivers and other obstacles. Bold experiments in the conduct of tactical missions were being tried out; using ground radar to direct the aircraft, an Auster could be flown by night many miles behind enemy lines to observe troop movements and engage any target rash enough to betray its presence. A whole new operational world was opening out and the only limitations, it seemed, were those imposed by the Auster's total lack of sophistication, especially its complete lack of blind-flying instruments.

Field Marshal Montgomery set the seal of approval on Bazeley's pioneering work when he had the following to say after the end of the war in Europe, 'The Air OP has proved its value in this campaign. It has become a necessary part of gunnery and we must press for a good aeroplane for the job. Very good Royal Artillery officers are required for duty in the squadrons and they must be selected with this in view. Primarily an Air OP officer must be a good gunner – it is not difficult to teach him to fly.'

Thousands of miles away from the European theatre, the light aircraft was proving indispensable in Burma, where Cochrane's Air Commando provided support for the 14th Army in its ultimately triumphant campaign. The Americans were joined in September 1943 by a British Air OP squadron whose pilots and groundcrews found the climate as dour an opponent as the Japanese. Despite appalling flying conditions they carried out their task throughout the monsoons, and were heavily involved in the desperate fighting of the Arakan campaign and in the crucial battles before the 'gateway of India' at Kohima and Imphal.

Until the end of the Burma campaign 656 Squadron's Austers continued to support the whole of 14th Army. They and their resourceful pilots and ground crews had exemplified everything that Parham had said could be achieved in his original 1933 essay; the Army had been given a new tool in the form of a simple aerial vehicle which could overcome the limitations imposed by terrain on conventional land vehicles and which endowed the military commander with something far more valuable than highly efficient fire control: he could use the Air OP as an extension of his own observation, himself move freely around the battlefield, regaining that close touch with his units which was second nature in the 19th century but which seemed to have been lost as warfare became mechanized in the 20th. The commander in his light plane, using radio to control his units, was restored to the mobility enjoyed by Wellington who controlled his army at Waterloo on horseback.

CHAPTER FOUR

First Blood

Throughout the dark winter months of 1939–40 the *Weserübung* team worked hard. Detailed planning was put into the hands of the officer selected to direct the operation, *General der Infanterie* Nikolaus von Falkenhorst, Commander of XXI Corps, a 63-year-old soldier of the old school with no evident political leanings. This shrewd soldier widened the scope of the plan to include Denmark in order to secure a clear route to the objective as well as guaranteeing the security of the narrow entrance to the Baltic. His initial plan visualized six divisions for Norway and two for Denmark; in the event, total success was achieved with far fewer airborne and airlanded troops. The initial assault was actually carried out by the equivalent of an infantry division and a parachute regiment of three battalions. The remainder of Falkenhorst's corps was landed from the sea at various points in both Denmark and Norway on 9 April, under close naval and air protection.

Even as the *Wehrmacht* bore down, the Norwegian and Danish Governments were presented with Hitler's ultimatum. They were ordered to accept German protection at once and without a struggle. This demand was placed by the German ministers in Copenhagen and Oslo at 5.20 am on 9 April. The Norwegians refused to yield; the Danes submitted. Their replies were irrelevant, for the war machine was launched at them in any case.

The airborne part of *Weserübung* was in the hands of a *Luftwaffe* officer, *Generalleutnant* Hans Geisler, commander of 10 *Luftflotte*, comprising medium bombers, divebombers for close support, single and twin-engined fighters, reconnaissance and maritime units, and 500 Ju52 transports. Because of the extreme range of the *Weserübung* objectives in mid and northern Norway, it was essential to seize Danish airfields on the first day, together with those at Sola near Stavanger and Fornebu just outside Oslo. The *coup-de-main* attacks against these were entrusted to parachute units under command of *Generalmajor* Süssman, nominated for the task by Student himself. An additional role for the paratroops was the seizure of the key bridge linking the small Danish island of Falster with Zealand, on which stands Copenhagen. Possession of this bridge secured the ferry link between Germany and the Danish capital.

If the seaborne part of *Weserübung* was boldly conceived, the airborne plan was a masterpiece of audacity. Just as victims of a smash-and-grab raid are paralysed by the violence of the onslaught, so did the Germans visualize the effect of their airborne arrival in Denmark. The force detailed to take the vital airfields at Aalborg in North Jutland was only one platoon of paratroops; they landed early on 9 April after the Danish Government's acceptance of the German ultimatum and quickly secured their objectives. The remainder of the company dropped with equal success to take the Vordingborg bridge whilst German ground troops quickly followed up from Falster and straight on into Copenhagen. Denmark was occupied with only a few shots fired.

In Norway, the airborne operation was far more dramatic. The key objective was the capital city, Oslo. It was the nerve-centre of the Norwegian communications network for southern and central Norway, and a boldly-executed attack here offered an additional bonus – the capture of the king and his government. The Germans therefore planned to land two battalions from warships near the city centre and two more by air at Fornebu airfield after its seizure by two

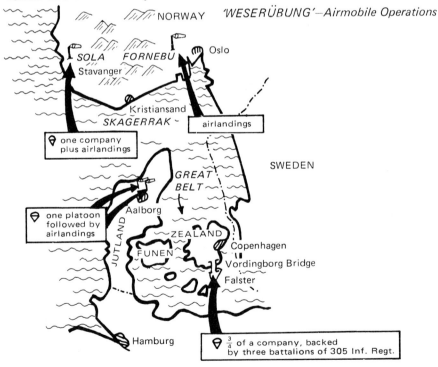

companies of paratroops. During the night the German ships approaching Oslo were detected and the heavy cruiser *Blücher* was sunk by the resolute defenders of the Oscarsborg fortress.

The Norwegians had now been thoroughly alerted and were thirsting for a fight. When German bombers and fighters, operating near the limits of their range, appeared over Oslo at dawn, they were gallantly engaged by *Gladiator* biplane fighters of the Royal Norwegian Air Force which shot down four, damaging two more. Whilst this air fight went on, the two parachute companies were flying towards Fornebu. Unexpected cloud, however, confused the crews of the transport aircraft and they were compelled to divert to Aalborg in Denmark, where the airfield was already in German hands. The aircraft carrying the airlanding element of the Fornebu operation were crewed by more experienced pilots and managed to find the objective in the murk. The leading Ju52, flown by *Hauptmann* Wagner, was approaching Fornebu when it received a cancellation order by radio, which Wagner ignored, believing it to be a hoax. He was not to know that the parachutists had failed to arrive and that the High Command had momentarily lost its nerve. A burst of Norwegian fire hit his aircraft as it approached to land, mortally wounding him, and his co-pilot took the plane into the air again.

Shortly after this, the escorting *Luftwaffe* fighters arrived on the scene; they had to land because of fuel shortage, and the defenders of the airfield surrendered. The main transport force quickly landed, and by 4 pm a battalion of German infantry, a band at their head, was marching into the centre of Oslo.

At Stavanger, the other primary airborne objective, a company of 1st Parachute Regiment jumped onto the airfield at 9 am on 9 April, to be followed ten minutes later by two battalions of the 193rd Infantry Regiment landing from Ju52s.

This drop was entirely successful and the first airborne phase of *Weserübung* was complete. The second phase was the exploitation of the initial landings; objectives further north were to be seized before the British and French could react and whilst the Norwegian army was still rushing to its mobilization positions. On 11 April 12 Ju52s flew to the far north and landed on the frozen surface of Lake Hartvig, carrying infantry and a battery of light mountain guns in a *coup-de-main* attempt to seize Narvik, where British, French and Polish troops arrived from the sea four days later, driving off the Germans for the time being. On 15 April a bold attempt was made to cut the Oslo–Trondheim railway at Dombas, 150 miles north-west of Oslo, when a company of paratroops was dropped ahead of the main German overland thrust. The Norwegians, however, counter attacked promptly and after four days of brisk fighting the surviving Germans were compelled to surrender.

After the failure at Dombas, Student retrieved his units; they returned to their bases in Germany and the applause of the homefront. The airborne troops had undergone their baptism of fire, and the making of a new mythology was under way. Bold handling of small units following a dramatic arrival on the battlefield made for good reading in the lavishly produced war propaganda journals, such as *Signal*, which sold well at every German bookstall. Wagner's audacity at Fornebu, where he had pressed his landing home at the cost of his own life, appealed to a nation which tends to exalt the war hero. Student was well pleased with this début. There was, however, another side to the coin. More than one in five of *Luftflotte* 10's Ju52s had been lost, through weather, enemy action or in crashes on unprepared landing grounds; and a dangerously low standard of airmanship had been displayed by many of the transport aircrew. Lavish fighter support and prompt re-supply from the air had contributed much to ultimate success, but a number of problems remained unsolved: control of the force en route to the objective, lack of heavy weapons in support of the parachute assault, and the inability of the paratroops to jump with any but the lightest small arms were the chief of these. Failure to solve these problems came near to costing the Germans success at Crete in the following year.

Meanwhile, a far greater enterprise than *Weserübung* was about to be launched. Hitler now went ahead with his plans for the conquest of his enemies in the West. The master plan encompassed the invasion of Holland and Belgium, by-passing and out-flanking the Maginot Line on which the French had pinned their hopes, and driving for the Channel Ports to cut off the British Expeditionary Force.

Apart from the rapid neutralization of the Low Countries the mortal thrust against the Anglo-French Armies was to be through the Ardennes, fondly thought by the French High Command to be impassable to motorized formations. The main attack was expected to follow the pattern of the right hook of 1914 and the French and British were poised to react to this with a general advance into Belgium.

The Allies awaited developments with confidence. To the south lay the impregnable fortress line. They felt that they could forestall any German move through the Low Countries. With the Belgian and Dutch armies at their side they outnumbered the Germans two-to-one in manpower and had more tanks. What they failed to appreciate was the spirit of the *Wehrmacht*, its superior fighting doctrines, and above all, its readiness to use the newly developed airborne arm to achieve overwhelming surprise. The intended victims lay behind their useless defences, unaware of the fate in store.

A new dimension was about to be added to the science of war. The *Wehrmacht* had been carefully trained and organized to break through opposition with its tanks, supported by motorized infantry, artillery and close-support aircraft. Resistance was to be by-passed and left to the slower-moving follow-up forces with their marching infantry and horse-drawn transport and guns. The techniques of inter-service and inter-arm co-operation, high-speed staff work and radio control had been evolved and practised to perfection on innumerable exercises and wargames. Certain special operations had been meticulously rehearsed in utmost secrecy; these were the airborne *coups-de-main* aimed at the Belgian barrier fortress of Eben Emael and the core of the Dutch defensive system. For Holland had now been added to the list of victims, and was about to receive an airborne assault of novel boldness and ferocity.

The Dutch, whilst remaining neutral, had been amongst the first nations in Europe to mobilize in September 1939, having leapt to arms on the second day of the invasion of Poland, since when they had stood to their defences at a high state of readiness. The defence of Holland against land attack from Germany was not easy. In the north-east the provinces of Drenthe and Gelderland lay wide open, with virtually no natural obstacles. In the south, the 'Maastricht appendix', a tongue of Dutch territory extending down to the Aachen–Liege area, was equally indefensible. The Dutch High Command had therefore established two first lines of defence south from the Zuyder Zee to the Belgian border, where they rested on the Peel marshlands. These were known as the Grebbe and Peel lines, and the territory behind them, containing the great cities of Rotterdam, Amsterdam and the centre of government at The Hague, was known as 'Fortress Holland'. There were plans to augment its fieldworks by opening the dykes to admit the sea – the historic method of defending the Low Countries. Against a conventional overland attack these expedients would have been effective; recognition of them may well have saved Holland from invasion in 1914. This time there would be no reprieve; the Germans, recognizing the threat posed to their *Panzers* by strategic flooding, decided to seize a number of key bridges over the rivers Maas, Waal and Merwede with airlanded and air dropped troops who would hold on until relieved by the advancing ground forces. This was, in effect, an 'airborne carpet' up which the mechanized spearheads were to rush. It was also the concept which was so nearly to succeed for Field Marshal Montgomery over four years later.

Simultaneously with the laying of this 'carpet' paratroops and air-landed units were to go for selected airfields and landing grounds around The Hague, with the aim of capturing the Queen of the Netherlands and the rest of the royal family and of crippling the national centre of government.

This daring plan would have three other results if successful: it would stop the movement of Dutch reinforcements from the area of The Hague across to the threatened Grebbe–Peel lines; it would block any move of the French army to succour the Dutch by advancing north-east across Belgium; and it would deny the use of the military airfields in Fortress Holland to the RAF's light bomber force.

The land offensive against Holland was entrusted to the relatively weak 18th Army under *General* Georg von Küchler. His spearhead consisted of the 9th *Panzer* division and a motorized SS regiment, followed by a division of cavalry and six infantry divisions. The novelty of the attack lay in the airborne forces assigned by Student to von Küchler's support – his own 7th *Fliegerdivision* of three parachute battalions and an airlanded infantry regiment, and von Sponeck's 22nd Infantry Division, also trained in the airlanding role. The air transport force available amounted to some 400 Ju52s.

As the day for *Fall Gelb* drew closer, tension mounted. The Ju52s were massed at airfields well back from the German frontier, at Münster, Loddenheide, Lippspringe, Gütersloh, Paderborn, Lippstadt and Werl. After 11 false alarms, the troops and aircrew finally stood to on the evening of 9 May as darkness fell over the Westphalian plain. Those with furthest to fly were airborne first; the 1st battalion of 2nd Parachute Regiment in 65 Junkers took off for The Hague at 4 am, followed an hour later by 100 more aircraft carrying the airlanding troops commanded in person by *Generalmajor* von Sponeck. As this armada droned westwards towards Holland every officer and man knew that he was in the van of the *Wehrmacht* and that a famous victory was in the offing.

As already mentioned, the Dutch were not entirely unprepared for invasion. In particular, Fortress Holland was garrisoned by tough, well-trained troops, many with long years of soldiering in the East Indies behind them. The Netherlands Marines and Grenadier regiments in particular could be counted amongst the finest in Europe, sharing battle honours dating back over three centuries, gained in dour campaigns against Germans, French and British alike. In command of the Dutch Army was *Luitenant-Generaal* Henri Gerard Winkelman, a thoroughly professional soldier fully aware of the airborne threat to Fortress Holland, who repeatedly warned his subordinates to take the necessary precautions. Most of them, however, were set in their ways; they trusted in the Grebbe and Peel lines, the inundations, the promises of French help.

Von Sponeck's force flew on, now at low level as it crossed Dutch soil. The alarm was sounded, and anti-aircraft guns fired wildly. A company of parachutists was dropped at 6.30 am on each of the airfields at Valkenburg, Ockenburg and Ypenburg and more aircraft arrived with airlanded troops an hour later. There was initial success, but at Ypenburg in particular the defenders kept their heads and shot down 12 Ju52s as they landed. The sight of the burning wreckage heartened the defence and fierce counter attacks were launched. At Valkenburg three resolute battalions of Dutch grenadiers drove the Germans off the field, and at all three airfields the anti-aircraft defences began to shoot down numbers of Ju52s. The second wave of transport aircraft circled uncertainly overhead; far from enjoying the unopposed landing they had expected, the pilots looked down apprehensively at scenes of mounting confusion; clearly a hornet's nest had been aroused. The air commander ordered a diversion and planes started to land on the beach at Katwijk; after seven had been wrecked in soft sand disorder began to reign, with Ju52s attempting to set down on near-by roads and any available open space. Thanks to Winkelman's foresight, obstacles had already been set up on the main

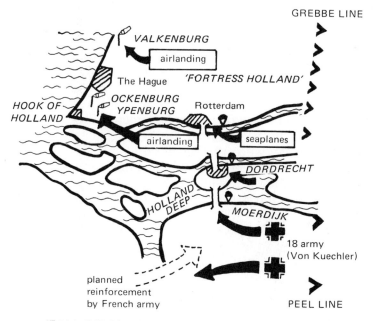

'FALL GELB'—Airmobile Operations Against Holland

49

roads and large numbers of aircraft crashed into these, with great loss of life. The airlanded units which got onto the ground were hopelessly mixed up and disorientated, and those who had survived at Katwijk were quickly rounded up or eliminated by Dutch infantry. As the day wore on, von Sponeck's predicament worsened. The 1st Battalion of Netherlands Grenadiers retook Ockenburg airfield, whilst the 2nd and 3rd Battalions recaptured Ypenburg. In Valkenburg village, whither they had been driven from the airfield, the hard-pressed Germans dug themselves in under continuous artillery fire and only held the Dutch counter attacks off with great difficulty.

At last light on 10 May, von Sponeck's division was therefore fighting for its life in four separate battles and had been driven off all its objectives. The primary aim of eliminating the Dutch High Command had failed, and so the third wave of transport aircraft was diverted to the Rotterdam area, landing more or less intact on Waalhaven airfield as darkness fell.

The operations to seize the key bridges on the overland route to Rotterdam had gone much better than von Sponeck's airlandings. At Rotterdam itself, a subaltern and 30 paratroops landed north of the bridge over the river Maas, commandeered some tramcars and drove boldly onto the bridge in them. As they arrived, 12 floatplanes carrying a company of infantry alighted on the river. The troops swarmed up onto the bridge, removing the demolition charges pre-placed by Dutch engineers. The two parties of Germans were then assailed from both ends of the bridge by the Dutch army, but held grimly on to their prize, thus denying its use to Winkelman's troops. At Dordrecht, two platoons of 3rd Company, 1st Parachute Regiment took the bridge over the River Merwede within minutes of landing and removed the demolition charges but were ejected by a prompt Dutch counter attack. German reinforcements then arrived on the scene and recaptured the bridge; it was held against successive Dutch attacks until 13 May when the vanguard of 9th *Panzer* division appeared and finally drove off the stubborn defenders. The hoped-for French relief operation from the south was stopped in its tracks on 13 May at Breda and thrown back across the Belgian border. By this time, however, Queen Wilhelmina, her family, and the Dutch Government had crossed to England, and much of the Dutch Army had extricated itself from the line of the River Maas and joined the garrison of Fortress Holland. The defenders of The Hague continued to fight successfully until 14 May, when the *Luftwaffe* heartlessly bombed the magnificent old city of Rotterdam whilst armistice discussions were actually taking place between the Dutch and German High Commands. A further terror raid was made on Den Helder later that day and the spirit had gone from the defence. Student himself became a casualty when, during the surrender of the Dutch troops in Rotterdam, German ground troops arrived on the scene and, unaware of the situation, began firing. The German commander was hit in the head, his life being saved only by the prompt work of a Dutch surgeon.

So ended the airborne assault on Holland. It was the biggest operation of its kind yet attempted, a bold plan carried through despite reverses and heavy casualties. The surprise of an airborne landing caused initial dismay but the Dutch army rallied quickly and denied von Sponeck his primary aims. It was clear that whilst resolutely opposed airlandings were not a valid operation of war, the moral effect of such outflanking landings could outweigh the purely tactical advantage (especially if rumour could be enlisted to spread despair) and that brave, aggressive and well-motivated men can use surprise to achieve results wholly disproportionate to their own numbers. The Germans ruefully faced up to an unexpectedly large 'butcher's bill' for this performance; 117 Ju52s were lost beyond repair – mostly due to landing accidents. In the 22nd Division alone nearly half the officers and more than a quarter of the rest became casualties; 1600 paratroops were taken prisoner and removed to England.

*　　　*　　　*

If the airborne attack on Holland had been messy but ultimately successful, the *coup-de-main* also launched early on 10 May against the fortress of Eben Emael and the Albert Canal bridges must surely take its place as one of the most outstanding airborne operations of all time. It combined the action of glider-borne troops, parachutists and ground troops who, trained to perfection and employed with great economy, brought off a stunning tactical victory.

The invasion of the Low Countries was planned by okw from the start to be secondary to the master-stroke against France. The German High Command correctly assumed that any move against Belgium would compel the French and British to wheel forward onto the line of the Dyle; once this move had been initiated, the main onslaught would be aimed at the weak hinge on the advancing Allies' right; this coincided with the supposedly 'difficult' Ardennes, opposite which stood low-calibre French divisions of Corap's 9th Army, blissfully unaware that they were destined to face *Generaloberst* Gerd von Runstedt's Army Group 'A' which included no less than four *Panzer* Corps commanded by stars like Guderian and Hoth. Von Runstedt's task was to punch through Corap's weak army and then, instead of hooking left and south for Paris as in the old Schlieffen plan, to go hard for the Pas de Calais, thereby trapping the French 1st and 7th Armies and the BEF – the Allies' best formations – in Flanders. *Generaloberst* Fedor von Bock's Army Group 'B' had the dual task of knocking out the Dutch Army and of offering itself eagerly to the Allies as it thrust across the Albert Canal just north of Liège. The Albert Canal had to be crossed at the outset if the Allies were to be convinced that the main German attack was to come through Belgium. This formidable task fell to *General* Walter von Reichenau's 6th Army.

The Albert Canal line was built by the Belgians after the First World War specifically to deter any repetition of the 1914 German invasion. Extensive fortifications combined with the water obstacle of the Albert Canal and the River Maas just across the Dutch border in the 'Maastricht appendix' and it was clear that these defences had to be cleared with a running jump. The key to the defensive system presented in itself the hardest problem. This was the fortress of Eben Emael, widely believed to be the most powerful and impregnable in the world, set on the west bank of the Canal and capable of dominating with its guns all crossing sites on the Maas and the Albert Canal out to a range of 16 kilometres. Work on it had been completed only five years previously. It was entirely dug out of a granite hill looming nearly 50 metres above the canal water level. Outwardly it was a grassy mound with a flat top measuring 200 by 400 metres. Surrounded by carefully sited moats and anti-tank ditches, its four roof-top casemates could retract into the ground. It bristled with guns: two of 120mm with all-round traverse, and a range of 16 kilometres; sixteen 75mm quick firers; twelve 60mm high velocity anti-tank guns; anti-aircraft machine guns on the roof, and 25 twin machine guns for close defence. The fort's guns were only part of an elaborate system of fire control in which the firepower of the Eben Emael was interlinked with neighbouring field works. The garrison of nearly 1200 officers and men were comfortably and safely housed 25 metres below the roof of the fort, supplied with water, food and ammunition to sustain an indefinite siege. The bridges over the canal were equally well cared for. Each one had a close garrison of an officer and 11 men with anti-tank guns and automatic weapons, to guard expressly against *coup-de-main* assault. Reinforcements were close at hand. Each bridge had two demolition systems: an electric one, and, as insurance, a conventional fuse system which could blow the charge after a two-minute delay. For 600 metres each side along the west bank were blockhouses with machine guns.

For many months in 1938–39 the Germans quietly studied this formidable defensive system, accumulating so much detailed knowledge that they were able to build replicas of it in order to devise special methods for its conquest. Hitler took a personal interest in this difficult problem, and after advice from an unusual quarter he came up with the victorious solution. His adviser was the vivacious Hanna Reitsch, already a well-known aviatrix (and incidentally one of the handful of women with whom Hitler ever seems to have established a lasting relationship – the others being his cousin Geli Raubl who shot herself, Eva Braun who eventually took poison in the *Führerbunker*, and Leni Riefenstahl the gifted film director). *Fräulein* Reitsch was an expert sailplane pilot; given the problem of Eben Emael she at once suggested a silent assault using troop-carrying gliders. Hitler, delighted, summoned Student who at once confirmed the plan's feasibility and nominated a young officer whom he knew stood a good chance of bringing it off. This was *Hauptmann* Walter Koch, one of his staff.

The glider to be used was the DFS230, which Student had developed several years earlier for just such a task as that now entrusted to the eager Koch who buckled down to the arduous training required, which took place in utmost secrecy deep inside Germany. On the remote training area at Grafenwohr near the old Czech border a replica of Eben Emael was subjected to all manner of demolition techniques, and special 50kg hollow charges were devised in order to pierce reinforced concrete. These would be operated by teams of gliderborne sappers, for Koch concluded that the fortress could best be taken by actually landing gliders on its grassy roof. His plan, which he personally presented to Hitler, gained the *Führer*'s enthusiastic approval and detailed planning and practice went on through the autumn and winter of 1939–40. Koch's force was divided into four parties, each 100 strong, organized and equipped for its own particular task. Three groups were assigned to the key Albert Canal bridges and one, commanded by *Leutnant* Witzig, to Eben Emael. Each group contained its specialist weapons: flamethrowers (to spread terror and neutralize the blockhouses), machine guns, anti-tank sections, mortars and demolition teams. Each man was trained in two roles and the preparatory training laid stress on ability to fight in small groups. Endless rehearsals were carried out; initially by day but soon by night, for Koch decided that the hour before dawn was the best time to secure maximum surprise and moral effect. After a final series of successful night rehearsals at Grafenwohr and Hildesheim, Koch moved his force up to airfields near Cologne, and waited for the order to go. H-hour was finally selected as 0530 hrs on 10 May, to synchronize with the attack on Holland. Koch, on his own initiative advanced his private H-hour to 0520; he was determined to achieve total surprise. At 0415 the glidertugs started to take off, climbing steadily in circles away from the frontier into the chill night air over Germany. In the gliders the men sweated and shivered alternately. Two of the DFS230s destined for Eben Emael became detached from their tugs and force landed on German soil in the dark; one of them was *Leutnant* Witzig's. Undismayed, he immediately started to make arrangements for another tug aircraft to take him on, whilst the other nine gliders bounced on towards the border at a height of 2500 metres. Although Koch had ordered the gliders to cast-off well beyond the target and approach from the dark western sky, they mostly did so almost overhead the fortress. Despite this, the glider pilots expertly wheeled down towards the unsuspecting Belgians. In the gliders the air thundered and drummed at the canvas skins and whined through the wingstruts, but from below the approach to battle was inaudible, as Hanna Reitsch had predicted. Accurate landings at two of the bridge sites resulted in total surprise and success, but at the third the garrison blew it in the face of the Germans as they arrived.

At Eben Emael, where surprise was crucial, it was triumphantly gained. The nine gliders, streaming brake parachutes, skidded to rest with a grinding run-on of around 20 metres. The sappers dashed out and began placing their deadly explosive charges on the inconspicuous

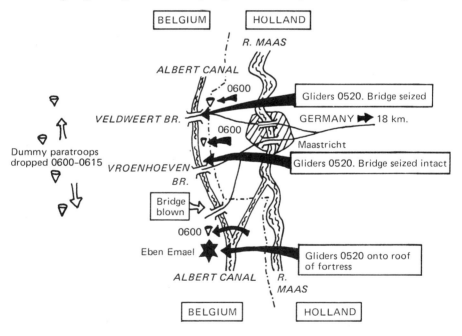

'FALL GELB'—Airmobile Operations Against Belgium

roofs of the casemates and the dawn was signalled by deafening explosions; so effective were the hollow charges, punching a pencil-like blast through three metres of concrete, that one Belgian soldier, 20 metres down below at the bottom of the stairway, was killed in his tracks. The stupendous noise paralysed the garrison who, deprived of all outside vision, could only guess at what was happening above. At first light, swarms of *Luftwaffe* divebombers appeared overhead, sealing off all reinforcement routes to the stricken fortress. Paratroops arrived with daylight to reinforce the assailants, and shortly afterwards a lone glider circled overhead and landed amidst cheers on the roof of Eben Emael. It was the irrepressible Witzig who had successfully obtained a second lift. Swarms of dummy parachutists were dropped to the west, further mystifying and confusing the defence.

Meanwhile, having crossed the border before dawn, Von Reichenau's *Panzers* were fighting through across the Maas. The Dutch demolitions partly failed at Maastricht, and 4th *Panzer* Division rushed the damaged bridge, sweeping aside all resistance as they pressed on towards Brussels. By 1430 hrs contact was made with the paratroopers and glider infantry at Veldwezelt bridge, and the armour poured across.

Throughout 10 May Koch's men worked patiently away atop Eben Emael, whose guns were totally unable to interfere with the proceedings. The garrison were forced to huddle unhappily in their underground barracks, powerless to act against their tormentors. All through the night the Germans continued to batter away with their explosives and at 1230 hrs on the 11th the fort surrendered. Sixty of its garrison had been killed and 40 wounded and over 1000 men marched sheepishly out to be taken prisoner. Koch's entire force had lost 6 men killed and 19 wounded.

The German offensive thundered victoriously on. Army Group 'A' punched through Corap's 9th Army and although isolated French units elsewhere fought splendidly, the writing was on the wall. In Belgium the BEF and French were forced first to look nervously over their shoulder then to make for the beaches to avoid envelopment as Von Runstedt swung north for the Channel. The valiant Dutch had been shocked into capitulation on 14 May and two weeks later the King of the Belgians followed suit. The British Army, now cut off from the main body of the French, retired to the Dunkirk perimeter, from which it was extricated in a superhuman *ad hoc* operation by the Royal Navy and a fleet of amateur small-boat enthusiasts. The French finally began to sue for armistice on 17 June and laid down their arms eight days later.

The strength and vigour of the *Blitzkrieg* amazed the world. A combination of opportunism, inspiration, training and martial expertise had produced for Hitler in 42 days the results for which a generation had died in 1914–18. The German nation rose in acclamation of the ex non-commissioned officer whose genius, it seemed, had redeemed the nation's honour. Those victorious troops not required to garrison the conquered lands returned home, many to be demobilized; it seemed that victorious peace was assured and that only the minor business of settling the British remained, even assuming they rejected the *Führer*'s generous terms. Unfortunately for the Germans, Hitler's appetite was far from being sated; and Britain, now under Churchill's resolute leadership, was in no mood to treat with the dictator.

The performance of the airborne forces in the Low Countries was enthusiastically treated in the press. To Student, slowly recovering from his severe wounds, it appeared that his star was in the ascendant. 7 *Fliegerdivision* was firmly established with three regiments of paratroops (who were also trained as glider troops) and Koch's special force, crowned with glory for its conquest of Eben Emael, was expanded into an airborne assault regiment. The 22nd Infantry Division, its casualties soon replaced, remained assigned to the air-landing role. All these formations were placed under command of XI *Fliegerkorps*; back in their old training grounds, they buckled down to preparation for an operation which never took place – *Seelöwe* (Sealion), the attack on England. The atmosphere in the parachute battalions was euphoric; had they not been the spearhead of victory? They confidently awaited their next test, certain of their prowess, having given conclusive proof of the value of shock tactics and high morale. Had they seen inside Hitler's mind, however, their enthusiasm would have been dampened, for he considered that the chief value of airborne operations lay in their ability to paralyse the unprepared victim. In time, Germany's opponents would train in anti-parachutist techniques, capitalizing on their lack of cohesion after landing, on their lack of heavy weapons, and on their almost total lack of mobility once committed to the land battle. Because of this, Hitler secretly believed that the value of airborne forces would steadily depreciate, an opinion which seemed to be confirmed after the assault on Crete in 1941.

CHAPTER FIVE

The German High Tide: Crete

By the late summer of 1940 Hitler's gaze had turned eastwards towards Russia. Stalin, though still nominally his ally, was clearly edging south-west down into the Balkans. In mid-1940 the Soviets had marched into Bessarabia and part of Bukovina; their goal was evident – the rich Ploesti oilfields without which Hitler could not fight a prolonged mechanized campaign in the east. Hitler would almost certainly have wished to gain Ploesti, together with primacy in the Balkans, through a process of diplomatic engulfment without the need for a military campaign, but his hand was forced by the unannounced antics of his new Italian allies. Mussolini, having hastily joined what appeared to be the winning side in June 1940 as France tottered to defeat, now decided to provide his people with bread and circuses in the form of a grand Balkan military triumph. The Italian army, already in occupation of Albania, crossed the Greek frontier on 28 October on what the Duce and his generals imagined would be a processional march to Athens. The Greeks declined to observe the rules and fought with spirit, flinging back the Italians in disarray. More significantly, the British reacted positively in support of the outraged Greeks; they occupied Crete on 31 October and during the next week had established air bases in southern Greece within easy range of the Ploesti oilfields. Hitler had no alternative but to rush to the help of his importunate ally. It was the worst possible time of year for a Balkan campaign, and initially the Germans relied on political moves whilst preparing for a military stroke in the spring of 1941. An alliance was sealed with Bulgaria and an attempt made to lure Yugoslavia into the Berlin–Rome axis. Just as this seemed about to succeed there was a *coup* in Belgrade and the pro-German regent Paul was ejected by a military junta unsympathetic to the Axis. Now only military force would accomplish the task and Hitler invaded Yugoslavia on 6 April. Within a week the Germans were in Belgrade and an armistice was signed on 17 April. In a textbook operation, *Generaloberst* Maximilian von Weichs's Second Army, rapidly concentrated overland from all over Europe, smashed the Yugoslavs at a cost of less than 600 casualties, taking 344,000 prisoners. The Allies had been given a further insight into the power and virtuosity of the *Wehrmacht*.

In Greece, where in the depths of winter the Italians floundered unhappily, a German rescue operation was indicated. Towards the end of February 1941 a British expeditionary force arrived to bolster the Greek defence, but when the German attack came, under the direction of *Feldmarschall* Wilhelm List, it struck unerringly at the vulnerable and ill-defended sector where the British and Greek flanks joined. List's Twelfth Army, of 12 divisions, quickly gained momentum. Salonika fell on 9 April, the Greek Second Army laid down its arms, and with resistance broken in the north-east the German thrust through southern Yugoslavia drove the British into retreat; falling back towards the Peloponessus the Greeks surrendered on 20 April, and it was clear to List that if he could seize the bridges across the gorge of the Corinth Canal he might prevent much of the British force escaping to Crete and Egypt.

Here was a splendid task for airborne troops; the cutting off of a withdrawal route had been regarded as a classic paratroop role since the Soviet demonstrations of 1935–36, only no one had ever actually tried it in war. Student's XI *Fliegerkorps*, athirst for further battle honours, had been moved from Germany to Bulgaria the previous month to take advantage of just such a tactical opportunity and was fretting unemployed on its airfields – a situation in which Allied airborne troops were to find themselves throughout the summer of 1944.

The British were using the single road bridge across the canal for their getaway. The task of seizing it was entrusted to the reinforced 2nd Parachute Regiment of *Oberst* Stürm, who elected to drop a group of 52 sappers onto the bridge in order to defuse the demolition charges, his 1st Battalion north of the bridge, and the 2nd Battalion to the south. These would then form a close perimeter to hold on until German ground forces came to the rescue.

The defenders had appreciated the airborne threat and assigned a scratch force to hold the bridge. On 24 April this consisted of a detachment of Australian sappers who were to blow the demolitions after the last retreating forces had got across, some 3·7in anti-aircraft guns, two companies of Australian infantry and four light tanks from the 4th Hussars with their regimental HQ. By dawn on the 26th, additional troops had been added and on paper the garrison looked fairly powerful – there were now ten anti-aircraft guns, four companies of infantry, a troop of armoured cars, the HQ of the 4th Hussars (Lt-Col. Lillington) and his four tanks. Lillington as the senior officer assumed command, but in the absence of adequate radio or telephone communications was unable to exercise much control once battle was joined.

On the morning of 26 April the Germans clambered into their aircraft before dawn and took off from Larissa at 0500 hrs for the two-hour flight. At 0700 hrs a swarm of German fighter aircraft started to attack the British anti-aircraft defences and within 40 minutes the garrison were under incessant bombardment by nearly 100 fighters and 20 Ju87 *Stukas*. It was an unsettling experience for tired troops who had been on the run for two weeks and who had seen very little in the way of friendly air support. Just before 0800 the strafing suddenly ceased and before the defenders could adjust to the silence Stürm's two battalions were dropping at opposite ends of the bridge. They were on the ground by 0810 and not a single Junker was shot down. As the paratroops came down, 12 gliders landed at the bridge, which was immediately rushed by the combat engineers. A ferocious battle broke out, in the course of which the bridge was destroyed, perhaps by accidental detonation or a supreme act of sacrifice by some Australian sapper. The fighting died lamely to a close. A thousand Imperial troops were taken prisoner at a cost to the Germans of 63 dead and 160 wounded.

The assault, spectacular though it was, had actually failed in its primary aim. It was launched too late to prevent the British forces getting across to the Peloponessus, and through the blowing of the bridge the headlong German pursuit was held up. However, it demonstrated the brilliant use of ground/air co-operation perfected by the *Wehrmacht*, with close-support fighter-bombers acting as artillery up to the last seconds before the parachute landing. It gave the Germans the idea that opposed parachute landings were now feasible, and illusion which was shortly to cost them dear.

The Imperial forces were able to withdraw, more or less intact, to Crete and Egypt, for command of the sea still remained firmly in the hands of the Royal Navy. A garrison of some 6000 Imperial troops had been stationed in Crete since the previous October in order to provide security for the naval anchorage in Suda Bay and to defend the island's landing grounds at Maleme, Retimo and Herakleion. As the result of the evacuation from Greece, these forces were greatly augmented and now totalled about 30,000, predominantly Australians and New Zealanders, with more than 10,000 Greek troops. The British commander was Maj.-Gen. Bernard Freyberg, a New Zealander who had won an astounding Victoria Cross fighting the Turks at the Dardanelles in 1915 and had commanded the New Zealand division in the recent Greek campaign. He was given the daunting task of holding on to Crete in order to deny it to the

Germans as an air and naval base. Early in May his plan was ready; it was geared to the defence of the three landing grounds and the Suda Bay naval anchorage, all of which lay on the island's exposed north coast. The most westerly, Maleme, was assigned to the New Zealand Division of two brigades and additional units, commanded by Brig. Puttick. Canea and the Suda Bay area were held by a hastily assembled force of mixed units and part of the Royal Marine Mobile Naval Base Defence Organisation (MNBDO) under Maj.-Gen. Weston. Retimo was defended by the 19th Australian Brigade (Brig. G. A. Vasey) and Herakleion by the British 14th Infantry Brigade under Brig. Chappel. The Greeks were divided between these sectors and instructions given to all units for a constant look-out against landings from the sea. There were no reserves, other than the nomination of one of the New Zealand brigades and a British battalion as 'Force Reserve'. Strung out along the narrow coastal plain the sectors could not support each other, and as most of their transport had been abandoned in Greece, the defence was virtually immobile. The few heavy anti-aircraft guns were concentrated around Suda Bay and Canea and there was a dire shortage of field artillery, as well as of much needed tools and defence stores – sandbags, mines, timber and barbed wire.

Freyberg considered that a combined sea and air assault could come within 10 or 14 days and the defenders began to dig and wire their positions. For a time, the RAF kept some fighter aircraft on the island, and this little band of *Hurricanes* and *Gladiators* fought valiantly against increasing odds and without hope of reinforcement. Realizing their struggle was hopeless, Freyberg agreed to their final withdrawal on 19 May. Only seven were left at this stage. The Germans now had undisputed command of the air, the vital prerequisite for success in airborne operations.

The German plan for the capture of Crete was entrusted entirely to the *Luftwaffe*. Student's advocacy of his airborne troops convinced Göring that here lay a chance to recover the prestige of his service after its repulse over Britain. Hitler agreed somewhat unenthusiastically to the plan now put forward, but only on condition that it was carried through quickly. He was not convinced that the seizure of Crete was essential to the master plan which now totally absorbed him – *Barbarossa*, the invasion of Russia. Student and the *Luftwaffe* generals, on the other hand, visualized a whole series of 'island-hopping' assaults, of which Crete was only the first. Malta and Cyprus would be next on the list; the eastern Mediterranean, dominated by German air power which would drive off the British fleet, could then become an Axis sea, permitting free movement in all directions for amphibious landing forces.

In charge of the whole operation was *Generaloberst* Alexander Löhr, the commander of 4 *Luftflotte*, comprising VIII and XI *Fliegerkorps*. The first of these formations was commanded by *General der Flieger* Freiherr von Richtofen and was specifically organized and equipped for the close support of land operations; a balanced force of long-range bombers based in Greece and Bulgaria, with reconnaissance aircraft and fighter-bombers operating from southern Greece and the Aegean islands. Additional aircraft were on call from X *Fliegerkorps* in north Africa to reinforce von Richtofen's 228 bombers, 205 dive bombers, 230 fighters and 50 reconnaissance aircraft; all their crews were well versed in the close-support role, having driven the Greek Air Force and the RAF from the Balkan skies only a month earlier, and before *Merkur* started they enjoyed almost total mastery of the air over Crete.

A few days before the operation von Richtofen had just over 514 serviceable aircraft. Student's XI *Fliegerkorps* possessed more than 500 transport aircraft and 72 gliders, which had been moved forward to rapidly-constructed landing grounds in southern Greece.

Student established his HQ amidst the fading splendours of the Grande Bretagne hotel in Athens, where behind shuttered windows he and his staff got down to the complex detailed planning of *Merkur*. From the outset this was carried out on wildly incorrect intelligence information. It was assumed that the British were ill-prepared and demoralized, and the German estimate of the defenders' numerical strength listed only a third of the troops actually on the ground. The attitude of the Cretan population was similarly misjudged; it was believed that a sizeable pro-German element would take up arms when the operation started, identifying themselves with the enigmatic codewords 'Major Bock'. The value of the Greek troops on Crete was also discounted; in the event, mixed in with Imperial units as they were, they would fight valiantly. Under Freyberg's energetic direction, all his units were well dug in by 17 May and their camouflage and track discipline was so good that the majority of their battle positions were not detected by *Luftwaffe* reconnaissance aircraft which flew freely over Crete in the weeks before the attack. Freyberg, near despair on 1 May, had then signalled Gen. Wavell, his Commander-in-Chief, that although he could and would fight, he could not hope to repel invasion without full naval and air support, and that if these were not forthcoming the holding of Crete should be reconsidered. By 16 May he was more optimistic and after touring the defences was able to assure Wavell that his troops were fit, their morale high and that they were well entrenched. He now had 45 field guns with adequate ammunition, and two 'infantry tanks' (i.e. heavily armoured vehicles built for close support of infantry) were positioned at each landing ground. More vehicles were being landed by sea, another battalion of good regular infantry, the 2nd Battalion of the Leicestershire Regiment – the famous 'Tigers'. 'I do not wish to be over-confident,' concluded Freyberg, 'but I feel that at least we will give excellent account of ourselves. With help of Royal Navy I trust Crete will be held.'

Löhr and Student initially failed to agree on an outline plan of attack for the airborne troops. Löhr believed in staking all on the two western landing grounds at Maleme and Canea and achieving over-whelming supremacy there. Student wanted to land in seven places and then spread out, reinforcing success as it occurred; he called this his 'oil-spot' theory. The problem was put to the distant Göring who settled for a compromise: landings at Maleme and Canea on the morning of D-day 20 May, and at Retimo and Herakleion in the afternoon. From 14 May the *Luftwaffe* stepped up its attacks on the island and the incessant bombardment was to sap the morale of many of the defenders.

The time came for Student to brief his subordinates and they con-verged on the Grande Bretagne Hotel: *Generalleutnant* Süssman, commander of 7 *Fliegerdivision*'s three parachute regiments, who was to land by glider with the leading elements and command the battle from the Canea–Retimo area; *Generalmajor* Meindl, in command of the Assault Regiment (one of whose battalions was commanded by *Major* Koch of Eben Emael fame); *Generalleutnant* Ringel of the 5th Mountain Division – tough soldiers made available for this operation, four regiments of them to be flown into the landing grounds in Ju52s; *Generalmajor* Konrad whose XI *Fliegerkommando* was to provide the airlift; and the commanders of the supporting troops who would go by sea, in hurriedly commandeered Greek fishing *caiques*. One of the parachute battalion commanders remembers that pregnant briefing vividly: *Major* Freiherr Friedrich-August von der Heydte was then the 35-year-old commanding officer of the 1st Battalion, 3rd Parachute Regiment. An aristocrat, classical scholar and incurable romantic, educated at an American university, he epitomized the best type of German soldier, good with his men, professionally skilled, courageous and chivalrous. More than almost anyone else in this story he represents those rather sad figures – brave men (and women, like Hanna Reitsch) destined by Fate to serve a rotten cause. Von der Heydte sensed the atmosphere in the shuttered ballroom of the hotel and Student's 'vibrant voice' as he outlined the plan. At 0715 hrs the first wave of parachutists would land around Maleme landing ground and Canea town; at 1515 hours the second wave would strike at the eastern objectives, Retimo and Herakleion. Each attack would include gliders and parachute troops. The follow-up would be airlanded from Ju52s and there were to be landings from the sea. *Generalmajor* Meindl (Western Group) was in charge at Maleme, Süssman (Central Group) at Canea. The Eastern Group was under *Generalleutnant* Ringel.

Before dawn on 20 May the first wave emplaned at their dusty and over-congested airfields. Von der Heydte's battalion, only 120 strong, had spent the night amidst choking clouds of dust as the Ju52s tested their engines. Equipment in containers was fixed to under-wing racks and the men checked their parachute gear and personal weapons – light automatics and grenades, for all heavier equipment still had to be dropped separately. The battalion was to be dropped south-west of Canea into what became known as 'Prison Valley'. The two battalions of 3rd Regiment assigned to the first wave were accompanied by a unit of parachute engineers and glider detachments of the Assault Regiment.

The defenders of Crete had become used to the *Luftwaffe*'s early morning raids. Col. Kippenberger, an Engineer officer commanding the *ad hoc* 10th New Zealand Brigade, had his HQ in the village of Galatos, barely two miles north of the prison which gave the valley its name. He awoke to the usual fine cloudless morning, noted the customary German reconnaissance aircraft at dawn and cast an expert eye around his positions to check camouflage and ensure that no movement gave them away. He was shaving in his HQ, a house in Galatos's main street – when the first ground-attack aircraft arrived, flying low over the town firing their guns indiscriminately. As he ate his breakfast in the back garden, four gliders suddenly passed low overhead, the silence of their flight momentarily stunning the New Zealanders. To the north, a crescendo of firing announced that battle had been joined. The 10th Brigade stood to arms as the main parachute lift thundered low overhead with parachutists leaping out by the hundred. Kippenberger and his men had heard about airborne troops and had indeed been expecting them for days, practising anti-parachutist tactics. They were experienced troops who had fought a hard withdrawal down through Greece, always harried by the *Luftwaffe*; even so, like the Dutch and Belgians before them, they were unprepared for the moral impact exerted by the massed arrival of the Germans. Nevertheless, they rushed to the battle. Kippenberger's brigade was a mixed bag – remnants of the Divisional Cavalry (armoured car) regiment, a battalion of gunners whose field guns had been lost in Greece and transport drivers without vehicles, a machine-gun platoon and two battalions of Greek infantry.

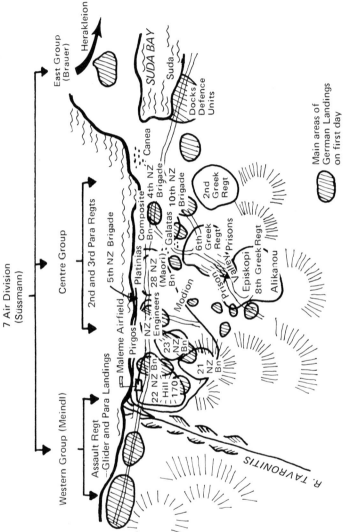

THE ASSAULT ON CRETE

7 Air Division (Süssmann)

East Group (Brauer)

Centre Group

Western Group (Meindl)

Assault Regt — Glider and Para Landings

2nd and 3rd Para Regts

Herakleion

SUDA BAY

Suda

Docks Defence Units

Main areas of German Landings on first day

Canea

5th NZ Brigade

Platinias

4th NZ Brigade

10th NZ Brigade

2nd Greek Regt

Galatas

Composite Bn

28 NZ (Maori) Bn

6th Greek Regt

Prison Valley Prisons

Episkopi

8th Greek Regt

Alikanou

Maleme Airfield

Pirgos

NZ Engineers

Modion

23 NZ Bn

Hill 107

22 NZ Bn

21 NZ Bn

R. TAVRONITIS

At Maleme, the experiences of the defenders were much the same. The daily air attack began at dawn, and by 0800 hrs had reached a climax; suddenly through the smoke and dust clouds, gliders were seen diving towards the western edge of the airfield, followed by hordes of parachutists. The German drop was not very accurate, and instead of a concentrated landing on the pre-planned dropzones small detachments landed all over the Maleme area. Ferocious fighting broke out as the parachutists tried to locate their weapons containers; the scattered dropping meant that many units never formed up at all and were compelled to link with others. Within minutes it was clear that instead of achieving rapid success, the Germans were fighting for survival. They were also leaderless; *Generalleutnant* Süssman of Centre Group had perished with his entire staff shortly after taking off when the wing of his glider failed and it crashed on the island of Aegina. The commander of Western Group, *Generalmajor* Meindl, was seriously wounded whilst still in his aircraft and played no part in the battle.

At Maleme airfield, held by the 22nd New Zealand Infantry Battalion, with the 21st and 23rd Battalions echeloned to the east on rising ground, the fighting was the fiercest of all. The New Zealanders had built elaborate field works on the terraced fields and olive groves overlooking the field and enjoyed excellent visibility and fields of fire. During the morning, no Germans were able to get onto the landing ground, despite the fact that the 22nd were pinned down in their positions by continual fighter-bomber attacks, and the 23rd actually had a parachute battalion of the Assault Regiment land right into their defensive position. The 21st, to the immediate south, also had landings within their perimeter; they quickly disposed of these and repelled every other attempt at a break-in. To the west of the Maleme landing ground there were no New Zealanders; here lay the valley of the Tavronitis river, now dried up; its rocky bed was far from ideal as a landing area but many German gliders were skilfully put down there, as were numerous parachutists. Out of sight of the airfield's defenders, they were able to form up unmolested.

The CO of the 22nd was an experienced and gallant First World War soldier, Lt-Col. Andrew. Like Freyberg he had won the VC in the earlier war. Now, approaching middle age and commanding a young battalion which he had brought safely out of Greece, he found himself in a novel situation for which no training had prepared him. Sensing the rising pressure of the German attack from across the airfield he called for a counter attack by one of the other battalions, the 23rd; but they were now locked in close-quarter battle with the parachutists who had landed amongst them. The aerial bombardment was cutting his field telephone links to the supporting artillery and successive runners were failing to get through with their messages. Andrew therefore launched an attack from his own dwindling resources. The two infantry tanks clanked forward with a platoon of infantry in support. Disaster struck; both tanks broke down, and the platoon, caught in the open without close support, was virtually wiped out.

It could be said that the loss of this forlorn hope was a turning point in the battle, for with it Andrew lost confidence; as evening drew on, when long-awaited reinforcements were actually on their way to him, he pulled back his forward company from their commanding position overlooking the airfield. In the dark they met the reinforcements, two relatively fresh companies, and in the sort of confusion which tends to take place on battlefields in the dark, when men have been tried to the limit, all three companies headed away from the decisive point.

At dawn on the 22nd the situation in the Western sector was therefore as follows. In the Tavronitis valley the Germans had assembled a force of parachute infantry and assault regiment, whose headquarters now assumed control. Andrew's battalion positions, unknown to the Germans, lay empty save for the dead. The 21st and 23rd still stood firm on their ground, having fought off every attack and inflicted appallingly heavy casualties on their assailants.

The initial attacks of the now leaderless German Centre Group had fared even worse than those against Maleme. As in the Western sector, the parachute drops were badly executed, possibly because the Ju52 pilots were disorientated by the pall of smoke and dust from earlier bombing and distracted by the storm of fire which greeted them from the ground. The vigour of the defence amazed the Germans, who had expected a relatively easy landing. Instead, they found themselves descending under a hail of accurate fire (which killed and wounded many in mid-air) and landing on rocky hill-sides. A good landing on smooth ground was difficult enough with that parachute, but under fire and onto a rough slope it was virtually impossible. There were heavy landing casualties. In Prison Valley the Germans were pinned down by fierce fire and the attacks on the high ground overlooking Canea and Suda Bay failed completely. It seemed as night fell on 20 May that having overcome their initial surprise, and despite the withdrawal of the 22nd Battalion at Maleme, the defenders were still in command of the battle. Freyberg's signal to Wavell that evening was cautiously optimistic but he reported that the margin by which his men were holding on was a bare one, ending: 'Everybody here realises vital issue and we will fight it out.'

It was clear at Student's HQ by noon on the 20th that all was not well with *Merkur*. The transport aircraft from the first lift began to return to their Greek airfields between 0900 and 1000 hrs. Some, damaged over Crete by small arms and anti-aircraft fire, and with wounded crews, crashed on landing; others careered into them in clouds of choking dust. The second lift was supposed to take off at 1300 hrs but delays of up to three and four hours set in. Chaos reigned on the bumpy, dust-choked airstrips as mechanics struggled to refuel and repair the aircraft. Units emplaned out of sequence, and weapons containers were fitted to the wrong aircraft. All organization at the mounting airfields broke down. When the lift eventually got under way it was piecemeal, with single aircraft and small groups searching – often in vain – for their dropzones and landing fields. Throughout the late afternoon and early evening they continued to arrive over Retimo and Herakleion. Many troops instead of being dropped away from defended localities, landed amidst fully alerted and aggressively held positions, to be killed before they could rally and regain their weapons containers. At Retimo, *Oberst* Brauer managed to collect part of his Eastern Group as darkness fell; he had entirely failed to take the airfield as planned, so as to admit the air-landing troops of the Alpine Division. The most he could hope for was to resume the attack at first light on the 21st.

At the end of the first day Student was obliged to face the fact that his initial attack had failed. None of the three landing grounds was in German hands and the defenders were clearly far stronger numerically and in terms of morale than German Intelligence had prophesied. Unknown to Student, Freyberg was now in possession of German Operation Orders which gave him a good idea of the planned development of *Merkur*. This may have led him to an over-optimistic view of his position, for when he signalled Wavell that night, he was not aware that Andrew had pulled back off Hill 107 overlooking Maleme landing-ground; and this is where the battle of Crete was lost for the Allies.

During the night the Germans cautiously probed across the airfield from the direction of the Tavronitis valley. Apart from intermittent shelling – for the area was well within range of the British artillery – all was quiet, especially at Hill 107. Eventually, a patrol reached this vital feature. To their amazement they found it empty. This news was radioed to Athens and it lifted the deep gloom lying over Headquarters XI *Fliegerkorps*. Student at once elected to reinforce success at Maleme, with which he had good communication thanks to sterling work by the Assault Regiment's signallers, who had repaired a radio damaged in the first drop. Early on the 21st Ju52s began landing on the beach to the north of Maleme landing ground, bringing much-needed supplies of weapons and ammunition. A single Ju52 carrying one of Student's staff officers made an audacious landing on the field during the morning to determine its condition but was driven off by well-directed artillery and mortar fire. Postponing the air landing of a mountain battalion, Student sent in another parachute drop of two companies during the afternoon. One had the singular misfortune to land amidst a unit of Maoris and the other on an engineer unit. Both were very severely dealt with. At the same time the Assault Regiment launched an infantry attack across the airfield at the 23rd Battalion, and whilst these fights were going on, the first Ju52s began to land with the mountain troops aboard. Although the airfield was still under fire, and despite numerous crashes whilst landing, the German reinforcement went on throughout the evening. Student now had a firm foothold on the island.

During the night of 21st/22nd, another battle raged out at sea, where the German seaborne troops were intercepted by the Royal Navy. It was a brutal and one-sided encounter – none of these German units arrived in Crete. On the island, the hard-pressed Germans stared gloomily out to the north at the flash of gunfire and the glare of burning fishing boats. They now knew that if Crete was to fall, it was entirely up to them. Although reinforcements had arrived at Maleme, the survivors of the units dropped in and around Prison Valley were surrounded by New Zealanders and Greeks who were determined to keep them pinned down. Von der Heydte's remaining men were almost out of ammunition and food after two days' hard fighting and could make no contribution to the battle other than dig in and hold whatever ground they had managed to secure. For their part, the defenders lacked the means of ejecting them, and confined themselves to frequent bursts of artillery and mortar fire; to betray their positions by using infantry weapons would call down the accurate attentions of the *Luftwaffe*, whose aircraft wheeled ceaselessly overhead attacking anything that moved.

Late on the afternoon of the 21st a council of war was held at Freyberg's HQ at which Puttick reported on the situation at Maleme. Plans were made for a counter attack during the night – German air superiority made it impossible to move the two selected battalions forward to their forming-up points in daylight. In order to maintain the strength of the defence in the Canea area, from which one counter attack battalion (the 20th New Zealand) was drawn, a third battalion, the 2nd/7th Australian, was to be brought by lorry from Georgeopolis, some 20 miles further to the east. The lorries, having debussed the Australians, would then carry the 20th forward a further eight miles where they would join forces with the 29th Maori Infantry Battalion; from there it was still over four more miles on to Maleme airfield, through an area heavily infested with parties of Germans who, though operating in small groups and mostly separated from their parent units, were still full of fight and ready to take on any target that appeared.

At best, this was a lame plan; counter attacks against airborne troops need to be launched as quickly as possible after landing, before the parachutists have gained cohesion and located their heavy weapons. The defenders now fell victim to what Clausewitz called 'friction': there were delays in assembling the transport for the Australians; misunderstandings over routes; orders were laboriously transmitted down the various command levels over defective telephones and despatch riders went astray. Worst of all, the Australians were located by the *Luftwaffe* when on the move from Georgeopolis and heavily bombed. The Maoris waited on for the 20th to join them. Like the Germans, they had a grandstand view of the battle out at sea where the Royal Navy was shooting the invasion flotillas out of the water, and this served to raise morale. By 0300 hrs only part of the 20th had joined the 28th, and although there was no sign of the remaining rifle companies, Puttick ordered the attack to go ahead. Daylight was not far away, and with it the dreaded return of the divebombers.

The Maoris are the original inhabitants of New Zealand; Polynesian in origin, they initially accepted the arrival of European settlers in the early 19th century with good grace. Later, the greed and stupidity of some settlers led to feuds over land and eventually to the Maori Wars in which British troops came to regard the Maoris as the finest fighting men they had ever encountered, whose chivalry and humanity matched their courage. These qualities had been tested and proved again in the First World war, and the performance of the 28th in their forlorn attack on Maleme showed that the great warrior tradition was still alive. The attack got under way at 0330 hrs; almost at once, small parties of Germans were encountered, and fierce hand-to-hand fighting broke out. As dawn broke, bringing the inevitable swarms of German aircraft, the Maoris were still 1½ miles short of their objective, which to their enduring credit they reached in broad daylight. On the edge of the airfield they were pinned down by mortar and machine-gun fire and subjected to incessant air attack. The attempt to retake Maleme had failed, having been made a day too late and with pitifully inadequate forces. Student continued to fly in his reinforcements, the Ju52 pilots disregarding any fire that the hard pressed New Zealanders could bring to bear. The airfield was now littered with the hulks of crashed and burning aircraft – an air photograph taken that day shows more than 50 – and still the Germans arrived.

Freyberg ordered one more attempt to retake Maleme airfield, but three days of non-stop fighting had begun to sap the endurance of even the brigade commanders. Hargest, detailed to attack with the whole of what was left of 5 Brigade, declined to throw his exhausted men into a further assault against ever-increasing numbers of enemy and proposed withdrawal to the east instead, a course of action in which he was supported by his fellow brigade commander, Puttick. Disappointed, but sympathizing with his brigadiers, Freyberg agreed. It was the beginning of the end, for once the British artillery observation officers were denied a view of the Maleme area Student's aircraft could land unmolested; and this they did. Hargest's dispirited troops were extricated on the night of 23rd/24th, and the centre of pressure of the battle moved east to the area of Canea. Here, the Germans prepared an all-out attack which was launched on the afternoon of the 25th against the area held by Kippenberger's 10th Brigade. The attack was planned and commanded by *Generalleutnant* Ringel who, as commander of the 5th Mountain Division now took over 'Group West'. He had four battalions of fresh airlanded Alpine troops, the badly-mauled remnants of Meindl's Assault Regiment, and all those elements of the 3rd Parachute Regiment which had been able to join forces. Almost immediately this formidable group, lavishly supported by artillery, mortars and divebombers, forced a breach in the New Zealanders' positions, but Kippenberger borrowed two rifle companies from Hargest's brigade and these, supported by two boldly-handled light tanks of the 3rd Hussars, stopped the Germans and repulsed them. It was, however, a brief respite. Freyberg realized that with Maleme the island was lost, and that without air support he could not hope to retake it. He was now painfully aware that naval support was unlikely to continue much longer, for after their successful destruction of the German seaborne force on the night of 21/22 May, the Royal Navy had taken a terrible beating from the unchallenged *Luftwaffe*. As day broke, the victorious ships were discovered by enemy aerial reconnaissance and subjected to incessant bombing. The destroyer HMS *Greyhound* was the first to go, followed by the cruisers *Gloucester* and *Fiji*; both these ships were caught with near-empty magazines; *Fiji*'s guns were firing practice shells as she finally rolled over and sank. Elsewhere, the 5th Destroyer Flotilla, under Capt. Lord Louis Mountbatten, had spent the 22nd sinking *caiques* and boldly shelling Maleme airfield; whilst withdrawing to Alexandria next day for fuel and ammunition HMS *Kelly*, Lord

Mountbatten's ship, and her companion HMS *Kashmir* were over-whelmed by 24 divebombers to the south-west of the island. The *Luftwaffe*'s supremacy was complete; the RAF had been driven from the skies to allow the airborne assault to go in without aerial oppo-sition, and now the British fleet, bereft of friendly air cover, was being driven off the sea. If anyone was to escape from Crete, the decision to evacuate was imminent.

Some effort was now made to try and redress the wholly adverse air situation. The aircraft carrier HMS *Formidable* launched ten air-craft to attack German airfields on the Greek islands, but the task force to which she belonged received the full attention of the *Luftwaffe* on the 26th. *Formidable*, her destroyer escort, and the battle-ship *Barham* were all badly damaged and compelled to withdraw. From the 23rd the RAF launched attacks on Maleme airfield: and a few fighters were actually flown back onto Herakleion, but not in suf-ficient numbers to influence the battle. What support was given by the RAF's Egyptian-based fighters was equally ineffective because their endurance permitted them so short a time over the combat area. Furthermore, German fighters were now operating with impunity from Maleme.

Even though the effects of German airpower were all too visible to the defenders of Crete, the Chiefs of Staff in London were unwilling to concede that the island could be carried by air assault alone; the naval and air commanders in the Middle East were directed to do all in their power to prevent further landings and it was in compliance with these unrealistic instructions that Admiral Cunningham, com-manding the Mediterranean Fleet, was obliged to expose his ships to air attack by daylight without proper air cover; the same directives led to the RAF's belated and necessarily inadequate re-entry into the battle.

After the fighting of the 25th and the temporary respite brought by Kippenberger's counter-attack, the German reinforcement con-tinued. Captured British tanks were used to remove wrecked aircraft from Maleme airfield and on the 26th a further regiment of the 5th Mountain Division was airlanded there. Canea was finally taken on the 27th and Suda Bay on the 28th; by now the Fleet anchorage was littered with burning wrecks, victims of the incessant bombing, and was dominated by the stranded wreck of the British heavy cruiser *York*, crippled some weeks earlier in a daring attack by an Italian motor boat. On the 29th, Ringel's troops at last made contact with the beleaguered Eastern Group, comprising the survivors of *Oberst* Brauer's 1st Parachute Regiment.

On the 26th Freyberg faced the facts and signalled Wavell that the end was in sight. The C-in-C was in a cleft stick; he was fully aware of Freyberg's predicament but was himself receiving strings of signals from Churchill in person stressing the need to hold on, reinforcing the garrison from anywhere in the Middle East; as these signals poured in from London, a convoy bound for Crete was being driven back to Egypt by heavy air attacks. Freyberg went ahead with plans for evacuation and the survivors began to make their way to the south coast. The resultant rescue was an epic in itself; units struggled across the rugged terrain, following the one road leading to Sphakia, the harbour selected for embarkation. The Royal Navy has often rescued the British Army from tough predicaments but seldom has it shown the devotion it displayed on the four terrible nights of 28–31 May when 17,000 men were taken off. It was a repetition of Narvik, Dunkirk and the Peloponessus; once more a British expeditionary force had been committed to battle without proper air cover and against the advice of the air commanders, whose warnings went unheeded but proved all too horribly correct.

Merkur had been a triumph for air power. It was the only victory won by any of the contestants in the Second World War with the sole use of airborne forces; British sea power, albeit at sacrificial cost, had destroyed the German seaborne force and had rescued a significant proportion of the garrison to fight again. The moral effect of the combination of close air support and shock tactics had not only secured a major strategic victory for the Axis, but had further spread the myth of invincibility with which the German airborne were now endowed.

Yet it was the high-water mark for Student. He himself was near broken by the casualties incurred, all old comrades with whom he had worked to bring on the new fighting arm: Süssman of 7 *Fliegerdivision*, the co and both company commanders in the first day's drop at Maleme; almost all the company commanders in 3rd Para Regiment; von Plessen, a leading glider specialist, killed on landing. Von der Heydte met his leader in Canea after the fighting – 'There was no evidence in his features that he was joyful over the victory – his victory – and proud of the success of his daring scheme. The cost of victory had evidently proved too much for him. Some of the battalions had lost all their officers and in several companies there were only only a few men left alive.' ★

On 28 April Churchill had signalled Wavell warning him of the impending airborne attack and adding, with his customary gusto 'It ought to be a fine opportunity for killing the parachute troops. The island must be stubbornly defended. . . .' Within the constraints im-

★ *Daedalus Returned*, London, Hutchinson & Co, 1958.

posed by lack of air cover, Freyberg had been fairly successful. At a cost of nearly 18,000 killed, wounded and prisoners, the Imperial forces had inflicted 6500 casualties on the enemy, or about 1000 more than the German losses for the whole campaign in the Balkans. One in three of the Germans who landed on Crete was killed, wounded or taken prisoner.

Two months after the battle, Student visited the *Führer* in the *Wolfschanze*, his command post in the East, where he invested the airborne commander with the Knight's Cross and congratulated him on the part XI *Fliegerkorps* had played. Almost in the same breath he pronounced sentence on all that Student had worked for. 'The day of the paratroop is over,' said Hitler, and went on to give his opinion that surprise – the key to successful airborne operations – would not be achieved in any subsequent attack, and that casualties in any large scale airlanding would be even more unacceptable than in Crete. Dispirited, Student left the presence.

Back in Germany, the veterans of *Merkur* were fêted as the heroes they undoubtedly were. Lacking heavy weapons, short of small arms and ammunition, and met by an opposition of unexpected vigour, they had somehow held on despite crippling casualties, displaying commendable qualities of initiative and aggression. The fact that anyone survived to enthral hometown audiences in Braunschweig and Hildesheim was almost solely due to Student keeping his head and feeding the 5th Mountain Division in at Maleme, leaving his men to work out their own salvation when their attacks at Retimo and Herakleion failed. Throughout the campaign he displayed all the qualities of a great airborne commander. Fortunately, it was three years before he had another chance – at Arnhem, this time in the role of a defender on the ground.

By dismissing Student with his forecast for the future (or lack of one) for airborne forces, Hitler was seemingly exorcizing from his mind the idea that the Allies might also be raising airborne troops. This ostrich-like tendency of ignoring what he did not wish to know was at last to prove his downfall; for over a year previously, the new techniques began to be tentatively adopted in Britain.

CHAPTER SIX

The Allied Answer: 1940–42

'Every journey of a thousand miles starts with one step.'

Chinese proverb

On the morning of 15 February 1941 *The Times* of London carried a small item of war news drawn from an Italian official communiqué reporting a landing by British parachutists on the night of 10/11 February in the Lucania district of Calabria, Italy's southernmost mainland province. These men, it was reported, had been equipped with automatic weapons and explosives, with which they had unsuccessfully tried to destroy the regional water system ('a magnificent achievement of the Fascist régime which made possible an agricultural revival throughout the district'). According to the communiqué the parachutists were quickly rounded up by Carabinieri, farmers and armed citizens. The British Ministry of Information duly produced its own version of the episode and this appeared in the London *Times* two days later: 'Soldiers in recognized military uniform have recently been dropped by parachute in southern Italy. Their instructions were to demolish certain objectives connected with the ports in that area. No statement can be made at present about the result of the operation, but some of the men have not returned to their base.'

In this way, reading the report of an operation which had clearly gone off at half-cock, the British public learnt that they now had a parachute force; it was not exactly the resounding sort of début the Germans had achieved in the previous year and it did not take a very clever reader to deduce from the inane phraseology of the official British statement that something had misfired badly, if not ignominiously.

Although tentative military parachuting trials had been run under RAF auspices since the early months of 1940, the accepted launching of Britain's airborne forces was Churchill's minute of 6 June in which he directed the War Office to investigate the formation of a corps of at least 5000 paratroops. An immediate call for 1000 volunteers from each of the Home Commands went out, and while results of this appeal were awaited, a training organization was hastily improvised. The first trainees, pending the arrival of the volunteers, consisted of Number 2 Commando, a specialist raiding unit formed earlier in the year as the result of another Churchillian memorandum. The men of this unit had come from all regiments of the British Army, drawn by the prospect of early action and the attractions of a somewhat unconventional life-style; Commando units were not housed in barracks, each man being given a daily allowance of six shillings and eight pence (equivalent in today's currency to 33p!) and told to find his own billet. As the parachute training centre was at Ringway airfield near Manchester, the citizens of that area quickly found that they had some unusual lodgers on their hands.

On receipt of Churchill's minute, the War Office had quickly started to arrange a paratroop training organization. Clearly an accommodation had to be made with the Air Staff so that some signs of progress could be shown to the impatient Prime Minister. The choice of Ringway – Manchester's civil airport – was due to circumstances beyond the control of the Ministries concerned; it was located far north of the main Army training areas on Salisbury Plain and its climate was hardly conducive to good flying conditions. When rain was not falling – and Manchester's rainfall has long been a British music-hall joke – the industrial murk of Lancashire's mills and factories hung mournfully in the leaden skies. The new organization, named The Central Landing School and formed on 19 June 1940, had little or no military parachuting experience to go on. Its staff, drawn from the Army and RAF, had never seen each other before and had only the vaguest idea of their task. The first commanding officer was Sqn Ldr Louis Strange, a much decorated First World War veteran; the senior Army member of the staff was Maj. John Rock of the Royal Engineers, a dedicated and conscientious regular soldier who despite his total lack of experience in this field at once got down to the study of training and organizing airlanded troops. He could only draw on the pre-war experience of the RAF, who had provided a somewhat hair-raising parachute familiarization course for any pilots rash enough to try it. (Most aircrew, then as now, regarded as little short of lunacy any voluntary departure from a perfectly serviceable aircraft in mid-air.) The RAF training technique, known as 'strut-clutching' meant that the jumper clung for dear life to the vertical wing strut of an ancient Vickers *Virginia* biplane bomber until the pilot signalled to him to jump. He then steeled himself to pull the ripcord. The parachute opened, and he was snatched bodily away from the strut. It was described as a 'miserable and terrifying experience' and there were numerous legends of parachutists clutching the strut so convulsively that they took it away with them when the canopy opened.

The provision of aircraft, parachutes and instructors was a multiple problem. Somehow it was quickly met. The Air Ministry allocated six *Whitley* bombers to the school, with 1000 training parachutes. Initially these were not of the static-line type, and the first Ringway students were obliged to jump from an improvised platform in the tail of a *Whitley*, using a variation of the 'strut-clutching' technique. Within a few days a back-pack parachute had been modified for use with a static line and a hole let into the floor of the *Whitley* out of which the troops made their exit. Almost at once a fatal accident occurred when a soldier using this modified parachute crashed to his death on 25 July – the 136th jump at the school. It was an unnecessary death, because several years earlier, after seeing a film of the 1936 Russian massed drops, Raymond Quilter, a director of the GQ parachute company, had offered the War Office the use of his firm's design for a safe static-line parachute. The offer had been politely declined. Unlike the RAF training parachute, in which the canopy opened first, Quilter's was a 'rigging line first' chute, in which the weight of the jumper's body unfolded the rigging lines before the canopy opened, thereby reducing the risk of entanglements. The new equipment, known as the 'X' type, soon acquired a very high reputation for reliability and until 1956 (when the British Army reluctantly fell into line with its Nato Allies) was used without a reserve, so great was the troops' trust in it.

By 9 July 1940, the industrious Rock had drafted his paper, in which he aimed 'to examine the present system of training and organization of airlanding troops and to try to find methods of improving it'. There were plenty of problems to overcome. Nobody knew just how many paratroops there were eventually to be; the War Office and Air Ministry – still horribly suspicious of each other – had to sanction any changes and this held up decisions; Ringway was in the wrong place (but there was nowhere else to go). The Commandos' weird terms of service were reminiscent of the 18th century, with their 6/8d billetting money and a tendency to get into all sorts of scrapes with the civil authorities. There were no proper transport aircraft. Rock's ingredients for a successful airborne organization were a good airfield, spacious practice drop zones, a good climate permitting maximum flying, and a total revision of the commando terms of service, with adoption of a special cap badge (they still wore those of their many parent regiments), substitution of parachute pay for the lodging money, and a general tightening of discipline in proper barracks accommodation.

With the formation of the Central Landing School came the suggestion that the glider was probably a better way of getting men to battle than the parachute – the men arrived on the ground as a formed body, carrying their equipment and heavy weapons with them. The idea of a glider force to complement the paratroops was accordingly put to Churchill on 10 August and he enthusiastically approved it. The example of Eben Emael was there for others to copy and the speed with which the Air Ministry produced the thousands of gliders used later in the war was a triumph of superb staff work and organization.

A momentous meeting was held in the Air Ministry on 5 September, convened in order to thrash out the future organization of Britain's airborne forces. Air Marshal Barratt, Vice-Chief of the Air Staff, was in the chair and around the table was an array of soldiers and airmen confronted with the hard fact that past differences had now to be resolved and a working partnership formed. The principal decisions reached were that airborne soldiers would be provided by the Army – a departure from the German policy of using *Luftwaffe* personnel – and that the Army might also provide the glider pilots, who would however be trained by the RAF. Some quaint ideas were fielded at this conference. One was a suggestion to try out a new invention called a rotorchute – a folding contraption of rotor blades which, when spread, acted in the same way as an autogyro. The theory was that instead of parachutes, men could be persuaded to jump wearing these devices; further inquiry revealed that the inventor – a Mr Raoul Hafner (later to be well known as a distinguished helicopter designer) – was not available to explain his machine. He had been interned in the Isle of Man under the provisions of the Defence Regulations as an 'enemy alien'. The idea was dropped.

It was stressed by Barratt and his staff that airborne operations could only expect to succeed given conditions of air superiority such as the Germans had won in the Low Countries and again achieved over Greece and Crete. Various scenarios were discussed – raids on enemy-held territory followed by sea or air evacuation; operations on land, using airborne forces as a spearhead; even the wildest concept – a raid on the German homeland in order to induce alarm and despondency.

It was agreed that a force of 3000 parachutists could be trained by the spring of 1941, that a glider lift be provided as soon as possible for a brigade-size formation of 2700 combat troops, and – most imaginative of all – that large gliders capable of carrying light tanks and similar loads should be built.

Within a fortnight, progress was in hand as the result of Barratt's meeting. The Central Landing School became The Central Landing Establishment under the command of an RAF officer, Gp-Capt. Harvey, with Wg-Comdr Sir Nigel Norman as his chief staff officer. Both these men were to give immeasurable service to the airborne cause, and Norman his life as well. Rock remained on the staff, and the organization now consisted of a Development Section, a Glider Training Squadron and a Parachute Training School.

At the end of 1940, plans were under way for the production of four types of glider: an 8-seater, originally designed in imitation of the German DFS230, but never used operationally; a 25-seater, which became the celebrated *Horsa* and the backbone of the glider force; a 15-seater known as the *Hengist*, which was produced only in small numbers as an insurance against failure of the *Horsa*; and the huge *Hamilcar* to meet the requirement for the airlanding of light tanks, artillery and large quantities of supplies. Pending the arrival of the 8-seaters, to be known as *Hotspurs*, the Glider Training Squadron pressed on, using a collection of small sailplanes and training gliders commandeered from civilian clubs. The initial students were a mixed bag of 37 soldiers and 18 RAF volunteers. The very idea of soldiers flying gliders was still abhorrent to some senior RAF officers – in December 1940 the Deputy Chief of the Air Staff expostulated that 'The idea that semi-skilled, unpicked personnel (infantry corporals have, I believe, even been suggested) could with a minimum of training be entrusted with the piloting of these troop carriers is fantastic. Their operation is equivalent to force-landing the largest sized aircraft without engine aid – than which there is no higher test of piloting skill.' The Air Marshal's views on soldiers' abilities were mirrored in War Office correspondence of the same period, fuming at the RAF's apparent refusal to produce aircraft solely for use by airborne forces but clearly not appreciating that the over-riding priority in the winter of 1940–41 was the creation of a truly strategic bombing force which alone could take some form of offensive home to the German people.

By early 1941 a proper doctrine for the employment of the as yet unformed airborne forces was being worked out at the Central Landing Establishment. Initially, the War Office and Air Ministry had been obsessed with commando-type raids and the capture of enemy airfields to the exclusion of almost everything else; now, Rock produced a methodical list of additional roles:

- the attack of an enemy defensive position in the rear, in conjunction with a frontal assault by ground troops.
- isolation of the battlefield by landing in the enemy's rear and blocking the forward movement of his reserves.
- seizure and holding of important river crossings and defiles to prevent their demolition, or deny their use by a retreating enemy.

– to carry out flank attacks.

– to disrupt the enemy's communications.

– to make distractive feint attacks, to draw off reserves.

With few variations, these were to remain the standard types of airborne operation for the rest of the war.

Meanwhile, the training of the officers and men of No. 2 Commando had gone ahead at Ringway. In November 1940 the unit received a new title – 11 Special Air Service Battalion (later, it was to become 1 Parachute Battalion). By the end of September 1940, 21 officers and 321 soldiers had been accepted; 30 of them declined to jump, 2 were killed through parachute failures at Ringway, and 20 others eliminated through injuries or what was tersely described as 'unsuitability'. The greatest deterrent was apparently the method of exit from the gloomy and cramped fuselage of the *Whitley* through the hole in the floor, during which it was quite easy for the trainee to smash his face against the side if his exit technique was faulty, a mishap jocularly known as 'ringing the bell'.

Having formed a trained cadre – if the average of two or three jumps completed could be said to constitute training – the War Office looked for an operation on which the paratroops could be blooded. In that winter of 1940–41 the Army's prestige at home was low despite a series of scintillating victories over the Italians in North and East Africa. A good 'propaganda' operation was indicated, preferably at low cost and minimal risk. Southern Italy was duly selected as the ideal theatre; the opposition in rural Calabria would, it was thought, be virtually non-existent, and there would be a good return in the form of public alarm and despair throughout Italy. The target chosen by the War Office was the Pugliese aqueduct, part of an elaborate scheme built in the 1930s to carry water to several southern Italian ports now in use for the supply of Axis forces in the Balkans. After the blow had been struck, the sparsely-populated region would be easy for the parachutists to traverse on their way to the sea, for recovery by submarine.

Planning for operation *Colossus*, as the enterprise was somewhat wrily called, went on at Ringway throughout January 1941. A detailed model of the aqueduct was built and committed to memory by the raiding party. Major T. A. C. Pritchard of the Royal Welch Fusiliers was in command, with Capt. G. F. K. Daly of the Royal Engineers in charge of the demolition party. The aircraft from which the men were to drop were *Whitleys*, manned by picked crews under Wg-Comdr Tait; his task was to train the force to navigate accurately by night and to drop the paratroops with great precision from a height of 500 feet. A full scale 'mock-up' of the target area was built in great secrecy at Tatton Park near Ringway and on the night of 1 February a full-dress rehearsal was carried out in high winds which left several men stuck in the tops of trees, out of which they had to be rescued by the local fire brigade. A week later, Tait's eight black *Whitleys* left RAF Mildenhall to fly through the night to Malta, from where the raid would be launched during the next few nights in order to make use of the full moon. With the raiding party went an Italian interpreter, Signor Picchi, a patriot who had worked in a London hotel for many years and loved the land of his adoption.

At 1820 hrs on the 10th, six *Whitleys* took off from Malta carrying paratroops and two carrying bombs, which were to be dropped on the port of Foggia as a diversionary effort. Five of the paratroop aircraft found the target and dropped their men accurately. The sixth, carrying Daly and most of the sappers with their explosives, dropped its party in the wrong valley and they never succeeded in joining the main party. The only engineers to reach the bridge were a small group under 2nd Lt Patterson, who piled all his explosive – about quarter of a ton – against one pier of the aqueduct and blew it shortly after midnight. Although there was a huge flash and a gratifying explosion, little damage was done, for the aqueduct had been built of reinforced concrete and not, as the War Office had fondly believed, of brickwork. The sound of the explosion brought the local Carabinieri to the scene and they, aided by the civilian population, had little trouble in rounding up both parties of paratroops, none of whom reached the rendezvous with the submarine. The luckless Picchi was summarily shot for his pains. It was small wonder that the Ministry of Information in London elected to play the operation in a very low key.

It was a dismal launching ceremony for what was to be the élite striking force. Instead of triumphant banner headlines, *The Times* carried a modest item on 20 February by 'a special correspondent', 'It may now be stated that the Army, with the co-operation of the Royal Air Force, has a force of parachute troops who are regularly making practice descents. Their recent landing in Southern Italy revealed them in action for the first time . . . in a recent exercise . . . I saw detachments of them make their descent well in advance of an armoured column with the objective of seizing river crossings and attacking an "enemy" headquarters. . . .'

Unseen by the general public, a lot was going on at Ringway, where the CLE's Development Section was working hard on the evolution of special equipment for use by parachutists. Rock, in particular, had an obsession about paratroops' clothing and personal

Colonel Templer glares down from
the basket of his balloon at Aldershot.
The year is 1894. His crewman,
obviously resigned to an uncomfortable
ride, looks on with an expressionless
face which yet speaks volumes.
(Imperial War Museum)

A mobile balloon detachment of the Royal Engineers at Laffan's Plain, Aldershot,
in the mid-1890's. The men on the left are carrying out the prescribed drill for
folding the deflated gas-bag, which will then be loaded onto the waggon. (Imperial
War Museum)

Above: *The Sikorsky R-4A first saw active service in Burma in 1944, when one was used in Colonel Cochrane's Air Commando. This one was in RAF service at Andover in 1946, and was known as the 'Hoverfly Mk I'. (Imperial War Museum)*

Right: *Departing from a 20-year adherence to biplane designs, the RAF's Army Co-operation Squadrons began to re-equip in 1938 with the Westland Lysander. Although technically a remarkable machine, it was too cumbrous and vulnerable to survive against the Luftwaffe—as Baxeley had prophesied—and was hurriedly withdrawn from Army Co-op duties after a disastrous debut in 1940. (Imperial War Museum)*

Below: *An early photograph of the German Focke-Achgelis helicopter showing the side-by-side arrangement of its main rotors. For its day—1938—it was an astonishing piece of engineering, but only a few were made. (Imperial War Museum)*

Soviet paratroops in 1936. They are jumping with rip-cord parachutes from an ANT-6 bomber, scrambling forward from the rear hatch and sliding off the wing at the bidding of the jumpmaster who signals with a flag from the gun position in the nose. (Imperial War Museum)

The assault on Holland, 10 May 1940. Badly shot-up JU-52s straddle a ditch after crash-landing on a main road near Ypenburg airfield. (Imperial War Museum)

Left: *General Kurt Student, (1893–1978), the pioneer of methodical airborne warfare and the victor of Crete.* (*Imperial War Museum*)

Right: *Brigadier General McCauliffe, whose resolute defence of Bastogne in Christmas week 1944 demonstrated the versatility of airborne troops even when mis-employed as conventional infantrymen.* (*Imperial War Museum*)

The practical visionary. Lt. General Hamilton Howze, US Army, whose foresight, patience and professional ability turned an idea into a versatile weapon. More than any other man he has earned the title of 'father of airmobility'. (*US Army Photograph*)

The founders. Against the bleak background of Salisbury Plain Major Chatterton poses with a group of the first glider pilots. On his left is Captain Cooper of the Cheshire Regiment, who was to die in Sicily two years later. At the ends of the front row are the two outstanding drill sergeants who quickly imposed the standards of the Brigade of Guards on this assorted collection of men—Sergeant Major Briody (Irish Guards) is on the left and Sergeant Major Cowlie (Coldstream Guards) on the right. (AAC Centre, Middle Wallop)

Operation Thursday—Burma 1944. Major General Orde Wingate with Colonel Phil Cochrane. Between them, they planned and launched an outstandingly bold airborne raid behind Japanese lines. (Imperial War Museum)

Near Nijmegen, during Operation Market Garden, an American CG-4 overturns on landing. In the foreground, a dead paratrooper lies in his harness. (Imperial War Museum)

A USAAF C-47 Skytrain drops its stick of paratroops onto the golf course at Corregidor, 16 February 1945. Many discarded canopies from earlier sticks litter the broken and cratered ground below; this remarkable photograph dramatically illustrates the difficulties under which the drop took place. (Imperial War Museum)

Precision. Aftermath of the magnificent coup-de-main which seized the bridge over the Caen canal early on the morning of June 6 1944. The further glider is the one which was piloted by Staff-Sergeant Wallwork, and carried Major John Howard. To the left of the picture, and on the far bank of the canal is M. Gondree's estaminet – the first building to be liberated in France. (Imperial War Museum)

American glider pilots disliked flying the British Horsa glider, which was larger and more demanding of its pilots than their own Waco CG-4. Here, eight American soldiers lie dead beside the wreck of their Horsa in a Normandy field after a disastrous landing. (Imperial War Museum)

Prior to Operation 'Varsity', USAAF C-47s and CG-4 gliders are massed on an airfield in northern France. This picture vividly illustrates the difficulty of mounting a massed-landing glider operation and the absolute need to keep the enemy's air force away from such an easy target. (Imperial War Museum)

The Rhine crossing. American paratroopers and gliderborne infantry rally near the wreck of a British Horsa. *Note the poor visibility—less than 300 yards in this part of the battlefield. (Imperial War Museum)*

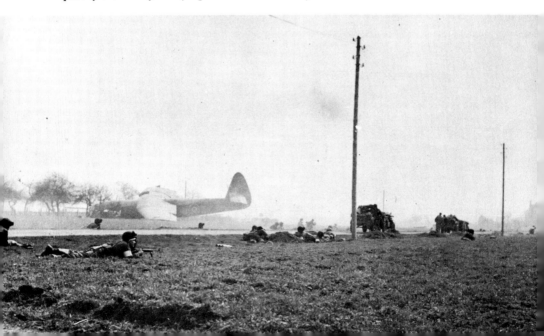

equipment; having steeled himself to undergo the training (for he was a man with a highly developed sense of duty, which eventually would kill him), he quickly qualified for the award of the coveted parachutist wings and busied himself with the design of a whole wardrobe of helmets, tunics, protective padding, even an absurd pair of boots with sprung soles to ensure a well-cushioned landing, which proved totally unsuitable for marching. In the end, British paratroops would use mainly standard infantry clothing and equipment, over which was worn a loose-fitting camouflage garment known as the Denison smock, still in service in the late 1970s, as much a part of the sartorial mystique as the red beret. Close examination had been made of German parachutists' equipment captured in the 1940 campaign, in particular the containers used to drop ammunition and weapons. Before the war the *Luftwaffe* had developed the *Waffenhalter*, a box 5 feet long and 16 inches square which was carried under the Ju52 to be dropped as the paratroops left the aircraft. Fully laden with stores it weighed 260 pounds and incorporated an ingenious frame and two wheels so that it could be moved around like a golfer's trolley. The need for such a container was imposed by the design of the German troop parachute which prevented men from jumping with anything more than light hand guns and grenades. From the start, British paratroops jumped complete with their rifles and light machine guns wrapped in a valise. They soon found themselves staggering to the aircraft under the additional burden of a kit bag crammed with extra ammunition. The valise and kit bag were strapped to the man's leg and released on a cord prior to landing. Separate containers were also developed which could be pitched out of the door as part of a paratroop 'stick'. This was only the start of a huge programme of methodical research devoted to the airdropping and airlanding of heavy equipment, a process into which the American Army was later to be drawn. The CLE's small Development Section would soon expand into a trials and experimental organization, far too large to remain at Ringway. As the Joint Air Transport Establishment it still thrives (1979) at Brize Norton in Oxfordshire.

1941 was a year of steady progress which saw the nucleus of Ringway expand into the Airborne Forces Establishment, the creation of a separate glider pilot training organization and the introduction of a new parachute training syllabus which continues in more or less the same form to the present day.

Although there had been much heated (and often peculiarly ill-informed) inter-service debate in Whitehall, things were far easier at working level. Of the Army–RAF relationship at the Central Landing Establishment in the late summer of 1941, an official historian was to write '. . . it is worth noting, not for reasons of sentiment but from a purely practical point of view, that excellent co-operation had been achieved between the two services. The RAF, in general terms, was responsible for producing the aircraft, gliders and parachute equipment and teaching the methods of dropping, training the glider pilots, teaching the troops their air technique, flying them or towing them to the target area and putting them down correctly at the right time. The Army had to submit to the teaching of this new art, organize and arm itself to suit its means of conveyance, and still, by training and the careful selection of personnel, produce a good worthwhile fighting force for the battle. Theirs was an expensive "approach march" to the battlefield and only the best was worth carrying. Each service learned to rely implicitly upon the other, and from this trust was developed an intimate co-operation at all levels which formed the basis of planning for the future.')*

The day before No. 1 Glider Training School opened its doors to the first course, an immaculately dressed and newly promoted Major-General moved into a small country house close to Netheravon airfield on Salisbury Plain and set up the HQ of the 1st Airborne Division. General 'Boy' Browning was a Grenadier. He had fought with distinction in the First World War, and between the wars had risen steadily in his profession. At one point he was adjutant at the Royal Military College, Sandhurst, originating a custom which has since become hallowed tradition. Left alone on the parade ground after the graduating class had marched slowly up the steps of the great portico and away to their new lives as commissioned officers, he decided to set his grey charger at the steps in their wake. He was one of the most elegant and eligible officers in the Brigade of Guards, combining a witty and cultured mind with a degree of professional dedication unusual in those inter-war years, when life even in an élite regiment like the Grenadier Guards could settle down to a numbing routine of exercises on Salisbury Plain and the pageantry of Public Duties in London. It came as no surprise, therefore, when he married the gifted and successful author Daphne du Maurier, a partnership which was to prove durable and happy until his relatively early death in 1965.

Browning's division was far from complete as he opened the HQ. On paper it consisted of 1st Parachute Brigade and 1st Airlanding Brigade. This was the formation selected to go to war in gliders. Until recently it had been training in the depths of Wales for service as a mountain brigade, using pack mules for its transportation. The four battalions comprising the brigade were therefore fit and hard,

* *Airborne Forces*, The War Office, 1951.

used to soldiering on light scales of equipment and, as regular battalions with a high percentage of long-service officers and men, well disciplined.

In the last weeks of 1941, 1st Airlanding Brigade moved to its billeting area, that marvellous stretch of countryside just to the south of a line joining Newbury and Basingstoke and reaching down to Barton Stacey near Winchester. Here, the battalions got down to re-training for their new role as best they could. They still had not seen a glider; but a mock-up *Horsa* fuselage had been built up at Ringway, into which the CLE staff were trying to fit every conceivable type of vehicle and equipment. A milestone was reached in November 1941 when with the blessing and enthusiastic co-operation of Lt-Col. Tom Wells, the American Military Attaché in London, the first jeep to arrive in the United Kingdom was crammed into the mock-up by a perspiring team of senior officers. It fitted; and for the first time the prospect of real ground mobility was held out to airborne forces. The USA was at this time a month before Pearl Harbor, still neutral, but Wells' connivance (and active participation) in the jeep trial was but one of the myriad generous acts which did so much to seal the great alliance before America entered the war.

It was not long before the first glider pilots were coming out of the Operational Training Unit; in the absence of *Horsas* they had completed their training in 8-seater *Hotspurs* but all had gone well and it was clear that the RAF's excellent training system was going to produce pilots of the skill and character required. John Rock was now promoted to become commanding officer of the glider pilots. In order to tidy up the personnel management of airborne forces, an Army Air Corps was formed on 21 December 1941 to include all parachute troops and glider pilots; the separate Glider Pilot and Parachute Regiments evolved within this corps shortly afterwards. At Ringway, Rock had insisted on qualifying as a parachutist, and now he himself took the first 40 members of the Glider Pilot Regiment to Elementary Flying Training School on 2 January 1942, leaving his newly joined second-in-command to raise the first battalion in his absence.

It is difficult to raise a new battalion of a well-established regiment or corps. When the new unit lacks any precedents, even a cap-badge, and is drawn together from all sorts and conditions of men from every regiment in the British Army (to say nothing of a few glider enthusiasts who have somehow escaped from the RAF) the problems are Herculean. From the start, the new unit must establish its own 'style', for this will form its ultimate character and the ability to go on performing its job even when the cause seems lost. The regiment needs a soul, and the man chosen by Browning to be the first second-in-command of the glider pilots was – once more – the right man at the right time.

George Chatterton was educated at the Nautical College Pang-bourne, which despite its name is almost as far from the sea as it is possible to get in England – all of 75 miles. It was founded to provide young officers, primarily for the great merchant fleets which were the backbone of British power in an age when politicians understood seapower. Chatterton, ever an individualist, elected to join the Royal Air Force on leaving and did so in 1930. His extrovert character and quick wits secured him a place in a fighter squadron – No. 1 at Tangmere on the south coast, equipped with that most eleg-ant of biplanes, the Hawker *Fury*. He became an expert at aerobatics and flew for 1 Squadron in the great Hendon air displays of 1934, and in the team which performed all over Canada that summer. He sur-vived a mid-air collision and flew in the celebrated King George V Silver Jubilee review at Mildenhall in 1935 (when visiting German aviators could not believe that the RAF's front line aircraft were so antiquated; they asked to see the *real* equipment and had to be told there was none). Shortly afterwards, his short-service commission having expired, Chatterton left the RAF. In 1938, to his dismay, he was told that his Reserve Commission was not in the aircrew branch. With a marked distaste for paper work he transferred into a Reserve unit of the Army, the 5th Battalion of the Queen's Royal Regiment.

During the 18 months leading to war, Chatterton learned the art of command as well as the skills of the infantryman in this fine battalion of part-time soldiers, and when it mobilized in September 1939 he went with it to France. After the collapse of France, Chatterton, posted to another battalion of the Queen's, found himself guarding the Kent coast in defensive works originally built to repel Napoleon's projected invasion of the early 1800s. It was a dispiriting existence and when the call came for volunteers to be glider pilots he jumped at the chance.

The camp allocated to the Glider Pilot Regiment was at Tilshead, a bleak collection of rusting corrugated iron and wooden huts on the edge of the Larkhill gunnery ranges. In high summer this stretch of country has a special ageless quality; gently rolling downland, treeless save for a few uneasy clumps and plantations, pitted with innumer-able chalkwhite shell-scrapes. The grass is springy, and larks sing incessantly. The intermittent thump of distant guns and the crumps of their arriving shells are a constant but nearly subconscious back-ground noise. Neither is the sound of aircraft engines absent for much of the time. This was where the founders of the Royal Flying Corps build their first airfields, at Upavon and Netheravon; their huddled buildings and hangars still crouch over the Plain like ships momentarily seen on the crests of a great undulant swell. Near at hand lies the airfield at Boscombe Down at which all new aircraft are tested prior to entering service. Away to the east, the School of Artillery, and the windswept garrison towns of Tidworth and Bulford added to the martial activity. Now Browning's 1st Airborne Division had arrived and training activity increased. It was a time for new developments and Chatterton, surveying the miserable camp at Tilshead, felt it was good to be alive, even though it was the depth of winter and Salisbury Plain almost Siberian in its bleak grandeur.

Chatterton had only three weeks before the first batch of 300 men arrived. He already knew what sort of regiment was needed and sensed the problems of creating it from men who would all be of the rank of sergeant and above. These pilots would not only have a dangerous flight to the battle but, if they were to be of any use at the other end – and more important, if they were to be available to fly in subsequent operations – they must be able to fight as fully trained infantry. To perform the dual role of soldier–pilot they needed discipline, and to Chatterton this meant the discipline of the parade ground, to knock a sense of corporate spirit into the heterogeneous crowd he accurately foresaw. He went to Browning, asked for a pair of Foot Guards drill sergeants, and got them at once.

The first draft of men arrived; as Chatterton had expected, a mixed bunch, reflecting the best and worst of the British Army. They shared only one thing: the thirst for adventure – and those who survived were not disappointed. Chatterton's opening address had a predictably electrifying effect and is worth quoting at length, '. . . we will forge this regiment as a weapon of attack, but in order to do so we will have to find inspiration. Now we consider ourselves to be unique in that not only will we be trained into pilots but also we will have to fight on the ground. Therefore we must be *total* – in all and everything. We shall fly, master all infantry weapons, drive tanks, jeeps and trucks. We shall learn to command and obey, use wireless sets. . . . But in order to do this we must instil in ourselves the highest form of discipline and *esprit de corps*. . . . Let me say that I make no apology for talking to you like this. May I add that I shall be quite ruthless. Only the best will be tolerated in loyalty and discipline – if you do not like it then go back whence you came; it would be far better.' This is the authentic moment in which a new regiment came to life. A number of men gave up and vanished back to their regiments, but the majority stayed.

When Rock returned from his glider course to assume command of the battalion, the fruits of Chatterton's work were evident; Tilshead camp had been transformed into something approaching the Guards depot and seethed with every type of martial activity: arduous physical training, weapons instruction, range work and map reading, driver training and vehicle maintenance – the Guards sergeant-majors reigned supreme on an immaculate parade ground, brasswork shone, and boots were universally brought to that glossy finish only obtained by hours of work with spit and polish. Rock was not accustomed to this; he resented the fact that Chatterton had been able to create, in a few months, a regiment in *his* image; the two men, of totally opposite characters and talents, clashed from the start. This confrontation was tragically resolved when Rock, determined to show that he could do all his men could do, was fatally injured when attempting a night-flying trial totally beyond his experience. Chatterton – who had been posted to the newly raised 2nd Battalion to get him away from Rock, returned to command the 1st.

Meanwhile, the second parachute operation had taken place. During 1941 the Germans had erected a chain of radar stations along the Channel coast which, it was clear, had enhanced their ability to detect and track British bombers on their way to attack targets in Germany and occupied Europe. Nothing was known about German radars and the only solution was to obtain the key parts from one of these new installations. A raid from the sea anywhere on this heavily defended coastline would almost certainly result in loss of surprise and bloody repulse. An airborne attack was suggested; it would achieve total surprise, could be mounted accurately against a pin-point target and there was a good chance of extricating the raiders by sea if the operation took place by night. The radar selected was at Bruneval, near Le Havre; it stood near high cliff tops overlooking the sea and was guarded by a garrison estimated to be 100 strong but billetted 400 yards away. More German troops were quartered in a near-by village for coastal defence and the whole area was patrolled at night.

The intelligence briefing was thorough and accurate; a detailed large-scale model of the area was built and a newly trained unit of paratroops selected for the operation, 'C' Company of the 2nd Parachute Battalion. The officer in command was Maj. John Frost, who had already displayed outstanding qualities of command and leadership in training and was carefully chosen for what would clearly be an operation on which the future of the parachute force depended. A repetition of *Colossus* could not be tolerated. Great care was taken to ensure absolute secrecy over the preparation of *Biting* as this operation was codenamed, especially as much special equipment had to be obtained, and an elaborate sea evacuation plan devised. HQ Combined Operations, under Cdre Lord Louis Mountbatten – last heard of as a survivor of HMS *Kelly* off Crete – provided two specialists to accompany 'C' Company: a radar expert and a German interpreter, both of whom were given a short parachute course at Ringway to prepare them for the operation.

In January 1942, when the raid was planned and 'C' Company selected, many of the men had not completed their parachute course, which was delayed by appalling weather and the need to practice embarkation drills with the naval units responsible for the evacuation phase. Consequently, many of Frost's men were not fully qualified as parachutists when the meteorologists' forecast for the night of 27/28 February led the overall commander of the raid, the Naval C-in-C Portsmouth, to order 'Carry out operation *Biting* tonight'. At 2145 hrs 'C' Company climbed aboard their aircraft at Thruxton airfield near Andover. The *Whitleys* from which they were to drop were commanded and led by the celebrated Wg-Comd Pickard, one of Bomber Command's aces, who had featured in the much-praised propaganda film *Target for Tonight* as the captain of the bomber 'F for Freddy'. In his hands, Frost and his men felt confident. They were divided into three parties, named (in deference to the Senior Service on whose skill they relied for the return trip) after famous admirals. 'Nelson' was directed to deal with the shore defences and the garrison in Bruneval village, 'Rodney' the larger garrison near the radar, in a group of buildings known as *La Presbytère*, and 'Drake' – led by Frost, with Flt Sgt Cox the radar expert – was to go for the installation and hold onto it for as long as it took Cox to examine it and purloin the vital parts.

As the planes came in over the French coast they met some flak but the drop was successful; some of 'Nelson' Group were dropped two miles away but quickly rejoined the main operation; total surprise was achieved; the *Presbytère* garrison proved to be remarkably torpid and all other resistance was overwhelmed. Cox, working fast and skilfully, assessed the radar and dismantled it and although the beach defences proved tougher than those at the radar site the evacuation, under heavy fire, was a brilliant success. Before dawn the flotilla was well back on the friendly side of the Channel.

Efficient planning, superb leadership by Frost and tremendous dash displayed by 'C' Company had brought off a spectacular coup, and much was made of its propaganda value, even to comparing *Biting* with Drake's raid on Cadiz. Winston Churchill, who loved such historical parallels, gave the seal of approval to airborne forces. The radar experts in England were delighted with Cox's loot. Above all, the paratroops' casualties had been miraculously light – one killed and seven wounded.

Just over a month before *Biting* a further organizational development had taken place which would seal the alliance now developing between the Army's airborne forces and the RAF. On 15 January 1942, 38 Wing RAF was formed under Gp-Capt. Sir Nigel Norman with the role of co-ordinating the operations and training of the RAF bomber squadrons now being allocated to the support of airborne forces. Shortage of aircraft was to Browning what a lack of frigates had been to Nelson 140 years earlier. At the beginning of the war the RAF had virtually no transport planes save for a few obsolete models unsuited for parachuting or glider towing duties.

After watching an airborne demonstration at Netheravon on 16 April 1942 Churchill sent a minute to the Chief of the Air Staff (Portal) directing him to make 'discarded bombers' permanently available for the support of airborne forces. Portal replied that there *were* no 'discarded bombers' – the obsolescent *Whitleys* were urgently needed in operational training units now springing up all over England to produce aircrew for the new four-engined bombers at last reaching front-line squadrons. To divert *Whitleys* from OTUs at this stage would prejudice the all-out bombing offensive which Churchill himself had ordered against Germany. The best that 38 Wing could hope for was one more exercise squadron of *Whitleys* and even this depended on the production of more propellers, for lack of which over 100 aircraft were grounded. Norman knew that if 38 Wing was to be credible to the Army he must produce a continuous supply of training aircraft and he renewed his fight for a minimum of four squadrons, a total of 96 aircraft. His courageous stand against the Chiefs of his own service produced an unexpectedly welcome result; Churchill appealed directly to Roosevelt and asked for a share of the American aircraft industry's booming production of transport aircraft. The President replied that in the short term none could be spared, but that the United States Army Air Force would send four of its transport groups – 208 aircraft – to England as soon as possible, and more in November, to give a total of 416 fully dedicated to supporting the British airborne forces.

This generous offer did not, however, solve the immediate problem; throughout the summer of 1942 38 Wing struggled to give the Army what support it could in the face of hostility from the Air Officer C-in-C Bomber Command (Harris) whose obsession with strategic bombing not only blinded him to any rival claims for aircraft but so influenced Portal that he also declined to make Churchill's 'discarded bombers' available. When Harris was invited to present his argument to the Chiefs of Staffs Committee he questioned the value of airborne operations compared to that of the strategic bombing of Germany and went so far as to declare that if any aircraft were milked off to 38 Wing the bombing offensive would have to be halted. Whatever Portal, Chief of the Air Staff, thought of his wayward protégé's pronouncements he tacitly supported him, commenting, 'I certainly do not think that a case has been made out for the use of Airborne Forces for a full scale invasion of the continent.' In fact, nobody had suggested their use as the primary arm in such an invasion. The War Office tried to placate these senior airmen, restating the need for airborne troops and pointing out that their use in the rear of the German defences might well be the only way of guaranteeing a lodgement on the beaches. As a further inducement, the CIGS offered the prospect of seizing landing grounds in France, off which the Tactical Air Force would be able to operate within a few days of the invasion.

This head-on collision between War Office and Air Ministry had an immediate and, it seemed, calamitous effect. On 23 October 1942 the Chiefs of Staff Committee, still unable to reach agreement, submitted a report to Churchill stating the Army and RAF cases. Within a week the Prime Minister's reply dashed the hopes of the advocates of Airborne: a stand-still was imposed on the production of gliders (already being made in quantity by leading furniture manufacturers) and on the posting of RAF personnel to 38 Wing; at the same time all airborne training was slowed down.

At this time the aircraft situation in 38 Wing was pathetic. Apart from 60 tired *Whitleys* (which could only tow the *Horsa* glider unladen) and a handful of *Albemarles* – unsuccessful medium bombers made of wood to save on strategic metals – the barrel was empty. It was clear that no heavy bombers would be forthcoming; but at this dark hour the greatest transport aircraft of all appeared on the scene. The Douglas C47 *Skytrain* – to give it its USAAF name – had entered American military service in January 1942. It was an adaptation of the DC3 passenger aircraft which had been in service with numerous airlines since 1935, and which had in turn been developed from the celebrated DC2 of the earlier 1930s. It became available as the *Dakota* to the RAF during the winter of 1942–43, and more than 1900 were eventually to be supplied under the terms of the Lend–Lease agreement. This marvellous aircraft was powerful enough to tow a fully laden *Horsa*, or two Waco CG4s. It could carry 18–20 paratroops or in the airlanding role 28 men and their personal weapons and equipment. The initial reaction of the Air Staff to the idea of using unarmed aircraft in the combat transport role was one of disbelief; but the time was now fast approaching when the Allied Air Forces would wrest command of the air from the Axis to obtain exactly the conditions in which the *Dakota* could operate.

In that same dark winter of 1942–43, when the tide of war was at the very moment of change, the Airborne Forces were put again to the test in operations as geographically different as they were in their nature. They took place respectively in North Africa and in the hills of southern Norway.

★   ★   ★

At this point, the first American paratroops enter the scene. During the inter-war years there had been desultory experiments with military parachuting, and in several army manoeuvres of the 1930s troops had been airlanded tactically to seize airfields or harass the opposing side from the rear. In the autumn of 1940, the US Army's first parachute battalion, the 501st, had been raised at Fort Benning. By February 1942 four battalions were in existence and these in turn served as the cadres around which four parachute regiments were formed. When rapid expansion is indicated, the US Army is seen at its matchless best, and the creation of a great airborne force now got under way with typical enthusiasm, attention to detail and the impressive backing of the Pentagon. In August 1942 the existing 82nd motorized division was split to form the 82nd and 101st Airborne divisions; the motorized battalions were re-roled to become glider infantry units and one newly raised parachute regiment of three battalions was added to each division. By November 1942, the 82nd and 101st were in their sixth week of collective training. The British, who had been struggling to form an airborne division all that year, could boast only one brigade remotely ready for action, with two still forming.

The advanced guard of the US Airborne forces had actually arrived in England in midsummer 1942, when the 2nd Battalion of the 503rd Parachute Regiment arrived at Churchill's express invitation, to be placed under Browning's command in 1st Airborne Division. At once they started training on Salisbury Plain, where their ability to call freely upon the USAAF's C47s was envied by the British paratroops, still grappling with the discomforts and terrors of the *Whitley*.

In September, the Allied Planning Staffs were deeply involved in preparing for operation *Torch* – the landings in French North Africa designed to end the desert campaign by forcing an Axis withdrawal to the European mainland and to seize a secure base from which the 'soft underbelly' could be attacked. Browning was told that the 2nd/

503rd would be needed for *Torch*. At once, seeing a heaven-sent chance to launch his green troops on a major airborne operation, he offered his one combat-ready parachute brigade, the 1st, to join in. No RAF aircraft could be made available, so the British had to re-train on the C47, learning the new art of jumping from the side door instead of the dreaded *Whitley* 'hole'. During this hasty re-training period there were a number of casualties, and whilst these were being investigated many troops of 1st Parachute Brigade were flown off to North Africa without ever having made a side-door exit.

The first airborne operation in *Torch* was something of an epic. The 2nd/503rd, commanded by Lt-Col. Edson D. Raff, were loaded into 39 C47s in Cornwall on the evening of 7 November, with the task of seizing Tafaraoui airfield near Oran, destroying all Vichy French aircraft found there and then taking another airfield, La Senia, used by the Vichy French as a maintenance unit and by the Germans as a terminus for their long-range transport aircraft. This was an ambitious aim at the best of times, and a number of imponderables militated against success. The whole operation hung on the ability of the C47 crews to navigate over 1500 miles, mostly at night across the sea. None of the pilots had seen action; the navigators were so inexperienced that the RAF had to provide 25 out of 39, and only a few of these had full sets of air charts. Fourteen C47 crews were hastily assembled only hours before the take-off. No formation training had been carried out even in daylight, and the hurried take-off meant that in order to conserve fuel the planes had to set course in the gathering darkness independently of each other. RAF fighter cover was provided until the straggling force reached the middle of the Bay of Biscay, after which the anxious crews flew on, navigating by dead reckoning. The weather was appalling, and it was to their great surprise that the pilots found at daybreak that they were mostly in sight of each other, in general agreement that the coastline visible to the south-east was that of Africa. Encouraged by a landfall on the right continent, the force followed the coast towards the east. Fuel was now running low, and an element of comic opera began to take over. The officer commanding the air group landed in order to make inquiry of an Arab he had seen on the ground, whilst the rest of the force straggled on to the airfield at Lourmel, where it was greeted by a brisk fusillade from the Vichy garrison. The other pilots declined to stay in the area in order to drop the parachutists but some, running out of fuel, had to land near by. Seeing what he thought were enemy troops, Raff ordered his men to drop, to be greeted on the ground by elements of the 1st US Armored Division feeling their way south from the coast.

Having delivered their passengers to the theatre of war the C47s, on their last few gallons of fuel, landed on a dried-up salt lake where their crews were promptly arrested by French policemen. Colonel Raff, having been told where he was by the 1st Division tank crews, marched energetically off at the head of his battalion towards Tafaraoui, his primary objective. On arriving there some distance ahead of the main body he found to his chagrin that it had already been captured by the ubiquitous 1st Armored, who had pressed on in the direction of Oran. Raff, left to defend Tafaraoui, and uncertain what to expect from the Vichy French, started to rally his scattered command by ferrying the men in by air. After three C47s had been shot down by French fighters, he commandeered every bus he could lay hands on and in this way the tired and frustrated battalion closed in on the airfield.

The Americans' first attempt at an airborne operation had been as discouraging as had the British. The men had stoically endured the long and at times demoralizing flight to Africa and had arrived exhausted to take on an unknown enemy. There had been little real planning beforehand; intelligence was almost non-existent; the aircrews, though willing enough, lacked training in combat flying – especially in navigation; there was no radio contact with friendly forces on the ground, and only good luck had prevented a pitched battle between the 2nd/503rd and the equally mystified 1st Armoured Division.

It remained to be seen how the British 1st Parachute Brigade would fare. Their approach to battle was less traumatic; having emplaned the 3rd Parachute Battalion (Lt-Col. Pine-Coffin) in England on 9 November, their aircraft landed at Gibraltar to refuel and late on the following afternoon they were airlanded at Maison Blanche airfield near Algiers to prepare for an attack on Bône with 6 Commando. The rest of 1st Parachute Brigade, with its commander, Brig. Flavell, was still at sea aboard its troopships. The 3rd Battalion were rapidly caught up in the campaign; on 12 November they were flown to Bône in order to forestall the expected arrival of the Germans. By now, the rest of the brigade had disembarked, and soon received their baptism of fire.

On 10 November, Raff's 2nd/503rd Battalion had been told to attack the airfield at Tebessa, in eastern Algeria, again to forestall the Germans; air reconnaissance revealed a more suitable target at Youks-les-Bains, some ten miles north-west, and at the same time the British 1st Parachute Brigade was ordered to go for another airfield just inside Tunisia, at Souk-el-Arba. As these drops formed part of a co-ordinated operation, Raff's battalion, now re-titled the 509th, was placed under Flavell's command, although no proper liaison or communication facilities existed. HQ 1st Army, under whom Flavell was serving, had little or no idea of planning, co-ordinating or controlling airborne operations, so the airborne unit commanders were left to grapple with the labyrinthine problems of getting the attack under way. 15 November was the day selected; the mounting airfield was Maison Blanche. At 0730 hrs the American battalion took off and managed to get to their objective where, on reaching the ground, they were greeted with open arms by the now friendly Vichy French. The British 1st Parachute Battalion failed to drop on the 15th because of bad weather, but arrived 24 hours later at Souk-el-Arba, where they, too, were greeted enthusiastically by the French. Their CO, Lt-Col. Hill, commandeered a fleet of buses and moved on to Béja, from where the Allies, in the last week of November, intended to launch an attack on Tunis.

On 23 October, 1200 miles to the east, Montgomery's 8th Army had launched itself at the Axis forces at El Alamein. The Axis forces in North Africa were now theoretically in a vice; to the east, the 8th Army was laboriously pushing back Rommel's *Afrika Korps* and their unenthusiastic Italian allies whilst the Anglo-American forces landed as Operation *Torch* made for Tunis to deprive the Germans of the base from which they could reinforce the North-African campaign.

The German High Command acted quickly to prevent the Allies achieving their aim. By 10 November it was reported that German paratroops had begun to arrive in Tunis, and from now on the resistance met by 1st Army as it fought its way eastwards was to stiffen dramatically. The operation to which Flavell and Raff were now committed was a last attempt at seizing airheads sufficiently close to Tunis for Allied troops to be flown in and capture the city. It failed due to a mixture of poor weather (which held up the British drop for 24 hours), inadequate resources at Maison Blanche, where the airborne troops were left to improvise as best they could, lack of support from the Allied airforces and the inability of the paratroops to drop with vehicles or any equipment other than their own light weapons.

The plan in which the British 2nd Parachute Battalion was to be used visualized a drive eastwards from Béja, where the 1st Battalion had been fighting stubbornly since 10 November against increasing German opposition. The 2nd Battalion's task was to drop on Depienne airfield, south of Tunis, whilst British Commandos and American Rangers landed from the sea to cut the Béja–Bizerta coastal road. In command of the 2nd Battalion was Lt-Col. John Frost, promoted since his brilliant handling of the Bruneval operation. On the morning of 29 November he led his men aboard 44 C47s of the

USAAF's 62nd Troop Carrier Wing. A 400-mile flight lay ahead, to a landing zone no one had ever seen, as no form of reconnaissance had been possible; maps were scarce and there were no aerial photographs to assist in planning the attack. Nothing was known about the enemy, or even if the objective was defended. The force arrived overhead Depienne early in the afternoon; there was no sign of occupation, nor was there any hostile fire. The field was deserted and had been ploughed up. Frost and his men jumped unopposed, to be rallied by the now familiar sound of their commanding officer's hunting horn. Once he had formed up his battalion and carefully checked to see that all weapons and equipment were serviceable, Frost decided to march north and attack Oudna airfield, which was only 10 miles outside Tunis. The battalion kept on the move throughout the night and seized Oudna at dawn on 30 November. Here, too, they found a deserted airfield. The Germans, momentarily taken off guard by this bold intrusion, reacted strongly, attacking the 2nd Battalion with fighter bombers and tanks, against which the paratroops had no defence.

On the following day the hard-pressed Frost learned to his dismay that the ground forces ordered to link up with him had been halted. His battalion was now in the situation in which no parachute unit should ever be found – isolated, without air cover, vehicles or heavy weapons, short of ammunition and food, and with no hope of resupply. Frost made his decision quickly; he would save as much of his unit as possible by marching west towards the now retiring main Allied force. At last light the exhausted men of the 2nd Battalion headed for the hills. For the next three days they were relentlessly harried and pursued by German air and ground forces. It was a terrible test for a newly formed unit, but the quality of its leaders was up to it and the men responded with a display of endurance and courage worthy of Sir John Moore's retreat to Corunna.

This discipline had been instilled since the battalion's formation a year earlier. An NCO, recalling those days, wrote that 'either our old units wanted to get rid of us, or we rid of them'. To knit such a collection into a fighting unit called for the imposition of draconian discipline, to the initial dismay of all. But collective misery is often the gateway to corporate pride, and within months the new unit had acquired a panache and spirit worthy of a 300-year-old regiment, and an unquenchable morale that would see it through North Africa and Sicily and to the grisly end on the bridge at Arnhem, still under its indomitable commander John Frost. Some of the junior officers in the 2nd Battalion were eccentrics as well as martinets. One, remembered vividly by the same NCO, was 'dead regular . . . doing everything by the book', even insisting that during night exercises his platoon marched cross-country in step. When on manoeuvres he would not share his men's food, insisting that his rations be prepared in the officers' mess and brought separately to him; he would then sit aloof from his men to eat his meal. At the same time he cared for them jealously, possessively, investigating their family welfare problems, meticulously inspecting their clothing and insisting on near-impossible standards of turn-out. He died as he had lived, working to the book. Given incorrect intelligence he marched his immaculate platoon, washed and shaved to a man, down a road thought to be free of enemy, in threes as though on parade. When they came suddenly across a German roadblock he took the first burst of machinegun fire himself, then formally handed his platoon over to his deputy as he lay dying by the roadside.

Frost's battalion – or what was left of it – reached the Allied lines at Medjaz on 3 December. Small parties of stragglers, cut off from the main body, continued to arrive for nine more days, but of Frost's splendid unit of some 500 officers and men, more than half had been killed, wounded or were missing. It had been a bloody introduction to war. There were many contributory factors to what had almost been a disaster: lack of experience by the American C47 crews, and of the British paratroops in jumping from these aircraft; the long approach flight to the combat zone; disagreement over command and control (which had led to Raff's men being arbitrarily dropped on a point selected by the commander of the transport force). There had been little or no collective training beforehand, and it was now apparent that in any subsequent airborne operation there must be total mutual confidence between the aircrew and the parachutist or glider pilot.

Browning's staff had leapt at the chance to use the 1st Parachute Brigade in action, believing that it would enhance the Airborne cause. It almost had the opposite effect; the logistic problem had been seriously under-estimated and the anti-airborne school now triumphantly claimed that airborne operations demanded a ridiculously expensive effort to mount them whilst yielding little or no operational dividend.

There had, however, been an immeasurable gain; and it came from a wholly unexpected source. Shortly before their departure from England, all airborne troops had been issued with a distinctive headdress; a maroon-coloured beret. In the British Army, minor distinctions of dress count for a great deal – almost as much as the pride of wearing one's own regimental cap badge and buttons. The 'red beret' was not welcomed at first by many parachutists who until then had continued to wear the regimental dress of their parent regiments. In North Africa, the paratroops discarded their cumbrous helmets on landing and fought, for the sake of comfort, in their red berets. Shortly after the end of the operation, Flavell received a signal from Browning. It read, 'General Alexander directs that 1 Para Brigade informed that reliable information from German forces in Tunisia states "1 Para Brigade have been given name by Germans of Red Devils". Gen. Alexander congratulates the brigade on achieving this high distinction. Such distinctions given by the enemy are seldom won in battle except by the finest fighting troops.'

Whilst the Anglo-American parachutists were learning their trade the hard way in North Africa, the first British glider operation took place. As early as 1941 intelligence had reached London indicating that the Germans were at work on the development of an atomic weapon. One of the ingredients of their experiments was deuterium oxide or 'heavy water', which had been made for some time before the war by the Norsk Hydro plant at Vermork, in a remote area some 60 miles west of Oslo. The factory was situated on a ledge, 1000 feet above the floor of a steep valley, making it a near-impossible target for bombers and almost invulnerable to ground attack. The Special Operations Executive (SOE) in London considered it essential to cut off the heavy water supply and several attempts were made by specially trained saboteurs parachuted in from England. As an insurance, it was decided to land a party of sappers by glider in the Vermork area with the aim of rushing the plant and blowing it up.

In October 1942 Maj.-Gen. Browning and Gp-Capt. Sir Nigel Norman made their plan. Because of the need to get large quantities of explosive to the target, a parachuted operation had to be ruled out, and it was decided to use two *Horsa* gliders, towed by *Halifax* four-engined bombers. Two groups of 16 men were trained in great secrecy. The *Halifax* crews and the glider pilots were carefully hand-picked for their skill, particularly in navigation by night. On the night of 19/20 November the *Halifaxes* towed their gliders off a remote airfield in the northern extremity of Scotland and quickly disappeared into the murk. It was planned that the glider landing site in the Norwegian hills would be located by use of a small radio beacon on the ground, called *Eureka*, which had previously been dropped with one of SOE's Norwegian agents. When this was switched on it would indicate its position with great accuracy to a navigational device called *Rebecca* in the *Halifax*, ensuring that the gliders were cast off above the landing ground, which was manned by the Norwegian resistance, standing by to light beacons of brushwood. The first *Halifax* made a good landfall, but then its *Rebecca* failed;

the navigator continued on dead-reckoning and the map, but the air-craft then flew into dense cloud, and began to ice up. The glider, too, began to gather ice, as did the tow rope. Glider and tug started to lose height despite use of emergency power by the captain of the *Halifax*; they were just north of Stavanger when the tow rope failed altogether. Down into the blackness went the glider; somehow the pilots, Staff-Sgt Strathdee and Sgt Doig, managed a crash landing in a blizzard on top of a mountain, but they died instantly in the wreck, as did six others. Four of the survivors were desperately injured. On Gestapo orders they were given lethal injections by the German doctor who attended them; the remaining five were executed two months later. The other *Halifax* and glider also made a good landfall but the *Horsa* was cast off prematurely, landing amongst hills near Helleland. Three of its occupants died instantly; the rest were quickly rounded up, taken to the German camp at Egersund and summarily shot. The *Halifax* hit a mountain top near by, killing all its crew.

Vengeance is not an attractive sentiment, but it is cheering to know that because of the dedication of the Norwegian Resistance movement and the sworn evidence of certain others, the perpetrators of this vicious war crime against soldiers correctly dressed in uniform were brought to justice in 1945, to pay the only penalty acceptable under the circumstances.

It is paradoxical that at the beginning of 1943 the airborne forces of the American and British armies, though well launched on their respective expansion programmes, faced their biggest crisis. The failures of *Colossus* and *Freshman*, the inconclusive results of the North-African intervention, and the ever-increasing demands made on transport and bomber aircraft resources, were drawing fire from all directions. There was a strong body of opinion which, whilst acknowledging the value of small-scale airborne raids such as the Bruneval operation, strenuously opposed any attempt to mount operations on a brigade or divisional basis. The airborne school countered that the forthcoming entry into Europe called for large-scale parachute and glider landings in order to confuse the defence, cut lines of reinforcement, paralyse the Axis command system and secure the flanks of the seaborne assault. So far, for reasons entirely beyond their control, the airborne arm had not justified themselves, and were uncomfortably aware of the fact. Little did they realize, as plans were made for their use on a larger scale in the invasion of Sicily, that the results of this operation would produce an even fiercer debate.

CHAPTER SEVEN

The Break-in: Sicily and Normandy

The ejection of the Axis powers from North Africa and their final surrender in Tunis on 13 May 1943 was the outcome of a laborious and difficult campaign, the first in which the Americans and British had fought side by side. Planning for the next step – the invasion of Sicily, known as Operation *Husky* – had actually started in January, aiming at a landing during July. A special Allied planning staff was set up in Algiers in February but its work went ahead at snail's pace, hampered by the fact that British and American staffwork was incompatible, and also by the fragmentation and geographic separation of the various planning staffs. The Alliance was still in its early days and working at times with great friction. All this led to poor inter-service co-operation throughout the Sicilian campaign and to some costly misunderstandings.

Ideally, *Husky* should have followed hot on the heels of the Axis collapse in Tunisia, where Italian and German losses had been huge in the final stages; about 180,000 of their battle-tested soldiers were taken prisoner in the last two weeks, having been flung into the battle after the Germans' initial successes over Eisenhower's inexperienced forces. Since then, however, the Axis had lost control of the air as well as of the sea. In March, Rommel, sensing imminent disaster, had flown to Hitler's command post in East Prussia to plead for immediate withdrawal to Europe, there to re-group and await the Allied invasion with well-equipped seasoned troops. The *Führer* had refused point-blank; his earlier inspiration had now, it seemed, deserted him; from now on his generals had simultaneously to fight his idiotic directives as well as the Allies. Retreat, even when indicated as the only sensible solution if armies were to be kept intact for the final battle, was out of the question.

The Axis immediately began preparations for the defence of Sicily. There was an Italian garrison of four moderately good infantry divisions, and six static coast divisions of very dubious quality. German reinforcements prudently withheld from Tunisia were formed into two scratch 'divisions' – the 15th *Panzergrenadier* and the 'Hermann Göring' *Panzerdivision* and were in position (behind the Italians, to ensure that the frailer ally would fight properly) by the end of June. Both these formations, whilst nominally under command of the Italian Gen. Guzzoni, were actually commanded by *Gen. Leutnant* von Senger und Etterlin whose orders were to take firm control in the event of an Italian collapse. It was an uneasy alliance.

The outline plan agreed by the Allies in March was for two main amphibious landings in Sicily. The British were to land in the southeast corner of the island to seize airfields and the key ports of Syracuse and Augusta whilst the Americans landed at three points on the south coast to secure further airfields. The airborne plan involved parts of the British 1st and the American 82nd Airborne Divisions. The problems of mounting 1st Airborne's task were particularly daunting. Whereas the 82nd was already in North Africa, together with its Waco gliders, the 1st was still in England. To make matters worse, Browning handed over command of 1st Airborne in March to Maj.-Gen. 'Hoppy' Hopkinson, an ambitious, energetic and amusing man who was determined to make a name for himself as well as for his division in the forthcoming operations. Browning now became Airborne adviser to the Allied commanders, Generals Eisenhower and Alexander, and immediately began grappling with the problem of getting 1st Airborne into Sicily. Due to shortage of aircraft for the parachute lift it was decided to use the division's three brigades in successive landings ahead of the leading British sea landing formation, VIII Corps. The objectives selected were the Ponte Grande bridge to the south of Syracuse, where a glider landing would be carried out, with parachute assaults against the high ground inland from Augusta and the important road bridge at Primasole to the north of Syracuse.

There now remained the problem of providing gliders for 1st Airlanding Brigade's attack on the Ponte Grande. An astonishing ferry operation involved the towing of 36 *Horsas* from England to North Africa, and the assembly of American Waco gliders by their British crews (who had never seen them before) on dusty Moroccan landing grounds.

At Kairouan in Tunisia, the mounting base for the Sicilian operation, Chatterton had taken command of a situation which threatened to be chaotic. Nineteen *Horsas* had survived the hazardous long-distance ferry operation and by dint of superhuman work by the glider pilots themselves 140 Wacos were now ready. The crews had to be quickly re-trained to fly them, a tall order in the limited time available. Chatterton's problem was compounded by the fact that he knew much more about the plan for operation *Ladbrooke* – as the airborne part of *Husky* was codenamed – than his glider pilots. It was to be a

night attack and he knew that his crews, who were badly out of training in any case, would find it difficult to carry out precision landings
in the unfamiliar Waco, a glider with radically different handling
characteristics to the British *Horsa* on which they had been trained. It
was much lighter, having been originally designed to the pre-war
German philosophy of a high-level cast-off some distance from the
target and therefore had a flat gliding angle and low rate of descent.
The *Horsa*, on the other hand, was fitted with huge flaps like barn
doors. With these fully extended – a condition known as 'heavy flap' –
it could be set at the ground from 1000 feet or more to dive at the
phenomenally steep angle of 70 degrees; the flaps, acting as dive
brakes, retarded the glider's speed to around 140 miles an hour;
having got near the ground the pilot, assisted by the co-pilot, pulled
out of the dive and landed. This technique enabled the glider, released close overhead its target, to reach the ground in the shortest
possible time. To reduce its run-on, the *Horsa* was later fitted with a
retarding parachute which could be streamed in the final stage of the
landing. The undercarriage could also be jettisoned, and a short skid
was provided on which the glider could be landed in a zone the size of
a football pitch.

The British airborne plan for *Ladbrooke*, with its night landings,
had been adopted by Gen. Montgomery as the result of a curious bit
of military intrigue. Maj.-Gen. Hopkinson was a keen amateur pilot,
and as such believed himself to be an expert on flying matters; without informing Browning he secured an interview with Montgomery –
whose ignorance of airborne forces' capabilities and limitations at this
time was if anything more profound than Hopkinson's – and obtained
the enthusiastic blessing of the 8th Army's Commander.

Chatterton, on the other hand, was a highly skilled aviator; his
professional training with the RAF had left him with no illusions as to
what was possible and what was not. He asked to see Hopkinson and
expressed his doubts as to the ability of the gliders to reach their
objectives. The general offered him the alternative of being relieved
of his command on the spot or carrying the night landing through.
Believing he could be of more service to his pilots by staying on,
Chatterton returned to the training airfields. He had three weeks to
bring his force to concert pitch. During this time as much night
flying as possible was done; characteristically Chatterton was the first
to demonstrate a tactical night landing in a Waco with only the moon-
light as an aid. He also flew along the Sicilian coast in a night fighter
to assess the chances of readily identifying the targets. There was an
encouraging lack of anti-aircraft fire and the loom of the land below
stood out well. However, three uncalled-for factors were to turn the

glider landing into a shambles. On the night of the operation a 45–50 miles an hour wind had risen, making towing doubly difficult in turbulent conditions; the tug aircraft, mostly American, were crewed by men who until recently had been plodding up and down civil routes in the USA and were totally untrained for war; and the fly-in routes led over that most mortal hazard to Allied pilots, the trigger-happy Anglo-American invasion fleet.

The same problems bedevilled the parachute landings. On the south coast of Sicily the first American drop was to be by the 505th Parachute Infantry Regiment whose commander, destined to be one of the great airborne leaders of the war, was Col. James M. Gavin. His augmented regiment was to support the amphibious landings of the 1st US Infantry Division at Gela by dropping inland and blocking the routes down which Axis reinforcements would try to move.

Having achieved this aim, the 505th were to seize the near-by landing ground at Ponte Olivo in order to permit rapid reinforcement by air. A full-dress rehearsal in French Morocco went well and the 505th approached their first big operation with confidence. On the evening of 9 July Gavin's men clambered aboard the C47s of the USAAF's 52nd Troop Carrier Wing and Brig. 'Pip' Hicks's 1st Airlanding Brigade strapped themselves into their gliders, which were towed by a mixed force from the 51st Troop Carrier Wing and 38 Wing RAF. 127 Wacos, each carrying 14 men and a handcart, were towed by C47s; the 10 *Horsas*, carrying 32 troops, were towed by *Albemarles* and *Halifaxes*. The flight plan was already complicated by the differing towing speeds of the tugs and the preference of American pilots for flying in 'vics' of three whilst the RAF chose to fly in a 'stream'. The route to Sicily involved three hours' flying; the first leg was to Malta, identified by cones of searchlights, and then by dead reckoning to a point south-east of Sicily where the parachute and glider streams were to split. A high wind produced severe turbulence and airsickness racked the whole force. Far worse, it soon became apparent that the training of the C47 aircrews was hopelessly inadequate. Many navigators had only the remotest idea of their position and some had the wrong charts or none at all. These crews had been hurriedly transferred to the USAAF from civil airlines; they were competent at peacetime navigation from radio beacon to beacon, but now, on a dark stormy night and under strict radio silence, their nerve began to fail. Few landmarks were recognized by the crews of Gavin's aircraft as they flew west along the south coast of the island, and the situation got even worse when the Allied fleets below opened up at them with every available gun. The sky filled with tracer and shell bursts and planes began to fall. Pilots flew up and down the coast and nervous jumpmasters started to despatch the men of the 505th into the void below. Few of the dropping zones had been identified as the pathfinders had not arrived to set out their lamps. There was no mass drop at Gela. Gavin himself landed, fuming, over 30 miles away and some of his units were 60 miles from their objective. Only one unit of the 505th landed on target, many of its men badly injured as they landed in a 30-mile-an-hour wind amidst a rock-strewn landscape.

During the night about an eighth of Gavin's force managed to rally around this company, and established a roadblock on the high ground overlooking Gela. Meanwhile, the rest of the 505th, operating in scattered groups and even as individuals, displayed tremendous initiative and fighting spirit by taking on any enemy they met. Innumerable small actions broke out along a 60-mile stretch of country, striking alarm into the Italian defence and thoroughly misleading von Senger und Etterlin's staff as to the Allies' intentions.

Whilst the 505th were grappling with their problems, a tragedy struck the 1st Airlanding Brigade. After separating from the force carrying Gavin's men, the leader of the glider stream flew north from Cap Passero up the coast towards Syracuse. The plan was for eight *Horsas* to land at the Ponte Grande at 2315 hrs with two rifle companies of the South Staffordshire Regiment, and for the remainder of that battalion and the whole of the Border Regiment, in Wacos, to land about two miles away, knock out a coastal battery, then pass the Border Regiment over the Ponte Grande to attack Syracuse by first light, leaving the Staffords to hold the bridge until relieved by units coming up from the beaches. The tug pilots had been briefed to cast off 3000 yards from the coast, over the water. Instead, most of them did so far out at sea, away from the anti-aircraft fire which was coming up from friend and foe alike. Sixty-nine Wacos crash-landed in the sea, amongst them the one flown by Chatterton and carrying Hicks, the Brigade Commander, and over 600 men drowned without firing a shot. Over the Ponte Grande the sky was full of wheeling aircraft and gliders. Only two *Horsas* got down on the target; 22 came down within a mile and 49 more scattered around a 10-mile radius. From those two battalions who had set out from Kairouan that evening less than a platoon's-worth reached the bridge on time.

There now ensued an heroic fight; Lt Withers of the Staffords and 14 men were in glider number 133. Flown by Staff-Sgt Galpin it was on tow behind an *Albemarle* which was hit by flak as it approached the coast; the tug pilot, Flt Lt Grant, flew on even though his plane was on fire and launched Galpin accurately at his target before making for his distant base; it is pleasing to note that he got his plane and crew safely home. Galpin, caught in a searchlight beam which providentially lit up his target as well, made a good landing, and joined Withers's men at the bridge. After first light, stragglers began to converge on the objective and by mid-morning some 80 infantry and glider pilots were fighting for their lives against successive Italian counter-attacks. By mid-afternoon the situation was critical; ammunition began to run out and still there was no sign of the Border Regiment. No one realized that most of them were at the bottom of the sea. When they were finally overwhelmed at 1600 hrs only 15 men were left unwounded. The Italian victory was shortlived, for within an hour the Royal Scots Fusiliers appeared on the scene and re-took the Ponte Grande. This time it stayed in British hands.

As in the American sector, much confusion was spread in the enemy's ranks by the bold actions of small groups which had either landed far away from the objective or straggled ashore from their sinking gliders. Indeed, the Italians were now convinced that several Allied airborne divisions were at large on the island. At this point the Germans moved forward into the battle, and the fighting took on a new intensity. On the morning of 11 July, whilst the Americans were still bringing their 1st, 3rd and 45th Divisions ashore on the south coast, a major counter attack came in with the dreaded Tiger tanks against the American paratroops north of Gela, who hung grimly onto their blocking position as the 1st Infantry Division and some Ranger units were drawn into the fight. Further to the east, Gavin had rallied a number of small units to his command and fought all day to stop the Axis troops reaching the beaches. General Patton, commanding 7th US Army, now decided to use paratroops in the airborne reinforcement role by dropping two battalions of the 504th, a light artillery battalion, and an engineer company within the American beach-head at Farello airfield, three miles east of Gela. The drop was to take place during the night of 11/12 July. This time the troop carriers found Malta easily but again as they neared Sicily they were greeted by a hail of fire from Allied ships. Twenty-three out of 144 C47s plunged into the sea or crashed inland and 37 were badly damaged. Due to violent evasive action by the pilots, many jumpmasters despatched their loads of paratroops prematurely and out of 1900 men only 400 landed on Farello. Many of the rest, coming suddenly out of the night sky to land amidst American sea-landed units, were shot at once by their own side, and by the afternoon of the 12th only 558 officers and men of the 504th Parachute Regiment were fit to fight on.

The next British airborne action was the launching of Brig. Lathbury's 1st Parachute Brigade against the Primasole bridge. Lathbury visualized an operation similar to that attempted against the Ponte Grande, this time with paratroops instead of gliders. On the evening of 13 July the brigade emplaned in North Africa; once more the 51st Troop Carrier Wing were to be the transport force. An air of optimism pervaded the High Command; in his HQ Montgomery promised his staff that by the next evening he would be in Catania. He was rash to do so.

For the first time, the British used pathfinders – small squads dropped ahead of the main body to mark out the drop zones with lamps. The 1st Battalion was to drop at the north end of the Primasole bridge whilst the 3rd would land to the south. The 2nd was to take some rising ground about 2000 yards from the bridge, which it overlooked. A battery of 6-pounder anti-tank guns was to come in gliders. It was a simple and straightforward plan which looked good. Unfortunately, the Germans also had designs on the Primasole bridge; their reaction to the landings of the previous 72 hours had been decisive and well-considered, demonstrating yet again the flexibility of their military organizations and the professional efficiency of their staff system. The Italian Napoli division, judiciously stiffened by a strong battle group of the *'Hermann Göring'* *Panzerdivision*, moved swiftly south from Catania; Student, who had once more entered the arena, obtained clearance for the use of Heidrich's 1st Parachute Division, which was airlanded and dropped onto the Plain of Catania behind the German front line on the evening of 13 July, unobserved by the Allies because the jumps were cleverly timed to take place during gaps between the RAF's regular fighter sweeps. By sheer coincidence the 4th German Parachute Regiment had been given almost exactly the same landing zones as Lathbury's brigade and some of them got there first. To make matters worse for the British, 51st Troop Carrier Wing had another bad night; the C47s, flying this time in stream rather than their preferred 'vics' of three, were given an intricate route to fly in order to keep clear of the Allied fleets, whose gunners still tended to engage every plane in sight, a legacy from the days of German air supremacy. Off Cap Passero the ships opened up with every weapon and eleven C47s were shot down. A further 27 failed to reach the drop zone and returned their infuriated passengers to North Africa. Lt-Col. Alastair Pearson, commanding the 1st Battalion, went forward to the flight deck of his aircraft to find out where his pilot was taking him, to discover the navigator in hysterics and the rest of the crew panic-stricken. He drew his pistol and compelled them to find his correct dropzone. A chaotic battle developed as the British landed amidst the recently arrived Germans; it was an historic encounter, the first between two airborne forces.

Although 200 of his men with 5 guns actually seized it, Lathbury was forced off the bridge by the German parachutists during the night of 14/15 July, the overland relief having failed. The Primasole was not recaptured until just before dawn on 16 July when an infantry battalion was guided into a successful attack by Alastair Pearson, still full of fight despite 72 hours in action. This remarkable man became a legend in the Parachute Regiment and throughout Airborne Forces. He had taken command of the 1st Battalion in North Africa after its commanding officer Lt-Col. Hill, had been wounded. In Tunisia, whilst the battalion was in the line as a normal infantry unit, he had captured an entire regiment of Italian *Bersagliere*. At Primasole, after watching an unsuccessful attempt by a battalion of 50th Division to recapture the bridge, he offered to lead it in a night attack along with his own 1st Battalion. He had a masterly eye for country, acquired through years of deerstalking in his native Scotland, and was a great trainer of men, a leader capable of using physical force if need be to get the best out of a man on the battlefield. By the end of the war he had won the Distinguished Service Order four times, as well as the Military Cross. A comrade would write of him, years later, that he '. . . personified the early volunteer parachutist. He had all the qualities a parachute soldier needs, and as long as our Regiment exists, he will be the Star.' Coming from none other than John Frost, of Bruneval, Tunisia and the Arnhem bridge, this is praise indeed.

Although the Allied airborne assault into Sicily appeared to have been a costly failure which almost resulted in the cessation of developments in this field, the enemy were singularly impressed, not only by the quality of the British and American airborne troops, but by the disruptive effect of their operations. Student himself remarked on the delays imposed on movement of German reinforcements towards the beaches and considered that the Allied airborne landings had been a decisive factor in the loss of Sicily.

The irrepressible Chatterton survived his sea landing. He managed to get his Waco down, damaged by a burst of fire as he tried to alight on the water. The glider floated and its passengers clambered onto the wing; a searchlight caught them and machine guns opened up from the near-by cliffs. They took to the water and struggled ashore, narrowly escaping destruction as an Allied bomber crashed into the shallows behind them and blew up. The little party were mostly unarmed, their weapons and radios having gone down with the glider. Fortunately, they met with a party of Special Boat Service troops who took them on; a colonel of glider pilots, a brigadier and his staff, now quickly adapting themselves to a new role as infantry, guarding prisoners, always moving forward to find their own men. Chatterton reached the Ponte Grande after 24 hours, to be cheered up by the sight of Galpin's glider triumphantly lying within a stone's throw of its objective, and sobered by the sight of many more gliders lying wrecked with the bodies of crews and passengers still inside them.

The most encouraging fact to emerge from the operations in Sicily was the abundant evidence that the American and British airborne personnel selection procedures and training systems were producing the right sort of men – not the bristling desperado so beloved of fictional war film directors, but intelligent, brave and thoughtful soldiers with the ability to think for themselves when deprived of their appointed leaders. Chatterton's 'Total Soldier' concept in particular paid huge dividends, with glider pilots fighting confidently alongside the infantry they had flown into battle and showing themselves adaptable to any combat role. At the Primasole bridge three of them, Sergeants Anderson, Atkinson and Doig, fought as anti-tank gunners, receiving a short and urgent course of instruction whilst actually under close-range attack, replacing members of the original crew as they became casualties. Elsewhere, glider pilots seized a captured 88mm gun and turned it on its previous owners. Paratroops, dropped miles from the rest of their units, fought and marched across country towards the sound of guns. A tremendous fighting spirit was evolving, fed by the élitism stemming from the very fact that to qualify as a parachutist or glider pilot, a man had to overcome raw fear. In the last few seconds before his first jump a man learns a great deal about himself, and afterwards he is never the same man again. The experience was universal to all paratroops; *Generalleutnant* Brauer, a successful German parachute commander in *Weserübung*, Holland and Crete, rhapsodized over '. . . the almost superhuman sensation of the parachute jump. It alone compresses into the space of seconds feelings of concentrated energy, tenseness and abandon; it alone demands a continual and unconditional readiness to risk one's life. Therefore the parachutist experiences the most exalted feelings of which human beings are capable, namely that of victory over one's self. . . .'

The American and British airborne leaders were therefore reasonably satisfied that their new arm had proved itself in battle, and that their capabilities and limitations were coming to be recognized by the higher command. Before the end of 1943, however, there were to be further battles for survival. In the Pentagon, senior generals were divided on the issue; Eisenhower, beset by doubts after Sicily, convened a board of officers under Maj.-Gen. Joseph W. Swing to see if the airborne concept was valid at anything above battalion level. After much deliberation, the Swing Board concluded that parachute and glider troops should not be sent on missions unsuited to their capabilities, or on tasks which could be more economically, or equally well, be performed by other means. Eisenhower accepted the board's findings and from then on demonstrated his whole-hearted support for the large-scale use of airborne formations; unfortunately, his innate caution, reluctance to shed blood, and total lack of combat command experience hardly qualified him as the supreme arbiter when it came to deciding how and when to use airborne forces in the assault on north-west Europe. More American generals changed their allegiance after the success of a minor parachute operation in New Guinea in late 1943 – dealt with later in this book – and still more after Maj.-Gen. Swing, by now commanding the 11th US Airborne Division, had conducted it through a highly successful exercise in the United States in December of that year. The Chief of Staff, Gen. McNair, generously wrote to Swing after this exercise in these words: 'After the Airborne operations in Africa and Sicily, my staff and I had become convinced of the impracticability of handling large airborne units. I was prepared to recommend to the War Department that the airborne effort be restricted to parachute units of battalion size or smaller. The successful performance of your division has convinced me that we were wrong, and I shall now recommend that we continue our present schedule of activating, training and committing airborne divisions.' This was the watershed. The American military establishment has often showed itself to be as purblind as any other, but has also bred senior officers like McNair, big enough to change their mind in public.

There were also signs that the Allies as well as the Germans were tackling that most intractable problem facing an airborne force once committed to battle – its inability to extricate itself at will from a dangerous situation or to redeploy elsewhere in the same theatre of operations. So far, glider and parachute operations had been conducted strictly on a one-way ticket and had been launched on the assumption that relief by advancing friendly ground forces could be accomplished within a few days. The wastage of equipment used to deploy an airborne force was huge; even though energetic steps were taken to retrieve parachutes, containers and gliders, a large proportion remained on the landing zones as scrap. One answer was to put engines onto gliders so that they could be flown into battle and then used as cheap transport aircraft for resupply and reinforcement.

The Germans were the first to develop the idea. They had realized after the 1940 campaigns that their DFS230 assault glider had the drawback of being able to carry only personnel, and the firms of Messerschmitt and Junkers were directed to design and build huge prototype transport gliders which could carry vehicles and artillery, large numbers of troops, or bulk cargo. The Messerschmitt glider, known as the Me321 *Gigant* (Giant) was chosen to go into production. Its wingspan of over 180ft, length of 92½ft and height (to tip of fin) of 33ft coupled with a payload of 48,500lbs in its cavernous hull made it easily the largest warplane in the world. Its sheer bulk created problems in getting it off the ground. The normal method was for a formation of three Me110 twin-engined fighters to act as tugs. A more bizarre expedient was the use of the Heinkel He111Z – two He111 bombers joined together to form a five-engined monster. The *Gigant* itself required strong pilots with even stronger nerves; control forces were great, and the drama of take-off behind the weird combinations mentioned above was heightened by the use of booster rockets and the need to jettison the huge undercarriage as the glider left the ground. This did not deter the extraordinary Hanna Reitsch from test-flying it. The Me321 was used extensively in Russia in the aerial resupply role, but never in an airborne assault. Its derivative, the Me323, was even more startling; it was essentially an Me321 fitted with six French-built Gnome-Rhône engines, enabling it to dispense with tugs and converting it into a rudimentary assault transport, the forbear of today's C130s. Clamshell doors in the nose admitted large pieces of equipment such as 88mm guns; a complete (if apprehensive) infantry company could be flown in one load. Again, the Me323 was never used in the assault, but it played an important logistic role in Russia and was used in quantity to keep Rommel's army in North Africa supplied.

The increasing availability of American C47s and surplus four-engined bombers in support of airborne operations reprieved the British from having to build gigantic imitations of the Me323. What was apparent by late 1943, however, was that airborne operations after Sicily would be on an ever-increasing scale, and that elaborate staff and administrative organizations would have to be created in order to ensure the smooth planning and execution of the landings now assumed to be a necessary feature of the invasion of France.

Browning had believed for some time that with the creation of yet more airborne formations, a separate headquarters was required to relieve the hard-pressed staff of 1st Airborne Division. In May 1943 he was appointed to the post of Major General Airborne Forces and by the end of the year a new organization, HQ Airborne Forces, was created with Browning – now a Lieutenant General – as its head, responsible for advising the War Office and the Supreme Allied Command on airborne matters, to supervise airborne training, to co-ordinate the development of all specialist airborne equipment, and to ensure that the RAF were kept fully up to date with the Army's requirements for aircraft and gliders. His was a difficult task, calling for firmness, professional expertise and diplomacy of a high order.

A second British airborne division, the 6th, was raised during the late summer and autumn of 1943 and was ready for operations by 1 February 1944. In its brief active service life it was to take part in two of the greatest military operations of the war in the West, the Normandy landings and the assault across the Rhine.

The American airborne forces had continued to expand at high speed. By early 1944 their 82nd and 101st Airborne Divisions were training hard in England and had been earmarked with the British 1st and 6th for the invasion of Europe – Operation *Overlord*. It was essential that the Allies trained together and collaborated closely over the use of the air transport force available. In January 1944 Browning's suggestion that an Anglo-American Airborne Base Organization was set up, with the aim of co-ordinating and running the impending operation.

As 1943 gave way to 1944, on their airfields and training areas in southern England, the 82nd, 101st, 1st and 6th, the IXth Troop Carrier Command and 38 and 46 Groups got to know each other and trained hard. By now, Chatterton had won a long battle to get his glider pilots living on base with the crews of the tug aircraft and this produced a tremendous spirit of comradeship which was to prove invaluable.

Other specialist Army units had to be formed to keep pace with the airborne expansion. The techniques had been developed for loading guns and vehicles into *Horsas* and the as yet untried *Hamilcar*, the biggest glider used by the Allies, into which a light tank could be driven through great clamshell nose doors. Airborne gunners, engineers, signallers and armoured reconnaissance troops had now joined the parachute infantry.

The administrative functions were not neglected. Special units were formed to load and despatch stores, equipment and heavy weapons by parachute; to clear the dropzones of these items once they had landed; medical units with specially designed field surgical equipment; even chaplains with lightweight communion plate.

Scientists, trials teams and experimenters of all sorts worked furiously to cut down the weight and size of guns and vehicles so that they could be loaded into aircraft and gliders or dropped by parachute in panniers and containers. Miniature motorcycles, folding bicycles, stripped-down jeeps, and fieldguns with shortened axles were all tried out and adopted. The 6-pounder gun, developed in Britain to counter the improved German armour in the Western Desert, was found to be air-portable with its towing jeep in a *Horsa* glider and enthusiastically taken up by the Americans as well.

A vast communications network was required to run an airborne operation on the scale now contemplated; the equipment and the staff to run it had to be scraped together only a month before D-day and the organization, badly strained, only just coped. The main difficulty was the passage of essential information through a command link of great complexity. To get a gliderborne operation, for example, to its target at the right time involved weeks of planning, training and rehearsal. The gliders, correctly loaded and in the right sequence, had to be lined up in a vast queue with its head at the downwind end of the take-off runway. The tug aircraft, also in strict sequence, had to be 'married' to their gliders, coupled up and despatched every 60 seconds. Often, the glider/tug combinations had to be ranged parallel on the actual take-off runway, which denied a good proportion of its length to the first aircraft taking off. A sudden change of wind direction involving a shift to a different runway was a catastrophe, as any delay meant changing the highly complicated plans whereby relays of fighter aircraft escorted the transport fleet on its majestic voyage to the target. For all these operations, air supremacy was essential. The mounting airfields required heavy anti-aircraft protection against intruder aircraft and continuous defensive air patrols overhead. Elaborate security measures were needed to mask the intentions and destinations of the huge force of aircraft and gliders. Extra fuel installations had to be built, protected against air attack or accidental fire. The bill for getting an airborne division to battle was hair-raising, and the mechanism for launching it delicate in the extreme.

*　　　*　　　*

The planning of *Overlord* had been in hand since the early summer of 1943, when the aim was the somewhat nebulous one of putting ashore a large Anglo-American force in order to inflict a strategic defeat on the German forces occupying north-west Europe. Although the shortest way across – from the Kentish coast to the Pas de Calais area – had much to recommend it, the Normandy coast was the early choice as it was within range of the overwhelming fighter cover considered necessary to achieve and maintain air supremacy, close to the great Atlantic ports in western France through which the Allies could receive massive reinforcement, and not as thickly defended as the Calais area. The Normandy beaches were also suitable for amphibious assault.

Despite the advantage of air supremacy and their command of the

English Channel, the Allies knew that the *Overlord* operation involved an element of risk almost too daunting to contemplate. France, Belgium and Holland already contained 60 German divisions under that hardened old campaigner *Feldmarschall* Gerd von Runstedt. Eleven of these were armoured. Within easy reach of the proposed beach-head were five infantry and six *Panzer* divisions, part of Army Group 'B' whose commander, Rommel, still exercised a near-hypnotic effect on the British even though they had eventually soundly beaten him in North Africa. On paper, the Allied invasion force looked impressive – two armies, the US 1st and the British 2nd, with three airborne divisions.

The airborne element of the plan was crucial to its success. For a number of reasons, the first day's sealandings were restricted to six infantry divisions, two special service brigades and an American Ranger battalion. The armoured divisions could only come in on subsequent sea lifts after the infantry had established a beach-head with enough room for tanks to deploy. A prompt counter-attack on the beaches by Rommel's *Panzers*, even in relatively small numbers, would therefore be catastrophic if it succeeded in over-running the airborne flank guards.

Everything depended on the weather. If it was not suitable for

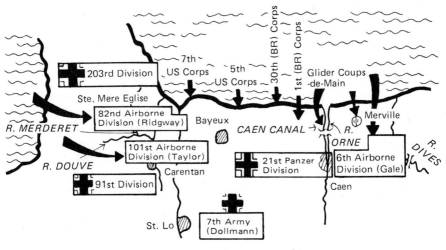

'OVERLORD'–The Airborne Plan

amphibious landings in the first days of June, the tides would not be right again for at least a month and it was doubtful if the security of the Allied plan would hold out as long as that; for a gigantic deception plot had convinced the Germans that the invasion would in fact be launched further north in the Le Havre–Calais area.

The final Allied airborne plan was the product of much debate on both sides of the Atlantic, a compromise between the views of the 'all-airborne' school who advocated a deep attack on the clutch of German airfields around Evreux – halfway from the beaches to Paris – and those who believed that widely dispersed airborne landings would create chaos and prevent the Germans from bringing decisive force to bear on the beaches. Eisenhower's natural caution prevailed; he elected to go for airborne landings in strength on the flanks of the seaborne assault. Even so, Gen. Marshall, in Washington, was persuaded that the 'deep' airborne invasion had much to recommend it. Having seen a convincing presentation of this concept he sent the planning team to England with a message for Eisenhower, '. . . give these young men an opportunity to present the matter to you personally before your Staff tear it to ribbons. . . .' The 'deep' plan is worth describing, for it would have demonstrated a use of the new aerial arm just as imaginative as that of the tank at Cambrai in 1917. The 'Marshall Plan', as it was known at the time, envisaged a landing by four Allied airborne divisions in the Evreux area to create an expanding airhead into which a massive airlift would bring reinforcements to attack the German lines of communication, especially those across the Seine. As soon as possible, sea-landed forces would make contact with the airborne lodgement and press on for Paris, aided by the French underground army which would have been called out to rally around the Evreux landings.

Eisenhower and his chiefs duly heard the presentation; inevitably they rejected it. The Supreme Commander was a great diplomat and strategist, rather than a combat soldier and was deeply conscious of his awesome responsibilities; the Allied Liberation Army had been entrusted to him, a compassionate and generous man whose selection for this post proved little short of inspirational. It is a measure of his humility and greatness that he had even composed, in his own hand, a gloomy little announcement which he, personally, would make on the radio to the world if the landings proved to be a failure. He wrote to Marshall rejecting the deep airborne plan, '. . . I agree thoroughly with the conception but disagree with the timing . . . vertical envelopment is sound – but since this type of enveloping force is immobile on the ground, the collaborating force must be strategically and tactically mobile.' He felt that in the early stages at least, his sea-landed forces would lack the striking power – the armour and artillery in particular – to smash their way out of the beach-head and to the relief of the airborne troops before their lack of armour and manoeuvring power led to their elimination by Rommel's *Panzers*.

It was therefore decided to commit the airborne divisions close to the beaches in the flank-guard role, even though Eisenhower's air commander, Air Chief Marshal Sir Trafford Leigh-Mallory, remained unconvinced of the value of large scale airborne operations and alarmed his master considerably at the last moment by prophesying casualties of up to 80 per cent.

On the opposite side of the English Channel the Germans were fully aware of the likelihood of an Allied airborne attack and since Rommel's arrival at Army Group 'B' there had been an intensification of anti-airborne measures. Posts up to 12ft high were placed in fields where gliders might land. Known as *Rommelspargel* (Rommel's asparagus) many were wired together and fitted with explosive charges to enhance their value. At Rommel's personal insistence the posts were sited at a density of 1000 to a square kilometre. Once they were laid out, cattle were allowed to graze amongst them to allay Allied suspicions. HQ Army Group 'B' published an instructive pamphlet in April 1944 entitled 'What every soldier should know about airborne troops', and many of Rommel's divisional commanders added their own booklets on the subject. There were frequent exercises to practise troops in anti-airborne operations, practice alerts, and officers' study periods devoted to the repulse of parachute and glider landings. A network of static observation posts connected by radio and land line and continual mobile patrols ensured that no airborne landing would remain undetected for very long.

The airborne formations selected for the initial assault were the 6th British and 82nd and 101st American. The 6th was commanded by Maj.-Gen. Richard Gale who had raised it from scratch and was determined to make it in his own image, rather than in imitation of 1st Airborne (whose men now sat fretfully around in reserve, athirst for battle but destined to remain unemployed until September). Gale, a masterly trainer and inspirer of men, worked with the aim of commanding a division complete in itself, not flung piecemeal into expensive battles as the 1st had been in North Africa and Sicily. He was a deeply read soldier yet a practical and down-to-earth leader with a gift for oratory which spell-bound his listeners.

The plan for 6th Airborne was to seize the two crucial bridges across the River Orne and Caen Canal in order to protect the left flank of the Allied landings, and to knock out certain fixed defensive works, notably the coastal battery at Merville which, if it survived the preliminary sea and air bombardment (and it could, being protected by massive concrete casemates) would cause terrible casualties to the landing ships as they negotiated the last five miles to the beaches.

The 82nd and 101st were to act as right flank protection for the landings. They were commanded by men destined for highly distinguished careers; the 82nd by Maj.-Gen. Matthew Bunker Ridgway and the 101st by Maj.-Gen. Maxwell Taylor. The 82nd was to land astride the River Merderet, take the town of Ste Mère Eglise – a focal point for road communications – destroy the crossings over the River Douve, and then advance to the west into the roots of the Cotentin peninsula. The 101st was to land north of Carentan, block the movement of German reserves towards the landing beaches, and seize the southern ends of the causeways leading off the western landing beaches along which the American armour and artillery would have to move. The divisional commanders were thus confronted with differing problems. Even the terrain into which they were to drop varied from division to division.

Gale considered his tasks with care. He was aware of the successful capture of the Ponte Grande in Sicily by a single glider-load of men and of Koch's brilliant coup at Eben Emael, and he elected to go for the main river and canal bridges with gliders, to ensure total surprise. Brigadier Hill's 3rd Parachute Brigade Group was given the fearsome job of silencing Merville battery, destroying a number of bridges over the river Dives further east and preventing enemy movement into the divisional area from that direction. Brigadier Poett's 5th Parachute Brigade Group was responsible for the Orne and Caen canal bridges, the seizure of rising ground overlooking them, the capture of a coastal battery outside Ouistreham at the seaward exit of the Caen canal, and the clearance of landing zones in order to permit the safe arrival, on the evening of D-day, of Brig. the Hon. Hugh Kindersley's 6th Airlanding Brigade. This formation contained two infantry units originally in the 1st Airlanding Brigade, the 2nd Battalion Oxford and Bucks Light Infantry and the 1st Battalion Royal Ulster Rifles. It now also included the 12th Battalion of the Devonshire Regiment and a light armoured reconnaissance group carried in *Hamilcars* and *Horsas*. The airlanding brigade's timely arrival was crucial, as it included the much-needed anti-tank guns without which no defence could be offered against a resolute German armoured attack.

Two aspects of 6th Division's operation called for total surprise – the landing at the bridges and the taking of Merville battery – and it was clear that these must be the first military actions of D-day. Six gliders were allotted to the bridges, carrying a company of the Oxford and Bucks commanded by Maj. John Howard, who flew in the leading *Horsa* with Staff-Sergeants Wallwork and Ainsworth as his pilots. Before they set out on their momentous flight, weeks of meticulous rehearsal had been carried out. The infantry had practised assaulting the Countess Wear bridges just outside Exeter in Devon whose relative positions approximated to the targets in Normandy, and the crews of the six gliders refined their night landing techniques to a pitch of excellence which was to serve them well. Full-scale landing zones were marked out to simulate the small areas into which the gliders had to be placed. The crews were aware of the horrible risks attendant on the landing; although no *Rommelspargel* had been placed in the chosen landing zones (the Germans thought they were too small for gliders) it was essential to place the leading glider within a few yards of the block house guarding the end of the canal bridge; this was surrounded by barbed-wire entanglement which was possibly mined. Wallwork undertook to get Howard through the wire before stopping the glider. Privately, he and Ainsworth both knew that what they were attempting might cost them their lives; they had both seen the grisly results of a crash in which the frail perspex of a *Horsa*'s crew compartment had smashed in on its pilots, giving no chance of survival.

Howard was not finally told what his precise targets were to be until early in May when he was personally briefed by Kindersley his Brigade commander and provided with a wealth of carefully gathered information on the two bridges, their garrisons and even their structure. He was given the names of local French resistance leaders and told that the *patron* of the inn at the west end of the canal bridge was one Georges Gondrée, who could speak English (a fact which Gondrée had successfully concealed from the Germans, together with his best wines, for four years). A large-scale model of the bridges and their surroundings and huge aerial photographs taken during the past few days were also produced. Howard was left in no doubt that to him, as the first Allied soldier to set foot on French soil, had been given a task of overwhelming importance. He elected to set three platoons onto the canal bridge and three at the bridge over the Orne. The pillbox at the end of the canal bridge had to be dealt with at once with grenades under cover of smoke and the leading platoon would rush the defences on the far side. Having taken both bridges, Howard's company would have to sit it out until the first parachuted reinforcements arrived later in the night.

On 26 May, Howard received orders to move his men to Hurn airfield near Bournemouth. Here, they were 'sealed' in by barbed-wire fences, and deprived of all contact with the outside world. Only now could all ranks be given their final briefing on the model, which was committed to memory by every man. They were joined by their glider pilots and were greatly heartened by the evident competence and confidence of Wallwork and his fellow crewmen. At the last moment there was bad news; photographic reconnaissance on 31 May revealed that *Rommelspargel* had sprouted in the field in which Wallwork's glider was to land. Undaunted, he promised Howard that he would still get him through the wire, even if the glider lost both wings on the poles.

After a false alarm on the 4th of June, the final message to emplane reached Howard the next day, and at 2301 hrs the combination of *Halifax* and heavily laden *Horsa* took off. It was a quiet crossing, enlivened by the singing of the troops. Cast-off was at 5000 feet, and now all was silent in the glider; through the open door Howard watched the Norman countryside, easily picking out landmarks familiar from long acquaintance with maps, models and photographs. In the distance the city of Caen blazed under aerial bombardment. Down came the *Horsa*, making its final turn so as to come in from the south; at the back, men threw out the arrester parachute which steadied the glider and slowed it down. With a tremendous crash it hit the ground, hurtling and skidding towards the end of the bridge in a shower of sparks, coming to rest with its nose buried in the wire, the pilots' cockpit smashed in and Wallwork and Ainsworth trapped in the wreckage from which they extricated themselves with difficulty. Howard and his men had been delivered to within a few feet of their target in what was probably the most outstanding feat of glider pilotage ever known. Howard remembers this triumphant moment to this day, '. . . to my complete and exhilarating amazement I saw that the nose of the glider had gone right through the wire fencing . . . and less than 50 yards away was the tall tower of the bridge!' Within seconds a phosphorus bomb and explosive grenades were dealing with the pill box. From the far side of the bridge came the sounds of the German guards standing-to in the darkness, firing at the first platoon as they charged across the bridge and killing its commander. The other gliders were now arriving on the LZ and more men joined the fight on both sides. A runner came from the Orne bridge to report that the landings had gone well there too. Less than 20 minutes had elapsed since Howard's arrival, and now the steady roar of low-flying aircraft from the north announced the arrival of the first parachute drop. Enemy searchlights played on the great stream of *Dakotas* and tracer fire laced the darkness, but the drop went majestically ahead. Further inland could be heard the thunder of intensive bombing as the pre-planned air attack on enemy units got under way.

The party at the bridge settled down to await the arrival of the paratroops. As they did so, the Germans sent a small tank down the road from the west. It was engaged with a PIAT (Projector, Infantry, Anti-Tank) a strange device not unlike a medieval crossbow with which a hollow-charge bomb could be hurled fairly accurately to a range of 100 yards. In this case the PIAT man held his fire until the tank was almost upon him, then hit it with the first shot. It blew up spectacularly and burned for the rest of the night, its ammunition exploding intermittently and proclaiming the location of the Canal bridge to every British soldier within ten miles' radius. By 0300 hrs the 7th Battalion Parachute Regiment arrived in the nick of time to stiffen up the perimeter against German attacks which now grew in ferocity.

M. Gondrée at the café had been an enthusiastic spectator of the night's events and at first light celebrated the fact that his was the first house in Europe to be liberated by digging out of his garden a huge *câche* of champagne which had been kept there for four years for just this occasion. A festive breakfast was interrupted by a curious interlude. Two enemy gunboats were reported coming up the canal from the coast, obviously unaware that the bridge had changed hands overnight. They were engaged by the versatile PIAT, which again

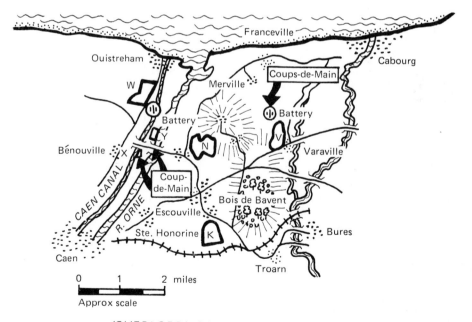

'OVERLORD'—6th Airborne Divisional Area,
showing Coup-de-Main Objectives and LZ/DZs

scored a direct hit, sending the leading boat out of control. Its crew were then forced to surrender.

There were, after all, no posts on Howard's landing zone but the holes for them had been dug, and during the morning two unhappy Italians, members of the *Todt Organisation* responsible for building the West Wall defences, turned up and insisted on erecting the *Rommelspargel*. After all, they told Howard, they had been paid to do so.

The Germans never retook the two bridges, which had been captured for the loss of only 2 dead and 14 wounded in Howard's force. It was the subsequent fighting which produced the casualties; on 7 June Howard took his company forward 110 strong; six hours later he only had 52, after a fearsome battle with the now fully aroused 21 *Panzer* Division.

This small but vitally important engagement has been described in some detail as it illustrates perfectly the characteristics of an airmobile operation. First, the careful planning and meticulous attention to every detail in rehearsal; then the skill of the pilots, as relevant now in the helicopter age as when Wallwork took his *Horsa* on its one-way journey; the simplicity of the plan, memorized by every man; above all, the priceless value of surprise, backed by the skill and aggression of the attacking force. Several years later, Howard received an unusual testimonial in the form of a postcard from a German prisoner of war. It read, 'On that night my friends and I were standing opposite you as sentries on the bridge. You were only 48 yards away from us but our whole company was so surprised and confused that we could not find each other. It was a master stroke that you and your people brought off.'

As Howard and his men were capturing their bridges the whole airborne plan was swinging into action. Pathfinding parties were to be dropped shortly after midnight on the four main parachute dropzones, 'K', 'N', 'V' and 'W' to set out their marker lamps. It was onto DZ (dropzone) 'N', the nearest to the bridges, that the main body of Poett's 5th Parachute Brigade Group dropped just before 0100 hrs; 3rd Parachute Brigade Group came down at the same time on DZs 'K' and 'V' and its men moved off at once to destroy the Dives bridges just over a mile to the east. At 0320 hrs the Divisional HQ was due in by glider onto DZ 'N', together with Gale's artillery and engineer staffs and a battery of anti-tank guns. This was the first time a massed glider landing at night – 68 *Horsas* and 4 *Hamilcars* – was successfully brought off. The lessons of Sicily had been taken to heart and in any case these glider crews had absolute faith in their tug pilots.

For a number of reasons, 3rd Brigade's drop ran into problems. Some of the pathfinders had been dropped on the wrong dropzone and set up their coded lamps unaware that they were 1000 yards out of position. Fourteen *Dakota* loads of the 3rd Brigade accordingly landed in the wrong place. Some more pathfinders were taken prisoner whilst setting out their lamps and 'K' was therefore left short of signal lights. At 'V' things were worst; the ground was virtually swampland and the difficulty of setting up lamps and 'Eureka' beacons meant that many of the sticks of parachutists destined for this DZ went badly adrift.

The Germans were now thoroughly awake to the fact that something drastic was happening. HQs opened up throughout Normandy, observation posts were manned, and mobile patrols began to scour the countryside, which started to resound with the noise of innumerable skirmishes. The air was filled with the sound of aircraft engines, but due to efficient jamming of their radars the Germans found it difficult to assess the scale of the operation now launched against them. There was inevitably confusion on both sides, to which the scattered parachute landings undoubtedly made a big contribution.

Against this noisy background the attack on Merville battery was timed to take place at 0430 hrs, when three *Horsa* gliders were due to crash-land within the heavily wired perimeter at the same time as it was breached by men of Lt-Col. Otway's 9th Parachute Battalion who were supposed to have been dropped on DZ 'V'. The drop was widely scattered; Otway himself landed in the yard of a farmhouse used as a German HQ but managed to get to his battalion rallying-point, where he was disappointed to find almost nobody. By 0300 hrs he had gathered together only 150 of his 600 men; he knew that he had 90 minutes to move into position around the battery, two miles away, in order to blow a gap in the wire and throw in his assault as the gliders landed. Looking around, he found he had 20 Bangalore torpedoes – tubes of high explosive used for cutting barbed wire entanglements – and one machine gun. Of his mortars and assault pioneers, key ingredients of the attack, there was no sign. He led his men towards the battery in the darkness amidst the crescendo of battle as the combatants groped for each other and began to fight.

It had been planned that 100 *Lancasters* of Bomber Command would bomb the battery before the airborne attack; unfortunately, this saturation bombardment was a total failure. The bombers mistook the village of Merville for the battery and virtually eliminated it. They also terrified the advance party of Otway's battalion who were crouching just outside the bombing pattern. By the time the gliders arrived overhead, a huge pall of dust and smoke added to their difficulties, and despite meticulous rehearsal and familiarization with the ground during their work-up training, they too could not identify the battery in the gloom. It had not been an easy ride across the Channel. Flying blind through dense cloud at 1000 feet, heavily laden with anti-tank guns, assault engineers and large quantities of explosive, they knew themselves to be highly vulnerable. A westerly wind had now risen to 28 mph. One of the three gliders broke its tow before crossing the English coast and another accidentally streamed its arrester parachute whilst still on tow in mid-Channel. This caused both tug and glider to stall (for towing speed was a bare 10 mph above the *Albemarle*'s stalling point). Somehow the parachute was cut free and the combination lurched on above the waves, the tail of the glider strained to near breaking point. Both gliders were hit by anti-aircraft fire after casting off. It is hardly surprising that the pilots were finding life difficult as they tried to crash-land their badly damaged aircraft into the elusive battery, especially as Otway's men had no flares, as had been planned, to signal their position; nor it is hard to see why the glider crews had wrily christened the Merville landing 'The vc Job'.

Otway struggled on with his main party and had just reached the perimeter wire as a *Horsa* swooped low overhead to disappear in the murk on the far side of the battery. This was Staff-Sgt Bone, who managed to get his load down intact a few hundred yards further on. The second glider, flown by Staff-Sgt Kerr, skidded to a halt just outside the wire. It was a splendid effort under the circumstances but Otway still had to fight his way into the battery and destroy it by 0450 hrs. There was now no alternative to an old-fashioned infantry assault. The Bangalore torpedoes were detonated and the men of the 9th Battalion, reinforced by the occupants of Kerr's glider, stormed through the gaps regardless of any mines. A bloody hand-to-hand fight followed and half Otway's men became casualties. The success signal, however, was fired by the battalion commander at 0445 hrs, to be seen far out to sea by the oncoming armada of landing ships. Otway's attack had been a triumph for leadership and aggressive spirit over a series of accidents any single one of which could have ruined the plan.

Whilst the British first lift was taking place in the early hours of 6 June, the 82nd and 101st were setting about their difficult tasks. Their dropzones and glider landing areas were far more difficult than those assigned to 6th Airborne and even harder to locate in the dark. Much of their divisional areas consisted of low ground flooded by the Germans. The glider landing zones were in small fields laced with *Rommelspargel* and surrounded by the high hedges typical of the *bocage* country of Normandy. Trouble began with yet another major navigational failure on the part of the C47 crews; the USAAF policy remained, incredibly, virtually what it had been at the time of the Sicilian operation: only the C47 formation leaders were trained and equipped for dead-reckoning navigation by night. This fact had alarmed Air Marshal Tedder, Eisenhower's deputy, who finally wrote to his Chief, a bare eight days before *Overlord*, raising all manner of obstacles to the success of the American airborne operation. He pointed out that the C47s were vulnerable to ground fire, lacking armour or self-sealing tanks and that the landing of gliders by night in the Ste Mère Eglise area would be highly dangerous. Eisenhower could only reply that he fully appreciated the risks but that the operation must go on. He must also have known that the training of the American glider pilots was nowhere near the standard of the British Glider Pilot Regiment, nor were they available in the numbers required. As late as November 1943, Gavin reported, there were not enough to provide one pilot for each glider. 'In the final invasion each co-pilot's seat was occupied by an airborne trooper . . . no training in either flying or landing the glider, and some of them found themselves with a wounded pilot and a fully-loaded glider on their hands as they came hurtling through flak-filled space on June 6. Fortunately the CG4 is not too hard to fly or land. But having to do it for the first time in combat is a chastening experience; it gives a man religion.'★

Maxwell Taylor's 101st began to jump south-east of Ste Mère Eglise at 0130 hrs on 6 June. The drop was a near-fiasco and the men were widely scattered, only 15 per cent landing close to their assigned objectives. Over half the division's para-dropped equipment landed in swampy ground and was lost. Ridgway's 82nd fared little better, as over-excited jumpmasters pushed out their sticks of paratroops regardless of the aircraft's position. Many were dropped at such low altitude, due to poor station-keeping by the pilots, that they crashed to the ground with undeveloped parachutes. Once on the ground, however, the American paratroops fought splendidly. As in Sicily, the wide spread of the drops generated enormous confusion amongst the defence. Ridgway assumed personal command of any men he could find, despatching them to deal with known German outposts and to ambush the roads, which they did with gusto. A terrible battle developed in the streets of Ste Mère Eglise, where a large number of parachutists died in their harness, shot by the defenders as they dangled helplessly from buildings and trees. All over the area covered by

★ Major-General J. M. Gavin, *Airborne Warfare*, Combat Forces Press, Washington DC, 1947.

the 82nd and 101st's drops, men searched for their leaders, formed *ad hoc* units, cut every telephone cable in sight, and generally injected chaos into the German defence system. Good leadership at platoon and company level ensured that the vital causeway exits were seized and the Merderet crossings secured, thus preventing German access to the right flank of the beach-head. The commander of the German 91st Infantry Division, at his wit's end for information and deprived of it because the men of the 82nd Airborne had cut his landline communications, set out from his HQ to make contact with his outposts; he was waylaid and killed in his staff car by a party of Ridgway's paratroopers. His division, instead of launching itself at the beaches, was engulfed in the widely scattered fighting all over the Ste Mère Eglise area; this was providential, for the American amphibious landings on Utah and Omaha beaches quickly ran into great difficulty because the preliminary air bombardment had failed to neutralize the beach defences. Had the 91st Division been able to form up and converge on the coastline it is highly probable that the landings of 1st US Army would have been bloodily repulsed, leaving the British 2nd Army to fight alone for its narrow foothold or be driven into the sea.

Before daybreak, the American glider lift came in, bringing wel-

US Airborne Operations in 'OVERLORD'

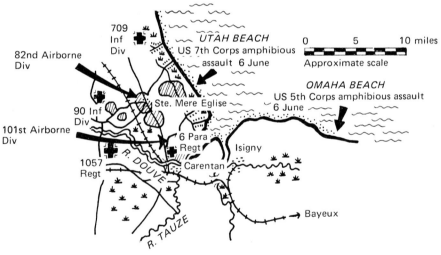

 Areas held by 82nd and 101st Airborne Divisions at midnight on D day, 6 June

Principal German formations in area, night of 5–6 June

Inundations

Causeway roads

come reinforcements but also sustaining heavy casualties and losses of equipment as the gliders smashed into hedgerows and buildings. In order to carry extra vehicles and light guns the Americans were using a number of British *Horsas*; these were unpopular with their USAAF pilots who lacked experience with them and who tended to land them much too fast, mistrusting their huge flaps and air-operated brakes. The small fields and farms of the *bocage* country became dotted with glider wrecks. Only 22 out of 82nd Division's 52 gliders actually landed their loads in the correct area. The 101st were luckier; theirs was easier terrain for airborne landings and 50 of their gliders reached the LZs; however, as daylight came, the full measure of the failure to place the parachute drops correctly became apparent. Only the high quality of the men in the two American airborne divisions had enabled them to perform the greater part of the task assigned to them. The 101st's efforts earned it a Presidential Citation – the first ever awarded to an entire division.

Daylight brought reinforcement to all three divisions; 101st received a mass glider landing at 0900 hrs, again with numerous casualties including their deputy commander, killed in the wreck of his CG4. The 82nd Division's second glider lift incurred even heavier losses, as it took place after dark onto LZs which were now coming under heavy fire. The second lift to 6th Airborne, on the other hand, was a great success; the LZs were large, cleared of *Rommelspargel* and well marked, and the Germans were unable to interfere effectively with the proceedings. 250 *Horsas* and *Hamilcars* wheeled in over the beach-head, bringing 6th Airlanding Brigade and the Armoured Reconnaissance Group. It was the greatest massed landing on one LZ ever attempted. To the watching Germans it was a portent; the Allies now had command of the air, and not a single *Luftwaffe* aircraft got near this tremendous, slow-moving and highly vulnerable armada as it crossed the Channel *en route* to the battlefield.

The Normandy campaign was far from over for the airborne men. 6th Airborne remained in the line until August, and the parachute battalions in particular had a very rough time; they had virtually no transport and apart from their infantry weapons and a limited number of 3in mortars and 6-pounder guns they were desperately short of the support weapons possessed by the battalions of the airlanding brigade. Virtually all their artillery support had to be obtained from *outside* 6th Airborne Division; but as this often included the 16in guns of battleships firing over the beach-head, it could be most effective.

The British glider pilots were extricated from the fighting within two days. Casualties had been remarkably light, and again the 'total soldier' doctrine had been convincingly demonstrated, in marked contrast to the unhappy spectacle of the American glider pilots who, armed with nothing more than pistols and not even possessing infantrymen's field equipment, could only huddle around the wrecks of their gliders hoping to be evacuated at the earliest moment.

The airborne landings in Normandy were the largest attempted so far by either side. Despite the wildly scattered drop of the American parachutists and the numerous hitches in the execution of 6th Airborne's plan, the use of paratroops and gliders in mass had been convincingly vindicated. The splendid fighting qualities of the 82nd and 101st had held the Germans off Utah and Omaha beaches, and Gale's division held firmly onto their ground at the eastern end of the Allied foothold. Junior commanders in all three divisions had displayed tremendous verve, obsessed with the need to take their assigned objectives whatever the cost. Battalion commanders willingly set aside their own tasks to work for the common good and this spirit permeated down to rifle-section level. Months of careful preparation and rehearsal paid off; Otway had made every man in his battalion draw a map of the Merville battery from memory on the day before they emplaned for Normandy.

On the debit side, it was evident that some lessons still remained to be learned. There was too much reliance on sophisticated navigation aids such as the 'Eureka' beacons which had a tendency to go unserviceable when most needed. The pathfinders, whose task it was to set out the dropzones, were given insufficient time to do their work and as a result many of the 6th Division's parachutists were dropped well off their DZs – some over 30 miles away. The pilots cannot be blamed entirely for this; they had enough problems of their own: station-keeping in the huge stream crossing the coast; bad weather; fierce anti-aircraft fire. There was a lot of formation breaking and some recrimination. The pilots of 38 and 46 Groups took this to heart and redeemed their failings over Normandy with honour when they next went into action. As it was, the RAF's achievement in getting 6th Airborne to battle was an outstanding feat of airmanship by any standards.

The case was otherwise for the Americans; following the distressing experiences of the 82nd and 101st there was a serious crisis of confidence which resulted in a refusal to drop by night again from USAAF aircraft. This had an adverse effect on subsequent operations, for if the British 1st Airborne had been able to land by night in the Arnhem operation, as was well within the capability of their transport and glider pilots, the outcome would have been very different.

The shortage of support weapons and means of mobility for parachute battalions was keenly felt in Normandy; when the Germans threw 21st *Panzer* Division against 6th Airborne it was only naval gunfire support and the use of airstrikes that prevented a major disaster. The immobility of parachute troops on the ground was compounded by the inadequacy of their radios. Many were broken or lost in the drop, most had inadequate range, and it was well-nigh impossible to communicate with Allied close-support fighter aircraft. This resulted in isolation of units; the airborne battle was essentially, in Normandy, a battalion commander's affair, with brigade and divisional commanders often struggling for information, impotently sitting around and unable to command properly.

With Normandy, airborne warfare had come of age; the ability of armies to wage war in the third dimension had been demonstrated beyond doubt. All the roles envisaged by the prophets of the '30s and early '40s had been put to the proof. The summer of 1944 would see if the Allied High Command knew how to wield the new-forged weapon.

CHAPTER EIGHT

Casting the Net – Airborne Operations World-wide, 1942–43

At this point it is necessary to leave the European theatre of war, where the two greatest Allied airborne efforts had yet to be mounted, and review the progress of parachuted and air-landed operations world-wide.

After their appearance at the 1936 manoeuvres Russia's airborne forces made little or no further progress; new equipment failed to appear, no new transport aircraft were introduced to replace the obsolete Antonov monoplanes from which the 1936 drops had been made, and little attention was paid to the serious study and development of new doctrine. All this stemmed from the fearsome purge of the Red Army's Officer class which got under way soon after the 1936 manoeuvres. The most important man to die was Marshal Mikhail Tukhachevsky, Chief of Staff since 1926; under his guidance the Red Army had evolved from the Bolshevik rabble of the revolutionary period into a mechanized host capable of waging war amidst the huge spaces of the Soviet Union. Encouraging the formation of airborne forces, he had watched their development approvingly. He fell victim to the Byzantine mind of his master and the backstage intrigue of the German secret service, which enthusiastically fed damning evidence against him into the *apparat* of the NKVD. It was the first successful stroke of Germany's intelligence war against the USSR.

On 22 June 1941, when Hitler's armies rolled eastward across the Soviet border, the Red Army was still recovering from the effects of the great purge. The numbers of prisoners taken by the Germans in the opening battles speak for themselves: at Minsk, 190,000; at Smolensk, 100,000; at Gomel, 80,000; at Kiev a staggering 665,000. Another 658,000 were taken at Briansk. The resilience of the Russians however was amazing; as in 1812, they withdrew into the heartland of Mother Russia. In the process, however, their élite troops were almost eliminated. What transport aircraft had been available for airborne operations were destroyed in the first onslaught and airborne units, desperately thrown in to stiffen the line or plug gaps, were wiped out. Despite this, paratroops were used in July and August 1941 in attempts to slow the German advance. Small parties were dropped as saboteurs and to stimulate guerrilla activity in the enemy rear. In October, as the Germans crept towards Moscow, Maj.-Gen. Gurjev gathered the remnants of the 5th Airborne Corps, a mere 6000 men, and landed them near Mtensk in an effort to head off the German advance from the key Soviet military base at Tula. Later that month, 40 Red Army paratroops were dropped onto a *Luftwaffe* airfield near Maikop in the Caucasus during a Russian night bombing attack. Before they were wiped out they accounted for 22 planes. All these operations were mounted on an *ad hoc* basis, making use of whatever resources came to hand. It was not until the front had stabilized in the perishing Russian winter that the Red Army's staff system began to recover to the extent of planning a major airborne operation.

In January 1942 the Soviet High Command decided to take the offensive against the German 4th *Panzer* Army which was sprawled about the area of Vyazma, a key road and rail centre on the Smolensk–Moscow highway. The plan was sound; the Russian 33rd Army was to attack frontally to the west in the area south of Vyazma with the aim of engaging not only the 4th *Panzer* Army but also luring two more German armies into a gigantic killing zone where they would be trapped by a massive left hook delivered by the Russian 10th Army. The role of the Russian airborne troops was to establish an airhead within the 4th *Panzer* Army area, into which reinforcements could be flown as this huge battle developed. The first phase therefore consisted of a number of drops and airlandings south of Vyazma to stiffen the partisan forces operating there, and to seize the airstrips necessary for the airborne build-up. On the night of 3–4 January 1942 a battalion parachuted onto the airstrip at Myatlevo, to find it feet deep in snow. Throughout 4 January they worked to clear a strip for aircraft, under continuous German fire; by last light it was clear, but heavy snow and freezing fog made it impossible for the planes to arrive on the 5th. The whole airlift was suddenly cancelled on the following day; it had been found impossible to keep the scarce transport fleet together for more than 24 hours in the face of a myriad claims elsewhere along the front. The parachutists formed themselves into a well-armed guerrilla band, wrought great execution and caused immense chaos in the German rear areas for a further two weeks, and successfully extricated themselves on foot to Russian lines. The main battle developed; on 18 January two more battalions were parachuted into the area of Lugi, south of Vyazma, with the aim of cutting 4th *Panzer* Army's main supply routes. They landed unopposed, and at once cleared an airstrip onto which, over a five-night period, transports arrived with reinforcements. Contact was made with advance elements of the 33rd Army on 25 January and the Russians decided that the moment was ripe for the commitment of the main part of 4th Airborne Corps. However, only 62 transport aircraft with untrained crews could be assembled. Only one battalion could be dropped at a time and the first went in after dark on 27 January. The men were scattered over a wide area and at least ten miles south of their planned dropzone; most of their heavy equipment containers were lost and a similar fate overtook the second battalion dropped that night. The Germans were now reacting strongly to the earlier landings; for a week they harassed the Soviet landing strips, destroying transport aircraft on the ground, burning stocks of fuel and food, and dispersing the Soviet troops into the forests where, their cohesion lost, they embarked on a battle of survival in the terrible cold. By 1 February the Germans were achieving the upper hand; their well-handled mobile combat groups had located most of the pockets of Russian airborne troops and had eliminated three of their brigade HQs. A ferocious stalking match now ensued.

The battle entered another stage on 3 February when the full strength of the Soviet 33rd Army moved forward. Instead of meeting a 4th *Panzer* Army racked by the activities of the 4th Airborne Corps, the Russians were assailed head-on and caught between two of

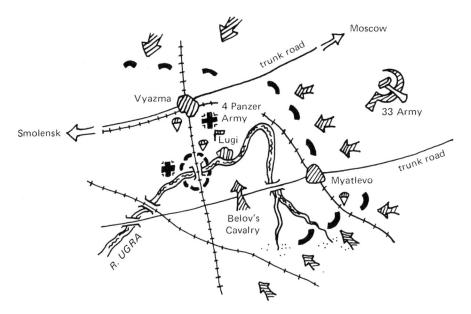

VYAZMA 1942—The First Major Soviet Airmobile Operation

the German armies they had tried to surround. The *Panzers* had observed the golden rule: when attacked by airborne troops in the rear, keep calm, act against them quickly and energetically, then stand firm against the inevitable main land attack. On the night of 23 February the Russians flung in their last airborne reinforcements; 7000 men and large quantities of supplies were flown into the Lugi airstrips, marked out by huge bonfires whose glare lit the skies for miles. There were now six Russian airborne brigades operating in the rear of 4th *Panzer* Army, although they had quickly lost cohesion and were fighting mostly in small partisan-type groups and on foot – a grave handicap in the snow and ice. These units, estimated by the Germans as 15–20,000 men, were now reinforced by Gen. Belov's 1st Guards Cavalry Corps, 15,000 mounted infantry with the high mobility conferred by their shaggy Mongolian ponies. Now it was the Germans who faced a crisis as they fought to keep their lines of communication open. By 7 March they had been compelled to throw in another corps and this proved decisive. The Russians, still fighting fiercely, were gradually driven into the forests. On 25 March the final drive against 33rd Army started and after nearly a month of confused manoeuvring and fighting the Soviets, or what was left of them, started to lay down their arms. The Russian airborne troops still lurked in the forests, supplied intermittently by air and demonstrating all the qualities of stolid endurance for which the Soviet soldier is renowned. On 18 April the great thaw started and the battle wallowed to a halt in a sea of mud; the Germans now grimly got on with the job of seeking out the remains of the 4th Airborne Corps and Belov's cavalry; this they did remorselessly, destroying them piecemeal as they dodged about the countryside, living like animals, cut off now from air supply. Some of them held out until the end of June.

Over a year passed before the Russians were able to mount another large airborne operation. By this time, in the early Autumn of 1943, the tide had finally turned against the Germans. Von Paulus and his luckless 6th Army had disappeared into the merciless grip of their captors at Stalingrad and the last great German offensive at Kursk, codenamed Operation *Zitadelle*, had failed disastrously. The Russians now rained a series of hammerlike blows against the invader, mainly on the central and southern fronts, inexorably closing in on the line of the River Dnieper behind which the Germans were clearly going to make a stand. By mid-September the Russian advance was threatening the great city of Kiev, but the out-numbered Germans fought skilfully, mindful of Hitler's incessant directives to fight to the last and not yield an inch of ground. The *Führer* reluctantly agreed to a withdrawal to the Dnieper line on 15 September, and Army Groups

Centre and South began the delicate business of retiring onto this 'Eastern Rampart' – as Hitler called it – whilst under heavy pressure from the Russians. Such a withdrawal, in contact with the enemy, is notoriously one of the most perilous operations of war. The Soviets determined to make it even more difficult for the Germans by using large numbers of airborne troops to seize a lodgement on the west bank and disrupt the delicate mechanism of the enemy's withdrawal. The chosen cockpit was the 'Dnieper Loop', a natural salient pointing eastward, formed by a huge bend of the sluggish marshy-banked river south-east of Kiev. The area of the loop had been in the hands of the partisans since the great German advance of 1941, when it had been by-passed and subsequently neglected. For two years the partisans had moved about freely, even openly using river boats. Now, the loop assumed a position of the utmost importance. There were several good crossings, but the river line was a natural ditch, the strongest defensive line in European Russia, which could have been prepared by the Germans well in advance – except that such defeatist tendencies were expressly forbidden by Hitler. The Russians, refreshed and strong, aimed to take the obstacle at a gallop, rushing the Germans off their feet and giving them no chance to stand and fight; in accordance

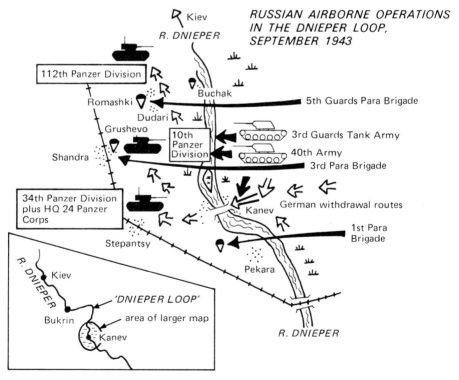

RUSSIAN AIRBORNE OPERATIONS IN THE DNIEPER LOOP, SEPTEMBER 1943

with what has become standard Soviet doctrine they planned to attack straight off the line of march.

On 22 September the German withdrawal towards the loop appeared to be going well. Three of their divisions, the 10th, 34th and 112th, were still on the east bank, moving towards the crossing at Kanev, at the southern shoulder of the loop. The commander of 4th *Panzer* Army had sent the 19th *Panzer* division south from Kiev to hold the loop until the three retiring divisions had safely got across and into the defensive positions assigned to them on the west bank. The Russians, hot on the heels of the retreating Germans, pursued them with tank formations; at the same time they began to infiltrate small parties of infantry across the river. On 23 September a battalion of Russian T34 tanks had got to within 3 miles of the Kanev bridge, across which German troops were still pouring. The situation hung on a knife-edge.

Meanwhile, 150 miles to the east, three Soviet airborne and three airlanding brigades had been mustered on airfields in the Poltava area; a total of 10,000 well-trained men who were to be pitched into the widening gap between 4th *Panzer* and 8th Armies. 5th Guards Parachute Brigade were briefed to seize the area of Grushevo, ten miles across the river. 3rd Parachute Brigade were to land at Shandra and cut the lateral north–south railway to stop the Germans moving reinforcements to the threatened flank. 1st Parachute Brigade were to drop close in behind the Kanev bridge to interfere as much as possible with the actual crossing. Because insufficient aircraft could be mustered there were no plans for launching the airlanded troops at this stage.

In the ranks of 1st and 3rd Parachute Brigades there were many survivors of the battles of Vyazma. Reorganized and retrained, both formations had been brought up to strength with young and enthusiastic recruits who were unaware of what lay in store for them. The veterans, having had one dose of fighting the Germans, were probably less optimistic, and with good reason. The paratroopers were given a cheerful briefing at their airfields. The Germans in the Dnieper Loop, they were told, were in panic-stricken chaos; little resistance was expected and a quick link-up with the Soviet ground forces was confidently predicted. In the event of delay, the airborne force would be contacted by the partisans swarming on the west bank. As all the dropzones would soon be in range of Russian artillery on the east bank, no field guns were to be dropped with the paratroops, who would go into battle with only their normal support weapons – anti-tank rifles, mortars and light machine guns.

It was planned to assemble some 180 aircraft at Poltava, plus two freight-carrying gliders and a few dozen sailplanes. However, the Soviet staff work collapsed miserably, and on the evening of 23 September only eight aircraft had materialized. To make things worse, the weather turned bad; with each hour of delay, and under cover of darkness, the Germans continued to pour back over the Kanev bridge. On the morning of the 24th some more aircraft started to arrive, but they were a mixture of types, and some were almost impossible to load. Passenger manifests and loading tables were scrapped. When aircraft were full to capacity the pilots insisted on unloading again, to count heads and weigh the payloads. All semblance of order broke down and the chaos became worse with the realization that refuelling arrangements were hopelessly inadequate. The Air Force moved some aircraft to other airfields, troops following by road. Units became separated, aircraft loads often comprising men from six or seven different units. Someone – it was never found out who – gave the order for aircraft to take off individually when loaded; this was about as helpful as the cry 'every man for himself' in a shipwreck. Few pilots knew where to fly to, and their passengers were equally ignorant. In a great undisciplined rabble, the planes flew westward.

On the afternoon of 24 September, units of 19 *Panzer* Division were moving east towards the loop, to act as covering force for the rearguard of the main body. As the leading German column approached Grushevo, a number of Russian transport aircraft appeared out of the murk overhead in twos and threes. Greeted by a storm of fire (the Germans were well provided even in 1943 with weapons the British Army lacks to this day – multibarrel automatics in the anti-aircraft role), the Russians were dropped far too high. This was 5th Guards Parachute Brigade, whose introduction to battle was most inauspicious. Those men who survived their prolonged descent were widely scattered and at once the Germans began to hunt them down. This went on throughout the night by the light of flares lit by the Germans to confuse succeeding waves of transport aircraft. The brigade commander and a small party of his men escaped into the forest, but the rest of his brigade had ceased to exist by midnight.

3rd Parachute Brigade's drop in the Shandra area came down right on top of a German Infantry Division and the HQ of 24 *Panzer* Corps. The paratroopers were subjected to a hail of fire throughout their descent and scattered into dozens of fugitive parties on landing. The only success achieved by the Russians was in the drop of 1st Parachute Brigade, which managed to concentrate in its appointed area to the south of the Kanev bridge, where work began at once on the cleaning and marking of airstrips for the planes bringing in the airlanding brigades. After dark on the 24th, the Russians crossed the Dnieper in an effort to link up with 5th Guards Parachute Brigade, which had by now been harried off the battlefield. Instead, the reconnaissance battalion of 19 *Panzer* Regiment lay in wait; before withdrawing to higher ground to the west at dawn on the 25th the Germans inflicted heavy casualties on the Russian infantry. Throughout the day that followed, most of 24th *Panzer* Corps had converged on the area of the loop, reinforced with mobile anti-aircraft units and fully prepared for a second wave of landings. None materialized, for the Russians had again run out of aircraft. Instead, they renewed the land assault, breaking out of their bridgehead in 1st Parachute Brigade's area on 26 September; their build up in the loop was dramatic – in a few days, they threw a tank corps and eight rifle divisions into the river bend. The Germans held firm, however, and during October and November they virtually destroyed the Soviet lodgement. The writing was on the wall all the same; Kiev, the holy city of old Russia, fell to the Russians on 6 November, and they finally gained possession of the Dnieper Loop by mid-January 1944.

Yet again, the Russian paratroops had displayed remarkable fighting qualities, especially at unit and sub-unit level. The commander of the shattered 5th Guards Brigade with only 150 survivors was driven off his dropzone but collected a battalion's-worth of stragglers and partisans and proceeded to wage his own guerrilla war for more than two months, deep in the German rear. His force subsisted off the land, captured German supplies, received irregular airdrops and was in continuous radio contact with the HQ of the Russian 4th Army. When finally relieved, this resourceful and energetic officer was still in command of over 1000 well fed, disciplined and aggressive troops.

This was the last attempt by the Russians at a major airborne operation in the Second World War; their High Command presumably decided that the paratroops' contribution to the land battle did not justify even the meagre air transport effort they were prepared to devote to it. At that time, airborne warfare was clearly beyond the technical capability of a vast but crude war machine geared to the mass deployment of armour, artillery and infantry.

★ ★ ★

In the Far East, the outcome of the war was decided by a combination of sea and air power. The Japanese recognized that a strong navy and airforce were essential to their plans for the conquest of South-East Asia and by 1940 had started to develop their own airborne forces. In the early stages of the Japanese onslaught conditions were ripe for the use of airborne troops. The Allied air forces, equipped with inferior aircraft, were defeated by the Japanese navy and army air forces, whose equipment proved far better than had been expected. They did not use their paratroops, however, until January 1942 when their naval airborne forces carried out their sole operation, a successful battalion-sized landing at Menado airfield in Celebes.

A month later, on 11 February, the Japanese brought off a major *coup* at Palembang, also in the Dutch East Indies, where Anglo-Dutch forces had started to demolish the huge refinery and storage facilities of the Royal Dutch Shell company. One hundred and thirty paratroops were dropped onto the refinery whilst demolitions were actually in progress; although the defenders succeeded in igniting some of the oil stocks, all the derricks were held intact by the Japanese within 24 hours, together with 250,000 tons of valuable oil. Only 25 Japanese paratroops were lost in this action, which enlisted the aid of confusion to defeat a far larger defending force.

Apart from a minor operation at Timor in February 1942, Japanese paratroops were not used again until 1944, when two desperate attempts were made to halt the Americans at Leyte in the Philippines. By November of that year the Japanese had been driven back from their far-flung conquests of 1941–42 by a relentless combination of air power and the strategic mobility enjoyed by the Americans, who methodically took island after island by amphibious assault, then established air bases from which to support the next move forward. The first Japanese airborne effort at Leyte was a total failure and all three troop-carrying aircraft used were shot down. In December they tried again. Using between 40 and 50 transport aircraft, their aim was to get onto the American forward airstrips and destroy as many aircraft as possible before they were themselves eliminated. There was no provision for the relief of this force, whose members were evidently primed for a one-way journey, having been issued with individual bottles of strong rice wine labelled 'not to be drunk until airborne'. They had also been well coached in the techniques of spreading confusion and kitted out with bells, horns, whistles and a lively repertoire of songs with which each sub-unit could identify themselves to their friends. A number of curious English phrases had also been carefully learned, although it is unlikely that the average American GI would have been fooled by such injunctions as 'Go to Hell, beast. Have done, all the resistance', 'Lay down arms, surrender quickly – if don't, shall die', and 'Kill a Yankee' (presumably aimed at Southerners).

The drop took place at dusk on 6 December. It happened that the area into which they descended was occupied by American airborne troops – Maj.-Gen. Joe Swing's 11th Airborne Division. Swing watched in amazement as the Japanese planes thundered overhead in the gathering dusk, then leapt for his radio to stand his men to arms.

The parachute landing had been timed to coincide with a land attack and by midnight on 6 December the Americans realized that a major threat was developing; Japanese infantry were fighting on one of the airstrips, from which they were ejected by one of Swing's formations, the 187th Parachute Infantry Regiment. Fighting went on in the glare of burning aircraft and fuel dumps and with the added distraction of the Japanese special sound effects. Swing's men were well up to the challenge, however. Their communications were good and they were in control within 48 hours. By 11 December the remnants of the Japanese were dispersing; the threat had dissolved. Once more, a disruptive effect out of all proportion to the forces used had been achieved, even though 18 of the troop-carrying aircraft had been intercepted and shot down *en route* to the target. The Americans' plans were delayed effectively for two weeks, huge stocks of fuel had been destroyed, and many aircraft damaged beyond repair in the fighting which had raged around them.

★　　★　　★

The use of airborne troops by the Allies in the Far East campaigns was long inhibited by the lack of suitable transport aircraft. Burma was notorious as the 'forgotten' theatre of war and it was not until a series of sharp defeats there at the hands of the Japanese that the Allied high command began to recognize the value of airmobility as a counter to the highly mobile tactics employed in the jungle by the enemy. The war in the East was essentially one which demanded air transportation rather than the spectacular use of glider and parachute troops, but in 1941, before the Japanese offensives began, approval was given for the formation of an airborne brigade in India, and for the creation of the necessary training establishment to produce parachutists in the quantities required. Because of delays in production of gliders by the then rudimentary Indian aircraft industry, an approach was made to the Americans for the supply of a quantity of Waco G4s but this came to nothing. After many delays the Air Landing School India was established by early 1942, using ancient Vickers *Valencia* biplane transports for parachute training. There was a dearth of parachutes and many of those in use proved to be faulty and badly maintained, giving rise in 1942 to a high incidence of fatalities in training and seriously affecting morale. Despite these early troubles, it was possible to start operations in mid-1942 when a small party from 153rd Gurkha Parachute Battalion were dropped behind the Japanese lines in central Burma, where they remained for six weeks, observing enemy movements and sending back a stream of useful information on enemy troop movements by radio to their base in India.

The first Gurkha paratroop volunteers were given a rousing presentation, in which was described the excitement of the jump, the departure from the aircraft at eight hundred feet and the splendid prospect of using their curved cutting blade, the *kukri*, in the subsequent battle on the ground. The audience listened intently. At the end, the lecturer asked for questions. A Gurkha rose sheepishly to his feet: 'Please sahib, is it possible for us to jump from two hundred feet?' He was told that this was impossible as there would be insufficient time for the parachute to open. Immediately there were wide grins of relief from the whole audience, hitherto impassive. 'Ah, sahib – so we have *parachutes*; that is very good.'

It was unfortunate that no further chance to use these splendid troops in operations occurred until the closing stages of the war in 1945, when they took part in the recapture of Rangoon. Although it was planned to use airborne forces for the subsequent recapture of Malaya the dropping of atomic bombs on Hiroshima and Nagasaki terminated the war. The major airmobile operations in Burma were actually carried out by American aircraft and gliders in support of Operation *Thursday*, the second Chindit operation against the rear areas of the Japanese field army. As an early example of the use of the air as a medium of mobility for men and *matériel* it was an outstanding performance.

The concept of deep penetration operations inside Japanese-held territory had been developed by an unusual British artillery officer, Orde Wingate. He was an inter-war product of the Royal Military Academy, Woolwich; but unlike the majority of his naturally conformist fellow students he was set apart, a lonely figure scorning convention, unpopular yet respected.

His subsequent military career reflected his behaviour at Woolwich. What Wingate wanted, he got; the chief requirement was air support, and as the result of his lobbying in high places Number 1 Air Commando, a tailor-made miniature airforce was produced by the Americans specifically for the support of Operation *Thursday*. Its composition was the outcome of meetings in Washington between Mountbatten – now Supreme Allied Commander in South-East Asia – Wingate and Gen. 'Hap' Arnold of the US Army Air Force. Arnold had long been a devout disciple of Billy Mitchell, but despite this and his resultant adherence to the creed of the indivisibility of airpower, he agreed to all Wingate's proposals. Instructions were given to form the Air Commando under Lt-Col. Philip Cochrane; by January 1944, so rapid was the American response, it was lying on its airfields in north-eastern India, ready to go. It was surely the most compact combat airforce ever formed. A small HQ commanded a squadron of P51 *Mustang* fighters, a squadron of B25 light bombers, 100 light aircraft fitted with a stretcher apiece for evacuating casualties from jungle airstrips; a squadron of light transport aircraft, some L1 spotter planes, 100 CG4 gliders – and one Sikorsky R4 helicopter, the first ever to see active service. A small signals detachment and an airphoto processing section completed the order of battle. For some 250 aircraft there was a total of no more than 500 officers and men – a staggeringly low man-to-aircraft ratio. It was a force capable of immediate response to any call for direct air support.

Wingate planned to launch Operation *Thursday* on 5 March 1944, with the aim of cutting the Japanese lines of communication to north Burma, thereby helping to trap their forces in that area, and to aid the advance of the Ledo road into China so that overland reinforcements, particularly stores and vehicles, could be passed through to Chiang Kai-shek's hard-pressed Nationalist armies. The second Chindit

BURMA AND THE 1944 CHINDIT EXPEDITION

attack was therefore a full-blooded operation of war and not in any
sense a guerrilla effort. It involved the airlanding of five brigades in
an area to the south-west of Myitkyina. The initial landings were to
be carried out by night in gliders; in order to achieve maximum surprise, there were to be no preliminary airstrikes. The spirit of the
enterprise was vividly expressed by Wingate in terms which surely
appealed to Churchill at his most bellicose – 'a hand in the enemy's
bowels'. The glider landings, having secured and cleared the landing
areas would be followed by a massive airlift: gliders bearing heavy
weapons and equipment, bulldozers, rollers, graders – all to be used in
making all-weather C47 strips. Once on the ground, with defences dug
around the airheads, the columns would strike out in all directions to
cut communications and gain absolute domination over the enemy
rear area. On 4 March, *Mustang* fighters trailing meat-hooks on long
cables flew up and down the Japanese lines of communication in
north Burma, severing every telephone cable in order to paralyse the
enemy command system; apart from this, no Allied aircraft stirred
over enemy-held territory except for a handful of photographic reconnaissance planes.

Three large open spaces, chosen during the previous year's expedition, were to be used for the initial glider landings; they were codenamed *Piccadilly*, *Broadway* and *Chowringhee* and Wingate decreed
that they were under no circumstances to be reconnoitred by air beforehand. Despite this, Lt-Gen. William Old, the commander of the
USAAF transport force, carried out a surreptitious flight over them in
February. Wingate discovered this and, coldly furious, declined to
confide in Old any more. This was not the only source of friction.
The Chindit leader quarrelled with Cochrane's staff over the glider
payloads; he demanded 4500 pounds when the operating manuals
stipulated a maximum of 3750. He was hazy about air matters despite
his awareness of the value of the air-arm in the logistic role, and his
abrasive manner was something new to the air commander. To
Cochrane's eternal credit, he supported his prickly ally with a loyalty
he did little to deserve.

On the evening of 5 March tension ran high; gliders and aircraft
stood loaded and with engines running on the airfield at Lalaghat.
General Bill Slim and his staff of HQ 14th Army had come to wish the
Chindits well. The bearded Wingate tensely awaited the result of a
last-minute photographic inspection of the three landing areas.
Minutes after the reconnaissance plane landed the pictures, still drip-
ping, were in his hand. Aghast, he saw that fallen trees lay all over
Piccadilly. There was an emotional scene and Slim was obliged to take
Wingate aside and give him a homily he almost certainly found pain-

ful. It calmed him down and the *Piccadilly* gliders were redirected to *Broadway* and *Chowringhee*. Many of the stripped-down C47s were towing two gliders apiece; some broke away in mid-flight, to be lost amidst the precipitous jungle-covered hills below. Fortunately the weather was fine and the navigators skilful. Thirty-four gliders reached *Broadway* and 33 got to *Chowringhee*. Although the ground at both was rough, the pilots skilfully landed more than 500 troops. Last in were the engineers' gliders, many of which crashed into other Wacos; but within 24 hours both strips were taking incoming C47s. In the first five days, 8000 men, 1300 mules and 250 tons of supplies had been flown in. The swelling force then set out towards the river Irrawaddy and set up another landing strip – *Aberdeen* – some 40 miles west of *Chowringhee* into which a further brigade was inserted on 23 March. There were now 12,000 men in the Japanese rear areas.

Tragedy struck suddenly on the following day when Wingate died in the wreck of his aircraft; his deputy, Brig. 'Joe' Lentaigne took over and the operation continued, but its mainspring had gone. Although the Chindits fought with splendid confidence and aggression, they became near-captives in their airheads, dependent on the air for their resupply and for the evacuation of their sick and wounded, but still limited to the tactical mobility conferred by their own feet and by their pack animals. After the first shock, the Japanese kept their heads, and showed that an Asian army could continue to function satisfactorily even with the enemy's 'hand in its bowels'.

★   ★   ★

By September 1943 the time was ripe for a full-blooded airborne assault against the Japanese in New Guinea. Colonel Kinsler's 503rd Parachute Infantry Regiment – one of the first to be formed in the United States – had been sent to Australia in the autumn of 1942 as an independent formation for use by Gen. MacArthur. Lack of aircraft prevented its employment for nearly a year, but it was decided to use paratroops in the offensive planned against the 11,000 Japanese in the Lae–Salamaua area. In outline, the 9th Australian Infantry Division, reinforced by American combat engineers, was to be landed from the sea east of Lae, whilst the 503rd were to drop onto an existing airstrip at Nadzab, some 20 miles inland and improve the landing ground to permit the airlift of the 7th Australian Division from Tsili Tsili, another airfield about 25 miles to the south. A force of 87 C47s had been assembled at Port Moresby. Five of them were loaded with the dismantled guns of a battery of the 2nd/4th Field Regiment, Royal Australian Artillery, which had been placed under Kinsler's command as the 503rd had no organic artillery of its own. The Australian gunners, all volunteers, were given some rudimentary training, but the jump onto Nadzab was, for all of them, their first.

At 0730 hrs on 5 September the force emplaned and the C47s took off, struggling to cross the 9000-foot-high Owen Stanley range. The troops in their jungle uniforms almost froze. Just after 1000 hrs the force arrived over the dropzone, which had been screened with smoke laid by low-flying aircraft. The first man to jump was Lt-Col. Tolson, commanding the 3rd Battalion, and the 503rd with its intrepid Australian gunners was on the ground within five minutes, as the C47s, unopposed by enemy anti-aircraft fire, were able to fly in tight formation. From high above, where his bomber circled the area, Gen. MacArthur watched approvingly. A closer inspection would have revealed that even in this unopposed drop there had been blemishes; most of Tolson's battalion missed the huge clearing around Nadzab airstrip and landed in the surrounding jungle. Hundreds of men in the other battalions landed in grass which proved to be twelve feet high and were exhausted when they finally struggled out into open ground. Had the Japanese been holding the airstrip, Nadzab could have been a disaster; as it was, it finally convinced the Chiefs of Staff in Washington that airborne operations at brigade level were a feasible operation of war, and led to the successful airborne divisional manoeuvres held in North and South Carolina in December 1943. The real value of the Nadzab drop lay in the securing of the forward airhead, into which 420 C47 loads of Australians were flown during the next week. Throughout the New Guinea campaign, Kenney's 3rd Air Force served the Allied cause magnificently; with its unflagging support the Australians managed to take the whole Markham Valley area in 15 days at an incalculable saving of men's lives, whether from disease or by enemy action.

★　　　★　　　★

There followed a pause in the use of airborne troops by the Allies in the Eastern theatre. General MacArthur was known to be anxious to use paratroops anywhere in the Pacific area and the eagerness of his staff in seeking the right opportunities almost led to a disaster in July 1944, at the tail-end of the New Guinea campaign. By this stage the Japanese had been forced into toe-hold positions, the strongest on the island of Noemfoor, where they had fortified a strong position defending the airfield. It was decided to use the 503rd Regiment again. Now commanded by Col. George M. Jones, it was based in Queensland, Australia, from where it flew to Hollandia, the mounting airfield several hundred miles east of Noemfoor. Only 38 C47s were available – barely sufficient for one battalion to drop at a time. The plan for the assault envisaged an amphibious attack on the island on 2 July followed by a parachute landing 24 hours later, when it was hoped that the airfield garrison (estimated at 3500), would be busily defending the beaches. The landings on 2 July went ahead as planned and the American 158th Infantry soon ran into stiff opposition. On receipt of an intelligence report that a strong Japanese counter attack was imminent, it was decided to drop the 1st/503rd right onto the airstrip on 3 July. The paratroops were out of practice, not having carried out a mass descent since Nadzab, ten months earlier; so, it seemed, were the C47 pilots, for as the result of a carelessly-set altimeter in the leading aircraft the jump was made from a dangerously low altitude – estimated in many cases to be as little as 200 feet. There was also much dispersion. Many troops landed heavily amidst a mass of close-packed Japanese engineer equipment or amongst the aircraft dispersals, and injuries ran at a high level. The 3rd/503rd followed on 4 July. Despite this auspicious date the drop was almost as bad, in terms of landing casualties, as the 1st/503rd's. Out of 1400 men dropped, 10 per cent were so badly injured as to be incapable of fighting. It was therefore decided to bring the 2nd/503rd in by sea. Fortunately, the strength of the Japanese garrison had been grossly overestimated and the 1200 or so on the island were soon over-run. Noemfoor illustrates admirably the pitfalls attendant on mounting an airborne operation with inadequate intelligence and without preliminary training or rehearsal. Once on the ground the 503rd were preoccupied with the own casualties in the dropzone, and with achieving tactical cohesion following the badly-muffed drop. They were lucky in that the Japanese, too, had their problems.

★   ★   ★

It was six months before the next American airborne assault took place in the Pacific theatre, at Tagaytay in the Philippines. Although the 11th Airborne Division had been in the theatre for some time it had not yet jumped into battle, but having been used extensively during the Leyte campaign in the infantry role its troops were seasoned and experienced soldiers. Its commander, the airborne pioneer Maj.-Gen. Joseph Swing, had imbued his men with a fine aggressive spirit and although they were out of parachuting practice he was confident that his division would acquit itself well in the drive for Manila. The overall plan devised by Gen. Eichelberger, commanding the US 8th Army, was to attack Manila from the north with two divisions (1st Cavalry and 38th Infantry) whilst 11th Airborne drove up from the south, its two glider infantry regiments landing from the sea whilst the 511th Parachute Infantry Regiment jumped into the hills along the Tagaytay Ridge to clear the road to Manila and deal with Japanese blocking positions known to be established around the Aga defile.

The landing of four battalions of the 187th and 188th Glider Infantry Regiments on 31 January 1945 at Nasugbu was made to look like the arrival of the entire 8th Army by means of a carefully orchestrated deception plan. There was little opposition, and cheered on by a delirious population the airborne infantry drove off towards Manila along Route 17. As predicted, the Japanese had blocked the road at the Aga defile and grimly waited for the Americans in well-prepared positions. On 1 February Swing ordered his pathfinders to drop, with instructions to set out dropzones on top of the Tagaytay Ridge behind the Japanese. The main drop was planned for 3 February. Yet again there were only enough C47s to permit one battalion to drop at a time; Swing therefore elected to put two battalions down in succession on the first day, followed by a third on 4 February. An error on the part of one of the jumpmasters came near to ruining the entire operation. The first waves of aircraft dropped

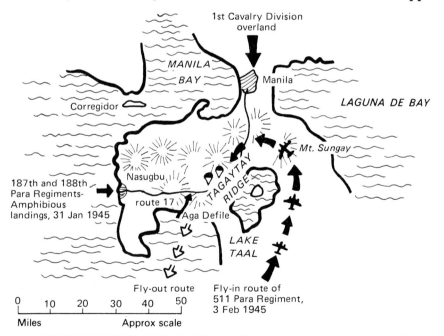

AIRBORNE ASSAULT AT TAGAYTAY—The Dash for Manila Jan-Feb 1945

their sticks of paratroops on the correct dropzone, but the next 30 planeloads were dropped prematurely and landed some miles to the north-east. All the C47 pilots flew too fast and the paratroops were badly buffeted as they left the aircraft at 135 instead of 110 mph. The pathfinders had managed to evade detection by the Japanese and the actual landings were unopposed.

The second drop in the afternoon also went wrong; as the C47s approached from the north-east the jumpmasters saw, on the ground, the discarded parachutes of the men whose drop had gone adrift in the morning and the whole of the second lift was duly deposited on the wrong DZ. On the ground, the two battalions took some hours to sort themselves out, but managed to put in a decisive attack on the Japanese at the Aga defile which, reinforced by the third battalion's arrival on its correct DZ on 4 February, cleared the route into Manila.

Two weeks later, the 503rd, out of action since the attack on Noemfoor, were launched into one of the most spectacular assaults of the whole war – the recapture of Corregidor Island. Known as 'The Gibraltar of the Pacific' this six-mile-long island stood sentry at the mouth of Manila Bay. In shape rather like a tadpole with its head to the west, it rose almost 500 feet above the sea. Before the war it had been a showpiece, with neat white colonial barracks, parade grounds and sports fields; there was even a small golf course on 'Topside', the highest point of the island, corresponding to the tadpole's head. In the 'tail' was a small airstrip and a lower hill – Malinta. Here also lay the only beaches across which an amphibious assault could be made. In May 1942 Corregidor had been the scene of the Americans' last stand when Gen. Wainwright, left behind with a garrison of 4000 after McArthur's departure for Australia, had finally capitulated to the Japanese. Since then the once-immaculate barracks had fallen into decay and by mid-February 1945, after several weeks of heavy bombardment by American ships and aircraft, the island was ruinous. Amidst the debris over 5000 Japanese, commanded by Captain Itagaki of the Imperial Navy, were resolved to defend the island to the last. Itagaki had concentrated most of his defending force on Topside and Malinta Hill, under which ran a series of tunnels concealing his reserves. Telephone cables connected all defence posts to the command post on Topside, but by the day of the American assault, 16 February, most had been repeatedly severed by the continuous aerial bombardment.

The forces assigned to the attack were Col. George Jones's augmented 503rd Parachute Infantry Regiment and, for the amphibious assault, the 3rd Battalion of the 34th Infantry. The plan was co-ordinated by Col. John Tolson of Nadzab fame, who gambled on the fact that although Itagaki might expect an airborne landing on the low-lying 'tail' of the island where the defence could pin it down with ease, he would not have been prepared for a parachute descent on Topside, where space was so limited and where the strongest defences lay. The whole concept was as bold as that carried out five years earlier at Eben Emael; but on Corregidor the defenders could be guaranteed to fight suicidally to the last man. Jones flew over Topside a week before the attack. He must have blenched at what he saw. The only places onto which his men could be dropped were the parade ground, perhaps 400 yards long and half as wide, and the old golf course, a little longer but even narrower. The troop-carrier aircraft would be across these DZs in just over five seconds, giving time for a maximum of only six or seven men to jump at each pass. Apart from the demands made on the parachutists, dropping into a certain hornets' nest, it was going to tax the pilots of the 317th Troop Carrier Group, whose commander, Col. John Lackey, had assembled about 50 C47s. Based on the airfield of Mindoro, they would be unable to return with the second lift until five hours after the first troops had gone down.

Neither Jones nor Lackey was aware of the real strength of the garrison or they would have been even more worried; they had been advised by Intelligence that there might be 600 enemy on the island – perhaps as few as 250. On this dangerous assumption it was planned that the 3rd/34th would attack from the sea at 1030 hrs on the south side of the 'tail' and link up with Jones's men who would have started to drop at 0830 hrs following a first-light airstrike on all known Japanese strong-points. Briefing for the assaulting force was meticulous; masses of air photographs were available and a detailed model of Corregidor, updated daily to include the latest bombardment damage, had been committed to memory by all ranks; in case of a logistic failure all the paratroops carried four days' assault rations, extra water bottles and ammunition, and the shared-out components of their battalion's heavy weapons. Thus festooned, and with the extra burden of the obligatory American reserve parachute – in this case of no more value than a lucky charm – the troops staggered aboard their planes.

It was a fiendishly difficult drop; as the leading aircraft approached the smoke-wreathed island it could be seen that a high wind was blowing from the north; the C47s were in parallel columns in order to drop simultaneously on the parade ground and golf course. The first wave of men, caught in a 20-knot wind, were slammed down south of their DZs in a wilderness of blasted tree stumps, ruined buildings and rusting barbed wire entanglements. Many of the over-burdened troops were dragged helplessly across the broken ground by their parachutes. The drop height was brought down from 600 to below 500 feet above Topside, and by a system of adjustment by trial and error the succeeding aircraft managed to place their men accurately on their correct DZs. Jones was quickly down amongst the leading troops, rallying and disentangling them. The Japanese, taken completely off balance, were hesitant to react and initially their counter-fire was sporadic. Itagaki, frantically trying to reach his outposts through a ruined telephone system, eventually gave up and left his command post, samurai sword in hand, to try and size up the situation for himself. Almost at once he died in a close-range action, victim of a well-thrown American hand grenade. Without its leader, the defence fought on without direction and the battle for Topside degenerated into innumerable close-quarter brawls, with bayonet, grenade and knife much in evidence.

When the amphibious attack came in two minutes ahead of schedule at 1028 hrs, the paratroops had gained possession of Topside apart from cleaning out numbers of snipers. The attack moved eastward towards Malinta and the 'tail' of the island, strengthened by the tanks and field artillery landed in the wake of the 3rd/34th's leading assault waves. Casualties to the 503rd had been mainly due to landing accidents caused by the appalling state of the ground and the excessively high wind. Out of 2050 who jumped on the first day more than 10 per cent were injured whilst landing. This led Jones to cancel the drop planned for the following day and bring in the balance of his troops by sea. During the next ten days the Japanese were remorselessly hunted down, despite their suicidal resistance; on D plus 1, 600 of them launched themselves in a screaming counter attack at Topside from which few survived. By 26 February it was all over; the bodies of over 4500 Japanese were counted, and many more lay entombed in the tunnels below Malinta Hill. Only 50 survived as prisoners, most of them critically wounded. The Americans lost just under 200 dead and 1000 wounded. It had been a triumph of sheer nerve.

Meanwhile the 11th Airborne Division had brought off a raid which must rank as one of the great parachute operations of all time. During the advance towards Manila the Americans became aware that out to the east, well off 11th Airborne's axis, there lay a prison camp in which the enemy were holding more than 2000 civilian captives, mostly American citizens who had been prisoners throughout the Japanese occupation. General Swing, despite his preoccupation with the main campaign, made it his business to find out about the camp and set his intelligence-gatherers to work. The camp was at Los Baños in a converted farm school; a recently escaped prisoner provided full details and it was soon possible to draw a detailed map and plot the organization and routines of the prisoners and their 275 Japanese guards. The camp lay two miles inland from Los Baños town; apart from the guards it was estimated that several thousand more Japanese were stationed within a few hours' march of the camp, making any rescue attempt an affair of precise timing and quick action. Many of the prisoners were known to be in poor health, unable to stand up to a physically demanding escape, so some form of transport had to reach them quickly for evacuation either across country or out to sea. It was therefore decided to employ a combination of airborne and amphibious troops to spring the internees. A scout unit of 11th Airborne, with a group of Filipino guerrillas, would approach Los Baños from the sea in fishermen's canoes, to act as pathfinders and to deal with any outlying Japanese patrols. One company of paratroops would then be dropped into the camp whilst three other companies would assault over the beach in amphibious tractors (Amtracs) to pick up the prisoners and take them back out to sea. A simultaneous attack would be made from inland in order to divert any Japanese units away from Los Baños, and to clear an alternative evacuation route if it was found impossible to get the Amtracs back to the beach.

In command of the operation was the commander of the 188th Glider Infantry Regiment, Col. Soule. He had a difficult task; so much depended on accurate intelligence and on the unpredictable reactions of the Japanese, about whom every available grain of intelligence was now assembled. Soule decided to launch the rescue on 23 February using the 511th Parachute Infantry Regiment for both the drop and the amphibious assault. This unit was actually in the line in the infantry role until 36 hours before the Los Baños attack, and had little time to readjust to its radically different new tasks. Only a surreptitious preliminary reconnaissance by air was possible; no rehearsals could be held, and only a few hours were available for the assembly of the units involved. On 22 February the parachute assault company, commanded by Lt Ringler, moved to Nicols airfield outside Manila, drew its parachutes and prepared to emplane. Ringler's men were veterans of the Tagaytay attack where their outstanding performance had earned them the honour of going in by air to Los Baños. As the tired men rested at Nicols Field, the pathfinders were edging towards the prison camp and the Amtrac battalion prepared itself further along the coast for its seven-mile dash towards the target. At dawn on the 23rd the tractors, having swung far out into the Bay of Lagona, set course for the beach. As they neared the shore, the pathfinders set off white smoke markers and the nine C47s carrying Ringler and his men, having come in almost at sea level, climbed at the last moment to drop their paratroops. The moment of attack had been carefully chosen; at 0700 hrs daily, the prison guards habitually laid down their rifles and indulged in half an hour's physical training. On this fateful morning they were hard at their exercises as the first paratroops landed amongst them. In a short and decidedly one-sided battle every Japanese guard was killed. One American paratrooper and one internee were slightly wounded; as the firing died away the prisoners were loaded onto the tractors as they burst into the camp. The subsequent evacuation went unhindered by the enemy, who had reacted to what they thought was a major threat from inland and were blindly casting about in the jungle far away from the camp.

This little-known operation succeeded beyond the wildest hopes of its planners. A tired parachute unit had achieved total surprise, acting with fearsome thoroughness in its despatch of the guards at minimal cost to itself. As a morale-raiser it was unbeatable. The psychological effect of airborne warfare had been demonstrated to the utmost.

★　　　★　　　★

Since the eclipse of the German airborne forces after Crete, their general employment had been as élite, highly trained and fanatically well-motivated infantry. In this capacity they excelled wherever they were employed. As early as the end of 1942 some were hurriedly flown to Tunis in order to arrest the advance of the Anglo-American forces landed in Operation *Torch*. They succeeded admirably; the British 1st Army, shaking down in its early skirmishes, rapidly acquired a marked respect for such units as the parachute engineer battalion commanded by *Major* Witzig – last heard of at Eben Emael when as a subaltern he had directed the firing of the deadly explosive charges to settle the fate of that fortress. By the end of the war in Europe a total of ten parachute divisions had been raised within the *Luftwaffe*; all fought with distinction in Sicily, Italy, Russia, the Balkans and north-west Europe – but the Germans never again used them in their proper role above battalion strength.

The most celebrated performance by Student's men was the 'rescue' of Mussolini in September 1943. The Italian dictator had been placed in custody by Marshal Badoglio following Italy's abrupt resignation from the Axis after the Allied invasion of Sicily. For political reasons, Hitler decreed that he be set free. It looked to be a particularly difficult job, and the *Führer* hand-picked the man to bring it off, Otto Skorzeny, attaching him somewhat cynically to Student's staff as a 'supernumerary aide-de-camp'. Student could not stand this fanatical and uncouth man, but nonetheless had to obey the *Führer*'s directive which opened all doors to Skorzeny and obtained for him any men and equipment he demanded.

Skorzeny discovered that Mussolini was held at the Hotel Campo Imperatore, 5900 feet up on Monte Corno, about 100 miles from Rome. All roads leading to the area were blocked by Badoglio's men and it was believed that no less than 250 troops were garrisoning the hotel itself. There was no road from the valley up to the hotel, the only means of entry being via a funicular railway. There was a small, steeply sloping field alongside the Campo Imperatore, and Skorzeny decided that a glider landing was feasible. His original plan was that a 'snatch' party would land in the field, release Mussolini and get him away down the funicular to a waiting light aircraft.

On 12 September, Skorzeny's gliders – 12 of the well-tried DFS230s – were assembled at Student's HQ on an airfield near Rome, which had been seized from the Italians a few days earlier by German airlanded troops. Amongst the 90 men chosen to take part were 18 of Skorzeny's disreputable 'irregulars', whose presence irked the regular paratroops. At 1300 hrs the force took off. Half were directed at the field by the hotel and half to seize the bottom end of the funicular. Skorzeny led the raid in person, flying in the leading glider, whose pilot was somewhat alarmed when his passenger hacked an improvised observation hatch out of the canvas covering of the fuselage and stuck his head into the airstream; despite this distraction he made a good landing on the steep slope by the hotel, streaming his brake parachute; three more gliders joined Skorzeny's and within minutes of landing the Germans had taken control of the Campo Imperatore from the mesmerized Italians. Five gliders landed at the bottom of the funicular and took that over without a struggle. There was now a snag; the light aircraft which was to fly Mussolini to safety was damaged in landing. Fortunately for Skorzeny Student's personal pilot, *Hauptmann* Gerlach, was orbiting the area in a Fieseler *Storch* aircraft having been sent along by his chief to observe the operation. Skorzeny called him in to land up at the hotel and pick up Mussolini. The *Storch* was a remarkable aircraft; heavily flapped and slatted, it had an excellent short field performance, but even an expert like Gerlach must have quailed as he flew low over the hotel. Down below, Skorzeny's men and their illustrious captive busied themselves moving the larger rocks from the steep field; even so it presented a fearsome sight as Gerlach committed himself to his final approach. He got down safely but he was horrified when Skorzeny, unwilling to lose out on the publicity aspects of this *coup*, insisted on bundling himself into the *Storch* with Mussolini. The protesting Gerlach faced his overloaded aircraft downhill and launched it over the precipitous edge of the field, plunging violently down into the void. Regaining control, he realized that one leg of the main undercarriage had been severely damaged in the headlong take-off, but superb airmanship enabled him to bring off a safe landing at Rome, from where Mussolini was whisked off in a Heinkel bomber to rejoin Hitler in his distant lair.

Hitler, however, had now become obsessed with other strategies: the war in the East, the business of holding off the Allies in Italy and the development of the terror-weapons with which he believed the whole balance of the war would be radically altered in 1944. Student remained outside the court circle. XI *Fliegerkorps* was already broken up and its divisions farmed out as reinforcements to the Russian and Italian fronts. Meanwhile the airborne depots in Germany continued to produce their quotas of high-quality troops. On paper, at least, German airborne forces still existed, with Student as their venerated head. In March 1944 his HQ was re-established at Nancy in France. Given the job of raising new formations, he had produced a complete Parachute Army by mid-1944, one corps of which was immediately committed as infantry to stem the Allied invasion of Normandy; the Parachute Army was destined to play a leading part in most of the subsequent operations, right up to the final surrender in May 1945. Some experimental work had gone on despite the airborne forces' apparent fall from grace; at Student's instigation a special unit was formed under the command of *Oberstleutnant* von der Heydte which carried out some startling trials with captured parachutes and new gliders; by the time these new techniques could be put to use, however, the war was irrevocably lost for Germany.

CHAPTER NINE

The Final Throw:
Arnhem, the Ardennes and the Rhine

It must have seemed to all those who fought under Eisenhower's command that August 1944 was the month of decision in the West. In the last week of July only the coastal districts of Normandy and Cotentin Peninsula had been taken by the Allies; six weeks later the American 1st Army had closed with the German border, Montgomery's 21st Army Group had captured Brussels and Antwerp and Gen. Patch's 7th US Army, having landed in the South of France on 15 August had driven up the Rhône valley and would make contact on 12 September north of Dijon with Allied troops coming south from the Normandy pocket. A decisive victory had been won and the way to Berlin was open.

Or was it? In fact, although total victory seemed within their grasp the Allies were no longer in concert. Eisenhower's HQ remained in Normandy and although he assumed direct command of ground operations on 3 September it was too late to resolve the conflict which had broken out between Patton, whose 3rd Army had charged spectacularly across France and who now wanted to lead the main Allied assault on into the heart of Germany, and Montgomery, whose 21st Army Group had borne the brunt of the fighting in Normandy as it wore the *Panzers* down in a bloody battle of attrition and which now smelt victory as its troops pressed across Belgium and up to the Dutch border. Eisenhower favoured a general advance on a broad front; his two most effective subordinates clamoured for the chance to lead the Allied Liberation Armies into the breach for the final victory and both, being men of pronounced views and strong characters, were convinced they were right.

Eisenhower, despite his genius for diplomacy, was also firm when necessary. He rejected the claims of both his juniors. At the same time, however, he agreed to the use of three airborne divisions to help Montgomery overcome the three water obstacles in Holland – the rivers Maas, Waal and Nederrijn (Lower Rhine). Having seized crossings over these, Eisenhower's staff hoped that this would outflank the strong German frontier defences, the Siegfried Line, and offer a further option if frontal attacks down its length failed to obtain an entry point into the German heartland.

When Eisenhower agreed to the airborne-led attack into the Netherlands the strategic outlook appeared rosy. The Allies, however, had reckoned without the incredible resilience of the German war machine which, after sustaining a technical knock-out in July and August, had retired groggily to its corner to emerge early in September as full of fight as ever. Hitler's remarkable gift for leadership had much to do with this. During the three months, June to August, the *Wehrmacht* had incurred more than a million casualties on the Eastern and Western fronts; the German cities had undergone an aerial bombardment, by day and night, of holocaust proportion; industry and transport systems were continually dislocated by air attack. Yet over ten million men were still under arms at the *Führer's* disposal. German industry, as the result of Albert Speer's brilliant management, was still rising to its peak war production. Heavy tanks, far superior to anything used by the British and Americans, were coming off the production lines, London and south-east England were under bombardment by the V1 and V2 weapons; and the new jet-propelled aircraft were reaching *Luftwaffe* units in quantity. Twenty-five new divisions were rapidly formed for the defence of the Western Front and more than 100 'fortress infanty battalions', hitherto considered fit only for home defence, were flung into the western defences. The faithful old warhorses *Generalfeldmarschall* Gerd von Runstedt, now in his 70th year but still revered by the German army as '*der Schwarze Knecht*' (the Black Knight) was restored to favour and to command in the West – he had been dropped after his failure to throw the Allies off the Normandy beaches. Hitler resolved to hold on at the Siegfried Line whilst he gathered strength for a decisive blow at the Anglo-Americans which would force them to negotiate a peace; after this, the *Wehrmacht* would devote its attentions to the Russians. Fantastic as this scenario now seems, there were moments in the autumn and winter of 1944–45 when it must have seemed to Hitler that it was actually beginning to take shape.

Having studied the results of the Allied airborne landings in Normandy, Eisenhower approved a new organization for a combined HQ which would henceforth command the British and American airborne divisions.

Eisenhower was also looking for a well-qualified commander for the 1st Allied Airborne Army, as it was to be called. This officer would require remarkable strength of character and would need to produce evidence of an outstanding track record if he were to be placed over such men as Ridgway, Browning, Gale, Gavin and

Maxwell Taylor. The man selected was Lt-Gen. Lewis H. Brereton. Since his early experiences in 1918 as Billy Mitchell's long-suffering staff officer, charged with the impossible task of launching the world's first divisional airborne assault without parachutes or aircraft, he had pursued a successful career in the US Army Air Corps. Now he found himself in command of an organization which would have gladdened Mitchell's heart, a total projection of airpower with an airman at its head.

Brereton's charter did not entrust him with the field command of airborne operations; this was vested in his deputy, Lt-Gen. Browning, who would act as a temporary Airborne Corps Commander whenever more than a single division was deployed operationally. Browning also doubled as commander of 1st British Airborne Corps. The other major components of Brereton's command were the XVIII US Airborne Corps under Lt-Gen. Ridgway, the British 52nd Division in the air transported role, and IX Troop Carrier Command USAAF. 38 and 46 Groups RAF were also to be placed under Brereton's command for specific operations.

Throughout the summer of 1944, those airborne units left out of the Normandy landing stood poised in England, ready for immediate use on operations which never took place.

Between 13 June and 10 September no less than 16 major airborne operations were planned at short notice by 1st Allied Airborne Army or 1st British Airborne Corps. All were cancelled, either because the situation they were designed to meet failed to materialize, or because the speed of the Allied advance rendered them superfluous.

By 11 September, the 2nd British Army had reached the end of a breathless 12-day advance which had taken it 280 miles from the River Seine to the banks of the Escaut Canal. As no major Channel ports had been taken, the lines of communication stretched back to the Normandy beaches. There was an acute shortage of logistic transport, Gen. Patton having appropriated the lion's share to provision his even more spectacular advance into Alsace-Lorraine. For the British, there was barely enough road transport to carry one corps forward from the Escaut Canal, providing opposition was of the lightest. Montgomery, now determined to use the Allied airborne forces to provide an 'airborne carpet' over the rivers, selected Lt-Gen. Brian Horrocks's 30th Corps as the formation which would drive up the 'carpet' and north from Arnhem to the shores of the Zuider Zee, cutting off the German forces in the Scheldt estuary and enabling the port of Antwerp to be opened as the Allied forward base.

Brereton's staff now turned to planning their part in this bold and ambitious operation, which was collectively named *Market Garden*.

Market was the airborne part, designed to assist 2nd Army in its advance towards the Zuider Zee, using the 1st Allied Airborne Corps, whose specific aim, as stated in the Corps Operation Instruction of 13 September, was to 'capture and hold crossings over the canals and rivers on 2nd Army's main axis of advance from about Eindhoven to inclusive Arnhem'. Operation *Garden* was the advance of 2nd Army from the line of the Albert and Escaut Canals in Belgium, up to the Zuider Zee.

Hitherto, 2nd Army had been advancing on an east-north-easterly axis. Now it was required to send 30th Corps off on a line running north-north-east, with undefeated enemy forces on each side of its axis. Only one road could be used; it ran up through flat open terrain imposing severe limits on free cross-country movement even by tracked vehicles. There were dozens of minor water-courses and drainage canals as well as the main water obstacles. For much of the way the road, which was only wide enough to permit traffic two abreast, lay on embankments above the flat landscape. Unlike the 'airborne carpet' used by the Germans in 1940, which had pointed like a spear directly into the vitals of the Dutch nation, the line of *Garden* lay off at a tangent. In the language of 18th-century warfare such an advance would have been defined as being 'formed to a flank' – a condition regarded as highly fraught with danger as it enabled a robust enemy to sever the supply lines to the attacking units at the spearhead of the advance; and this is exactly what happened to 1st Airborne Division at Arnhem.

In planning *Market Garden* the Allies gave way to a forgivable spirit of optimism. It was thought that if the airborne landings succeeded in taking the key bridges intact, 30th Corps would be on the shore of the Zuider Zee between two and five days after crossing the Dutch border. The weather forecast for the three days following 17 September, the selected D-Day, was good. A cheerful atmosphere was in the air following the delirious liberation of Brussels on 3 September by the Guards Armoured Division. Victory could be sensed and the 'home-by-Christmas' attitude was further encouraged when Eisenhower's HQ, from far away in the Cotentin Peninsula, issued a euphoric appreciation in the opening days of September describing the German Army as '. . . no longer a cohesive force, but a number of fugitive battle groups. . . . Organised resistance under the control of the German High Command is unlikely to continue beyond 1 December . . . (and) may end even sooner.' There had, in fact, been a short period in the first week of September when *Market Garden* would have succeeded, but Eisenhower did not move forward to Brussels until 10 September, a week after assuming direct operational command, and it was not until two days later that he at last gave a belated referee's decision favouring Montgomery's thrust in the north rather than Bradley's and Patton's in the centre. Montgomery had for weeks pressed for a single, 40-division on-slaught across the Rhine – either on his front or Bradley's. Eisenhower had so far stood out for steady pressure right across the front. This hesitation gave the Germans just enough breathing space to sort out their defences, get into position and await the inevitable Allied attack wherever it came. But whatever Eisenhower had decided in his Normandy HQ, 400 miles to the rear, was irrelevant; he was not even in direct radio or telephone contact with Montgomery and Bradley, his chief field commanders. Even after agreeing to giving priority to Montgomery's thrust-line he continued to assign the major share of his road transport resources to Patton's 3rd Army in Lorraine, allow-ing it to devour fuel, ammunition and supplies and privately carping when Montgomery protested that 2nd Army's attack had been in-adequately provisioned, a factor which accounts in part for the 30th Corps' hesitant advance to the relief of Arnhem.

The Germans, since their crushing defeat in Normandy, had acted with astonishing vigour to prepare the defences of the Fatherland. Early in August, virtually nothing but the remnants of 25 divisions had stood between the Allies and Berlin, yet between 12 and 17 September they doubled their combat strength in the *Market Garden* area alone. Eisenhower's delay in opting for the northern thrust gave time for Hitler to form the new divisions, calling up 16-year-olds, *Luftwaffe* ground crews, civilians in reserved occupations, training units, the medically unfit, invalids and convalescents, sailors without ships – all there thrown forward to the Rhine. The Allies expected that *Market Garden* would be opposed by nothing larger than a bri-gade and a few tanks and guns; on the other hand, they over-rated the German *Flak* defences and this resulted in many of the airborne dropzones being chosen too far from the objectives. But although the latter stages of the approach flight might be dangerous, the actual seizure of the bridges, it was thought, would be '. . . a matter of sur-prise and confusion, rather than hard fighting'.

The Germans had other ideas. Behind the Albert Canal lay the German 1st Parachute Army. Student had formed it within ten days of his appointment as its commander earlier in the summer. His presence generated high morale at once and he knew he had a good fighting force at his disposal despite its mixed composition; the ex-perienced parachutists had been reinforced with drafts from dis-banded *Luftwaffe* formations and even included aircrew for whom no planes could be found. Student's HQ was at Vught, near 's-Hertogenbosch, less than ten miles off the proposed 30th Corps axis, and his units were admirably well placed to act against the Eindhoven–Arnhem road.

More recently arrived in the area was an equally formidable formation whose presence was discounted entirely by British intelligence despite frantic but unheeded warnings from the Dutch Underground. Since 7 September II *SS Panzerkorps* had been in the Arnhem area. It was admittedly a shadow of what it had been in Normandy prior to the Allied breakout, but nevertheless a force to be reckoned with. At the beginning of the month it was still edging back across Belgium and got into Arnhem undetected, to refit and rest. Its commander was *SS Obergruppenführer und General der Waffen SS* Wilhelm Bittrich. He had the remnants of two *Panzer* divisions under command. The 9th *Hohenstaufen*, consisting of an armoured infantry regiment, an artillery battalion, two batteries of assault guns, an armoured reconnaissance battalion, a company of *Panzer* tanks and various engineer and signals units, was under the temporary command of *SS Obersturmbannführer* Walther Harzer. The 10th *Frondsberg* under *SS Gruppenführer und Generalmajor der Waffen SS* Heinz Harmel, had lost almost all its armour at Falaise; it could now assemble an armoured infantry regiment, two artillery battalions and one battalion apiece of engineers, anti-aircraft and armoured reconnaissance. Bittrich's Corps was therefore effectively down to the strength of a weak Division.

Apart from these units in the very areas where the Allied airborne force was to land was the HQ of *Generalfeldmarschall* Walther Model, commanding Army Group 'B', who had installed himself comfortably in an hotel at Oosterbeek, a suburb of Arnhem destined to become 1st Airborne Division's sacrificial altar. The fighting strength of the Germans in the Eindhoven–Nijmegen–Arnhem area was augmented by a number of units gathered from all arms and branches of the *Wehrmacht*.

Of the airborne forces comprising Browning's Airborne Corps, 1st British Airborne Division had seen no action since its mixed experience in Sicily over a year before. Now at full strength it had spent a miserable summer, constantly at a high degree of readiness for repeatedly cancelled operations. Frustration had taken its toll, and although many of its personnel approached the forthcoming operation with eagerness, many – convinced that this too would be cancelled – were either apathetic or overstressed. The American 82nd and 101st Airborne Divisions, however, had both been heavily involved in the Normandy landings; they had been rested and reinforced and were at concert pitch once more, as their subsequent performance would show. The 1st Polish Parachute Brigade was a newcomer to the airborne scene, having only been formed two months previously. It was commanded by Maj.-Gen. Stanislaw Sosabowski who from the outset foresaw a bitter fight ahead and who did not share the general feeling of optimism in the Allied camp.

Montgomery's plan for the use of the Allied Airborne Army in *Market Garden* was governed by a number of factors outside his control. He had chosen 17 September as his D-day, this being the earliest possible date by which 30th Corps could be readied for its dash up the corridor to Arnhem and beyond. As this was a moonless period a night airborne landing was out of the question, for although Browning and 1st Airborne Division had every confidence that 38 and 46 Groups RAF were capable of delivering them accurately by night, no such confidence in the USAAF existed on the American side; memories of Sicily and Normandy were still uncomfortably vivid. For the first time, therefore, the Allied airborne troops were committed to an assault in broad daylight. The condition for success was overwhelming air support to suppress *Flak* and to keep the *Luftwaffe* out of the sky and at last this was feasible. Daylight landings, argued the Americans, would result in great accuracy of landing and thus a quicker concentration, particularly of the parachute units, resulting in tactical surprise. However, the risk from unsuppressed *Flak* was far greater by day; not only would the transport fleet have to be very carefully routed to avoid the anti-aircraft defences along the Dutch coast and across occupied Holland, but the dropzones, over which the transports and gliders were particularly vulnerable, would have to be well clear of the *Flak* concentrations. One of these was known to be centred around Deelen airfield only three miles north of Arnhem bridge, and the RAF insisted on using dropzones well clear of this area of high risk, but up to seven miles away from the bridge itself.

The plan, in outline, was as follows. 1st Airborne Division, to be followed in later by 1st Polish Parachute Brigade, was to capture the bridges at Arnhem (one road and one rail, plus a pontoon bridge and a vehicular ferry) and establish a bridgehead on the north bank of the Nederrijn through which 30th Corps could advance towards the Zuider Zee. 82nd Airborne Division was to seize crossings at Grave and Nijmegen and the higher ground between Nijmegen and Groesbeek. Browning's Corps HQs, travelling by glider, would also land in this, the central divisional area. At the southern end of the 'airborne carpet', 101st Airborne Division was to capture the bridges and potential 'choke points' between Grave and Eindhoven. Once an airborne bridgehead had been secured at Arnhem, an American airborne engineer battalion and a battery of gliderborne light anti-

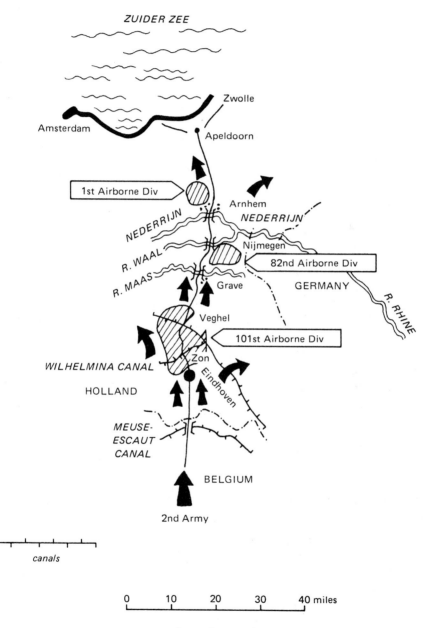

'THE AIRBORNE CARPET'
MARKET GARDEN: The Plan

ZUIDER ZEE

Zwolle

Amsterdam

Apeldoorn

1st Airborne Div

Arnhem

NEDERRIJN

NEDERRIJN

R. WAAL

Nijmegen

R. MAAS

82nd Airborne Div

Grave

GERMANY

R. RHINE

Veghel

101st Airborne Div

WILHELMINA CANAL

Zon

HOLLAND

Eindhoven

MEUSE-
ESCAUT
CANAL

BELGIUM

2nd Army

canals

0   10   20   30   40 miles

Approximate scale

aircraft guns would be landed to construct and protect additional airstrips into which the 52nd Lowland Division could be flown as soon as the tactical situation permitted.

38 and 46 Groups would provide the pathfinder and glider towing support for the Arnhem lift and Browning's Corps HQ as well as all subsequent aerial resupply to 1st Airborne Division; the US IX Troop Carrier Command would carry the main parachute drops for all three airborne divisions and the subsequent fly-in of the airportable formations. IX USTCC would also provide the entire airlift support for 82 and 101 Divisions. As there was insufficient transport aircraft to carry the Allied Airborne Army in one lift, the landings would have to be spread over three days. This, of course, meant accepting a loss of concentration in the first landings and was one of the factors prompting Browning's celebrated remark that perhaps 21 Army Group was going 'a bridge too far' in attempting to seize the Arnhem bridgehead. Both he and Maj.-Gen. 'Freddy' Urquhart, the commander of 1st Airborne, were uneasy about 30th Corps' ability to relieve them in 48 hours, as well as having to accept dropzones for 1st Airborne so far from the bridge; even if the landings achieved total surprise, their purport would be all too clear to any intelligent German in the area. It would be at least an hour before Urquhart's first troops could assemble and move off towards the bridge and it was impossible to believe that the Arnhem garrison, plus any other Germans in the area, would not be waiting eagerly to take on the British as they made their way through the built-up area of the town towards their objective. Chatterton, now Browning's Glider Commander, added his doubts, and volunteered to lead a glider *coup-de-main* onto the open ground immediately to the south of Arnhem bridge. Here, although the fields were small and a number of high-tension wires criss-crossed the land, there was a good chance of bringing such an operation off despite the risk; but the RAF would not expose their tug aircraft to the Deelen guns and to the considerable amount of light *Flak* certain to be posted in Arnhem town.

An elaborate offensive air support plan was planned. All known *Flak* positions en route to the combat area would be heavily attacked on D-day and throughout the following days. Twenty-four hours before the assault, RAF Bomber Command were to attack enemy *Flak* positions and fighter airfields in the area; they would also drop dummy paratroops elsewhere in Holland and near Emmerich on the Rhine on the night of 17 September. Armed reconnaissance in the dropzone area was to be carried out by 83 Group of the RAF's 2nd Tactical Air Force, but in order to avoid mis-identifications and confusion this would cease 25 minutes before the first landings. Further away from the operational area, diversionary activities would be staged by RAF Coastal Command.

By 15 September the troops, at their mounting airfields, listened to yet another briefing in their sealed camps with a mixture of indifference and cheerful cynicism. On the evening of 16 September, having received a good weather report for the morrow, Brereton signalled all units that the operation would take place the next morning.

D-day dawned fair, with slight haze and a light westerly wind. The pathfinders for 1st Airborne were away first, 20 minutes before the main stream which began to lift off at 1025. Within half an hour an aerial armada of 1544 transport aircraft had set course, bearing Browning's gliderborne HQ, all the paratroops of 82nd and 101st Divisions, a parachute brigade and half the airlanding Brigade of 1st Airborne. The offensive air support plan rose to a crescendo, watched with awe by the Dutch civilian population on their way to church, and with considerable suspicion by the Germans who, as yet, had no clear idea of what lay in store. None of 1st Airborne Division's aircraft or gliders was lost on the way, but 35 American transports and 13 gliders were shot down on their more southerly route. In the wreck of one of these gliders, brought down near Student's HQ at Vught, a full set of operation orders and marked maps for Operation *Market* were found on the body of an American officer who had taken them in wanton contravention of every principle of field security. Within two hours these papers were being studied eagerly by the Commander, 1st Parachute Army, and his delighted staff. They provided full details of all Allied dropzones, timings and objectives; the cat was well and truly out of the bag.

Major-General Maxwell Taylor's 101st Division encountered fierce anti-aircraft fire during the last 20 minutes of its flight but the landings were a huge success. His three parachute infantry regiments – 501st, 502nd and 506th – dashed off to take the Willems Canal bridge at Veghel, a bridge over the Wilhelmina Canal at Zon, and the key road junction of St Oedenrode. Brigadier General James Gavin's 82nd, tasked with the multiple objectives of the great Nijmegen bridge, the Groesbeek upland and the more distant Grave bridge, had possibly the most difficult job of all. Because of the *Flak* risk, they could not be landed close aboard the bridges and their dropzones and glider landingzones were all east of Groesbeek village, perilously close to the German frontier, which actually ran along the edge of both the glider fields. In full view to the south-east was the uninviting and sinister mass of the Reichswald Forest, which lay on German soil and from which Gavin correctly expected a lot of trouble.

Also landed in 82nd Division's area was Browning's Airborne

Corps HQ. Heading the cavalcade was the Corps Commander's glider, flown by Chatterton the senior glider-pilot officer, who was struck by the immense gaiety of the scene as the gliders were unloaded. Browning's turn-out was, as always, immaculate. With a flourish he undid a package containing a small silken flag bearing the Airborne symbol of Bellerophon riding his winged horse Pegasus.

The advanced HQ included a small signals detachment and Browning's personal chef, armed with a supply of additional delicacies and wine. It was a happy and well-knit HQ, for many of whose members this was an initiation into combat soldiering. During the first few hours there was some skirmishing as isolated parties of surprised Germans appeared to be promptly engaged by staff officers, clerks and signallers. Unfortunately, Browning's field HQ proved totally incapable of managing the battle for reasons which began to make themselves apparent within an hour or so of landing.

The Allied Airborne Army had been in existence for only a few weeks, and Brereton's organization for co-ordinating and commanding a major operation was in a rudimentary stage of evolution. The Airborne Corps signals units were even less effective, having been formed since the beginning of August with untrained drafts to support a minor operation in Brittany which never took place, then hurriedly expanded from 200 to 500 personnel for the *Market Garden* operation. Complex signals networks had to be improvised in a few days; there was no time for collective training or rehearsal and as there was no common cipher for Allied airborne forces a large increment of American signallers was included at the last minute. Their standard of training was poor, especially in the vital field of long-range high-frequency signalling under difficult atmospheric conditions. The British had not yet developed an organization to provide communications between front-line combat airborne units and the aircraft providing them with close air support, and American signals detachments were lent to 1st Airborne Division for the operation. Of the gliderborne ground–air signals party assigned to the Arnhem landing no trace has ever been found after their take-off from England in a CG4 glider. Extra American high-powered radio equipment loaned to 1st Airborne was manned by semi-trained operators who never had the chance of pre-operational practice and with no knowledge of British Army signal procedures.

The worst signalling problems, however, were associated with the high-frequency sets used for battle-field communication. Many of the key signals links were in the notoriously 'difficult' 15–18-mile range – from Browning's HQ forward to Urquhart's, and to 30th Corps, 2nd Army and 21st Army Group in the rear. The field signals plan had been put together with no time for consultation between Browning's HQ in England, the widely scattered Airborne Divisional HQs, and those of 30th Corps and 2nd Army in Belgium. A vast amount of information on ciphers, radio frequencies, codewords, callsigns and the allocation of radio equipment had to be drawn up and disseminated in the space of a few days. Frequency selection was a hit-and-miss affair, resulting in the selection of many which for technical reasons were ill suited to the *Market Garden* area or already over congested and in actual use by other formations in the theatre.

Very soon after landing, Browning's chief signals officer was obliged to tell his commander that although he was in touch with 82nd Airborne a few miles away, and with the rear Corps HQ back in England, there was no sound from 101st Airborne or – more ominously – from Urquhart. A liaison detachment from HQ 2nd Army were in contact with their own HQ, but that was all. Browning agreed to moving his HQ to see if more favourable radio reception could be found. As the operators worked to set up their aerials in the new location, darkness fell and high-frequency signals began to fade away altogether – a normal phenomenon.

Throughout the afternoon there appeared to be no great cause for alarm at Arnhem. The glider and parachute landings up on the heath land north-west of Arnhem had something of an air of a training exercise. Opposition in the early stages was sporadic, and the main difficulty was keeping the dropzones clear of curious and elated Dutch citizens who, convinced that liberation had arrived, threw caution to the winds and pressed long-hoarded stocks of food and drink on the bemused troops. There was an initial hold-up when it was found that a number of armed jeeps of the divisional airborne reconnaissance unit had gone astray or had been irreparably damaged on landing. Frost, as a battalion commander tasked with moving off at once towards the bridges, fretted impotently. He knew full well what every minute's delay meant; it gave the surprised Germans time to think things out, regroup, size up the strength of the landing and – above all else – to fling any troops they could lay hands on in the direct path of 1st Parachute Brigade as its three battalions at last set off on foot towards Arnhem.

The alarm had been sounded at the HQ of the 2nd *SS Panzer* Corps just before 1400 hrs. *SS Obersturmbannführer* Walther Harzer of the 9th *Hohenstaufen* Division had started the day agreeably by driving out to Deelen where he was to invest one of his officers, *SS Hauptsturmführer* Gräbner, with the Knight's Cross of the Iron Cross for his conduct in Normandy. As he prepared to make the award in front of the serried ranks of Gräbner's unit, all eyes turned upwards as a crescendo of aircraft engines was followed by the alarming sight of a stream of C47s, barely 500 feet above the trees. From the rear door of every aircraft trailed bundles of static lines, a sure sign that a massed parachute drop had come down close at hand. *Generalfeldmarschall* Model was enjoying his lunch in the Tafelberg Hotel at Oosterbeek when word reached him that parachutists and gliders were landing on Renkum Heath, just up the road. Model and his staff decamped rapidly and drove to join Bittrich.

On his way through Arnhem, the *Feldmarschall* called in on the HQ of the Arnhem Garrison whose commander, *Generalmajor* Küssin, was already carrying out his well-rehearsed counter-airborne plans. In a moment of misplaced enthusiasm, Küssin left the relative security of his HQ to contact his troops to the west of the town. He ignored their warnings, set out back towards Arnhem, and almost at once suffered the same fate as had the Commander of 91st Division in Normandy. Küssin's car ran headlong into a platoon of paratroops and he died in a hail of fire.

The closest German unit to the British dropzones was the *Panzergrenadier* Reserve and Training Battalion commanded by *SS Sturmbannführer* Sepp Krafft. He quickly divined 1st Airborne's intentions and deployed his men across the line of march from Renkum Heath to Arnhem town.

At Vught, Student and his staff watched the great stream of transports and gliders pass overhead. The airborne pioneer looked on with mixed emotions. 'How I wish that I had ever had such a powerful force at my disposal,' he remarked wistfully to his Chief of Staff.

Once Student had examined the operational orders taken from the crashed Waco, no time was lost in passing the crucial information to every unit within reach. So, although numerically thin on the ground (despite its resounding title, Student's Parachute Army had a fighting strength of less than 15,000) the Germans were able to apply effective force at all the most vulnerable points of the Allied operation. Of these, none was more sensitive than the route up which the Guards Armoured Division had set out earlier in the day, followed more slowly by 30th Corps' infantry. The Irish Guards, leading the spearhead, had run into trouble almost at once, losing tanks to fire from well-emplaced 88mm guns sited on the flanks of the advance. The narrow road became blocked with knocked-out tanks; behind them the rest of the Guards Division lay immobile and telescoped. By last light on 17 September the advance had ground to a halt fully six miles south of Eindhoven and only eight miles north of the start-line they had left so confidently at 1435 hrs.

H-hour for *Market* had been 1300 hrs and the first landings had gone in promptly at Arnhem. However, despite the imperative need to reach the bridges as soon as possible, the first units of Urquhart's command only started to leave their dropzones at 1500 hrs. They were all marching parachute battalions; the more heavily equipped Air Landing Brigade commanded by Brig. 'Pip' Hicks was to defend the landing areas and make them secure for the follow-up waves due in on the 18th and 19th. Although a quick rush for the bridges in any vehicles which could be assembled would have stood a good chance of getting into downtown Arnhem by 1400 hrs, the gambler's throw was not made. Such vehicles as did accompany the parachute battalions, some towing 6-pounder guns which subsequently played a leading part in the fight, moved off at walking pace with the troops, to the accompaniment of a rousing reception from the delighted Dutch.

As afternoon drew on into evening the opposition stiffened and the three battalions were increasingly forced to halt, deploy, locate the enemy and attack. The Germans, still thin on the ground but experts at this sort of fighting, proved almost impossible to pin down or elude. As darkness fell, Frost's 2nd Battalion, most of 1st Parachute Brigade's HQ less its commander, part of the brigade's parachute engineer squadron and a platoon of Royal Army Service Corps, all dog-tired, arrived at the north end of the road bridge, which they found abandoned by its immediate garrison of elderly reservists. A bold attempt to cross over to the south bank was frustrated by well-aimed fire and the British formed a tight bridgehead, determined to hold out until the vanguard of 30th Corps drove into sight from the south. At most, they expected to wait for 24 hours. The other two parachute battalions of the 1st Brigade never reached the bridge. They were engulfed in a street battle of great ferocity and before the end of the evening had begun to lose tactical cohesion. Their short-range radios performed badly amidst the trees and houses of suburban Arnhem and they lost contact with their brigade and divisional HQs early in the afternoon.

Urquhart, in his field command post on the edge of the dropzones, found himself in an unenviable position; he was out of contact with his own forward troops as well as his immediately superior HQ. With nightfall, the situation seemed worse. German probing attacks were now coming in from all sides against the airlanding brigade, and the limited amount of information coming from the Arnhem direction indicated that his troops were in trouble there. He called for Hicks, appointed him to act in his place at divisional HQ, and set out by jeep for the embattled town, little realizing that he would be absent, cut off by the fighting and a fugitive in hiding, for 39 hours; and although the follow-up waves duly came in on D + 1 and D + 2, his division and its battle were irreversibly lost by midnight on the first day.

A day-by-day account of *Market Garden* is outside the province of this book. The heroism of those involved on both sides has been recognized in literally hundreds of publications, and there is space here for descriptions of only a few incidents, chosen to illustrate the virtues and defects of airborne forces restricted, as were Browning's in 1944, by the physical impossibility of redeploying them by air, or even withdrawing them altogether, once it became apparent – as it did at Arnhem within 24 hours – that the Germans had reacted so effectively, not only to the local threat but also to that posed by the perilously exposed advance of 30th Corps up the Eindhoven–Nijmegen axis.

The 4th Parachute Brigade, which duly dropped onto the heath on the afternoon of D + 1, was commanded by an outstanding soldier–scholar, Brig. John 'Shan' Hackett. He had entered the army via Oxford University and was, unusually for the commander of a Parachute Brigade, a cavalryman. His brigade's task was originally to move onto the higher ground known as the Westerbouwing, north of Arnhem town, and hold it against the German counter-attacks which were bound to come from that direction. Back in England his men had been disappointed to hear that because of the shortage of aircraft they would be dropping 24 hours after the 1st Parachute Brigade and Airlanding Brigade. The rumour had even got around that by the time they arrived at Arnhem the Guards would have swept across the Nederrijn and that they would land amongst the administrative units moving up in support of the armoured thrust to the Zuider Zee. Hackett disabused his officers of this delusion and having discovered something of the progress of the first day's fighting was personally prepared for the worst. In the event, reality outdid imagination. He arrived at Arnhem to find himself under Hicks's command, for Urquhart was still lost and there was no trace of Brig. Gerald Lathbury, commanding 1st Parachute Brigade, or of the commanding officers of the three parachute battalions which had gone forward. Lathbury was in fact already badly wounded and in Arnhem. One of the colonels was dead. Frost was pinned down with his embattled force on the bridge. Hicks, though technically Hackett's junior, was in the unenviable position of having to dismember the newly arrived brigade and commit it piecemeal to a battle of whose actual course he was more or less ignorant. There was a flaming confrontation between the two men – Hicks, almost exhausted and still commanding the Airlanding Brigade in its fight to hold on to the dropzones; Hackett, fresh and untried as an airborne commander, impatient for battle and eager to launch his fine brigade at the enemy. By nightfall,

4th Parachute Brigade had virtually ceased to exist, having been drawn into a battle aptly referred to by the Germans as *Der Hexenkessel* – 'the witches' cauldron'.

As the second day drew to a close, *Market Garden* was proving to be a mixture of triumph and calamity. The 101st to the south had fought off a series of German attacks and were still in possession of their initial objectives; they had taken Eindhoven, made contact with 30th Corps shortly after midday, and by sundown had linked up with the Guards fighting up from the south. The 82nd, advancing into Nijmegen town, reached the great bridge and found it still firmly in German hands. As the day wore on, there was increasing pressure from the enemy in the Reichswald, but the welcome arrival of the divisional artillery by glider enabled the 82nd to fight off the challenge. Only two facets of the operation seemed to be in question – the advance of 30th Corps, which had made such disappointing progress – less than 9 miles in 24 hours, and Urquhart's hard-pressed division, with whom Browning was virtually incommunicado.

Aerial reconnaissance indicated that a tremendous battle was raging at Arnhem bridge, whose northern approaches were liberally spread with burning German vehicles. Beyond that, nothing was known. 1st Airborne Division, by the evening of 18 September, was in fact no longer a cohesive fighting formation. Bereft of its commander, and with virtually a total communications failure, it was acting like a beheaded wasp, writhing and stinging furiously, but deprived of all power of co-ordination.

Forty-eight hours on from the first landings, and two more factors were decisively weighing the scales against Urquhart's men. The weather over the British Isles had deteriorated and only a few airfields could be used by the aircraft meant to resupply 1st Airborne, the gliders bringing in the first lift of the Polish Brigade and gliderborne reinforcements for the 82nd and 101st. Of a total of 655 aircraft and 431 gliders which took off from England 226 transports and 185 gliders failed to reach the battle area and of these, 40 aircraft and 112 gliders were shot down or were lost as the result of enemy action.

By now, German opposition on the ground was stiffening hour by hour and heavy anti-aircraft reinforcements had been rushed to the area. The *Luftwaffe* had been quick to note the total absence of RAF combat aircraft when transports and gliders were arriving to succour 1st Airborne Division, and more than 400 German fighter aircraft were directed into the area as the resupply missions came in. Due to a communications error, the Allied fighter escort which it was planned should take the transports into the edge of the operational area failed to make the rendezvous and the slow-flying stream of C47s, *Stirlings,*

Albemarles and gliders faced the fire of hundreds of guns as well as wolf-packs of fighters as they flew at 500 feet through the murky sky.

The pilots had no radio contact with 1st Airborne Division below, whose dropzones were now under continuous attack and swept by enemy fire. The troops on the ground watched in anguish as the devoted crews of the 163 aircraft of 38 and 46 Groups which reached Arnhem delivered their loads with great accuracy onto a dropzone which unknown to them was already in German hands. Frantic attempts to mark out a new dropzone on ground still in British hands failed because of heavy German fire. The courage displayed by the RAF aircrew and their RASC air despatchers now reached sublime levels.

Flight Lieutenant Lord, the pilot of a C47 *Dakota*, was approaching Arnhem when his aircraft was hit by anti-aircraft fire which ignited his starboard engine. Instead of abandoning the mission he elected to continue, as he and his crew were aware of the urgent need for their supplies to reach the airborne troops. Losing height, Lord's aircraft, streaming flame and smoke, became the target for every German gun in range. Despite this he completed an immaculate first run and then, discovering that part of the load still remained on board, he turned round and dropped the rest. Only then, with fire engulfing his wing, did Lord give the order to abandon the aircraft. Not one of his crew had jumped until then, and only one survived to tell the tale, for the wing finally gave way and the aircraft, with Lord still at the controls, crashed to the ground. The whole episode had been watched in awe by the fighting men on both sides below. Thirteen RAF transports were shot down and almost a hundred more riddled with *Flak* as they pressed home this totally useless resupply drop.

Elsewhere in the battle area on this, the third day, the operation was meeting with some success; the 101st were reinforced by a glider-borne anti-tank unit just in time to repel a determined attack on the bridge at Zon and the 82nd continued to fight in the streets of Nijmegen despite increasing pressure on their right flank from the Reichswald. By now the Guards had joined them in Nijmegen and towards the end of the day a concerted attempt was made to take the bridge, which still remained intact and unblown. The attack failed, however, and it was decided to try again next day, 20 September, using assault boats covered by close-range fire from the south bank.

At nightfall on the 19th an air of optimism still pervaded Browning's HQ. The actual situation in Arnhem was, however, getting steadily worse. Although the fugitive Urquhart had regained his own HQ at 0800 hrs that morning after a series of hair-raising adventures, his command, 12 hours later, was on the verge of disintegration. The survivors, all hope of reinforcing Frost at the bridge abandoned, were beginning to concentrate in the area of the Hartenstein Hotel in the suburb of Oosterbeek, some five miles west of the road bridge. The day's aerial resupply, as already recounted, had gone almost entirely into enemy hands. Four of Urquhart's battalions had lost contact with his HQ and never regained it; their remnants, fighting stubbornly from house to house, were borne down by the gathering weight of the German attack before they could gain the Oosterbeek perimeter; of Hackett's whole brigade, only 300 men reached it. Urquhart was aware that Lathbury was out of action and unable to command his brigade for he had been with him when he had been wounded. In any case the only remaining part of the 1st Parachute Brigade was the rapidly diminishing band under Frost's command, still grimly holding on at the north end of the bridge and denying its use to the Germans. Nevertheless, Urquhart sent Hicks's deputy, Col. Barlow, into Arnhem town to try and take command. He was never seen again.

On 20 September the weather was so bad over the airfields in England that Brereton ordered the cancellation of all but parachute supply missions and the airlift of some further artillery to 101st Division. The most dramatic event of the day was the outstanding performance of the 3rd Battalion of the 504th Parachute Infantry Regiment; although they had received no training in the use of assault boats or even in elementary watermanship, they paddled their flimsy collapsible craft across the River Waal in the face of very heavy German fire. At the crossing point the Waal is 400 yards wide and the current runs at up to six mph. The attack was mounted with the help of fire support from the Irish Guards' tanks, and from every Allied artillery unit within range. The 3rd/504th fought their way across the river, took the north end of the railway bridge and stormed on to the road bridge, arriving at its north end as the tanks of the Grenadier Guards rushed it from the south bank. It was a magnificent effort of sustained courage for the defenders had every advantage – good observation of the actual crossing, excellent fields of fire across open ground on the north bank, which was also dominated by a strongly fortified and moated position. A brisk wind dispersed the smoke screen laid to cover the crossing and the Americans suffered heavy casualties; the ferocity and sustained momentum of their attack, once on the north bank, amazed the Germans, who fled.

The Allies had now arrived on the north bank of the last water obstacle before Arnhem, where Frost's men now at the end of their tether after 72 hours' sustained fighting, were only nine miles up the road. But the tanks stayed at Nijmegen bridge. There were however no infantry to go with them; they were running out of fuel and ammunition and to take tanks on up that straight road was an open invitation to the German anti-tank gunners lying in wait. With great reluctance, Maj.-Gen. Allan Adair, the Guards Division commander, halted the advance to await replenishment and the arrival of infantry. Browning agreed with his difficult decision and plans were made to resume the march as early as possible on 21 September; this decision was passed by radio to Urquhart. But it was too late; during the night the last survivors at the bridge were forced into the open as the Germans systematically flushed them out with close-range gunfire. Frost's marvellous stand had come to an end, and the Germans could now concentrate on the elimination of what was left of 1st Airborne Division.

The operation ground on for five more days. At 2200 hrs on 25 September the remnants of 1st Airborne stealthily made their way to the riverbank, where Canadian sappers waited with assault boats. The route to safety was manned by glider pilots, who had fought splendidly throughout the battle; the withdrawal was covered by fire from the artillery of 30th Corps, which was now within range.

About 2500 reached the south bank; hundreds of wounded had to be left behind, together with the devoted medical staff and chaplains. They were generally well treated by the Germans, who by now had also fought themselves to a standstill, and who freely expressed their admiration for 1st Airborne Division's fighting qualities. Ten thousand British and Polish airborne troops had been landed at Arnhem.

For the Poles it had been a tragic experience; their commander, Sosabowski, had harboured grave doubts about the whole operation since he first listened incredulously to his initial briefing, given by Urquhart on 12 September. As a professional soldier of long standing, he at once identified the glaring weakness of the plan – the separation between landing zones and objective; he also knew the German mind and was appalled at the way in which the British seemed to under-estimate the actual strength of the enemy in and around Arnhem, and to dismiss their fighting ability. Even although he did not know that Bittrich's *Panzer* Corps was even now arriving there, he was certain that the German lines-of-communication troops would fight well to defend the gateway to the Fatherland. It had been planned to land part of the Polish Brigade by glider on the Renkum Heath landing zones and to drop the rest by parachute south of the river at Driel, in order to secure the Heveadorp ferry which could be used to augment the Arnhem bridges as 30th Corps closed in from the south. The railbridge was blown on the evening of 17 September in the faces of 1st Parachute Brigade, and despite the heroism of Frost's force the road bridge was never taken. The Poles' gliders duly arrived on the third lift on 19 September, by which time 1st Airborne Division was fighting for survival. Their paratroops, delayed repeatedly by bad weather at their airfields around Grantham, were finally dropped south of the river on the afternoon of 21 September. As the result of bad weather and intense enemy fire, only a battalion's-worth of men – about 750 – actually landed on the DZ. They never got across the river and in any case arrived too late, and in the wrong place, to be of any value in the battle. Had the Poles been dropped – as Sosabowski wished – on 17 September, close in to the road bridge, the outcome could have been totally different.

The line now stabilized between Nijmegen and Arnhem, which remained in German hands – as did most of Holland – until the last few weeks of the war. The brave Dutch population, whose assistance in battle and conduct towards the British wounded will never be forgotten by those who experienced it, were severely punished; Arnhem was forcibly depopulated and the townsfolk spent a dreadful winter as refugees. Many, identified as resistance workers, were shot out of hand. Their beautiful town lay in ruins.

No single factor caused this disaster; it was the result of a complex inter-action between a host of chance happenings and decisions. There was a basic lack of understanding by senior Allied army officers of the real meaning of air warfare – even by some in senior airborne appointments. Quite early on it had been accepted that until the airborne troops landed, any operation was an *air* operation and therefore the entire responsibility of the airforce commander. This was essentially a sensible concept, but it did not allow the soldiers to insist on the choice of dropzones and landing zones. For the Arnhem landings, these were selected by the air commanders and they elected to go for Renkum Heath because it was clear of the known German *Flak* positions; the soldiers' protests were over-ruled and 1st Airborne Division lost its chance of achieving surprise – the key weapon of airborne troops – before the first aircraft took off from England. By landing so far out, the British gave the Germans time to deploy and for Model to escape from his HQ at Oosterbeek. Delays on the dropzone and the inexplicable loss of the reconnaissance jeeps allowed the advantage to slip almost at once from the attackers. The Germans had been underestimated in every possible sense; not only was Allied intelligence inaccurate, but no allowance was made for the surprising fighting quality of the *ad hoc* units thrown in against 1st Airborne Division. All these, whether administrative, training,

Luftwaffe or naval, had been well trained in anti-airborne drills: aggressive action; quick identification of the attacker's objective (all too obvious at Arnhem) and its occupation before the airborne troops could reach it; destruction of the airborne force before it could be resupplied or reinforced; its isolation from any ground troops sent to its relief; all these were achieved except for initial occupation of the Arnhem road bridges, and the brief German failure here was only because the old men detailed to guard it ran away.

It was sad that the offensive air support given to 1st Airborne Division failed to match that provided by the transport crews of the USAAF and 38 and 46 Groups RAF. In the original Airborne Corps *Market Garden* plan 83 Group RAF was specifically tasked with providing tactical air support with its fighter-bombers, and American 'air support parties' were attached to the three Allied airborne divisions, to Browning's Corps HQ, and to the 52nd Lowland Division, the formation assigned to Browning for use in the air-landing role. The task of these parties on landing was to open up their VHF radios, establish contact with aircraft overhead, indicate their own position on the ground with fluorescent panels or yellow smoke (which assumed the total absence of German aircraft) and direct fighter-bomber attacks onto enemy troops. As already mentioned, the two air-support parties allotted to 1st Airborne Division were never seen or heard from once the operation took off from England. The others proved to be undertrained and communications suffered as a result. Although 83 Group received copies of the operation instruction of *Market Garden* and were repeatedly asked by Browning's staff to exchange liaison officers, they did not acknowledge any of the Airborne Corps' signals, letters or messages. Once battle was joined on the ground, it was impossible for 83 Group's aircraft to fly over the *Market Garden* area whilst the transport lifts were in progress, a procedural weakness quickly exploited by the *Luftwaffe*. Apart from the lack of communications between the airborne troops and 83 Group, the weather (which had been confidently predicted as fair) had a consistently adverse effect on Allied air operations. Low cloud bases and poor visibility added to the troubles of all aircrew involved.

The final failure of joint service staffwork is epitomized in the haggling over provision of forward fighter airstrips in the *Market Garden* area, and over the use of the airfield at Oud Keent, two miles west of Grave. Its existence was unknown to the Allies when *Market Garden* was planned and 82nd Airborne Division were agreeably surprised to discover the grass landing ground during the first 24 hours. It was large enough for C47s to land and take off and would have been ideal as an airhead for the 52nd Division, assigned to Browning's command but not used in the role for which it would have been ideally suited – to augment the overstretched infantry of the 82nd in Nijmegen and then secure the flanks of the road north to Arnhem in order to allow the Guards Armoured Division to make their dash for the fateful bridge. The Airborne Corps post-mortem on the operation stressed the point that extra supplies and extra infantry would have been invaluable; these could easily have been flown into Oud Keent; instead, repeated attempts were made to drop supplies by parachute – at best an inefficient method of resupply and at Arnhem in particular a totally ineffective one – and of bringing in reinforcements by glider and parachute drop, neither of which was as accurate or economic as airlanding them in transport aircraft. In the end, Oud Keent fulfilled its role as an airhead for only 24 hours; on 26 September 209 C47s of the USAAF brought in supplies and reinforcements for the two American airborne divisions and evacuated the American glider pilots who, as in all previous major operations, had mostly been spectators of the fighting, not having been equipped or trained to take part in the land battle. Ironically, the airfield had been marked out for the occasion and was operated by surviving British glider pilots, whose versatility was now a by-word. The next day, Browning's headquarters was abruptly told that at 1930 hrs 83 Group would take over the field as an advanced fighter base and that air transport operations were to cease at once.

Even in defeat, the captured survivors of Arnhem continued to display the high standards of morale and resilience which had now come to be associated with airborne troops. Bittrich, in his post-combat report, wrote, '. . . I consider it a point of honour to do justice to our opponents in the battle area Nijmegen–Arnhem. These British troops were the same type of hardbitten soldiers with excellent professional training that had been fighting us since the beginning of the invasion . . . even after defeat these men left the battlefield with their morale intact.'

Many were resolved to escape as quickly as possible, despite grievous wounds and inadequate medical attention. Captain Eric Mackay, a sapper, had fought to the end at Arnhem bridge; wounded before capture, he was bayonetted as he lay exhausted in the road alongside the blazing house from which he had been flushed; within a few days he had escaped from his captors just inside Germany, paddled a small boat down the Maas to Nijmegen, and rejoined other 1st Division survivors as they passed through on their way back to England.

Brigadier Hackett, seriously wounded and left behind to be cared for by his captors, got away and was cared for by a succession of devoted Dutch people who willingly shared their scanty supplies of food in order to keep him alive. He, too, eventually returned to Allied lines.

Colonel Warrack, 1st Airborne Division's senior medical officer, stayed with the wounded and badgered their captors to ensure the best possible treatment; the Germans were themselves by now desperately short of medical supplies but did their best. Only when he was satisfied that everything possible had been done for his patients did Warrack make his escape; he, too, was cared for by Dutch families for many days until he could escape down-river into friendly territory.

Major Anthony Deane-Drummond of the Royal Signals was already a practised escaper. As a subaltern he had dropped in southern Italy for the ill-fated Operation *Colossus* and, escaping from prison camp, regained safety after a series of amazing adventures. At Arnhem his major preoccupation was with the establishment of communications between Urquhart's HQ and 1st Parachute Brigade as its battalions fought to reach Arnhem bridge on that first calamitous evening. Drawn inexorably into the dog-fight in the town, he and his party of infantry and signallers were trapped in a house for three days before being captured on 22 September. Temporarily held for interrogation in a house near Arnhem he hid himself in a cupboard where he remained for 13 days, subsisting on a few crusts of bread and some water. For most of this time the room in which he was hidden was occupied by Germans who used it for questioning prisoners. Eventually he extricated himself and was spirited by the indefatigable Dutch Resistance back to safety in Nijmegen.

★   ★   ★

After *Market Garden* both sides were in urgent need of a respite; the Allies to establish proper lines of communication and supply, the Germans to prepare for the decisive stroke which Hitler was certain would knock out his opponents in the West.

On 8 December Student was finally let into the secret of the great offensive long promised by Hitler and given the airborne task. He was horrified to be told that D-day was only eight days ahead, which gave almost no time to allot units and find transport aircraft. The OKW plan involved throwing the last reserves of the *Wehrmacht* at a weak section of the Allied front in the Ardennes with the aim of driving a wedge between the Americans and British and seizing Antwerp with its vast reserves of fuel and supplies. The forces available for the actual thrust were the 6th *SS Panzer*, 5th *Panzer* and 7th Armies, a total of 10 armoured and 14 infantry divisions.

Although often mis-named 'the Runstedt offensive' its command lay with *Generalfeldmarschall* Walther Model's Army Group 'B'. The plan was Hitler's own creation and 'Nicht abändern!' (not to be modified!) was scribbled in his own hand. He consulted neither von Runstedt the C-in-C in the West, nor Model. Although both of them begged to be allowed to try for a less ambitious objective, such as regaining the line of the River Meuse, they failed to move their warlord, who had recovered his optimism as the bombardment of London and Antwerp with the V2 missile intensified.

Lack of resources placed severe limitations on the scope of the airborne role in *Kondor*, as the operation was codenamed. The available transport lift permitted the drop of only two weak parachute battalions and even then the planes had to be scraped together from all over the *Reich* and assembled at the last minute on the launching airfields south of Hanover. Student chose the leader of the force with care – *Oberstleutant* von der Heydte, who had first made his name in Crete but who had not obtained subsequent promotion, probably due to his luke-warm support for the Nazi party.

Von der Heydte had fought in north Africa as an infantry battalion commander and had survived El Alamein and the subsequent retreat; later he was in Italy, where his parachute unit played a key role in the seizure of Rome after the Italians had changed sides in 1943. In Normandy his 6th Parachute Regiment fought so well that it became known as the 'Lion of Carentan'. During *Market Garden*, commanding his depleted regiment, he had fought to cut the narrow corridor from Eindhoven to Arnhem. Throughout the last year he had been in great pain as the result of a road accident which had broken his left arm and shoulder but was still jumping regularly and was now commanding a parachute training school. Even he blenched when given the task for his combat group in *Kondor*. He was to recruit a force of 1000 men, to drop deep behind the American lines in order to capture a series of important road junctions. There was only a week in which to gather his men, equip and restrain them, and assemble the transport force. Von der Heydte knew from the start that his chances of success were slender and he appealed personally to Model for the plan to be reconsidered or scrapped. Model agreed with Heydte's assessment but refused to alter the *Führer*'s plan.

Kampfgruppe von der Heydte was placed under command of 6th *SS Panzer* Army, whose commander, *Generaloberst der Waffen SS* 'Sepp' Dietrich, a rabid Nazi, knew little about airborne warfare. Von der Heydte was finally briefed at HQ 6th *Panzer* Army on 15 December. He had done his best to train his men as saboteurs in the few days available and to lay hands on as many of the hundred promised aircraft as he could. He now had only 12 hours to return to his unit and issue orders for the landing which was to take place at 0200 hrs on the following morning. It was to be the first combat night landing by German paratroops and to make things worse it was in heavily forested hill-country in the depth of winter, and from aircraft manned by inexperienced and untrained crews. The trucks in which the paratroops were to get to the airfields failed to turn up and at midnight on 15 December barely a quarter of the force had been assembled. This was a far cry from the efficient *Wehrmacht* of 1940–41, when operations like this could have been mounted with smooth staffwork and ample transport resources.

The parachute landing was postponed and *Kondor* went ahead as planned. Manteuffel's 5th *Panzer* Army cut into the astounded Americans with ease in the centre, as did Brandenberger's 7th Army in the south. Dietrich's shoddy staffwork soon became evident in the north, where his armoured columns ground to a halt in monster traffic jams. Despite the lack of progress on the ground, von der Heydte's men were launched into battle on the second night of the offensive. Their leader, despite his injuries, would jump at their head, wearing a captured Russian parachute of advanced design permitting its wearer to steer it down to the ground. Elaborate measures had been taken to help the inexperienced Ju52 crews with their navigation. Whilst their route lay within German-held airspace all went well. Searchlights were placed at key points, anti-aircraft guns fired bursts of tracer and Bonn airfield displayed all its lights. Unfortunately for von der Heydte and his men, a head-wind had blown up; the aircraft at the rear of the stream missed most of the pyrotechnic aids which only burned for a short time; some aircraft were shot down as they crossed the forward ground positions and others just got lost.

Bombers had been sent ahead to mark the dropzones with clusters of incendiary bombs and this they did with great accuracy; but the bombs had burnt out within 15 minutes and few of the transport pilots saw them. Only ten aircraft dropped their loads of troops on the correct dropzone; the rest of *Kampfgruppe* von der Heydte was distributed all over the Ardennes; many actually ended up within the German lines. Von der Heydte himself could assemble only 25 men at his rendezvous in the first two hours and by last light on 17 December, having laid low all day and sent out a few cautious patrols, he had gathered in a company's-worth of his own troops and a few prisoners. These were sent off, together with some injured paratroops, armed with a personal letter from von der Heydte to his old opponent Maxwell Taylor: 'We fought each other in Normandy near

Carentan and from this time I know you as a chivalrous gallant general. I am sending you back the prisoners I took. They fought gallantly too and I cannot care for them. I am also sending you my wounded. I should greatly appreciate it if you would give them the medical treatment they need.'

That night, von der Heydte received some encouragement in the form of a supply drop (it included, to his amusement, containers of drinking water) but on the following day his force was chased by American patrols. At noon on 20 December he knew that it was hopeless to continue; without radios, he had no contact with the nearest German ground forces, now only eight miles away. He could ask no more from his men and ordered them to split into small parties and try to regain the German lines. For two more days he wandered around in the hills, then gave himself up to an American unit. His well-fought war was over.

Despite the surprise achieved by the Ardennes offensive and its initial success against the thinly-held line of Hodges's American 1st Army, the Allies reacted quickly and effectively. Eisenhower soon committed his reserves in order to slow down the main German advance; his staff, recognizing the importance of the small town of Bastogne, from which major roads radiated in five directions, threw in the 101st Airborne Division, still recuperating from *Market Garden* in the Rheims area. The acting commander of the 101st was Brig.-Gen. Anthony McAuliffe, a robust soldier who quickly got his troops on the road and covered over a hundred miles in less than 24 hours on routes jammed with traffic and deep in snow, mud and ice. The division was in Bastogne at first light on 19 December, narrowly beating the German advanced guards who arrived as the paratroops were energetically digging in.

What followed is a minor classic of war, illustrating the fighting quality of good airborne troops employed in the infantry role. The Germans recognized the importance of the town and set a *Panzer* Corps against it. After two unsuccessful days of siege warfare the *Panzer* Corps commander, von Luttwitz, called on the Americans to surrender with a letter couched in terms more appropriate to the formalities of 18th-century warfare. He granted McAuliffe two hours to think it over. The reply of 'nuts!' has rightly entered American folklore.

McAuliffe's 11,000 men held out through that critical week, the battle rising to its peak of fury on Christmas morning when German tanks broke through the perimeter supported by infantry. The defenders stalked each tank down remorselessly and knocked it out, leaving 18 burning wrecks, and wiped out the German infantry. The attack was renewed on the following day but was dispersed by a relieving column from the south-west. The great German offensive ground to a halt, overwhelmed by Allied airpower and starved of fuel and ammunition. By mid-January the Allied lines had moved forward again to their original mid-December position. The Germans had made their final throw; all that remained was the crossing of the last barrier, the Rhine.

The Allies, who had reached the Rhine in the north by the end of *Market Garden* and to the south in the area of Strasbourg, were delayed by the Ardennes offensive but closed up to the Rhine along its length by 21 March. Although it was hoped to take a bridge intact by surprise – achieved in fact with a bold American stroke at Remagen on 7 March – it was clear that several crossings would have to be made, and in places where they would constitute a mortal threat to the *Reich*.

Montgomery's 21st Army Group was confronted with the biggest problem. On his sector, stretching from Roermond, through Nijmegen and thence westward to the sea, the Rhine constitutes the most formidable river barrier in Europe. It was to be assailed on a 30-mile frontage by 25 of Montgomery's divisions, against whom was ranged Blaskowitz's Army Group 'H', a very mixed bag indeed, ranging from the still unbroken remnants of the 1st Parachute Army to odds and ends drawn from training units and convalescent depots. Despite this, the attack was elaborately planned. For days a chemical smokescreen was used to conceal Allied preparations drifting eastward with the prevailing wind. Huge resources of artillery were massed and provided with millions of rounds of ammunition. The aid of Bomber Command was sought in order to eliminate the town of Wesel which lay on the right bank in the middle of Montgomery's sector, and the American XVIII Airborne Corps, which included the British 6th Airborne Division, unemployed since Normandy, was committed to a plan which in comparison with the imaginative concept of *Market Garden* was tame and cautious in the extreme.

The whole operation was named *Plunder* and the airborne part of it *Varsity*. Montgomery described his concept as follows: 'My intention was to secure a bridgehead prior to developing operations to isolate the Ruhr and thrust into the northern plains of Germany. In outline my plan was to cross the Rhine on a front of two Armies between Rheinberg and Rees using 9th American Army on the right and 2nd Army on the left. The principal initial objective was the important communications centre of Wesel.'

This operation had been studied some months earlier and its planning was conducted without haste. Major-General Mathew Ridgway, the commander of XVIII United States Airborne Corps, had two airborne divisions at his disposal. These were the 17th US Airborne, commanded by Maj.-Gen. William Miley, and the 6th British Airborne under Maj.-Gen. Eric Bols. Ridgway's deputy was Maj.-Gen. Richard Gale, who had so successfully commanded 6th Airborne in Normandy.

Since *Market Garden* strenuous efforts had been made to replace the huge number of gliders lost in that operation, nearly 700 at Arnhem alone. In addition the British had lost most of the glider crews who flew into that battle; only 48 officers and 666 sergeant pilots now remained of Chatterton's regiment. On the assumption that at least one more major glider operation would take place before the end of the war, he turned to the RAF for assistance and sought the aid of an old friend, Air Chief Marshal Sir Peter Drummond, who was in charge of all RAF aircrew training. Chatterton called on Drummond, accompanied by the Army's Director (Air), Maj.-Gen. Kenneth Crawford. They put their problem to the airman and he immediately agreed to their request. The newly acquired RAF pilots completed a short conversion course onto gliders and were then introduced to the Glider Pilot Regiment's ferocious ground combat course; many objected strongly to this, but all were to benefit in the final battle.

As the result of the fighting in the Nijmegen–Eindhoven area the Americans decided to adopt the 'total soldier' concept for their own glider pilots. They had seen how well the Glider Pilot Regiment had performed in all their earlier operations and the airborne generals had tried without success to get the US Army Air Corps to train its glider crews to the same standards. Major-General James Gavin in his post-Normandy report wrote that although a number of the glider pilots did excellent work individually and volunteered for combat missions, the majority were a severe liability, having no organization and no commanders. After *Market Garden*, the staff of 82nd Airborne considered that the addition of their 900 glider pilots, formed into an infantry battalion, could have released three parachute battalions from watching the Reichswald forest, enabling them to go straight for Nijmegen bridge on D + 1, and almost certainly leading to the relief of Frost's group at Arnhem on 19 September. Brereton now ordered that all the American glider pilots be given 'broader and continuing ground combat training, so that after landing they can be not only self-protecting but trained to contribute to the offensive ability of the airborne troops'.

Montgomery's plan for operation *Plunder* was carefully drawn up. Behind the 70-mile-long smoke-screen which was sustained for over a month, the build-up continued. The crossing was planned for the night of 23/24 March. By 23 March, Montgomery's Intelligence Staff had identified 12 German divisions across the entire frontage of 21st Army Group, a total of some 50,000 troops plus 35,000 *Volksturm* – elderly ex-soldiers and civilians of all ages hastily kitted out with weapons and uniforms. The *Luftwaffe*, it was thought, could put 1000 aircraft in the air for tactical operations along the Western front. It was believed that there were over 300 *Flak* guns, manned by 7000 men, in the area selected for the airborne part of the attack, operation *Varsity*.

The American 9th Army was to cross the Rhine south of Wesel, and the British 2nd Army to its north. The main crossings were to start at 0300 hrs on 24 March. Ridgway's Airborne Corps would land on top of the German gun areas at 1000 hrs. If all went according to plan, they would have linked up with the cross-river attack by midafternoon; there was to be no calculated risk this time. The dangers of making an airborne assault in successive 'lifts' had been noted in *Market Garden*. The *Varsity* plan therefore provided for a concerted onslaught in which the two airborne divisions would reach the ground in the shortest possible time, to give the *Flak* defences little chance of recovery. The adoption of this technique raised a serious problem for the glider pilots, as they could no longer use one or two large landing zones, coming down in successive waves. Chatterton therefore taught his men to land on several LZs simultaneously, placing their gliders in groups corresponding to the rifle and support-weapon companies of the air-landing battalions. The location of each of these smaller LZs was carefully prearranged and planned jointly by the glider pilots and their passengers.

The air transport force available for *Varsity* exceeded anything assembled before or since. Six hundred and sixty-seven aircraft carried the paratroops of both divisions, and IX Troop Carrier Command also provided tugs for over 900 CG4 gliders. The RAF's contribution from 38 and 46 Groups, was the tug force for 6th Airborne's fleet of 440 *Hamilcar* and *Horsa* gliders. This time there was to be no hitch in the provision of tactical air support. The Deputy Supreme Allied Commander himself, Air Chief Marshal Sir Arthur Tedder, had given absolute priority to the air effort supporting *Plunder*. Apart from the Allied Tactical Air Forces and the RAF's Fighter Command, Tedder called on the 8th US Army Air Force, RAF Bomber Command and even Coastal Command if required. The commander of the 2nd Tactical Air Force was the designated air commander, responsible for the movement and escort of the two great transport armadas as they converged – 38 and 46 Groups from

East Anglia and the Americans from their airfields near Paris – on the aerial rendezvous near Brussels and droned majestically on towards the Rhine. The tremendous air support plan had been launched days before the landings. Every *Luftwaffe* airfield within range had been strafed and pulverized. On the day itself, American bombers attacked Berlin to draw off the German air defence force. An elaborate plan had been devised to neutralize the German *Flak* defences, which were also under continuous artillery fire from the left bank of the Rhine. Fighter-bombers were allotted specifically to attack any position seen to be firing at the airborne troops as they reached the final stages of their journey.

Despite intensive Allied air attack on German defences enemy ground fire was intense as the transports and gliders came overhead the dropzones, which were shrouded in smoke caused by the smoke-screen, fires started by the preliminary bombardment, and pulverized masonry from the town of Wesel, shattered during the night by RAF Bomber Command and now in sniper-infested heaps of blazing ruin, impassable to any vehicle.

The area in which Ridgway's Corps was to be dropped lay just across the Rhine on low-lying ground, in the flood-plain. The highest point in the area was a wooded ridge barely 65 feet above river level,

OPERATION 'VARSITY'—The Rhine Crossing

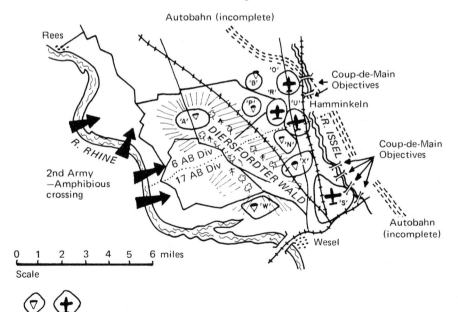

the Diersfordter Wald, through which ran the main lateral road linking the towns of Wesel, Rees and Emmerich. Although relatively in-
significant, this feature overlooked the river crossing sites of one of
Montgomery's assaulting corps and it was important to get the
Germans off it as quickly as possible. To the east lay level open
ground well suited for airborne landings, with scattered farms and
small hamlets. The eastern edge of the airborne corps area was
bounded by the River Issel, crossed by several bridges which needed
to be seized in order to prevent their destruction by the Germans and
also to stop reinforcing units reaching the Allied bridgehead. The
small town of Hamminkeln, lying on the Issel, was another important
objective as it provided cover from which German counter-attacks
might be launched.

Bols's 6th Airborne Division was given the task of taking the
northern part of the Diersfordter Wald, the town of Hamminkeln and
the three northern bridges across the River Issel, which were to be
seized by gliderborne *coup-de-main* parties and held at all costs. US
17th Airborne Division was given similar tasks in the southern part
of the corps area, with the additional responsibility of making contact
with the Royal Marines Commandos who had crossed the river near
Wesel during the night, narrowly escaping destruction at the hands of
Bomber Command in the process.

Both the airborne divisions had seen recent combat in the infantry
role – the 6th in Belgium, where it had been used as an emergency
reserve during the Ardennes offensive, and the 17th similarly employed in Luxembourg. Both were under strength when they were sent
quietly out of the line in February, but soon came up to strength and
were re-equipped with new weapons. A corps-sized exercize was held
early in March to test the complicated staff-work and one of the
American parachute regiments was retrained to jump from the new
Curtiss C46 aircraft, larger than the C47 but having one dreadful
weakness which only became apparent when it went into battle: its
fuel tanks, buried in the wing roots, were vulnerable to enemy fire,
and once ignited, the aircraft instantly became a great torch out of
which no one could escape.

A massed descent such as this, so close in front of the Allied amphibious river crossing, could hardly expect to achieve surprise. The
Germans were alert and standing to their guns as the huge swarm of
planes and gliders hove into sight through the haze. A storm of anti-
aircraft fire burst out as the first parachutes developed. The first
American combat team to land was commanded by Col. Edson Raff,
whose unfortunate experiences two and a half years earlier in the first
airborne assault in north Africa have already been described. Again,

he and his men were dropped inaccurately and came down over a mile from their appointed dropzone. Undismayed, Raff immediately led his men to the attack, over-running a battery of German field guns and mopping up hundreds of bewildered prisoners.

Keeping up the momentum of his attack and picking up more of his regiment all the time, Raff pushed up the slope of the Diersfordter Wald, taking the main German position there at the point of the bayonet. His parachute-artillery battalion showed equal *élan*, quickly coming into action over open sights at any Germans who appeared on the dropzone and breaking up any counter-attacks before they formed up.

The second regiment, Col. Coutts's 513th, landed even further off its dropzones than Raff's, but this was providential, as they came down in 6th Division's area right amongst a well-hidden 88mm *Flak* battery which was now causing terrible execution to the leading British gliders as they slithered to a halt right in front of the guns. The Americans went straight into the attack, thus saving hundreds of Bols's men from certain death. The other American parachute artillery battalion came in on target, but was at once attacked on the dropzone as the gunners struggled to assemble their pack guns. The whole battlefield was now blazing with action as streams of gliders nosed down through the haze and smoke. The American CG4s, because of their flat glidepath, were released at about 800 feet in order that they could get quickly onto the ground. The British *Horsas* and *Hamilcars*, on the other hand, were released at 2500 feet or more and suffered heavily on the way down; soon their landing zones were littered with blazing wrecks as German incendiary bullets set light to loads of petrol. The pall of smoke thickened.

The men of 6th Airborne underwent a similar experience to the 17th. The haze hanging over the battlefield made it hard for the glider pilots to see their landing zones but most landed with great accuracy. Major Tony Dyball of the 1st Battalion Royal Ulster Rifles, had the task of seizing one of the Issel bridges with his rifle company. He had flown by glider into Normandy and he and his men had enormous confidence in their pilots' ability to get them to their objective; this was fully justified, for as the glider ground to a halt only a few yards from its appointed place the pilot leant back and apologized to Dyball for being two minutes late; most sub-units arrived with similar accuracy – Bols and his divisional HQ party within a hundred yards of the place he had previously selected off an air photograph to be his initial command post.

The two parachute brigades of 6th Airborne had preceded the gliders. The 1st Canadian Parachute Battalion was greeted with a hail of fire as it came down and immediately lost its commanding officer, shot at close range as he hung in his harness from the tree in which he landed. The 12th Battalion of the Parachute Regiment came down on top of an 88mm battery and quickly put them out of action, then set out for the higher ground, picking up stragglers from the American battalions who had been dropped well away from their proper objectives.

Within two hours the whole Corps was on the ground and a large supply drop now took place, carried out by American *Liberator* bombers. Some of these were carrying cameras, and the pictures they took include some remarkable shots of wrecked gliders and the inevitable chaos following a large-scale airborne descent. By mid-afternoon all the primary objectives had been taken and contact made with the Allied troops now swarming across the Rhine in their amphibious and assault boats, whilst engineers rigged pontoon bridges across the swift and sullen stream. After dark German counter-attacks came in against the airborne perimeter, but it held; the newly trained American glider pilots now showed that they too could fight as infantry by repulsing the enemy.

Varsity was the last of the massed airborne attacks, for already it could be seen that they were desperately costly in terms of skilled manpower and equipment, absorbing disproportionately large amounts of badly needed resources for a return which at best was transitory. The waste was fearsome. Out of the 416 *Hamilcars* and *Horsas* used by 6th Airborne only 24 were salvaged for further use; the rest were either smashed, riddled with bullet holes or burnt out. However, there was as yet no really satisfactory alternative method of getting light armoured vehicles, field artillery or anti-tank guns onto the ground in support of the airborne troops. Even in 1945, after enormous efforts in research and the introduction of ingenious equipment, parachuted units, once dropped, enjoyed only a little more ground mobility than Wellington's armies.

Whilst armies had been acquiring – often painfully – the skills of airborne warfare, another line of development had been quietly gathering momentum. Soldiers were quick to see the value of the airborne observation post afforded initially by the balloon, later by the heavier-than-air flying machine. As the development of army aviation was eventually to merge with, then overtake and supplant that of conventional airborne techniques, it is necessary to retrace one's steps in order to see how it took shape.

CHAPTER TEN

Slack Water: the Post-war Years

At the end of the Second World War the victorious Allies were obliged almost immediately to dismantle their war machines. Within the space of six years their navies, armies and air forces had expanded and changed beyond recognition, and the influence of air power was evident as never before on sea and land. Maritime air power, whether projected from the decks of aircraft carriers or land-based, had toppled the battleship from its pedestal and played a co-equal part in the defeat of the German U-boat fleet. A new dimension had been added to the mobility of armies. The pressures of war had accelerated technological development in all fields of aviation; the successful development of the gas turbine offered a huge improvement in the performance of combat aircraft, and the world-wide requirement for aerial logistic support had produced equally significant advances in the capabilities of transport aircraft. At the same time an ominous question mark hung over the whole military scene; the nuclear age had arrived, and with it the capability of devising weapons with destructive power which could not easily be visualized.

In 1946 the future of airborne forces seemed dim. Heavy casualties to gliders and low-flying transport aircraft during operations *Market* and *Varsity* had indicated the growing risk from multi-barrel automatic weapons and radar-laid anti-aircraft guns. Above all, airborne forces, if used correctly in the strategic sense, are an offensive weapon; and no realistic scenario could encompass an aggressive operation into the Soviet-occupied states of Eastern Europe.

Some encouraging developments did, however, make their appearance in the airborne field during the immediate post-war years. In America, transport aircraft started to enter service which allowed vehicles to be transported within the fuselage, out of which they could either be dropped on platforms suspended beneath a cluster of parachutes, or airlanded and driven down a ramp after landing. The first of this new generation of freight aircraft was the Fairchild C82, which was no more than a metal box with high wings, two powerful engines and a twin-boom tail structure. Although Fairchild called the C82 the *Packet*, it and its successor the C119 were inevitably nicknamed 'Flying Boxcars'. The American airborne forces eagerly seized on the C82 and started to develop a variety of techniques for lifting and airdropping a wide range of standard army vehicles and weapons.

In Britain, no similar aircraft was under construction; it had been agreed early in the late war that the United States would concentrate on the development and production of military transport aircraft whilst all the resources of the smaller British aircraft industry were devoted to the production of warplanes.

★   ★   ★

The outbreak of the Korean war in 1950 took the free world by surprise. The two states of North and South Korea had been established in 1945 as a temporary expedient pending the conclusion of a satisfactory Peace Treaty between the Allies and Japan, whose dependency Korea had been since the early 1900s. The 38th Parallel of Latitude was arbitrarily selected as the frontier dividing the two states, which at once adopted forms of government reflecting their sponsorship; the North became a Stalinist tyranny under Kim Il Sung, and the South followed the American constitutional pattern under President Synghman Rhee.

On 20 June 1950 the North Koreans rolled south across the frontier and almost succeeded in over-running South Korea before American and United Nations reinforcements could reach the scene. General MacArthur assumed personal command of the UN forces and on 15 September launched a brilliant amphibious counter stroke at Inchon, retaking Seoul the South Korean capital on 26 October and shattering the North Korean army as it attempted to regain the safety of the 38th Parallel, taking along with it large numbers of Allied prisoners-of-war.

Late in September the 187th Airborne Regimental Combat Team arrived in Korea from Fort Bragg. Commanded by Col. Frank Bowen it was a self-contained formation with its own parachute artillery battalion, equivalent to a brigade group in the British Army. MacArthur, now determined to pursue the North Koreans across the 38th Parallel and destroy their army on its home ground, quickly decided to use Bowen's paratroops boldly in an attempt to cut the enemy's main escape route and rescue as many of the prisoners as possible.

On 15 October Bowen was ordered to prepare his troops for an airborne landing. The earliest date by which the requisite force of transport aircraft could be assembled and prepared was 20 October;

by the middle of the previous day 80 C119 *Boxcars* and 40 of the well-tried C47s had been lined up at Kimpo, just south of Seoul. The troops were out of practice and took 20 hours to load their jeeps and guns aboard the C119s, but all was ready by last light. In anticipation of a dawn assault the 187th were roused at 0230 hrs on the 20th, to be grounded at Kimpo by fog until after midday. The drop was put back to the early afternoon.

The dropzones lay 30 miles north of Pyongyang the North Korean capital where two railway lines and two main roads run north in parallel, a few miles apart. It was believed that the trains carrying the prisoners, together with a number of senior North Korean officials, were creeping north by night, hiding in tunnels during the day to avoid detection by the ever-present Allied air forces. The information on which this was based was actually more than a week old. Most of the enemy troops had slipped through two days earlier and the government officials had been gone eight days as had nearly all the prisoners apart from a party of 66, murdered in cold blood by their North Korean guards on the day of the airborne landing.

Bowen led his HQ and 1st Battalion out of the planes at 1400 hrs, landing virtually unopposed on dropzone 'William', the westerly one of the two selected. Apart from 25 of his overloaded men injured on landing and one killed by sporadic rifle fire, nearly 1500 men and 74 tons of equipment arrived safely on the DZ within a few minutes. Of the enemy expected to be swarming in the area there was no sign. The 1st/187th cleared the near-by town of Sukchon and set up road blocks to prevent the enemy re-entering the place from the north. The 3rd/187th, which soon joined them, set up road blocks to the south. Arriving at 1420 hrs on dropzone 'Easy' to the east of 'William', the 2nd/187th set up road blocks around the small town of Sunchon. By last light, after a relaxed afternoon's work in the early autumnal sunshine, Bowen's force was firmly installed across what was assumed to be the enemy's main escape route; 4000 men, 12 155mm guns, a troop of anti-tank guns and a small mountain of supplies and fuel were secured within the two perimeters. As he had done at Nadzab seven years earlier, MacArthur watched the drop from an aircraft overhead, firmly believing that he had cut off 30,000 North Koreans. On the following day at a press conference in Tokyo he confidently forecast the imminent end of the war.

The actual situation was very different. The only enemy troops still in action to the south of Bowen's force were their rearguard, the 239th North Korean Regiment, which was skilfully conducting a series of resolute delaying actions on the routes north from Pyongyang. On 21 October, after a quiet night, the 3rd/187th moved cautiously south from Sukchon astride the road and railway lines. They had gone six miles when they were attacked head-on out of the blue by an enemy battalion which over-ran the leading company of paratroops before melting into the low hills around the village of Opa-Ri. Three miles to the south-west another company of the 3rd/187th collided with more enemy troops and drove them off after a brisk fight. The 187th had come up against the 2500 determined men of the 239th Regiment, bent on regaining their own main force, and throughout the night of 21/22 October a savage battle raged at Opa-Ri as the North Koreans fought to break through to the north. The fighting was at point-blank range and mostly hand-to-hand. HQ Company of the 3rd/187th was assailed by a battalion of howling Koreans whilst the battalion command post and 'L' Company grappled with another 350 enemy troops. For a time, amidst the confusion attending such a close-quarter fight in the dark, the situation appeared desperate and the battalion won a Distinguished Unit Citation for its work that night.

Whilst the men of the 3rd/187th were fighting for their lives, the main Allied advance was closing up from the south, headed by the 27th British Commonwealth Brigade. Its leading unit was the 3rd Battalion Royal Australian Regiment, whose men could hear the battle raging through the night a few miles to the north. At dawn on 22 October they advanced rapidly to take the North Koreans in the rear. A classic infantry battle ensured as the Australians, armed with the antique short-magazine Lee-Enfield rifle of First World War vintage, fixed their 18in bayonets and charged, four rifle companies led by Lt-Col. Green and his small HQ party (who between them accounted for 34 Koreans). For the loss of only 7 men wounded, the Australians killed 270 and captured 200 North Koreans. The 187th and the 3rd RAR were left in triumphant possession of the field. In 48 hours the North Korean 239th Regiment, a formidable unit by any standards, had ceased to exist; 1075 of their men had been killed and 881 taken prisoner in an outstanding example of determination and aggression by the American and Australian infantry. Total casualties to the 187th were just over 100.

Only one more airborne operation was mounted in Korea. Towards the end of 1950, Chinese 'volunteers' arrived on the scene to rescue Kim Il Sung from what appeared to be imminent defeat. The Allies, having duly reached the Yalu River which marks the North Korean–Chinese border, would have crossed in hot pursuit if McArthur had been given his head; but he was dismissed by President Truman and succeeded by a distinguished airborne general, Matthew Bunker Ridgway, who had followed Browning as Brereton's deputy in HQ 1st

Allied Airborne Army in 1944. He was at once faced with hordes of Chinese, before whose attacks he was compelled to withdraw in the depths of the bitter Manchurian winter. Pyongyang fell, then Seoul, as the Chinese advanced into South Korea. Early in 1951 Ridgway launched a counter-offensive, retaking Seoul on 15 March. With the enemy apparently on the run, he decided to use the 187th again to disrupt the Chinese withdrawal. On 23 March, reinforced by two companies of Rangers, to a strength of 3300, the 187th dropped at Monsan-Ni, just south of the 38th Parallel. They met with little opposition, for the agile Chinese managed to evade the blow and got away. There was to be no repetition of Opa-Ri.

★   ★   ★

The glider had remained in British and American service in small numbers, as it was held to be the best means of delivering small parties of men with their vehicles, heavy weapons and equipment in the *coup-de-main* role. The growing threat from ever-improving air defence weapons indicated that such glider operations would have to be attempted at night or, if by day, against only the most unsophisticated opposition. Now, with the advent of the tactical transport aircraft, the glider's knell was sounded. In April 1952 the American Joint Airborne Troops Board at Fort Bragg pronounced sentence: '. . . gliders, as an airborne capability, are obsolete, and should no longer be included in airborne techniques, concepts or doctrine, or in reference thereto.' In Britain, the last of the gliders had been disposed of in the previous year, but the Glider Pilot Regiment, reduced to little more than cadre strength, continued to exist until 1957, mainly because it now provided a convenient source of non-artillery pilots to augment the Air OP squadrons and to carry out the increasing amount of 'non-Air OP' flying which was required, especially in the Far East. Airborne troops were used by the French in Indo-China where from 1949 a full-blooded insurgency was directed by Ho Chi Minh and his apostle, General Vo Nguyen Giap with the aim of ejecting the colonial power and establishing a communist republic. French paratroops generally fought as infantry because of a shortage of transport aircraft, but a number of parachute-landed operations were mounted. Results were mixed, however. The final dénouement took place as the result of a decision to set up a French tactical base at the obscure village of Dien Bien Phu. Giap's troops turned the tables, invested the French garrison, and despite repeated efforts to relieve it with parachuted reinforcements and air supply, it fell after a five-and-a-half-month siege.

187

The French in Indo-China never recovered from this blow, and communism marched on across the Far East. Despite the enormity of the reverse there was no lessening of the airborne spirit in the French Army, which like the British has always tended to derive stimulus from hard-fought defeat. If anything, the aggressiveness of *les paras* was fuelled by Dien Bien Phu and encouraged a mood of defiance towards the French Government which was finally to erupt in the repercussions following the Algerian war.

★   ★   ★

The next occasion in which the French airborne forces were to see action was at Port Said in November 1956 when they were joined by the British in one of the military curiosities of the 20th century.

The Suez Canal had long been regarded by the French and British governments as a strategic key to their Far Eastern possessions and both had considerable stakes in its finances and day-to-day management. Until the spring of 1956 a large British garrison had occupied the Canal Zone; when it was finally withdrawn large stockpiles of military stores and equipment were left behind in the care of civil contractors so that if necessary a British military presence could rapidly be restored. In July 1956, however, President Nasser of Egypt abruptly nationalized the Canal and impounded the British stockpiles. The political situation rapidly worsened and military tensions grew between Egypt and Israel, whose government had become alarmed by the seizure of the Canal and was in any case hypersensitive to shifts of power amongst its hostile Arab neighbours.

It was eventually decided to reoccupy Port Said at the north end of the Canal and move troops down towards Suez, and a joint Franco-British operation was accordingly planned for 6 November. But the Israelis could not wait. Secretly equipped by the French with modern aircraft and weapons, they decided on 27 October to strike against the Egyptians in Sinai and the Gaza strip with the aim of eliminating guerrilla bases and reopening the Gulf of Akaba to their mercantile traffic. Two days later they struck; a battalion of paratroops landed at dusk to seize the Mitla Pass, the key defile on the desert track south into Sinai. This took the Egyptians completely by surprise, and although they duly reacted to the presence of an enemy force less than 40 miles from the Canal, the paratroops had been quickly reinforced overland and easily repulsed all Egyptian counter-attacks. At this point the Israeli Air Force carried out a deadly blow against the Egyptians, virtually destroying their Air Force on its own airfield and attaining air supremacy at a single stroke.

The British Government, taken as much by surprise as the Egyptians, issued an ultimatum on 30 October to Israel and Egypt demanding the withdrawal of both sides from the Canal Zone; the Israelis agreed and halted their armour ten miles from the canal on 3 November. The Egyptians disregarded the ultimatum and British and French aircraft began to attack selected military targets in Egypt. Nasser responded by sinking blockships to close the Canal.

The Allied expeditionary force now stood poised for its descent on Port Said despite a thinly-veiled threat of Soviet intervention unless the operation was called off. The parachute landings scheduled for 6 November, to coincide with the amphibious assault, were brought forward by 24 hours and early on 5 November the troops emplaned in Cyprus. At this time the RAF could only produce enough *Hastings* and *Valetta* aircraft to lift a weak battalion group. The 3rd Battalion of the Parachute Regiment, commanded by Lt-Col. Paul Crook, was the unit selected; a total of 780 men whose heavy weapons consisted of six 106mm recoilless anti-tank guns, medium machine guns and 3in mortars. As the *Hastings* and *Valetta* were conventional troop-carrying aircraft, the battalion's seven jeeps, four trailers and the anti-tank guns had to be dropped on platforms suspended beneath the *Hastings*.

The 3rd Battalion's task was to jump onto Gamil Airfield, about four miles west of the Port Said canal entrance and, having taken possession, to advance into the town and link up with the troops who were to land over the beaches early on 6 November.

The French airborne contribution was a battalion of the 2nd Colonial Parachute Regiment under Col. Gilles, a Dien Bien Phu survivor, whose men were almost all seasoned veterans of the Indo-Chinese campaign. Their mission was to land on the east bank of the Canal at Port Fuad, move quickly into the built-up area and also seize the Raswa bridges immediately to the south of Port Said. The French battalion's dropzones were extremely cramped, and fierce resistance was expected. In fact, Port Said was not heavily defended, much of its garrison having been milked off to the Sinai and Gaza. A battalion of infantry was dug in at Gamil, where oil drums had been scattered all over the airfield to prevent aircraft from landing; in Port Said itself there was a further regular battalion backed by two battalions of jittery National Guards and a coast artillery regiment. A weak battalion guarded the Raswa bridges and succeeded in blowing one of them as the French drop began.

The twin streams of aircraft carrying the British and French paratroops crossed the Egyptian coast well to the west of Port Said, then turned to port into the rising sun; within ten minutes 668 of Crook's men were on the ground, rallying by platoons, then companies, unlashing the vehicles and equipment dropped by the lumbering *Hastings*, and picking up the 176 supply containers scattered over the airfield. The Egyptians fought back at first with some spirit although their fire was erratic; a pall of black smoke rose from the airfield buildings, set on fire during the preliminary airstrike and quickly seized by the paratroops. The battalion was in possession of the airfield within 30 minutes, its garrison fleeing eastwards into Port Said town.

The French paratroops were faced not only with dropzones far more cramped than that of Crook's battalion at Gamil, but with a more determined resistance on the part of the Egyptians. Within an hour of their initial landing, however, they had taken the surviving bridge at Raswa intact, thus securing the start-point for what the Anglo-French high command hoped would be a dramatic dash down the Canal to Suez on the following day. A second French parachute battalion was dropped into Port Fuad, on the east bank of the Canal facing Port Said, later in the day, whilst at Gamil a supply and personnel drop was carried out – a superfluous operation as Crook's men had cleared the airfield of obstructions by mid-morning and the addi-

THE ASSAULT ON PORT SAID, 5-6 November 1956

tional equipment and men could have been airlanded despite sporadic mortar fire from the western edge of the town. In the evening the Egyptian commander in Port Said negotiated a cease-fire, but as he failed to obtain authority for this from Cairo, the amphibious landings due at dawn on the following morning ran into unexpectedly fierce opposition. As dark fell over Port Said, the British had dug themselves in around the sewage farm on the outskirts of Port Said and French patrols skirmished with small groups of Egyptians who chose to ignore the cease-fire. The smoke and glare of numerous fires spread across the night sky.

None of those involved could realize that something of a military revolution had taken place.

CHAPTER ELEVEN

The Third Dimension

The paratroops who landed at Port Said in 1956 found themselves no more mobile, once on the ground, than their forbears at Arnhem or Tagaytay, and having been delivered to the battle by a vehicle of great strategic mobility – the transport aircraft – they became foot-soldiers once more in order to fight their tactical battle, dependent on early relief by forces brought to the scene by other means. Hitherto this had meant the timely arrival of conventional forces overland or an amphibious assault as in Normandy, and this was the case at Port Said where the main landings took place 24 hours after the parachute landings. But on this occasion the amphibious assault was accompanied by the use of troop-carrying helicopters; mobile operations would never be the same again.

The age of vertical take-off and landing (VTOL) had dawned well before even the Second World War. Although attempts to achieve VTOL flight had been made by many designers and builders, the first practical helicopter flew in 1938. It employed a technique known to man for thousands of years but which could not be tested successfully until power plants had been developed capable of getting a rotorcraft off the ground and sustaining it in the hover. Leonardo da Vinci was only one of the many designers thus frustrated. The invention of the internal combustion engine at last gave aircraft builders the essential ingredient for the power-hungry rotorcraft and early in the 20th century numbers of grotesque VTOL hopefuls thrashed and flapped themselves into heaps of wreckage without even leaving the ground. It was clear that power was not the only requirement and that rotating wings posed complicated problems of control and structure. For years, VTOL projects languished, until the Spaniard, Juan de la Cierva, solved the problems of controlling rotating flying surfaces in his autogyros and blazed the way for the designers of the first true helicopters.

Cierva's first successful model flew in 1923, and by the mid-1930s the RAF had formed an experimental flight which was used amongst other things for conducting artillery spotting trials at Larkhill, flown by RAF pilots with Royal Artillery officers as observers, using radio to transmit fire orders and corrections to the guns. The autogyro, it seemed, offered a splendid answer to Parham's plea of 1933 for an observation post operating from the gun lines, as its short take-off and landing performance far exceeded that of any fixed-wing aircraft. The idea, however, lapsed when the RAF declined to let artillery officers fly the autogyros whilst carrying out their observation role.

The autogyro was not a true helicopter; the main rotor was not powered, its rotation being derived from the airflow generated by the forward motion of the airframe, and this was obtained by means of a conventional propeller. The first practicable helicopter, capable of vertical take-off and hover in still air, was the German Focke-Achgelis Fa61 which made its appearance in 1938. The Nazis, eager to demonstrate this evidence of German technical skill, had it flown inside the covered stadium of the *Deutschlandhalle* in Berlin, with the versatile Hanna Reitsch at the controls. A larger developed version of this machine actually went into production – the world's first helicopter to achieve production status – in 1940 as the Fa223 for the *Luftwaffe*. Due to official indifference and wartime production difficulties the project ran down until, by 1945, only three specimens were still airworthy.

While the Germans toiled over their intricate designs in the mid-1930s, a rival was at work on the other side of the Atlantic. Igor Sikorsky, a Russian emigré who had lived in the United States since the Bolshevik revolution, had made his name as an aircraft designer before 1914 and his astounding *Bolshoi* biplane bomber remains one of the all-time wonders of the aeronautical world. As early as 1909 he had designed and built a rotorcraft which left the ground but ran into control problems, and Sikorsky shelved the idea for lack of time and resources. He returned to the field of vertical take-off in the 1930s, adopting a conservative line with a single main rotor-and-tail-rotor configuration. His concept remains the mainstay of Sikorsky design policy to this day. In 1939–40 he designed, built and (wearing a Homburg hat in the completely open cockpit, an aerodynamic achievement in its own right) test-flew the VS300. He refined its design, and in 1943 it went into production as the R4; one of these aircraft, flown and operated by the USAAF, saw service with Cochrane's Air Commando in Burma during the second Chindit expedition of 1944. In that year the Royal Navy began trials with Sikorsky's helicopter and the RAF followed suit, although they approached the new concept with many reservations, proclaiming that its initial cost, complexity, unreliability and limited performance, together with the disproportionately high maintenance requirement, outweighed its advantages. The R6, an improved version, followed the R4 into service. In the RAF the two types were known as the *Hoverfly*, Mks 1 and 2.

From the start, the War Office displayed great enthusiasm for the helicopter. Once more, it seemed, the solution to Parham's problem had appeared; a light helicopter, flown by a gunner officer and operated from the battery position, was surely the ultimate Air OP. The Air Ministry agreed to hold trials and in October 1946 some *Hoverfly* helicopters were issued to a flight of 657 Air OP Squadron RAF, whose Royal Artillery officers thus became the British Army's first helicopter pilots.

In these early days, little was known about the aerodynamics of the helicopter except that they were complex and unpredictable. The first pilots were mainly self-taught; not until the mid-1950s was the course of instruction rationalized by the RAF's Central Flying School and the pioneers were left to work things out for themselves. There were two notable hazards; one became known as 'Vortex ring' and occurred when a helicopter, making a near-vertical descent under power into a confined space, sank too rapidly into the mass of turbulent air caused by the downwash of its own rotors, causing loss of control and a headlong fall to the ground; the other peril was that of 'ground resonance' which occurred when a landing was inadvertently made onto one wheel, causing the helicopter to oscillate about its undercarriage, displacing the centre of gravity of the main rotor system and, unless the pilot took extremely rapid action, literally shaking the helicopter to pieces. It was some years before designers overcame this phenomenon and accidents due to ground resonance were fairly common.

Throughout 1947 the newly trained pilots of 657 Squadron carried out numerous trials and gave many demonstrations. History was made in September when Capt. Wilson of the Royal Artillery conducted the first-ever artillery shoot from a helicopter. Appropriately, it was at Larkhill, where less than ten years earlier Bazeley and his flying club had pioneered the technique with their de Havilland *Moths* and Taylorcraft. Some demonstrations came to grief when the temperamental *Hoverfly* declined to start. Its engine was notoriously difficult of access and hard to service. Oil consumption was excessive; '. . . as a yardstick, the oil-tank needs filling up twice for each fill-up of petrol', read one pilot's report. On one occasion a *Hoverfly* was fitted with an external stretcher in order to give a public demonstration of casualty evacuation. An airman, representing the 'casualty' was strapped down and taken aloft, exposed to the elements and the main rotor downwash. The matron of an Oxford hospital, who was watching and believed the 'casualty' to be a real one, remarked that she had always believed men to be capable of acts of raving madness and that her views had now been amply confirmed.

Despite the unintentional comedy element which attended most early helicopter operations, tremendous potential was clearly ahead. In America, Sikorsky had begun to build larger helicopters capable of lifting useful military payloads. The Marine Corps were quick to realize the value of 'vertical envelopment' in the assault and in December 1947 formed their first helicopter squadron with the air of testing and evaluating '. . . the concept of transporting Marines to the battle area by helicopter'. By May 1948 they were carrying out the first ship-to-shore trooplifts.

At first, the US Army lagged behind the Marines although this was not for lack of enthusiasm. The Army had taken to aviation as the result of its wartime experience with the light aircraft which were integrated with all field artillery units and by 1947 had started to acquire helicopters as well as larger fixed-wing aircraft. In that year, however, the US Air Force was formed as a separate service and at a single stroke the Army Air Force changed the colour of its uniform and, it seemed to the Army aviators left behind, its mental attitudes as well. The USAF, as the primary agency of the West's nuclear deterrence power, was stategically orientated and viewed Army aviators with suspicion and scorn. An arbitrary upper weight limit of 4000 pounds was placed on aircraft operated by the Army (an example which was duly followed in Britain by the Air Ministry when the Army Air Corps formed in 1957) and for a time this inhibited the development of Army airmobility.

The Korean War, which saw some of the last of the old-style airborne operations, was a testing ground for the new concept of tactical mobility as it saw the first use of the helicopter by the US Marines and Army as a battlefield aerial vehicle. The USAF employed helicopters as well, using them boldly to rescue airmen shot down deep behind enemy lines; but the most significant developments were in their use for the resupply of Army and Marine units high on inaccessible hills, and casualty evacuation from front-line positions in which role they were used most effectively in conjunction with the Mobile Army Surgical Hospitals, hilariously immortalized as in the 'MASH' film series but in fact one of the most outstanding advances in army medical services since Florence Nightingale's days.

There was much movement of troops by helicopter, but only a few trooplifts were attempted in the face of the enemy and none of these came under fire.

Three weeks before the first combat mission was undertaken by a US Army helicopter in Korea, the RAF carried out the first operational helicopter lift of the Malayan campaign. Infantry patrols operating in deep jungle often sustained casualties due to enemy action, accidents or disease, and until the arrival of helicopters in the theatre early in

1950 this meant carrying the victim to the nearest road or track – often several days' agonizing march. The morale effect of the helicopter was tremendous, for the soldiers now knew that if they became casualties their patrol could make a jungle clearing, using air-dropped saws and explosives, into which a helicopter could descend. Initially the RAF used British-built Sikorsky S51s, known as the *Dragonfly*, but a squadron of the larger S55s, flown by the Royal Navy, arrived in 1952. These gave the Security Forces a troop-lifting capability and even though in the higher parts of the country only three fully equipped troops could be landed vertically, a new dimension of mobility had been conferred on troops who could be moved in minutes to jungle clearings hitherto reached only by several days' hard marching. This new mobility was a godsend to commanders, who could achieve operational results with platoons which had hitherto demanded battalions. It was one of the turning points of this protracted 12-year war; the initiative henceforth lay with the Security Forces.

Elsewhere in the Far East the French began to use American-built helicopters in their ill-starred Indo-Chinese campaign. Initially used to relieve Piper *Cub* aircraft of liaison and casualty evacuation tasks, their versatility soon became apparent and within two years an 'Army Aviation Helicopter Group' had been formed. At that time the French Army and Air Force shared the responsibility for manning helicopters and light aircraft, but after the *débâcle* in Indo-China the Army broke away, changing the title of its aviation arm from 'Artillery Observation Light Aircraft' to 'Light Aviation of the Army' (ALAT). It was the French, in their later Algerian campaign, who pioneered the full integration of the helicopter into combat units; before discussing this interesting development, however, it is necessary to return to the British experience.

The performance of Royal Naval and RAF helicopters in Malaya had greatly encouraged the War Office, who were at last beginning to show every sign that their appreciation of air power extended beyond that of the close air support so lavishly provided on the battlefields of 1944–45. The Malayan campaign was actually a microcosm of air power in many aspects and deserves study. At the outset, in 1948, the RAF still maintained a useful presence in Singapore and Malaya and reinforced the Far East Air Force (FEAF) with fighter-bombers for ground attack, and C47 *Dakotas* for parachuted resupply of units operating in the jungle. This resupply role was brought to an outstanding peak of efficiency; the loads were prepared and despatched by men of the Royal Army Service Corps who shared the dangers of the supply-drop missions with the RAF crews on whose airfields they lived. It became a matter for joint pride that the troops in the jungle would not go short and missions were flown daily in conditions which demanded the highest standards of skill and dedication from the air-crew and their soldier-despatchers. Such operations inevitably claimed their toll. From time to time a supply dropping pilot, in his efforts to ensure an accurate drop, would place his aircraft in a position facing up a steep mountainous valley from which recovery was impossible; the waiting troops on the ground would hear, first the ominous sound of engines at maximum rated power, then the awful rending sound and explosion as the aircraft flew into the mountain-side. The resolution with which the RAF crews and their despatchers went on with their work, undeterred by such disasters, was of an order to be compared to Lord and his crew at Arnhem.

Offensive action with bombs, guns and rockets against unseen targets is a futile exercise. In the early stages of the 'Emergency' (as the anti-terrorist war in Malaya was officially termed) bombing attacks were launched against arbitrarily chosen tracts of jungle or mangrove swamp. It was thought that the distant rumble would have a tonic effect on the civil population; it would possibly deter potential terrorists contemplating the guerrilla life; there was even a remote chance that a bandit camp would be hit. The falsity of this line of argument is readily appreciated by anyone who has flown over Malaya (West Malaysia as it is now called). A range of densely jungled mountains, rising at the peaks to 7000 feet, runs like a spine for two-thirds of the way down the peninsula from the border with Thailand. To the west of the mountain chain lie the rich rice-producing areas of the State of Kedah. Further south are the open-cast tin mines of the Kinta Valley in the State of Perak. To the east of the near-impenetrable mountains are the rural, predominently Malay States of Kelantan, Trengannu and Pahang. The southern third of the peninsula mostly consists of the State of Johore, rich in rubber and oil-palm, but also covered with flat jungle and mangrove in which movement is severely limited and navigation a nightmare.

The peninsula is about as long as England from Hadrian's Wall to Plymouth Hoe. Somewhere in it, during the crucial years of the campaign, there were lurking a few thousand armed terrorists, supported with varying degrees of enthusiasm by a large Chinese working population.

The burden of the Malayan campaign fell on the infantry, for the only way to deal with an enemy operating from jungle bases is to close with him, destroy his camps and food supplies, and either persuade him to surrender or kill him. Many of the larger camps held several hundred of Chin Peng's men, and were used for training purposes, with a parade ground, classrooms, mess halls and living quarters. They were carefully sited in deep jungle, well defended and difficult to reach on foot. The light aircraft came into its own in these operations, for as the attacking infantry slowly made their way towards the enemy camp – often seven or eight days' march – they could be given an accurate daily 'fix' by putting up smoke; the pilot, far above, could see this seeping through the tops of the 200ft-high trees and quickly gave a grid reference, and course to steer, to the patrol leader. In the final stages of the approach march, the pilot would assist the commander on the ground as he positioned his sections to cut off the bandits' escape routes. To locate a bandit camp in the first place was extremely difficult; sometimes the only give-away was a small patch of well-trodden sunlit parade ground, momentarily visible as the Auster wheeled high above; closer inspection might reveal the corner of a hut, and little else. Easier to find were the minute clearings – seldom larger than a tennis-court – in which the bandits grew their vegetables in meticulous neat rows. For every camp or clearing found, a pilot would spend hundreds of hours' flying.

Some camps and clearings were too far into the jungle to be attacked by the infantry. In this case an airstrike would be mounted. By 1953 some of the Austers had been equipped with a bomb-rack on which were carried four parachute flares. With the introduction of VHF radio the Auster pilots could talk to the pilots of the RAF strike aircraft, with whom they established a very high degree of rapport. There were some heavy bombers on Singapore Island; a squadron of Avro *Lincolns*, each of which could lift a load of 14 1000lb bombs. A drill was devised by which a target could be accurately marked by an Auster as the bombers started their run-in. This gave the light aircraft pilot barely 90 seconds to release his flare at tree-top height and head away from the target to avoid the shockwaves as the great salvoes of bombs came down. The effect was startling; whole trees became airborne and a huge pall of smoke, bearing millions of eddying leaves, hung over the jungle. It was, admittedly, using a sledge hammer to crack a nut; and only rarely did an airstrike succeed in killing the occupants of a camp, for the bandits had well-practised emergency drills for evacuating their camps as soon as the marker flare came down. Captured terrorists, however, testified as to the terrifying psychological effect of these attacks, especially when they came by night.

Flying a light aircraft in Malaya could be a hair-raising business; the daily weather pattern was predictable and generally featured tremendous thunderstorms during the afternoon, when the aircraft would be seized by violent up-and-down draughts, and the pilot half blinded by lightning. The rain, slamming at the canvas covering of the plane, would often turn into hail, tearing the fabric away, denting the metal engine casing and cracking the perspex of the cockpit canopy. Water poured into the cabin from 100 holes. The radio was unusable, for the trailing aerial – 100 feet of weighted wire – had to be reeled in to minimize the risk of lightning strike. As there were no flying instruments in the Auster 6 and 7, the pilot had to maintain visual contact with the ground, and many owe their survival to their intimate knowledge of the terrain, for map reading was impossible under such conditions.

In 1949 the commander of a Guards Brigade, in a hurry to get across the central range during the afternoon, was lost with his pilot. Exhaustive search failed to locate the aircraft until it was found seven years later. No trace of the brigadier or his pilot was ever found. Some pilots were more fortunate. One aircraft, caught in a violent downdraught whilst trying to cross a ridge, hit the treetops, hung there for a few seconds, then crashed 200 feet to the jungle floor, bursting into flames as it hit the ground. Pilot and passenger struggled clear of the blazing wreck, unable to salvage their rifles or any of the survival kit carried in the cockpit because flares and ammunition were beginning to explode around them. Providentially, they marched in the right direction and reached safety later the same day, bloody, shaken, but thankful to be alive.

As the result of the Malayan experience, which showed that soldiers in light aircraft could relieve the RAF of many chores, permitting them to devote their resources to the application of air power, it was decided to form the Army Air Corps and this was done in 1957. It meant the severance of a longstanding association with the RAF who, since the days of Bazeley and 'D' Flight, had provided the light aircraft and the men to service them. It had been a mutually rewarding partnership, and soldiers and airmen had learned much from each other. However, the Army was now determined to move into the helicopter business and as the Air Ministry was understandably reluctant to pay for such expensive aircraft, or divert highly skilled manpower to service and maintain them, the Army was obliged to to its own way.

A similar situation had occurred in the US Army after the formation of the USAF in 1947. The French Army also moved in the same direction during the 1950s. Unlike the British, the French Army's association with the Air Force had not been a happy one. At the outbreak of the Second World War a few of the Air Force reconnaissance squadrons had 'army observers', but these were under-trained and they flew in antiquated aircraft. By the end of 1942, artillery units of the Free French Army were being equipped by the Americans and this included the provision of Piper Cub aircraft for artillery observation; these were flown by Air Force pilots and carried an artilleryman as observer.

It was the Algerian campaign, starting in 1954, which saw the creation of a separate French Air Arm. It was never, as proclaimed, a straightforward war of national liberation, but a carefully orchestrated plot to foment revolution in the classic Maoist mould, as its pattern of development clearly showed. At the outset the 'National Liberation Front' (FLN) pursued a 'guerrilla' campaign from sanctuary areas deep in the Atlas mountains. This was followed by the 'protracted' stage, a struggle of endurance with the security forces in which harassment, sabotage and ambush played a prominent part whilst the FLN avoided head-on battle. This was to cover the recruitment, and training outside Algeria, of their 'regular' army of liberation, the *ALN*, which was to be progressively blooded in a 'mobile' phase of operations and then thrown headlong at the exhausted French in the final stage of pitched battle – exemplified in Indo-China by the *débâcle* of Dien Bien Phu.

The secret of French military success in Algeria lay in mobility. The instrument of this was the helicopter, operated by Army and Air Force under a curious arrangement whereby the country was arbitrarily divided into two sections by a north–south line passing through Algiers. To the west of this line the Air Force operated a force of Sikorsky CH34s and to the east, ALAT flew their fleet of CH21s and CH19s. Each service handled its helicopters in its own way: the Air Force, true to the classic dictum that 'air power is indivisible' took this in its literal sense and concentrated their machines on a single airfield just outside Algiers; the Army's helicopters were usually grouped in support of a formation closely at grips with the FLN out in the countryside. The operational area was huge – initially 900 by 300 miles but shrinking to about half that as the security forces gained the upper hand – and distances from Algiers to the operational areas increased as the FLN were gradually driven out of open country and into the southern mountains.

Although the Air Force's arrangement led to highter serviceability because it was possible to centralize the workshops support, the Army's helicopters, living as it were in the field with the operational units, were far more responsive to shifts in the battle and more readily at hand when required by the ground commander, as they were organizationally integrated with the Army. 'Helicopter intervention detachments' or DIH were formed as an experiment; each consisted of two light *Alouette* helicopters for reconnaissance, liaison, and command and control, and six CH21s for troop-lift and logistic support.

A DIH could be redeployed quickly from one operational area to another, and took with it sufficient technical stores and equipment to permit operations away from its main base for several weeks.

After several years hard and generally successful campaigning the French Army had come to accept the helicopter not as some kind of mechanical freak but as a normal battlefield vehicle with the useful ability to move three-dimensionally. In the first two years of this campaign the scale of operations expanded rapidly; from a strength of 50,000 in 1954 the security forces had reached 400,000 in December 1956, but even so they were spread thinly, and only aerial mobility enabled them to react quickly to the attacks of an enemy who could chose the time and place for each attack. As one Foreign Legion regimental commander put it: 'Tanks, aviation and artillery are nothing but means of support, whereas in Algeria the helicopter represents the manoeuvre itself.' The rapidity of manoeuvre which was now possible was essential to success in Algeria, for throughout the campaign the security forces were inhibited by political directives which forbade them to undertake offensive operations unless they had been attacked first. Under these conditions one can only marvel that the French Army did so well right up to the end.

The British, after the early trials of 1946–47 mentioned already, were hesitant in developing the use of the military helicopter. A few Bristol *Sycamores* were in service with 1906 Air OP Flight for liaison and VIP passenger-carrying; the Air Ministry, which had to pay for these aircraft, was understandably reluctant to subsidize what was clearly an Army activity. Besides, there was a pressing need to provide additional helicopters for Malaya, where the RAF's original Far East Air Force casualty evacuation flight of Sikorsky S51s had been somewhat upstaged by the arrival, in 1953, of a squadron of Royal Navy S55s which were far better suited to the troop-lift role.

In 1955, the Air Ministry and War Office agreed to the formation of a joint Army/RAF unit, equipped with helicopters bought by the Army (the first aircraft purchased by the War Office since 1918) and called the Joint Experimental Helicopter Unit, or JEHU. The somewhat longwinded task of this unit was the '. . . collection of information by practical trials to enable the two services to determine whether helicopters were likely to be a practical, economical and efficient means of solving the Army's problems of mobility, organisation and administration in the field in a future war.' JEHU was commanded by Lt-Col. 'Jock' Scott, a wartime Air OP pilot, with an experienced RAF helicopter pilot as his second-in-command. One flight, equipped with Bristol *Sycamores*, was commanded by a soldier; the other, equipped with the Westland-built version of the Sikorsky S55 known as the

Whirlwind, was commanded by an RAF officer. Army and RAF pilots were mixed in both flights. The Army provided transport, soldiers and radios, and the RAF the technical support. By the end of 1955 the unit had shaken down well and was busy with a variety of trials, interspersed with demonstrations and exercises.

In the summer of 1956 it was intended to send JEHU over to Germany for field trials with the British Army of the Rhine, but as the Middle East situation deteriorated all trials work ceased and the unit was placed on a war footing. It embarked on the light fleet aircraft carrier HMS *Theseus* in order to acquire a new skill, that of the amphibious assault. The summer wore on and the British Army went through the convulsion of a partial mobilization. JEHU's vehicles were painted 'desert brown' and tropical clothing was drawn. It was clear what lay ahead. In order, one imagines, to allay the fears of prospective passengers the word 'Experimental' was deleted from the unit's title and the 'Joint Helicopter Unit' embarked for the seat of war on 26 October at Devonport, bound initially for Malta in *Theseus*'s sister ship HMS *Ocean*. During the voyage the aircrews practised emplaning and deplaning drills with the Marines of 45 Commando who came aboard at Malta. The helicopters were stripped of every non-essential component to ensure maximum payload, and second pilots' seats, doors and passenger seats were discarded.

On 3 November the Carrier Task Force sailed from Malta. The two ships were jammed with helicopters, men and equipment, and last-minute practice of emplaning drills went on until every man knew his part like an actor. During the afternoon of 5 November the helicopters were finally ranged out on the flight decks; as darkness fell a complete black-out was imposed and all hands stood to battle stations. Such news as had reached the ship indicated that the parachute assault on the morning of 5 November had succeeded but fighting was in progress ashore and a measure of opposition could be expected. Just before 0400 hrs on 6 November the two carriers anchored, about 1000 yards from each other, in the safe channel swept of mines. From ashore could be heard the sound of the preliminary naval and air bombardment, and as dawn broke a pall of black smoke rose from Port Said. A reconnaissance helicopter set off from HMS *Theseus* to check on the landing zones selected for 45 Commando. It came under heavy fire and was hit in 20 places; it returned hurriedly to *Theseus* where a new plan was made: the Marines were now to land near the canal entrance, close to the prominent statue of Ferdinand de Lesseps.

The Carrier Task Group was under the command of Rear-Adm. Sayer, who flew his flag in HMS *Ocean*. He was reluctantly joined on the bridge by Lt-Col. Scott, who had intended to fly the leading helicopter but was kept on board the carrier by the admiral as his adviser. The privilege of leading the first opposed amphibious helicopter assault therefore fell to his second-in-command, Sqn Ldr 'Danny' Kearns, RAF, who had spent much of the summer patiently initiating JEHU's newly joined Army pilots – mostly officers of the Royal Army Service Corps – into the art of flying the Westland *Whirlwind* Mk 2 helicopter. It was indeed something of an art, for unlike the Sikorsky S55s flown by the Royal Navy which had Wright Cyclone engines of more than 700 horse power the *Whirlwind* 2, though externally almost an identical aircraft, was powered by reconditioned 550 horsepower Pratt and Whitney 'Wasp' engines stored in RAF Maintenance Units since 1945 and unearthed as an economy measure to be installed in Westland's version of the S55. The *Whirlwind* was therefore considerably underpowered and JEHU's could take only five fully equipped Marines compared to the naval helicopters' seven. One flight of JEHU was equipped with the smaller *Sycamore* Mk 14 helicopter which carried three Marines. It was all a far cry from the troop-lifts which would be commonplace in Vietnam 15 years later.

At 0610 hrs (GMT) the first wave of helicopters took off from the deck of HMS *Ocean* amidst considerable speculation. Virtually nothing was known about the state of the defences ashore but the hot reception accorded to the reconnaissance helicopter had been evident as it landed back on *Theseus* peppered with bullet holes and with a slightly wounded pilot. The uncertainty of the whole operation was reflected in 'Commander's Daily Orders' aboard HMS *Ocean* on the previous evening: after detailing the routine for the early morning of the assault, with details of readiness and time of emplaning, the orders ended hopefully with, '. . . and the best of British Luck.'

In this spirit of mingled curiosity and endeavour, the assault went in. Within five minutes, JEHU's *Sycamores* were airborne and followed the *Whirlwinds* towards the beach; both carriers had weighed anchor and were steaming cautiously in towards the town, from which unmistakable sounds of battle were to be heard. Landing craft and tracked amphibians were also forging towards the beaches at their best speed, carrying the rest of the 3rd Commando Brigade. In all, JEHU and 845 Naval Helicopter Squadron each flew in seven waves of troops. Despite their small payloads, their helicopters flew the entire Commando ashore in just under one and a half hours, after which they continued to land stores and ammunition.

Men landed in the first waves were in action within seconds of landing. Both the signallers in the Air Contact Team which was one of the first units to be landed were wounded in the first few minutes; they were back aboard HMS *Ocean* on the surgeon's operating table within 20 minutes of emplaning, as helicopters returning empty to the carriers were pressed into service as flying ambulances. Out of 749 men flown ashore, 96 were flown back as casualties. Ashore, the Egyptians fired copiously but erratically. One helicopter, damaged by fire and drained of fuel, landed in the sea but its load of casualties were all saved. Another helicopter, one of JEHU's *Sycamores*, suffered engine failure on take-off and subsided ingloriously onto the flight deck. There were no casualties to the helicopter crews. One of the wounded brought back aboard was the Marines' commanding officer, Lt-Col. Tailyour, who survived this experience to become Comdt-Gen. Royal Marines.

Morale aboard the ships was tremendous, particularly when it was seen how quickly the wounded were being recovered, and sailors, soldiers and airmen cheerfully lined up to donate their blood. On the flight deck, it was evident that the endlessly repeated drills, by day and night, were paying handsome dividend. If no fuel was required, a helicopter returning from the beach could deplane its load of casualties, embark the next 'stick' of Marines and be off again in 90 seconds. Every second trip, so small was the fuel load carried, the helicopters stopped their engines, refuelled, restarted and took off again within seven minutes. In the early days of training this had taken up to 20 minutes; it was a remarkable tribute to the Royal Navy's instruction that men of all three services were now working together at such a high level of efficiency.

As the beaches were cleared of enemy and the Marines fought their way into the town, resistance began to fall off, and for the rest of the day JEHU was used to ferry troops and stores ashore. The 3rd Battalion of the Parachute Regiment, out on Gamil airfield to the west, were reinforced by a helicopter lift of men from the Royal Air Force Regiment, and the carriers eased into Port Said Harbour where they secured alongside the wharf. After two days of intensive activity, during which JEHU was used for cargo and personnel lifts as well as reconnaissance and liaison, the helicopters flew ashore and were based on Gamil airfield, still littered with the debris of the 3rd Battalion's earlier assault.

Out on Gamil airfield, the helicopters began to succumb to the effects of high humidity, salt-water corrosion and the abrasive effect of the desert sand, all of which have an alarming effect on magnesium alloys. On 22 November the *Whirlwinds* were flown aboard a carrier for evacuation to Cyprus, to be followed four days later by the *Sycamores*. At the end of the month the remainder of the unit embarked for the United Kingdom in a rusty tank-landing ship. It was a somewhat anti-climactic end to a novel operation.

With the helicopter landing at Port Said a milestone was reached in the development of the use of army aviation. The first combat operation of its type followed 24 hours after what may have been the last of the classic parachute assaults to be carried out by British troops. During the 1950s, all armies acquired confidence in the handling of aircraft, whether through experience with 656 Squadron's Austers in Malaya or in the increasing number of smaller helicopters which began to follow JEHU's *Whirlwinds* – which, because they exceeded the 4000lb limit, were quickly taken over by the RAF when JEHU disbanded in 1959. However, a tremendous amount of experience was gained, and may of the army pilots who had begun their flying careers in the RAF's Air OP Squadrons and had served in JEHU transferred to the newly formed Army Air Corps when it came into being in September 1957.

If the British had pioneered the use of the helicopter in Malaya, and carried out the first helicopter assault from the sea, it was the French in Algeria who showed how the third dimension could be used in land operations. From 1960 onwards, however, the United States Army was to lead the way, developing and refining the handling of airmobile units on a huge scale.

CHAPTER TWELVE

Air Cavalry

On 24 June 1956 the Russians celebrated Soviet Air Force Day with a display at Tushino airport which included an event calculated to excite the foreign attaché corps as much as had the massed parachute descents of 1936. A force of low-flying helicopters burst into view, landing in front of the crowd to disgorge troops complete with light vehicles, motor cycles and support weapons, who proceed to carry out an assault operation whilst the helicopters rapidly took off and flew away. Later waves of helicopters brought reinforcements, additional guns, vehicles, and loads of fuel and ammunition. Despite the artificiality of the occasion, its message was clear; the Soviet Army possessed a return ticket to battle. At last, a well-armed fighting force could be carried to any chosen point in the combat zone, put down as a tactically balanced formation, and recovered if necessary for reinsertion elsewhere. A solution had been found to the seemingly insoluble problems of mobility faced by 'conventional' airborne forces launched into battle by glider and parachute.

Although the Russians had obviously devoted much thought to the creation of an airmobile arm, they were far from being the first to use helicopters as a means of battlefield mobility. The French were already using them in Algeria in that savage campaign against an elusive enemy. Since 1950, British helicopters had flown on operations in Malaya. The Americans had built up a considerable force of them in Korea by the time of the 1953 ceasefire, and it was the US Army which led the evolution of battlefield airmobility in the free world.

Tactical mobility can be described as the capacity to move fighting strength at will to the point where a decisive result is required; moving freely across country with a degree of speed and secrecy which will ensure surprise. It also implies the ability to move not only fighting men but also their means of mobility and combat support once they have been deposited at their destination; mobility for the eyes and ears of the commander in the form of observation, reconnaissance and enhanced communications; for the commander himself and his key staff officers and subordinates, who can use the third-dimensional approach to command the battle by direct observation rather than remote control; for the sinews of war – fuel, rations, ammunition and stores of every description; for the inevitable casualties who must be evacuated quickly to receive medical attention.

Quite early in the Second World War, soldiers in a number of armies began to realize that even the rickety light aircraft operated for artillery spotting purposes were capable of fulfilling a number of 'mobility' tasks. The US Army, originally equipped with Piper *Cub* aircraft for artillery observation purposes, quietly acquired numbers of larger aircraft, and as soon as helicopters came on the scene they got hold of some of these as well. The infant air arm suffered a set back, however, in 1947 when the US Air Force was formed; USAF chiefs immediately obtained a Pentagon ruling that the Army's fixed-wing aircraft should not exceed 2500lb in weight, and its helicopters were limited to 4000lb. These arbitrary limits (a similar one was imposed on the British Army Air Corps when it formed in 1957) were slowly eroded and the US Army went ahead with its procurement of larger aircraft – but in an atmosphere of inter-service distrust and skirmishing which persisted until 1966 when a final agreement was reached with USAF on the scope and nature of army aviation.

From the start, the US Army attempted to use helicopters for every conceivable battlefield role, especially in the field of aerial armaments. In 1942 a Sikorsky R5 helicopter had been fitted with a 20mm cannon and by 1947 (when USAF put a temporary stop to these activities), numerous trials had been carried out with a variety of weapons; all suffered from serious limitations due to the sheer ballistic difficulties of firing from an inherently unstable platform, and the inadequate load-carrying performance of the early military helicopters.

In 1950 the ever-resourceful US Marine Corps, who had already pioneered the use of helicopters in assault trials, were the first to mount a battery of rockets on a helicopter. Shortly afterwards, the US Army, turning a deaf ear to strident USAF protests, made trials of helicopter-mounted rockets in the anti-tank role. These early trials, whilst invigorating and spectacular, showed that the effect was moral rather than physical. Fin-stabilized rockets were designed to be fired from a warplane in a shallow dive at speeds exceeding 250 knots; when launched from a helicopter struggling along at a maximum speed of around 80 knots, they behaved unpredictably, and films of these early trials show them colliding with each other in mid-air, veering off at right angles or even diving alarmingly to the ground beneath the helicopter from which they had been fired.

In Korea, automatic weapons were occasionally fired for self-protection from the passenger doors of helicopters, but no attempt was made to employ such weapons aggressively. Despite the evident failings of early trials it was held by some army aviators that the helicopter could be used to advantage as a weapons platform. The first methodical trials of heliborne rockets were held in 1953 on the US Army's Aberdeen Proving Ground. Physicists and ballisticians obtained much useful data from these firings – codenamed 'Project Sally Rand' – and their findings laid the foundation for the scientific approach to aerial weapons systems which reached fruition in Vietnam and will attain further developments with the Advanced Attack Helicopters of the 1980s.

In the early 1950s there were conflicting ideas on the role of armed helicopters. One school advocated their use in the shock assault role, preceding the troop-carriers with a carpet of rocket and cannon fire to neutralize all opposition. This was an extension of the technique of 'reconnaissance by fire' developed by the late Gen. George Patton and used with conspicuous success by his armoured divisions in their headlong dash from Normandy to the Rhine in 1944; instead of using the more deliberate tactic of 'fire and movement' favoured by the British, which involved one portion of an advancing (or for that matter a retiring) force halting in order to provide covering fire for the other, Patton encouraged a general advance with all guns firing on any cover from which enemy fire might be expected. Although horribly wasteful of ammunition, it seemed to work in 1944, and thus became enshrined as standard American tactical dogma. The more cautious school of Army Aviators recognized the fragility and vulnerability of the helicopter and argued that it was best used well out of reach of the enemy's weapons as an observation, troop-lifting or logistic vehicle, keeping to the rear of the friendly forward positions. The actual answer, as will be seen, lay somewhere between these two poles.

The enthusiasm and enterprise of the 'recce-by-fire' school led to the 'Sagebrush' trials of 1955, an ambitious – and as it turned out, premature – attempt to co-ordinate armed with assault and support helicopters in land operations. Light-armed helicopters were used in what amounted to a skirmishing role, and in the subsequent reports it was clear that they would have suffered appalling casualties from enemy ground fire at point-blank range in 'real' war conditions. The armed scout helicopters used in the trials were fitted with rifle-calibre machine guns of low hitting power and limited accuracy, and as they were flown with little regard to use of natural ground cover they were repeatedly 'caught' and adjudged destroyed. Other aspects of 'Sagebrush' went largely unnoticed in the subsequent flurry of argument; troop-carrying helicopters had succeeded beyond expectation in this and later trials and their development was pushed ahead.

Crossing the Rhine. A British Horsa *glider makes its final approach through the haze. In the foregound, American paratroops who, though dropped well away from their intended dropzone, were of great assistance in clearing the British glider LZs of German gun detachments. (Imperial War Museum)*

Operation 'Varsity' (The Rhine crossing). Immediately after the glider landings, this remarkable picture was taken from a supply-dropping USAAF Liberator; a British Horsa *glider, having smashed through a line of trees, lies wingless on the LZ. Such dramatic landings were fairly common-place and most were survivable. (Imperial War Museum)*

'*Total Soldiers*'—*two British glider pilots search the ruins of a school in Arnhem. A parachuted supply container—one of the few which reached 1st Airborne Division—lies in the door-way.* (*Imperial War Museum*)

Below: *This poignant photograph, taken by a German soldier at Arnhem, epitomizes the sacrifice of the 1st British Airborne Division—a paratrooper killed in the act of helping his stricken comrade.* (*Imperial War Museum*)

Above: '. . . *something of the air of a training exercise . . .*' *Troops of 1st Parachute Brigade land on the glider LZs at Wolfheze on the afternoon of 17 September 1944. In Arnhem town the Germans are already reacting to the arrival of 1st Airborne Division and deployed to block their advance to the bridges.*

Below: *One of the glider LZs at Arnhem. The first gliders to land were required to get as near to the upwind edge of the LZ (on the left of the picture) as possible, and several pilots in their zeal have crashed on into a plantation of young trees. Most of these gliders are Horsa Mk Is, which had to be split aft of the wings in order to unload. The larger glider, slight right of centre, is a Hamilcar, and the tracks made by the light tank it was carrying can clearly be seen leading off into the woods at the top of the picture. (Imperial War Museum)*

The assault on Port Said, 6 November 1956. In vics of three, Whirlwinds *of the Joint Helicopter Unit fly Royal Marines Commando troops ashore whilst the town burns under naval and air bombardments. (Imperial War Museum)*

Whirlwind helicopters of the Joint Helicopter Unit on Gamil airfield, Port Said, on the afternoon of 6 November 1956. The debris of the previous day's assault by 3rd Battalion, The Parachute Regiment, is in the foreground. (Air Ministry)

Air assault in Vietnam. 29 May 1965. Paratroops of the 173rd Airborne Brigade make for cover after landing from UH-1's in a rice field near Bienttoa. (US Army Photograph)

Vietnam. May 1966. Having landed the assaulting troops of 173rd Airborne Brigade, three UH-1Ds race away from the landing zone. (US Army Photograph)

Air assault in Vietnam, July 1967. In the An Lao valley, men of the 1st Cavalry Division have just attacked a Viet Cong base. A UH-1D is about to land to pick up enemy stores captured in the operation. (US Army Photograph)

Vietnam, 1969. All the drama and urgency of a casualty evacuation mission is captured in this photograph, taken during the operations in the A Shau valley. (US Army Photograph)

An armed UH-1 helicopter of the 502nd Aviation Battalion is prepared for its next fire support mission at Can Tho in May 1965. Until the arrival of the HueyCobra the UH-1 was in widespread use as an escort and ground attack machine. (Department of the Army, Washington)

Vietnam, December 1965. A UH-1B releases a cargo net filled with combat rations alongside a patrol of the 101st Airborne Division. (US Army Photograph)

Whilst the US Army forged boldly ahead with practical trials, some distinguished officers were beginning to think seriously about the military possibilities of the helicopter. It is interesting to note that in the forefront of this new wave were some of the most outstanding airborne soldiers of the Second World War. Here were men proven as leaders, respected in their profession and clearly heading for the top. Colonel John Tolson, who took part in every action fought by the 503rd Parachute Infantry Regiment in South-East Asia and who had master-minded the spectacular assault at Corregidor, qualified as an army aviator in 1957, later became Director of Army Aviation, then served in Vietnam in 1967–68 as commander of the airmobile 1st Cavalry Division. General 'Jim' Gavin, who had commanded 82nd Airborne Division in *Market Garden* with distinction, went on to round off a distinguished career as US Ambassador in Paris. During the early 1950s he was G-3 at the Pentagon, a highly influential post in which he was served by a young and brilliant team of staff officers. Tolson was one of them; as Gavin's Director of Doctrine and Combat Development he was well placed to assist his chief in the formulation of new doctrine and in whipping up powerful political support for the great army aviation expansion programme.

Although, to the outsider, the junior echelons of the American military system appear to be woefully deprived of the ability to make even the simplest decisions, the key posts in the Pentagon are filled by men who are not only masters of their profession but who have far less inhibitions than their opposite numbers in other Western nations about going publicly into print or stating their views in open debate. The candour with which the proceedings of Congressional Committees on defence issues are reported makes a startling contrast to the flat anonymity of a British Government White Paper. Gavin was no exception to the rule. A gifted and persuasive writer, he published an article in the mass-circulation *Harper's Magazine* in April 1954 which was generally acknowledged to reflect the drift of Pentagon policy. Entitled 'Cavalry, and I Don't Mean Horses!' it described a whole range of hypothetical organizations which the Army might adopt to perform the traditional 'Cavalry' roles with helicopters instead of tracked and wheeled vehicles. The article was an eminently readable, brilliant exposition of the vision which now beckoned the progressives. It described how, even on a post-nuclear battlefield, the essential tasks of reconnaissance, surveillance, screening and exploitation, for centuries the province of horsed cavalry, would still have to be performed. Tanks and armoured cars enjoyed the benefits of protection, but were limited in speed and by their inability to move other than two-dimensionally. The helicopter, argued Gavin, offered an even bigger breakthrough than the tank because of its ability to move freely over and across any type of terrain.

Nine years later, whilst ambassador in Paris, Gavin set the seal on his life's work with another important article, this time in the prestigious *Army Journal*. He entitled it 'The Mobility Differential'. It is possibly one of the most important doctrinal statements printed this century, for it finally resolves the problems which have confronted the 'conventional' airborne forces of the free world since 1945.

Gavin argued that *innovation* is essential to survival, and is usually decisive when applied to the science of war. A study of history, he claimed, showed that most of the truly outstanding examples of military innovation were the product of two functions – firepower and mobility, whether exemplified by the shock tactics of Alexander the Great's cavalry, the Roman legions marching rapidly from end to end of the Empire along a network of strategic roads, or the technique of *Blitzkrieg* employed by the Germans in 1939–40. In each of these cases, victory had gone to the side which enjoyed the advantage of a 'mobility differential' over its less nimble opponents. In the Second World War, the armour had taken over the cavalry role; by the early sixties, with the ominous Warsaw Pact build-up in Eastern Europe, the West, still reliant on tracks and wheels, had lost its mobility differential. The only way to redress the balance was to develop battlefield aerial vehicles to complement the conventional fighting arms. Up to 1945, airborne forces had been able to do this, often with great success; but the development of potent anti-aircraft weapons in the post-war period had driven the glider and the low-flying troop-carrying aircraft out of the sky over the combat zone.

The most telling message came towards the end of the article. Gavin, the paladin of airborne soldiers, felt himself obliged to write the epitaph of old-style airborne warfare: 'It is foolish, therefore, to assume that we can continue to employ the World War 2 type of airborne operations in the future. It is beautiful, spectacular, and demanding of courage, but it isn't war – not in the missile age.'

The 'traditional' airborne soldiers who read these words with horror probably threw down the magazine at this point. Had they read on, they would have seen what Gavin was driving at. He could see that an important role still remained for airborne units; there were many situations in which it would be impossible to use helicopters, especially for strategic troop deployments over long ranges, when airlanding was impossible and the prompt arrival of military force by the most dramatic method would still achieve results out of all proportion to the actual numbers of men used. The place for the battlefield aerial vehicle was the low-level airspace over the actual combat zone – the very area from which old-style airborne forces had been driven by the threat of vastly-improved anti-aircraft weaponry and the Warsaw Pact's undeniable strength in tactical combat aircraft.

Gavin's astounding article was rounded off with a summary of the uses which he and his Pentagon staff had devised for the whole family of aerial vehicles. At the point of initial contact, when the attacking enemy was attempting to brush aside the NATO defenders' screen of lightly equipped units, pairs of light reconnaissance helicopters would operate well forward, identifying the enemy, preventing him from achieving surprise, bringing down the fire of all available artillery and controlling Allied airstrikes in order to disrupt and delay. 'Support helicopters', capable of lifting up to 12 fully equipped troops, would give the defending commander tremendous mobility, seizing threatened points and holding them if necessary in order to buy time. 'Command helicopters' fitted with the necessary radios would be used to control the fast-moving airmobile battle. Larger helicopters would provide mobile logistic support, shifting stores, weapons, fuel and supplies up to the forward combat zone. Flying cranes – helicopters specially designed to lift bulky and heavy loads – would be used to lay temporary bridges and remove them again.

When Gavin's article appeared in print, the US Army had been operating helicopters in Vietnam for one and a half years, applying aviation techniques and using a family of aircraft thought out in the Pentagon almost ten years earlier. The sheer size of this undertaking is hard to visualize; for apart from the theorizing and political infighting which had gone on in Washington DC, some notable pioneering field-work had been going on in the US Army's schools and training centres.

In 1956 and 1957 a determined Army officer, Col. Jay Vanderpool, head of Combat Development at the US Army Aviation School, gathered a small staff about him, 'borrowed' some helicopters, strapped a variety of weapons to them, and started to evolve an entirely new tactical code for battlefield helicopters. He taught his pilots how to use natural cover and the agility of their machines to gain immunity from enemy observation. Instead of flying headlong in the general direction of the enemy, Vanderpool's pilots applied the skills of the stalker and sniper, carefully proving each piece of un-reconnoitred ground before moving across it, flying 'nap-of-the-earth' (NOE) and acquiring undreamt-of skills in airmanship and low-level navigation. Where necessary, 'recce-by-fire' was still used, but only as a last resort. Just as Bazeley and his little band of disciples had toured the United Kingdom in 1940 and 1941 preaching and demonstrating their gospel of aerial gunnery observation, so now did

Vanderpool's men, with their often hair-raising demonstrations, introduce the US Army to the techniques it would be regarding as commonplace a decade later in Vietnam.

In Algeria, the French were discovering the need for armed helicopters by dint of experience. They soon found that once the novelty had worn thin, their enemies could inflict heavy casualties on the unarmed assault helicopters. Improvised weapons systems were quickly lashed on in order to provide suppressive fire in the final stages of the assault. These proved inadequate, and an 'arms pack' was devised for the H21 'Flying Banana' helicopter; it comprised two rocket pods, each of eighteen 68mm rockets, and two machine guns in flexible mountings on the forward undercarriage strut from where they were remotely controlled by the co-pilot. Thus equipped, the H21 could lay down an effective curtain of fire, but its troop-carrying capability was seriously affected, and its lack of agility made it an easy target. The French accordingly fitted a weapons pack to the small *Alouette* 2 helicopter, for use in the armed escort and fire suppression role. The genesis of the gunship was at hand.

By 1958, when they appeared to be on the verge of military victory in Algeria, despite the crippling political constraints imposed on military commanders in the field, the French had begun to introduce the earliest helicopter-mounted wire-guided missiles. These are, in effect, pilotless miniature aircraft propelled by a rocket motor and 'flown' by a controller in the launching helicopter by means of a small control column, which passes the controller's commands to the missile's guidance vanes along a thin wire cable paid out as the missile flies towards its target. The earliest missiles, such as the Nord SS10 used in Algeria, were guided visually, the controller aided by a flare in the tail of the missile. With practice, a good controller could place his missile with great accuracy at ranges of 2000 metres. The SS10 proved most effective against enemy hiding in caves; the effect of the shaped charge exploding within such confined spaces was devastating and had a profound effect on enemy morale.

Whilst the US Army, with its relatively huge financial resources, was getting down to large-scale development in the armed helicopter field, and as the French put their experience to the proof of battle, tentative trials were afoot elsewhere. In 1958, the Joint Experimental Helicopter Unit, restored to its legitimate pursuits after the excitements of the Port Said escapade, undertook the first British trials with helicopter weapons. The incongruous choice of weapon was the Vickers Medium Machine Gun. The direct descendant of the Maxim Gun of the high Victorian age, it had served in two world wars and was the revered mainstay of the machine gun platoon in every British infantry battalion. Tripod mounted and water-cooled, it was served by a team of three gunners who handled it almost as a piece of artillery, using a dial sight to engage unseen targets at several thousand yards' range. The Vickers was noted for its capacity to fire steadily for hours on end rather than for its handiness or high rate of fire, and 20 years later its selection as a helicopter-mounted weapon seems bizarre. However, it was the only suitable belt-fed, sustained fire machine gun in British service at the time. Mounted in the passenger door of a *Whirlwind* on its tripod the old gun fired belt after belt of ·303in calibre up the Warminster ranges of the School of Infantry. The water in the cooling jacket boiled merrily and the cabin filled with the evocative mingled aromas of hot oily metal and cordite. Far down the range, spurts of white chalkdust indicated the fall of shot, apparently covering a huge area of Salisbury Plain.

At this time the British were looking everywhere for a light helicopter with which to replace their Auster light observation aircraft. The eventual choice was the *Skeeter*; it had been optimistically designed in 1946 as a businessman's runabout by the firm of Cierva, the builders of the earliest autogyros 20 years earlier. Difficulties over the engine imposed continual delays and the *Skeeter* eventually reached military service in 1958 after 12 years of development, which must be something of a record for a light aircraft. Even then, its lack of power forbade its use outside the temperate European zone, and its very limited payload severely constrained its military value. For five years, however, it was virtually the only helicopter available to the British Army, apart from a few French *Alouette* 2s, and it played a significant part in the at times laborious business of educating a naturally conservative military establishment in the business of army aviation.

The US Army's aviation arm continued to expand steadily. From a 1950 strength of 668 light aircraft and 57 helicopters it had attained a total of 5500 all types by the middle of 1959. As many were either obsolescent or of limited military value, a hard look was indicated at the creation of a 'family' of aerial vehicles for the next decade. Providentially, one of the helicopters selected in 1959 was the Bell XH40 which, originally designed as a flying ambulance powered by a piston engine, was to enter US Army service as the turbine-powered UH1, the immortal *Iroquois*, and to be the mainstay of army aviation throughout the '60s and '70s. This was a time of great activity in the American aircraft industry, which rose splendidly to the challenge thrown down by Lt-Gen. Arthur Trudeau, the Pentagon's Chief of Army research and Development, in December 1959. He called for design concepts for the Army's future aircraft inventory and 45 companies responded within weeks. Their outline designs were examined by the Army Aircraft Requirements Review Board (known as the Rogers Board) which, having closely studied the material before it, spelt out a requirement for three distinct types of aircraft: observation, surveillance and transport. Development of the most promising types went ahead, with a production target date of 1964 for the most successful. Although overshadowed by later developments, the work of the Rogers Board laid the true foundations of US Army Aviation's equipment programme.

New organizations for airmobile warfare were also beginning to appear. Hitherto, aviation resources had been widely dispersed, closely under control of their parent arm, whether Artillery, Armour or Transportation. In 1960 the commander of the 101st Airborne Division grouped all his aircraft under a single command and designated this the '101st Combat Aviation Battalion (Provisional)' – the forebear of all future units of this type.

As the American Army got down to organizing, equipping and training its exciting new combat arm, the French and British were still enmeshed in problems of imperial policing and counter-insurgency which dogged them throughout the post-war period; some were the inevitable result of a precipitate retreat from Empire, many bore the all-too-familiar stamp of Marxist–Leninist inspiration. British Government policy during this prolonged era of retreat began to veer towards strategic mobility for a global reserve force held at readiness in the United Kingdom. Stockpiles of heavy equipment were established in the Far East at Singapore, and in the Middle East at Aden. The RAF began to acquire, at last, aircraft with a convincing strategic transport capability; the turboprop *Britannia* and the turbo jet *Comet* came into service in the early '60s to displace the leisurely troopships which for decades had moved the British Army to and from its agreeable overseas posts. Tactical transports such as the huge *Beverly* and the twin-boom *Argosy*, both with rear cargo doors and thus suited for airdropping equipment on stressed platforms, had joined the squadrons rather earlier, displacing the four-engined *Hastings* and twin-engined *Valetta*. An even greater degree of strategic mobility was promised by the military version of the VC10, a four-jet airliner which would join the RAF in the later '60s. What was still lacking, however, was a transport with strategic range and cruising speed which could match the stage lengths of *Comet* and *Britannia* and deliver troops and equipment by parachute, if necessary, at its destination. Although the superb Lockheed C130 was already in service with USAF and in many other countries, the RAF was unable to acquire it for many years and because of the British aircraft industry's failure to produce such an aircraft (due to complex politico-industrial factors outside the scope of this book) Britain's ability to deliver a parachute force over strategic distances withered and died. It was a dismal period for 16th Parachute Brigade; highly trained, complete with its own parachuted artillery, armoured reconnaissance, engineers and all supporting units, it remained part of the UK Strategic Reserve but without a credible means of transport other than over the shorter ranges within the NATO theatre, where the chances of using airborne forces seemed to be diminishing steadily with the rise of Soviet airpower.

Within two years of the victorious end of the twelve-year counter-terrorist war in Malaya, another outbreak occurred in Borneo which reinvolved the British Army in jungle operations and emphasized the importance of airmobility for warfare in undeveloped terrain. The operational area was huge; a 900-mile frontier with Indonesia had to be kept under surveillance, enemy incursions detected and fought off, and isolated outposts sustained. With the aid of a small force of helicopters from all three Services the Director of Operations, Gen. Sir Walter Walker, fought a masterly campaign. He never had more than 10,000 combat troops; those he had were given tremendous mobility by intelligent use of the third dimension. General Walker later summarized his doctrine: '. . . The fewer helicopters you had, the more troops you required . . . give a hundred men helicopters and they will do the work of a thousand . . . a battalion with six Wessex helicopters was worth more to me than a brigade without them. . . .'

The British Army became embroiled in another counter-insurgency operation whilst the East Malaysian confrontation was in progress. This was in South Arabia, where a Yemeni-inspired campaign, backed by Egypt, stirred up the notoriously difficult tribes in the Western Aden Protectorate. The area into which a brigade-sized force was rapidly deployed must rank as one of the most awesome places in the world in which to fight a running anti-guerrilla war. The wild hills rise to well over 6000 feet; the average out-of-shade temperature is 115°F and, over most of the area in which the supporting helicopters were required to operate, the effects of heat, height and relative humidity produced an equivalent atmospheric altitude of over 10,000 feet. These conditions were more severe even than those encountered by the French in Algeria, but nevertheless the Radfan campaign, like that in Borneo, must rank as a minor classic of its type.

Aviation resources were limited, as the Borneo campaign had first claim on the British government's attention. The Radfan war was therefore successfully prosecuted by whatever forces could be scraped together. The Royal Navy was able from time to time to augment the

RAF's helicopter lift with *Wessex* aircraft disembarked from aircraft carriers. The RAF's helicopter lift was provided by a small number of *Belvederes* – twin-rotor machines of uncertain temperament, the result of a political decision to go ahead with the production of a semi-developed Bristol design which, had it been fully worked out, could have been a world-beater. As it was, the *Belvedere* was a great dis-appointment; but the skill of its crews and the devotion of grossly overworked groundcrews kept it flying in both Borneo and South Arabia. The Army Aviation resources available for the Radfan were ludicrously small – nine light aircraft and two *Scout* helicopters to start with. There was a grave shortage of Army helicopter pilots quali-fied to fly the relatively new *Scout*; this reached such proportions that the Director of Land/Air Warfare himself, Maj.-Gen. Napier Crookenden (who had qualified as a *Scout* pilot in England), was pressed into service during a short visit to Aden, and found himself flying supplies to infantry patrols on the highest peaks of the Radfan.

In both the Borneo and Radfan campaigns the Army was well served by the air; but it was noticeable that there were differences between the services in their methods of commanding and controlling their battlefield aerial vehicles. The RAF retained control at a high level, which often meant from a distant base headquarters, whilst Army Aviation was parcelled out for use by commanders on the ground according to their needs at any given moment. There were several crises in the Radfan when RAF helicopter support was arbi-trarily withdrawn at the height of a crucial operation. There were very sound reasons for this, of course; the larger RAF aircraft required complicated base servicing and, not being designed to live in the field, were not suited for easy maintenance away from their base hang-ars. A soldier in a forward position, however, does not take kindly to having his helicopter support withdrawn at a critical moment. Inter-service relations were severely strained; it was unfortunate that the recipients of the soldiers' wrath were the crews of the helicopters who had been trying so conscientiously to do their job, and not the distant air staff officers back in Aden.

Army Aviation in the Radfan was more responsive. The Army Air Corps commander and his staff were installed in a huddle of tents on the forward airstrip and his meagre resources could be quickly switched from task to task to meet the demands of the brigade com-mander. If, for example, a platoon-size picket on an outlying peak had to be relieved, a battalion would be allotted two *Scout* helicopters for one hour; a fresh platoon, with water, rations and ammunition for 72 hours could actually be lifted 3000 feet up to its perch in 30 minutes and the outgoing pickets brought down to the valley below. This was a technique laboriously acquired and practised by the British and Indian armies during a century of frontier wars; an elaborate and risky operation which formerly took the best part of a day was now performed in a matter of minutes with the aid of two small helicopters.

Two decades had now passed since the end of the Second World war and a new combat arm, that of Army Aviation, had emerged. Its experimental use in a variety of combat situations had proved most encouraging. There were still, however, some urgent problems to be solved – command and control, tactics, organizations, all were still in a state of flux. Moreover, the different requirements and circumstances of the various national armies involved demanded a variety of approaches. One thing was abundantly clear – alone of all the Western allies, the British had elected to divide the responsibility for battlefield aviation support between more than one service; the Army, though now operating its own light and utility aircraft, remained dependent on the RAF for support in the troop-lifting and cargo roles. More significantly, the RAF's largest helicopters remained the *Belvedere* – withdrawn finally from service after its unhappy career in 1969, and the *Wessex*, a turbine-powered version of an old Sikorsky design (the S58) which had first flown in the early 1950s. There was no helicopter heavy lift support for the British Army; several attempts to acquire a small number of Boeing-Vertol CH47 *Chinooks* during the later '60s and early '70s foundered due to lack of funds, and *Chinook* will not enter RAF service until the 1980s.

Whist other nations had been dabbling with the new dimension, the Americans had been hard at work. The foresight of their Army aviators during the 1950s was to bear fruit in abundance throughout the bitter and eventually unresolved struggle in Vietnam, with which the next three chapters are mainly concerned.

CHAPTER THIRTEEN

Vietnam 1: The Proving-ground

The arrival of the small aircraft carrier USNS *Card* at Saigon on 11
December 1961 went almost unnoticed. At this point in the war,
American involvement in the internal affairs of the Republic of
Vietnam was confined to the activities of military advisory and
specialist groups whose mission was to help organize and train the
Vietnamese armed forces for what promised to be a prolonged strug-
gle against Ho Chi Minh's carefully prepared campaign, controlled
from Hanoi.

The *Card*'s deck cargo consisted of 32 H21 helicopters, which,
speedily disembarked, were soon being flown by two US Army
Transportation Companies from near-by bases in support of the
Army of the Republic of Vietnam (ARVN). Their arrival was the result
of a visit to Vietnam earlier in the year by President Kennedy's
Military Adviser, none other than Gen. Maxwell D. Taylor, the commander of 101st Airborne Division in the great days of *Market
Garden* who, like 'Jim' Gavin, his fellow airborne leader, was now an
ardent convert to the idea of battlefield airmobility. The additional
American aid which followed Gen. Taylor's mission to Vietnam was
the beginning of a gradual build-up of US Army Aviation support.
Within a month the *Card* was back off the coast of South Vietnam
with another load of H21s, which were flown ashore to the Da Nang
airbase. In April 1962 the first US Marine Corps helicopters arrived;
from then on a steady stream of Army and Marine aviation units
joined in the fight, for it was apparent that tactical mobility was
essential for the South Vietnamese and their allies in a rapidly escalat-
ing fight for survival.

The early days of helicopter operations in Vietnam were fraught
with adventure. The Vietcong seemed to be everywhere; helicopters
were continually under fire, but at this stage the enemy also had
much to learn. One H21 pilot had an unnerving experience when, on
landing in a rural area, he was confronted by a platoon of Vietcong
who opened fire at a few yards' range. Fortunately for him, they sla-
vishly obeyed their instructions for engaging aircraft and aimed ahead
of the helicopter, which was unscathed. However, the prowess of the

Vietcong – heirs of the Viet Minh who had triumphed in the same area in 1954 – was quickly recognized. Newly arrived pilots would be shown the hilltop overlooking the Mang Yeng Pass, on the road from the coastal town of Qui Nhon to Pleiku in the Highlands, where the graves of 4000 French troops bore testimony to a bloody defeat in 1954. It was a sobering introduction.

At first, the American helicopter units were concentrated and based centrally on a few airbases, rather as the French Air Force had operated their helicopter force in Algeria. This was a sensible course to adopt while the pilots learned their job and before a proper system of staff procedures and deployment drills had been evolved; it also helped to conserve the limited amount of spare parts available and made life easier for the handful of technicians who worked phenomenal hours to keep the machines in the air. There was also the formidable task of educating the ARVN in the use of helicopters. The Vietnamese – contrary to much ill-informed criticism – quickly showed themselves to be excellent soldiers when properly equipped, trained and led, responding well to the tuition and example of their American advisers. As airmobile training became widespread in the ARVN, US Army aviation units were integrated with Vietnamese formations; the aviators found themselves drawn more and more into the struggle and were able to pass their experience back to the United States, where wide-ranging studies and trials of airmobility had now started.

The man at the centre of the great expansion of American Army aviation in the 1960s was Lt-Gen. Hamilton Howze, who must be regarded as the 'father' of battlefield airmobility. Howze had been a member of the Rogers Board of 1960, but his interest in army aviation extended back to the Second World War. As a senior staff officer in the Pentagon during the later 1950s, he had followed Gavin's example and made a number of searching studies of the likely shape of future land warfare. His assistant in these was Col. Claude Sheppard of the US Artillery; Sheppard had been one of the earliest army aviators and a Piper *Cub* pilot during the war. He had subsequently served in Korea as a military adviser to the South Korean Army and as an artillery battalion commander. In this latter capacity he had made a point of meeting the British light aircraft pilots in the Commonwealth Division, with whom he would spend many congenial hours discussing the future uses of battlefield aviation. Now, he and Howze plunged into their work. Their starting-point was a pile of classroom exercises used at the Staff Colleges and Arms Schools of the US Army. Substituting a super-mobile Air Cavalry Brigade of their own devising for the conventional armoured divisions of the exercise narrative, they war-gamed their way through every conceivable phase of military operations.

The hypothetical Air Cavalry Brigade conjured up by Howze and Sheppard was able to move quickly around the combat area. Its engineers, carried forward by air with their demolition gear, mined and obstructed the routes along which the enemy advance was expected to come. Stay-behind parties with powerful radios would be deployed by helicopter, or dropped by parachute, to keep observation on the blown bridges and blocked defiles; then, as these became choked with enemy traffic, artillery and missile fire were brought down. Because the forward elements of the defence could be brought safely back to the main position by helicopter, demolitions and mining were carried out on an unrestricted scale; minefields laid by slow- and low-flying helicopters to impose delay, and channel the enemy's advance in to the areas preselected by the defence as killing zones, where the enemy armour, massed in the open, could be engaged by the defence's own tanks, heliborne anti-tank guided weapons, artillery controlled from observation helicopters and devastating airstrikes. Howze was looking ahead ten years, for at that time (1957–58) no helicopter had been fitted with a serviceable anti-tank guided weapon. He was mindful, however of what Gavin was preaching to all who would listen – that those charged with the planning of future operations could not afford to be conservative, and that history proved beyond doubt that the requirements for future wars had been consistently underestimated. It was no use, Gavin would point out in 1963, to plan for the next war on the basis of better ways to fight the last.

Howze's brilliance as analyst and prophet served the Rogers Board well, but his great chance came in the autumn of 1961 when the US Army produced a curiously hesitant statement of its future aviation requirements. Secretary of Defence McNamara, dissatisfied with this document, wrote a memorandum to Secretary of the Army Elvis J. Stahr requesting a full study into the Army's aviation requirements. This was signed on 5 October and McNamara called for an answer by mid-November. He got it on time and having studied it pronounced it to be far too conservative. In a decisive note to Stahr on 19 April 1962, he nominated a panel of senior Army officers to conduct a far-reaching new study. McNamara's nominee as chairman was Lt-Gen. Howze, backed by a number of senior officers, aviation consultants and the resources of the Rand Analysis Corporation. Howze must have savoured McNamara's punch line: 'I shall be disappointed if the Army's re-examination merely produces logistically oriented recommendations to procure more of the same, rather than a plan for employment of fresh and perhaps unorthodox concepts which will give us a significant increase in mobility.'

The die was cast. Seldom can a defence planning committee have been given a clearer or more encouraging directive, or such generous political support. Howze and his team set to with a will. The importance of the work in hand was evident to all members of the board. It did not require a particularly gifted imagination to see what lay ahead in Vietnam, where the first three companies of H21s were already hard at work. Even so, for three years US Army Aviation participation there was to remain at quite a low level; the full weight of American military effort was not applied until 1965, when it seemed that the overstretched ARVN was about to collapse; and a force of 13 US Army aviation companies in the theatre in April of that year was expanded to 110 by mid-1968.

Howze was well placed as President of the US Army Tactical Mobility Requirements Board (which was inevitably referred to thereafter as the Howze Board). As Commanding General of XVIII Airborne Corps, of the Strategic Army Corps and of the US Army Airborne Centre at Fort Bragg, he had ready access to well-trained units for trials purposes. General Wheeler, Chief of Staff of the US Army, later described the Board at work:

> Over a period of 18 weeks the Board conducted an extensive series of field tests, war games, operational research and other studies, to see how many Army helicopters and light fixed-wing aircraft might replace in part or augment the current ground systems of the truck, ground fire support, and the armed combat vehicle . . . in brief, the Board considered air mobility as the capability of a unit to deploy in battle, fight and sustain itself using air vehicles under the control of the ground force commander.

The Board's findings were presented on 20 August 1962. They included a recommendation that an airmobile division be formed without delay, as well as two other types of unit – Air Cavalry Combat and Air Transported Brigades. Logistic support for these units was to be provided in the combat area by the Army's own large cargo-carrying helicopters and short-range transport aircraft, which would pick up their loads from the Air Force's most forward airstrips and carry them up to the fighting troops. The increased mobility provided by these new units would give the commander in the field tremendously improved capabilities in finding, surprising and getting to grips with the enemy, by-passing natural obstacles or enemy strong-points; and in the ability to concentrate force quickly at the point of decision with maximum secrecy and minimum casualties.

These proceedings were strongly endorsed by Mr Cyrus Vance, who had succeeded Stahr as Army Secretary, but energetically opposed by the strong Air Force lobby in Washington, headed by Senator Barry Goldwater (who maintained that the Army had flagrantly trespassed into USAF territory) and Gen. Curtis Le May, the father-figure of Strategic Air Command and a true-blue apostle of Douhet and Billy Mitchell (who objected to the Army's use of armed aircraft). Le May, however, withdrew his objections after it had been shown conclusively that the USAF lacked the motivation as well as the equipment to carry out the armed helicopter role; and after a certain amount of sparring – during which the Army agreed to give up its *Caribou* transport aircraft in return for an unobstructed passage for the creation of its medium-lift helicopter force – the Army–USAF controversies eventually died away.

Back in Vietnam, both sides were learning new lessons. Helicopter operations were still fairly limited and consisted mostly of the combat deployment of the ARVN against the Vietcong. An important secondary role was that of casualty evacuation. American ground combat troops were not yet deployed in the country and US aid, though steadily on the increase, was still 'advisory' in character. However, the Vietcong soon showed that they, too, had been studying airmobile operations. Documents captured late in 1962 showed that their troops had been carefully instructed in the techniques of airmobile operations, and had been given useful training in the use of their weapons against helicopters. Casualties started to increase despite the fitting of machine guns in the doors of the ageing CH21s. It was clear that additional armed helicopters were needed to escort the troop carriers and provide suppressive fire during the highly vulnerable phases of landing in, and taking off from, unguarded landing zones.

In September 1962 the first helicopter unit specifically formed and equipped for the Fire Support Role arrived in Vietnam. It consisted of 15 UH1A *Iroquois* helicopters fitted with an interim locally-made weapons pack of two ·30-calibre machine guns and sixteen 2·75in rockets. Two months later, eleven of the more powerful B model UH1s arrived, carrying four guns in an improved weapons pack. Immediately before the arrival of the armed 'Hueys' (as the UH1 was universally called) the Vietcong were obtaining one hit on an American helicopter for every ten hours flown; once the troop-lift missions were escorted by armed 'Hueys' the hit rate fell sharply by over 25 per cent. Confidence was restored and troop-lift missions began to be pressed home again with the old gusto. In its first five months in Vietnam the armed helicopter unit accounted for an estimated 246 Vietcong with its suppressive fire, and although 11 of its helicopters were hit by ground fire, none was brought down.

The H21 was nearing the end of its life, and by mid-1963 it was being replaced as a troopcarrier by the UH1B, which could carry ten ARVN soldiers at a pinch (but was usually limited to eight). The Vietnamese were now sufficiently well trained to be able to undertake battalion-sized helicopter assault operations – a great step forward from the non-tactical troop-lifting which was all that could be attempted during 1962. The basic organization of the Utility Tactical Transport Company comprised an armed platoon of UH1Bs with guns and rockets, and two platoons of troopcarrying UH1Bs without weapons packs. It was soon discovered that the armed 'Huey' was slower in the cruise than the troopcarriers ('Slicks') it was escorting. This was hardly surprising; the extra drag of the weapons with which they were now festooned slowed them down to 80 knots. Apart from the four guns and the rocket pods of their arms pack, and the gun ammunition, each armed 'Huey' carried two waist gunners with ·30-calibre weapons. Their weight, and that of the additional guns and ammunition, brought the UH1B up to its maximum all-up weight, and seriously impaired its agility. For all its drawbacks, the armed *Iroquois* did a sterling job at a critical stage of the war.

Before long, battle drills and standard operating procedures were evolved. If enemy fire was encountered on the way to an LZ, the after escort commander decided whether to engage the enemy or continue the flight at a safe altitude. If the fire was persistent and effective, the escort commander would indicate the target, which was engaged in succession by each escort helicopter with continuous fire as the force passed overhead. Wherever possible, engagements were at maximum effective range in order to minimize the risk of hits from ground fire. Although the aim was to return fire without departing from the line of flight – because of the difficulty of catching up again after turning away to engage a target to a flank – it was sometimes necessary to detach one or more escorts for a rocket attack, accepting the resultant dilution of effort. The escort commander normally travelled up at the head of the formation, navigating from a map on which known hostile areas were marked, and flying at 1500 feet.

The threat in the first two years in Vietnam came almost entirely from rifle-calibre small-arms. The Vietcong compensated for their initial lack of automatic weapons by training their troops to fire volley after volley at aircraft passing overhead at which they became extremely skilful; they also began to mine and ambush likely LZs, displaying considerable insight and skill. Pilots' reports began to reflect a growing disquiet, and operating procedures were developed to

SOUTH VIETNAM—THE SEAT OF WAR—The country was divided into four ARVN
Corps areas. American formations, part of Field Forces I and II, were assigned with other
allied forces as follows: I CORPS AREA—US Marine Corps, operating from enclaves at Phu Bai,
Da Nang and Chu Lai. II CORPS AREA—The Northern half, comprising the strategically vital
Central Highlands was assigned to US Army formations. 1st Cavalry Division (Airmobile) was
usually to be found operating in this area. In the Southern half lay the US Army and Air bases
with US Army garrisons. The South Korean Capitol Division also operated in this area. III and
IV CORPS AREAS—US Army Units at Bien Hoa and Vung Tau in support of ARVN III CORPS.

a higher pitch; the experience gained during the years 1962–65 was to be put to good use when the storm eventually broke.

By the end of 1963 the drill for an air assault into terrain known to be held by the Vietcong was as follows. The decision to mount an assault was made at the ARVN Corps Tactical Operations centre by the commander and his American Advisory Staff. The details were then passed to the officer commanding the aviation battalion supporting the Corps, who would assign his companies to their specific tasks. This was normally accomplished by last light on the day preceding the operation in the case of a 'deliberate' or preplanned assault; however, an operation could be planned and launched in an emergency situation within an hour, so effective was the staff and communications system. If possible a reconnaissance flight would be flown, on which the commander of the assault unit flew with representatives of the aviation battalion; during this flight, the in-and-out routes would be drawn in on the map together with any known details of the enemy, landing zones selected and the flight plan determined. In order not to arouse the enemy's suspicions, the reconnaissance flight was normally flown with extreme caution and at a safe height well out of small-arms range. Considerable thought was devoted to selection of the most suitable formation, so that the airlanded force could arrive as far as possible simultaneously on one or more LZs. A 'V' formation was most frequently used as it permitted easy and safe changes of direction in flight and was also easy to control in the final stages of the assault. A small group of armed helicopters flew ahead of the main body whilst others flew on each flank of the 'Slicks' and yet more – if any were available – flew at the rear, ready to pounce on any enemy who tried to interfere with the flight to the target. Every effort was made to deceive the enemy by using different routes to and from a target and approaching LZs from different directions. In the event of an ambush being detected by the leading armed helicopter, one of several alternative LZs would be used. By dint of repeated training, a formation of 12 helicopters could be climbing hard for safety within two minutes of the leading 'Slick' touching down. The LZs varied enormously, from open spaces in which the whole group achieved the ideal of a simultaneous landing, to confined spaces surrounded by scrub and jungle in which the Vietcong could always be lying in wait, undeterred by any amount of preliminary 'softening-up' by strike aircraft, artillery and the armed 'Hueys'. In the reedy swamps of the Mekong Delta the luckless infantry would be landed in chest-deep water whilst the helicopters hovered just above the surface. Elsewhere they might be dropped from the hover into 10ft-high grass.

It is hardly surprising that the aircrews found service in Vietnam to be an extremely gruelling experience; they flew intensively under appalling conditions, the only compensation being that at least they normally operated from a semi-permanent and secure base airfield. As the pace of operations increased, and as the Vietcong gained confidence and began to bring more and more helicopters down, new drills and techniques were introduced. One of these was the 'Eagle Flight' – a highly-trained heliborne intervention force which could react within minutes to any emergency. The unit would be commanded from an armed 'Huey' by the US Army Aviation commander and the commander of the ARVN unit which formed an integral part of the Eagle Flight; six or seven unarmed 'Hueys' would carry the infantry element; five or six armed 'Hueys' provided close fire support and acted as escort; and an additional 'Huey', fitted with stretchers and crewed by medical assistants, acted as a flying ambulance. The Eagle Flight concept had been brought to such a pitch by late 1964 that every aviation company had formed one from its own resources; morale was high and an excellent spirit of mutual confidence and admiration existed between the US Army pilots and their affiliated ARVN units.

At the beginning of 1964 the US Army was operating 248 helicopters and 140 light fixed-wing aircraft in Vietnam. An aviation company or US Marine Corps aviation squadron now supported each ARVN division, and additional aviation support was allocated to each ARVN corps. Not all these aircraft were employed in the straightforward troop assault role. Two types of fixed-wing aircraft flown by the Army at this stage are of particular interest: the OV1 *Mohawk* and the CV2 *Caribou*.

The Grumman OV1 entered US Army service almost by accident. It had started life in the 1950s as the result of a US Marine Corps requirement for an aircraft with outstanding STOL characteristics capable of providing effective close support for the ground troops and also for tactical reconnaissance. The Marines dropped the requirement when a prototype had already flown; Grummans turned to the Army, who were impressed by the performance of this ugly aircraft, with its two powerful turbo-prop engines and three tailfins. At this stage the OV1 was visualized primarily as a surveillance aircraft which could operate in all weathers, day and night, using advanced electronic aids to observe enemy dispositions deep in hostile territory without actually crossing the front line itself. This, indeed, is the role for which later models of the *Mohawk* are intended in the European theatre. Its crew of two are accommodated side-by-side in the nose, enjoying excellent fields of view, the reassurance of highly effective ejection seats and a considerable amount of armoured protection. *Mohawk* had begun to enter US Army service in 1961, and in the autumn of 1962 six of them were deployed to Vietnam for use in the armed reconnaissance role, in which they proved to be outstandingly successful. Their high-grade camera equipment produced volumes of information and the observers acquired an almost uncanny degree of skill at spotting the Vietcong in their well-camouflaged hide-outs. Much of this success could be ascribed to the *Mohawk*'s quietness and speed – its maximum was 255 knots – which frequently enabled its crews to surprise parties of enemy out in the open. The 'A' model originally used in Vietnam was fitted with ·50-calibre guns in addition to its cameras; later models dispensed with armament and carried electronic surveillance gear such as side-looking airborne radar (SLAR) and infra-red sensors. This was mobility for the observer carried to the utmost; a far cry from the resources available ten years earlier to the British in Malaya.

The CV2 *Caribou* began to enter US Army service in 1959 and was from the start a flagrant challenge to any weight restrictions the USAF sought to apply. Designed and built by de Havilland Canada, it represented a huge step forward from the six-seat U6 D.H. *Beaver* of 1950 and its larger cousin the U1 D.H. *Otter*, which had both been designed for light cargo and passenger service. The *Caribou*, however, was in the 20,000lb class, a twin-engined transport with tail-gate door, capable of lifting 32 passengers or a 3-ton payload. Immensely rugged, its powerful engines and ingeniously-flapped wings gave it an astonishing STOL performance, even off ploughed fields. The first *Caribou* to arrive in Vietnam was sent there for field trials in August 1961 and quickly demonstrated a vastly superior performance to the aged C47s still in use by the Vietnamese Air Force. By mid-1963 two companies of *Caribous* were serving in Vietnam, flying in and out of the most primitive airstrips in appalling weather conditions. The USAF looked askance at the Army, and the dash with which the CV2 pilots were performing their task. The nearest comparable USAF aircraft was the C123 *Provider* but it was twice as heavy as *Caribou* and had nowhere near its STOL performance.

As an indication of the operating standards to which the US Army's *Caribous* were working in Vietnam, two examples must suffice. One of the airstrips in the delta area south-west of Saigon was at Cao Lanh; it was described as 'an aircraft carrier's deck about three feet out of water', only 55ft wide. The main landing wheels of the *Caribou* are 26ft apart, so all landings on the 430-yard 'runway' had to be made with great precision, especially in a crosswind when the pilot, crabbing in on the final stages of the approach, had to exercise extreme care not to land at excessive speed. During the rainy season (May to September) the shoulders of the strip were turned to mud, and after landing the aircraft had to be manhandled round to face the other way for a down-wind take-off. The most hair-raising experience for *Caribou* pilots, however, was at Tra My in the far north of the country. It lay at the bottom of a steep valley and even an air-drop mission required a maximum power climb-out to clear the surrounding hills. At each end of the original 280-yard strip was a steep bank. The first pilot to land there put his aircraft down after three aborted attempts, only 12 feet from the upwind end of the strip with the aircraft's nose overhanging the far embankment. The *Caribou* proved to be an invaluable workhorse in Vietnam for air landing as well as for parachuted resupply missions; by 1964 it was also capable of performing ultra-low-level supply drops in which an extractor parachute pulled the sledge-mounted load out of the rear door as the aircraft flew down the dropzone at a height of about five feet.

Although the US Army continues to use *Mohawk* to this day – now equipped with highly advanced sensors as part of an extremely complex intelligence-gathering system – the *Caribou* could hardly be described as a battlefield aerial vehicle and was correctly, if reluctantly, handed over to the USAF in 1966 on condition that the Army was allowed to develop its medium- and heavy-lift helicopter capability.

As the struggle in Vietnam slowly escalated towards the point where full-scale American participation began, the studies and trials initiated by the Howze Board came under close scrutiny. In almost any country but the United States it is certain that the board's proceedings would have been shuffled from desk to desk, gathering comments from Treasury officials and the more conservative members of the military Establishment, finally gathering dust in an obscure pigeon-hole. Fortunately this was not the course adopted by the Pentagon; the momentum of Howze's findings was sustained by the Army Staff and by the Department of Defense. On 7 January 1963 orders were given by the Deputy Chief of Staff for Operations for the formation of an experimental air assauult division and of an air-transport brigade.

The formation selected for the trials were the resuscitated 11th Airborne (renamed 11th Air Assault Division) and an *ad hoc* 10th Air Transport Brigade. Troops and aircraft had to be scraped together from all directions and the initial total strength of the trials units was little more than 3000 personnel with 125 helicopters and 29 fixed-wing aircraft. With these cadres Brig.-Gen. Harry Kinnaird got to work, content to await reinforcements as and when they materialized. Kinnaird was a clever choice for commander of the experimental force. He had served in 101st Airborne in the Second World War, had filled a number of key airborne staff appointments at Fort Bragg during the post-war years and came to his new job from the deputy commander's seat at 101st Airborne. Like many others of the progressive airborne arm of the US Army, he had qualified as an army aviator.

Kinnaird and his staff faced a severe challenge. Most of the troops in 11th Air Assault had no prior experience of working with helicopters; new organizations and staff tables had to be drafted; pilots had to undergo intensive training in close-formation and tactical flying, in the handling of armed helicopters, assault techniques, nap-of-the-earth navigation, communications; the divisional staff had to jump from thinking solely in terms of the land battle to handling units moving three-dimensionally in the low-level airspace over the combat zone. An imaginative approach was adopted in order to harness the enthusiasm and wide experience of all ranks: Kinnaird's staff set up an 'ideas group' which welcomed suggestions – however outlandish – and carefully analysed the resultant flood of advice which poured in.

The first field trials, at company level, were held towards the end of April, and as reinforcements began to arrive at Fort Benning, the trials centre, additional training areas had to be acquired. One thing was already clear – an airmobile division could take on a vastly greater operating area than any type of conventional formation. This brought administrative problems, for the new division's fuel requirements were enormous. New methods of rapid refuelling in the field had to be evolved, with equipment for providing and safely storing the unprecedented quantities of aviation fuel. A system of 'refuel–rearm points' was successfully tried out and incorporated into standard operating procedures.

The entry into service of the new medium-lift helicopter, the Boeing-Vertol CH46 *Chinook*, added a new dimension to airmobility; it could carry, underslung, the standard 105mm artillery fieldpiece and its crew, as well as a generous supply of ammunition; mobility for the guns had taken an even bigger leap forward than when the British Army introduced Horse Artillery batteries in the Napoleonic wars, which could gallop across country to keep pace with the cavalry. Weapons were developed for armed helicopters, notably the 'flying rocket battery' in which UH1s were fitted with 3·5in rockets for quick-reaction fire support. Already, the Air Assault Division was overcoming a weakness pounced on by its early critics – that of lack of hitting power.

Using experience gained in Vietnam by the troop transport helicopter companies, Kinnaird's staff evolved standard assault drills for their potent new instrument. On receipt of his mission the airmobile commander planned his manoeuvre scheme – if necessary whilst airborne himself in a reconnaissance helicopter – aiming to deploy his resources to obtain maximum shock effect. An artillery and airstrike fire plan would be prepared by the formation's artillery commander in close concert with the division's USAF representative, with the aim of suppressing enemy fire on the way in to the assault as well as on the actual LZs. For the final stages of the fly-in, this fire support would lift, to be taken over by the rocket-firing armed helicopters in the van of the attack, while artillery and air support shifted to targets further out from the LZ in order to disrupt any counter-attacks. Overhead, the commander controlled the operation from his command-post helicopter, and airborne observation posts circled the area to keep watch on any enemy movements.

By mid-1964 the trials had succeeded beyond expectation, and the major test, Air Assault II, was set for the middle of October. It was to consist of a two-sided exercise over large tracts of North and South Carolina, in which 11th Air Assault were pitted against the élite 82nd Airborne. Kinnaird, though with only six actual battalions plus a 'simulated' brigade, made an excellent showing with his Air Assault Division. The post-exercise analysis was quick to point out the salient weaknesses of the Airmobile Division: its lack of mobility once deployed by helicopter; vulnerability to attack by heavy armour; inability to operate in really bad weather; and the adverse effect of aircrew fatigue. However, these were heavily outweighed by the advantages. The Division had sustained an incredibly high tempo of operations, had reacted far more quickly to tactical changes than a 'conventional' formation and had sustained its operations over a huge geographical area without recourse to a cumbrous logistic 'tail'. It could conduct several operations simultaneously, required less of a reserve because of the speed of aerial redeployment and could regroup very quickly to meet unforeseen situations. Its fire support, thanks to the medium-lift helicopter, was prompt, flexible and devastatingly effective (within a year, field batteries in Vietnam would accept 20 heliborne moves in 48 hours as normal). The Airmobile brigade repeatedly showed its ability to find the enemy, pin him down and destroy him with a free use of fire and movement, a technique which had seemed to be all but lost. In low-intensity operations, the Airmobile formation had shown that it could assert a powerful military presence over wide areas of countryside, enabling a small force to do the work formerly undertaken by much larger conventional formations. In the type of high-intensity operations visualized in Europe, airmobility clearly offered an attractive solution to the difficult problem of finding a nimble screening force and also a mobile and responsive reserve.

At the end of 1964, with the results and findings of these trials in the hands of the Pentagon, it became clear that the ARVN was steadily being worn down by the Vietcong and that something more than the existing system of American military aid was essential if Vietnam was to survive. Early in 1965 the Army Chief of Staff, Gen. Harold K. Johnson, visited Fort Benning for discussions which it was clear would lead to selection of the first US Army formation to go to the aid of South Vietnam. As it existed at the time, 11th Air Assault Division was far too weak to take to the field for active service. On the other hand, it was the repository for virtually all the hard-earned experience of the previous year's trials in which it had been augmented by large drafts from 2nd Infantry Division. A compromise solution was produced; 11th Air Assault was deactivated; its men and aircraft were then transferred to 2nd Infantry Division, which then exchanged identity – and even its colours – with the 1st Cavalry Division, then carrying out the dreary and thankless task of frontier-watching in South Korea. The 'new' 1st Cavalry Division (Airmobile) was formally activated on 3 July 1965 and warned to be ready for overseas service by 28 July. Despite the short time available it was possible to put two of the three battalions of the division's 1st Brigade – which was also designated as an airborne formation – through a ten-day parachute refresher course.

The new division, commanded (as was proper) by Maj.-Gen. Kinnaird, now consisted of 16,000 officers and men, organized into eight battalions. The battlefield airlift was provided by the 10th Air Transport Brigade and there was a divisional air cavalry squadron. An aviation maintenance battalion provided technical support. The division had its integral artillery brigade, engineer and signals battalions. There were 434 aircraft, of which all but a handful were helicopters. Wheeled transport, at 1600 vehicles, was cut to less than half the establishment of a conventional infantry division.

By superhuman efforts, final preparations for embarkation were completed on time. Enthusiasm ran high; the 1st Cavalry contained many army aviators who had already completed operational tours of duty in Vietnam and every officer and man in the division was eager to take part in the test which lay ahead. On 2 August, advance parties left Fort Bragg for the long flight to Vietnam; two weeks later the aircraft carrier USS *Boxer*, her flight and hangar decks crammed with 1st Cavalry's aircraft, put to sea from Mayport, Florida. She was the first of 20 ships which left the east coast of the United States during the next five days, heading for the war zone.

CHAPTER FOURTEEN

Vietnam 2: Into Battle

By 19 September all the ships bringing Kinnaird's division to Vietnam had docked at Qui Nhon.

Fortunately, their landing was unopposed. Advance parties had already arrived and gone inland to An Khe to mark out an area which was to be the division's first main base, the famous 'Golf Course'. The rest of the month was spent in clearing scrub, digging defensive works, patrolling the area and building temporary accommodation. By 28 September the division was ready for limited action and by the end of October it had been blooded. The regular North Vietnamese Army (NVA) was now entering the field in strength with the apparent aim of cutting South Vietnam in two by a drive to the coast. On 19 October Kinnaird was informed that a Special Forces camp at Plei Mei, 60 miles to the south-west, was under heavy attack by a regiment of North Vietnamese. An ARVN relief column backed by 1st Cavalry's air-lifted artillery, whose batteries were leapfrogged into position under the powerful new *Chinook* medium-lift helicopters, fought through to Plei Mei from the provincial capital Pleiku, 25 miles to the north. The enemy was repelled but not defeated; the siege continued and on 27 October Kinnaird received orders from the US Military Commander, Gen. Westmoreland, to move his division into the area to 'find, fix and destroy the enemy forces threatening Plei Mei, Pleiku and the Central Highlands'. It was a tall order, for no less than three North Vietnamese regiments had now been identified in the area. Kinnaird immediately threw in his 1st Brigade – three air-lifted infantry battalions, an artillery battalion and his divisional air cavalry squadron, which was organized in troops, each of three teams: 'White' (light observation helicopters), 'Blue' ('Hueys' in the troop assault role) and 'Red' (armed 'Hueys'). Despite the unfamiliar terrain and the difficulty of learning the art of airmobile warfare while fighting their first battle, the 1st Brigade at once got to grips with the enemy who, clearly disconcerted by the sheer speed of airmobile operations, began to withdraw towards the Cambodian border and safety. By mid-November the NVA had been forced back into an area between Plei Mei and the border which they were reluctant to abandon as it contained several regimental base camps, carefully hidden amongst the steep valleys in the northern slopes of the Chy Pong mountains.

The enemy had underestimated the observation skills of Kinnaird's pilots, who succeeded in locating two of the base camps of the North Vietnamese 66th Regiment. The 1st battalion of the 7th Cavalry under Lt-Col. Hal Moore was flown in to the attack, achieving almost total surprise. The enemy, with a strong American force astride his main escape route into Cambodia, reacted violently with repeated attacks by regular NVA and Vietcong against Moore's battalion. On 16 November before dawn the 1st/7th, now reinforced by two more battalions, was attacked by waves of enemy attempting to fight their way out of the trap. The 2nd/7th, moving on foot through the bush, collided head-on with a battalion of the NVA 66th Regiment and a ferocious hand-to-hand fight ensued; 151 Americans were killed, but the bodies of over 400 of their opponents were counted.

It had been a bloody and sobering introduction to the campaign, but despite the heavy casualties, morale in 1st Cavalry Division was high. Operations had been sustained by day and night, and the division had brought off several night troop-lifts; the drills and procedures for close artillery fire support and airstrikes had been highly successful. Although frequently exposed to close-range enemy fire, the division's doctors and medical teams had performed splendidly and the rapid evacuation of all wounded had been a fillip to morale. Hundreds of hits were sustained by the helicopters but only two were forced down, and these were recovered within two days by *Chinooks* acting as flying cranes. The ferocity of the close-quarter fighting came as a shock even to veterans of Korea and the Second World War. The body of one of Moore's platoon commanders was found in his foxhole, five dead NVA soldiers within five paces; in a neighbouring slit-trench a dead American soldier and a North Vietnamese were locked together in the act of mutual strangulation.

Reviewing the Pleiku campaign, fought within weeks of his division's arrival in Vietnam, Kinnaird had every reason for pride. During its three-week duration there had been no less than 193 separate company troop-lifts, 6000 helicopter sorties and 27,000 hours of combat flying. Thirteen thousand tons of ammunition, supplies and fuel had been moved by helicopter. Batteries of artillery had been moved complete on 67 occasions. Only four helicopters had been irretrievably lost.

The pattern of operations was beginning to take shape. Some of the many battles, ranging from small patrol actions to full-scale battalion-size engagements, had started as the result of helicopter reconnaissance, others from head-on encounters between marching infantry. The effectiveness of the helicopter–infantry team was now proven beyond doubt, and the previous summer's training in the Carolinas was paying dividends. Airmobility enabled the infantry to establish contact with the minimal amount of fruitless 'jungle-bashing' and to sustain a relentless pressure on an opponent who, though resourceful, skilled and fanatically brave, was only as mobile as his own feet could make him. 1965 closed on a high and hopeful note.

The war into which 1st Cavalry Division had been so violently pitched came as an entirely new experience for the US armed forces. They were confronted with a far more intractable problem than either the French or the British in their post-war counter-insurgency campaigns, for these had been fought within the framework of well-tried and established systems of colonial government. In Malaya, often cited as the sole example of the defeat of a Maoist-type insurrection by a European neo-colonial power, the British were in full control of the civil service, police and armed forces as well as the judicial machinery of the courts. The population, once it was apparent that the security forces were mastering the situation, was sympathetic to the cause of law and order and stood to gain by the triumph of the legitimate government. In Vietnam the Americans were brought in at a late stage to bolster up the flagging government and its overstretched armed forces; it was a campaign in a foreign country, where the Americans could only advise the government and could not take control of the whole politico-military structure – an essential factor if insurgency is to be tackled effectively.

By the opening months of 1966 President Johnson had honoured his promise of the previous summer to raise the US military presence, now known as 'US Army, Vietnam', to a troop strength of 125,000. American units, on arrival, were deployed into the four ARVN corps areas to bolster them up in their fight against the NVA and the Vietcong, and in an attempt to 'win the hearts and minds' of the people of Vietnam who were now in the grips of a ruthless campaign of subversion, terrorism and coercion. In Malaya it had been possible to isolate the vulnerable Chinese section of the population from terrorist influence by resettling some thousands of jungle-fringe 'squatters' into well-guarded 'new villages'. In Vietnam this was attempted with some success, but the geography of the country and its far denser rural population made it impossible to run a full resettlement scheme.

The ARVN, though capable of fighting heroically, lacked the training in depth which is essential if a counter-insurgency campaign is to be won; its sudden expansion had diluted the limited supply of good leaders at all levels, and by mid-1965 the government forces had lost the initiative, tending to sit tight in garrison towns and fire bases from which they would emerge by day to scour the countryside fruitlessly, abandoning it at night to the Vietcong who went almost unchallenged. The Americans found themselves conforming with the ARVN's pattern of operations. 1st Cavalry Division, though lavishly equipped with the means of airmobility, was dangerously deficient in technical-support facilities and thus to operate from heavily entrenched and protected bases like An Khe. Infantry divisions arriving from the USA were faced with the equally intractable problem of the high personnel rotation rate induced by the 12-month tour of duty, and of training unenthusiastic draftees to be proper jungle soldiers. Although the higher percentage of long-service men in the élite US Marine Corps and 1st Cavalry (and later, the 101st Airmobile) divisions justly earned them a splendid reputation, some of the other formations never got down to sustained jungle operations in which the Vietcong and NVA would have been relentlessly hunted and met on their own ground with the vastly superior resources available to the US Army Commander.

Vietnam is a rural country and apart from some two million living in Saigon and a small number of large towns, its population of about 17 million are country folk. It is a beautiful land, but a difficult one in which to fight a war; there are wide differences between the terrain of the Mekong Delta, the rice-rich coastal plains, the central plateau and the rugged jungle-clad mountains running north–south along the Cambodian and Laotian borders, populated by aboriginal Montagnards and laced with hidden trails linking a multitude of enemy bases, military schools and depots. The American Special Forces units assigned to these remote areas performed wonders, at enormous risk and cost to themselves, to bring the Montagnards onto the side of the government, but they could do nothing to prevent the free movement of enemy forces into South Vietnam across the 900 miles of its borders with Laos and Cambodia. Although the country is 600 miles long, it is as narrow as 50 miles in the northern province. The weather alternates between hot-and-wet and hot-and-dry depending on the stage of the tropical monsoon; whereas in the south the winter months are dry, they are wet in the north, with a reversal of climate in the summer. In many areas, over 120 inches of rain could fall during the five or six wet months. Flying conditions could be appalling, with the hills shrouded in dense cloud. The need to fulfil missions regardless of weather was quickly appreciated, and all helicopter pilots trained at the US Army Aviation School at Fort Rucker, Alabama, received instruction in basic instrument flying in case it

235

was necessary to enter cloud during operational missions in Vietnam.

Nineteen sixty-six was a year of hard slogging for 1st Cavalry, which started the year in the Central Highlands where the ARVN's 22nd Division and the awesome South Korean Capitol Division were attempting to reimpose the writ of the Saigon government on an area which had been effectively under Communist control since 1945. The coastal plain area with its treasure of huge rice crops was dominated by the NVA's 3rd Division whose three regiments, the 2nd, 18th and 22nd, operated from secure and well-hidden bases up in the hills. Kinnaird's plan for the use of 1st Cavalry was made in consultation with the ARVN and South Korean divisional commanders and with the South Vietnamese and US Marines controlling the area to the north, who would prevent the NVA escaping in that direction. The base selected for 1st Cavalry Division was Bong Son, where there was a good fixed-wing airstrip and a Special Forces base; this was duly occupied during January and Kinnaird opened the campign on the 28th of the month with the move of a 105mm field-gun battery and an infantry battalion into an area to the north-east, where units of the NVA 2nd Regiment had been identified. It was like prodding a hornet's nest; fierce fighting broke out at once around the fire-base and on the landing zones being used by the 2nd/7th Cavalry. Twelve helicopters were hit as they flew reinforcements in and the 1st/7th joined the 2nd Battalion in the mêlée. At one stage a *Chinook* bringing a 105mm gun into the area was forced down; the gun was nevertheless brought immediately into action, firing over open sights at the enemy swarming around the LZs. Early the following morning a third battalion, the 2nd/12th Cavalry, was flown into LZs to the south of the continuing battle and the 22nd ARVN Division came in from the east, brushing aside enemy resistance. After 48 hours the enemy broke, split into small groups and fled south-west for the relative safety of the hills, leaving 500 dead.

After a further ten days of patrolling and reconnaissance Kinnaird felt sure that he had located the two remaining regiments of the 3rd NVA Division. For the first time he committed his entire division in battle, to a radically new plan. He was certain that the 2nd and 18th NVA Regiments were installed in the Kim Son Valley, a dark, dank and sinister place long known to be an enemy sanctuary area. Heavily bombed for months by B52s, huge areas of defoliation punctured by crater fields gave evidence of earlier efforts at ejecting the Communists. The operation was entrusted to the newly promoted Brig.-Gen. Hal Moore and his 3rd Brigade. He flew small parties into positions all round the area to set up ambushes at the heads of all the

smaller tributary valleys. The main assault went in on 11 February,
landing – to the total surprise of the enemy – right in the middle of the
Kim Son Valley; a battalion with a battery of field artillery and two
air cavalry companies which at once struck out to force the confused
enemy up the smaller valleys and into the jaws of the carefully sited
ambushes. By mid-afternoon it was clear that the plan had worked;
from the firebase at the valley bottom could be heard the sounds of numerous skirmishes up at the heads of the lesser valleys. These vicious
encounters went on for two days. The enemy turned out to be from
the 2nd Regiment, one of whose battalion commanders was captured.
Under interrogation he talked freely and as a result the HQ of 2nd
Regiment itself was quickly located, up in the hills to the east of the
Kim Son Valley. It received the undivided attention of all three battalions of Brig.-Gen. Ray Lynch's 2nd Brigade, flown in to bring off
a text-book vertical envelopment resulting in the killing of more than
300 enemy troops. The Americans lost 82 killed and 318 wounded.

The 1st Cavalry had by no means finished with that part of
Vietnam. It was to remain one of their principal operational areas
until the latter stages of the war, for they had demonstrated conclusively that in such difficult terrain, lacking roads or even rough tracks,
the helicopter held the key to success in combat.

BONG SON—1st Cavalry in Vertical Envelopment -

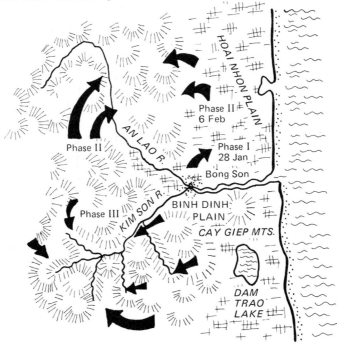

237

One of the great successes of Vietnam was the medium-lift helicopter. After careful consideration during the later '50s, a competition was held to decide the type to be acquired by the US Army. The Boeing-Vertol submission was adjudged the winner by a joint Army–Air Force panel and by the beginning of 1966 over 150 *Chinooks* had entered Army service. The *Chinook* was designed from the start as a transport and not an assault helicopter; despite this, it featured in numerous desperately fought landings in Vietnam. *Chinook* proved to be a classic in that the basic model was capable of tremendous development; successive improvements to its rotor system, transmission and power plants enabled it virtually to double many aspects of its performance. Its ability to carry field artillery pieces has already been mentioned; this was put to excellent use in a technique known as the 'artillery raid', where an entire battery would be lifted deep into an area of enemy territory which was well out of range of existing fire bases. Once landed, the guns would be ranged rapidly onto targets chosen as the result of intelligence reports and reconnaissance flights. A number of targets would be engaged and destroyed or neutralized; then, before the enemy could react, the *Chinooks* would return to lift the guns back to safety. One battery was actually lifted in this way to 36 different fire positions in a 24-hour period.

Another use for *Chinook* was as a bomber. Using the tail door, it was possible to eject $2\frac{1}{2}$ tons of napalm in drums onto entrenched enemy positions. The 40-gallon cans were fused by means of a static line which armed them when well clear of the helicopter. It was also possible to drop heavy charges of high explosive, fused to explode several feet above the ground, in order to blast landing zones out of the jungle. Chemical agents such as irritant gases were dropped onto enemy positions in an effort to 'smoke out' their occupants. The most spectacular variant of *Chinook*, however, was the 'Go-Go Bird'. Three were tried out in Vietnam to produce overwhelming close air support; they were armed with a mixture of twin 20mm Gatling guns, ·50-calibre heavy machine guns and 40mm grenade launchers. Thus equipped and bristling with additional ordnance fastened on wherever a space could be found, the 'Go-Go Bird' could lay down a devastating pattern of fire and so impressed the enemy that they immediately fled at its approach. Its effect on the morale of the troops it was supporting was tremendous. Unfortunately, two of these aircraft were lost to enemy ground fire – almost certainly due to the over-enthusiasm of their crews who pressed home their attacks with a sublime disregard for danger – and the immense logistic problem of providing such vast quantities of ammunition eventually led to abandonment of the project.

An important organizational decision was made in 1966 as the result of 1st Cavalry's first six months of combat. It arose because the US Army was finding it increasingly difficult to maintain the Airmobile Division and its integral helicopters in the field while trying to provide Army Aviation support in steadily increasing quantity for the other Vietnamese, American, Korean and Australian units now involved in the battle. Although some of these had a modest number of their own helicopters these were mainly for observation and reconnaissance and for light transport only. There was a desperate shortage of *Chinooks* and UH1Bs and it soon became clear that all non-1st Cavalry aviation resources would have to be pooled in order to make the best use of them. The 1st Aviation Brigade was accordingly formed as an experiment on 1 March. Its commander, Brig.-Gen. 'Phip' Seneff, was an expert in airmobility and had played an important part during the previous year's 11th Air Assault Division trials in the Carolinas.

The creation of a 'centralized' aviation brigade raised shudders in many army circles; to some, it looked like an attempt to deprive armour, artillery and engineer combat units of 'their' aviation and to create a separate 'Air Corps'. This was anathema to most American soldiers, although it is exactly what the British Army *had* done in 1957. A compromise was arrived at by which, although Seneff commanded all the units comprising the 1st Aviation Brigade, their operational handling was in the hands of whichever ground commander they might be supporting. The growth of the brigade was phenomenal; when first formed it consisted of 680 aircraft and nearly 11,000 men serving in the equivalent of 36 aviation companies. By mid-1968 it disposed of 2000 aircraft, 25,000 men and 110 companies. As a rule, each non-airmobile division had the equivalent of an aviation battalion placed under its operational control, consisting of two aviation companies, a general support company and an airmobile company. Further units were deployed in support of corps troops. In this way a reasonable solution was found to the clamorous demands for helicopter support now streaming in from all quarters. It was beginning to look as if the ARVN and their allies were becoming 'over-helicopterized', at the expense of the sustained close-quarter infantry war of attrition which was really now needed to put the Vietcong and NVA out of action.

The expansion of 1965–66 was causing almost unbearable strains right back down the line to the training organization and even to the American aircraft industry. In January 1966 Gen. Westmoreland, continually badgering the Pentagon for more army aviation support, had been warned that a serious shortage of aircrew was imminent.

Many now flying in Vietnam were on their second or even third tour of active service. Pilots were being posted to the theatre irrespective of rank and many units were top-heavy with disgruntled majors; morale began to deteriorate when aviators found themselves back in Vietnam within a year of leaving it; theirs was a perilous assignment and the statistics indicated one of the lowest survival rates. The personnel branch of the Department of the Army revealed the full measure of the famine in mid-1966; by 1 January 1967 there would be 9700 army aviators to fill an estimated 14,300 cockpit seats. The gap would widen even more alarmingly in 1967. At once the trainee pilot intake was stepped up from 120 to 410 per month, and aviation units in other overseas theatres were cut to the bone to find more pilots. There was a dismal response to urgent letters sent to 2000 reserve pilots; only 60 bothered to reply and only a handful of these expressed a burning desire to return to the colours in Vietnam. Lurid television news coverage had rivetted the American public to what was happening in South-East Asia and national disenchantment was already making itself felt.

If the strain was taking its effect on pilots, less evident symptoms of stress were impairing the performance of the technicians, responsible for ensuring high availability of the complex helicopters whilst working under appalling conditions – often under fire from snipers, rocket launchers and mortars. Crew chiefs would be logging up to 150 hours' flying a month and after a full day in the air, very frequently under heavy fire, would have to work long into the night rectifying minor faults, changing assemblies and repairing battle damage; this work might have to be done in the open by the light of carefully shaded torches, in torrential rain or choking dust clouds. The pilots could not be guaranteed an unbroken night's rest, for it was often necessary to test-fly the aircraft long before daybreak.

The pace of operations continued to increase, and by the beginning of 1967 it seemed that a military victory over the NVA and Vietcong was at last a possibility. Even though the South Vietnamese and Americans still tended to operate by day from a network of strongpoints and firebases, the possession of so much airmobility gave them an ability to seek and destroy the enemy which was beginning to tilt the scales. The most advanced aids to reconnaissance and surveillance were in widespread use and huge firepower resources could be harnessed in support of even the smallest military operation. As pressure on the Vietcong mounted, however, there was disturbing evidence of increased participation by the regular NVA, and of the use by the enemy of more sophisticated anti-aircraft weapons. In the earliest stages of the war, damage to helicopters by ground fire had usually been the result of hits by rifle-calibre weapons. From December 1961 to the end of January 1963 about 25,000 combat missions had been flown by rather less that 200 Army helicopters; 189 of them had been hit by ground fire but of these only four were totally destroyed, and only one received irreparable damage. By mid-1967 the scale of operations had vastly increased; the Army had over 2000 aircraft in Vietnam and the Marines another 275. Since early 1962 over five million combat sorties had been flown, nine million passengers carried and 645,000 tons of combat stores lifted. In any one week of 1967, 9800 sorties were flown, with 127,500 troops and 14,000 tons of freight. During five years of intensive operations over 900 American helicopters had been lost, of which about 300 were the result of combat. The high non-operational accident rate could be attributed to pilot fatigue, and the skimped training of aircrew and technicians in order to meet the incessant manpower demands of the campaign. Casualties to aircraft would have been far higher had it not been for the use of *Chinook* and the Sikorsky CH54 *Skycrane* to recover helicopters forced down by ground fire. By mid-1968 more than 4700 aircraft had been recovered in this way and subsequently repaired.

Although 1st Cavalry Division had gone to Vietnam with two of its battalions trained in the parachuting role, they were never used in this way. The first and only parachute assault took place on 22 February 1967 as part of a large-scale operation ('Junction City') which involved the 173rd Airborne Brigade, two us Infantry divisions (1st and 25th), the 11th Armored Cavalry Regiment and a number of ARVN units. The objective was a series of known enemy bases north of Tay Ninh and it was decided to use paratroops to close the most distant sector of the cordon so as to free troop-carrying helicopters for the actual assault. The unit selected for the jump was the 2nd Battalion of the 503rd Infantry which had acquired much lustre from its Second World War exploits at Nadzab and Corregidor. The last us Army combat jump had been in Korea in 1951 and the men of the 2nd/503rd were eager to prove their worth in this operation, for most of them a baptism of fire.

The plan for the drop was prepared in utmost secrecy in order to avoid landing on an enemy-held dropzone. At 0900 hrs the commander of the 173rd Airborne Brigade, Brig.-Gen. Deane, personally led the men of the 2nd/503rd to the attack. Total surprise was achieved and the dropzone was quickly secured so that the subsequent cargo drop could be called in. When this had taken place the 1st/503rd were brought in by helicopter. Due to lack of familiarity with this type of operation many of the helicopter pilots landed too close to the discarded parachutes littering the dropzone and several aircraft were damaged when the nylon canopies flew up into their rotors. After the drop the 2nd/503rd were deployed, like all the other units in 'Junction City', in the infantry role; for 12 weeks the enemy was harassed and worn down, losing 2700 dead and huge quantities of stores. It was a successful operation, but the parachute assault had been something of an anti-climax. Whereas the 2nd/503rd had to wait for most of their equipment to be dropped to them the 1st/503rd, though chafing at missing the jump, were brought fresh to the battle by helicopter, complete with their support weapons and essential stores. Even that most ardent airborne admirer, Gen. Tolson, felt obliged to comment that:

> Every man with jump wings was eager to prove his particular mettle in Vietnam. However, this special talent was not often suited for that enemy, that terrain, and that situation. Nevertheless, I firmly believe that there is a continuing requirement for an airborne capability in the US Army structure.

In April 1967, Tolson assumed command of the 1st Cavalry Division. It was a post for which he had been professionally readying himself for years and under his leadership the division excelled. He returned with it to the old hunting grounds in the north where the three regiments of the NVA 3rd Division still lurked in their mountain fastnesses, and in conjunction with the US Marines began to harry the enemy by day and night. As much of this operation took place within gun range of the coast, the US Navy provided fire support, and a high degree of integration was achieved with the Navy and with the US Marines and the USAF, whose support ranged from thunderous B52 airstrikes to logistic support with their newly acquired, ex-Army *Caribous*. Tolson demonstrated the flexibility of his division not only through its excellent operational performance but by the ability to create fixed-wing airstrips, lifting in tons of engineer equipment so that the strips were operational within two days. As the USAF *Caribou* units gained the confidence of the cavalrymen and acquired the novel skills of operating unarmed aircraft right inside the combat area, Tolson used them increasingly to shift troops around the battlefield, especially on the longer hauls which were uneconomical for the slower and less capacious UH1Bs.

Throughout 1967 pressure was sustained on the Vietcong and NVA, who now found themselves under attack in sanctuary areas which had never been penetrated the the Government forces and had in fact been Communist enclaves for up to 25 years. One such was the Song Re Valley into which Tolson directed a reconnaissance in force in

August. The valley appeared peaceful and innocent from above, although heavy anti-aircraft fire was invariably directed against low-flying reconnaissance aircraft. The rice crops were well tended and fat cattle grazed in the fields; only the absence of a civilian population indicated that something was amiss.

The choice of LZs was hard. It would clearly be suicidal to assault into the bottom of the valley, exposed to every gun within range, but the surrounding hills provided few suitable sites. One was eventually selected on higher ground overlooking the valley, which could take up to six 'Hueys' simultaneously. On the morning of 9 August the leading elements of the 2nd/8th Cavalry landed after a short but intensive artillery barrage. One platoon had deplaned when a tornado of enemy fire burst onto the LZ from the surrounding slopes. As the rest of the leading company arrived, two 'Hueys' were shot down and the rest were repeatedly hit. The lift was abandoned, a routine performance suddenly transformed into a rescue operation. 'A' Company of the 2nd/8th had landed, by sheer mischance, amidst a carefully concealed NVA position in which at least 80 enemy troops were dug in with three 12·7mm Russian anti-aircraft cannon, numerous mortars and recoilless guns. Adjoining the NVA position, and also overlooking the LZ, was a company of Vietcong. From all directions, more enemy troops could be seen hurrying towards the fight.

What seemed to be a hopeless situation was successfully retrieved through the fighting qualities of 'A' Company, the speed of 1st Cavalry's reaction, good radio communication and the stunning array of firepower now brought to bear on the enemy. Two of the *Chinook* 'Go-Go Birds' were on call and these fired an incredible eight tons of ammunition at the enemy position and on all likely enemy reinforcement routes, thereby sealing off the battle area. The division's integral aerial rocket artillery quickly came to the rescue, and USAF support followed. The cavalrymen on the LZ quickly regained the initiative, flushed out the enemy and destroyed an anti-aircraft position. Seventy-three enemy corpses were counted, and 'A' Company brought back the bodies of 11 of their comrades when they were finally flown out to safety.

Tolson and his staff used the affair at Song Re as a test case and its lessons were put to effective use in 1st Cavalry's subsequent battles. Meanwhile, a new aircraft was entering US Army service which would give aviation units the offensive fire power for which they had been searching so long.

The defects of the armed 'Huey' had long been recognized. It was slow, cumbersome, presented a large target to enemy gunners and lacked protection against hostile fire. Although the Department of the Army had already recognized this and initiated a competition for the design of a custom-built armed helicopter, or 'gunship', there was no sign of it materializing for several years at least. As so often happens, however, the American aircraft industry was equal to the problem, and the Bell Helicopter Company, builders of the UH1, came up with a private-venture design. Using many of UH1's standard components, including power plant and transmission system, the *Hueycobra*, as Bell's design was christened, was a streamlined aircraft with a crew of two, greatly improved armour protection and the ability to carry an impressive variety of weapons. Its slender fuselage and greatly reduced head-on profile made it a difficult target, and this was further helped by *Hueycobra*'s high speed – over 50 per cent faster than UH1B – and tremendous manoeuvrability. As the long campaign moved into its climactic final phases, *Hueycobra* began to replace the armed 'Hueys' in all 1st Cavalry Division's aviation units, and its appearance alone over the battlefield was often enough to put the enemy to flight.

CHAPTER FIFTEEN

Vietnam 3: Climax

Two years after its formation in March 1966 the 1st Aviation Brigade had expanded to a size which made it one of the largest air forces in the world. Its 2000 aircraft provided a hitherto undreamt-of degree of mobility for the US, South Vietnamese and South Korean infantry divisions, whose confidence and offensive spirit was at its height. Study of dozens of combat reports from this period shows how accustomed the infantry of the line were becoming to airmobile operations. It also gives the lie to the ill-informed opinions of journalists on both sides of the Atlantic who poured scorn on the performance of the US Army and paraded it as a demoralized body of drug-addicted misfits. The real picture is perhaps given by an account of a typical small-scale action, one of thousands which took place in 1968.

The HQ of the 25th US Infantry Division was in the small town of the Chu Chi, about 25 miles north-west of Saigon, together with one of its brigades, the 2nd. The area for which 2nd Brigade was responsible consisted mostly of flat tracts of scrubland and bamboo thickets providing good cover for the Vietcong, interspersed with patches of cultivation. The brigade commander usually had four or five battalions under command with an artillery battalion for fire support. Each day he could rely on the use of ten 'Hueys' from 1st Aviation Brigade for troop movement, giving him a lift of 60 fully equipped men. Also available, if required, were one or more Light Fire Teams (LFTS), each consisting of two *Hueycobras* and a light observation helicopter (LOH). The sequence of the action which took place on this particular day now follows chronologically as it illustrates the sheer speed with which airmobile operations were conducted.

1500 hrs The duty officer at HQ 2nd Brigade receives a message from HQ 25 Division that a LOH mission has spotted a squad of Vietcong three and a half miles north of the Brigade HQ and has brought fire down from its two escorting *Hueycobras*; three enemy dead can be seen on the ground and a number of concealed bunkers have also been detected. The brigade commander immediately takes off for an aerial reconnaissance accompanied by his Artillery battalion commander and his Operations staff officer or S3. Within minutes the command helicopter, a 'Huey' with additional radios fitted, is overhead the contact area. No bodies are to be seen; the LFT, out of fuel and ammunition, have left the scene to replenish. The brigade commander turns to his artillery commander; he is sure that the enemy is still present, and to keep him pinned down he calls for 15 minutes of fire on an area of scrub 400 yards square. Only 30 minutes have passed since the first contact by the LFT. Whilst the first rounds of gunfire begin to come down, the brigade commander's helicopter returns to Cu Chi where a company of the 4th battalion, 9th Infantry Regiment is now standing by for helicopter insertion if required.

1600 hrs The Brigade commander, back on the ground in his command post at Cu Chi, hears on the radio that the refuelled LOH is back in the contact area. He takes off again in his own command helicopter and joins the LOH, whose pilot immediately sees signs of movement in the area of the recent artillery target, and drops a smoke marker. The brigade commander directs the recce helicopter to go down to tree-top height for a closer look. Using his rotor downwash to part the foliage, the LOH pilot reports a dead Vietcong, equipment lying on the ground, and many newly dug foxholes, bunkers and tunnels. Although it will be dark within two hours, the brigade commander orders a reconnaissance in force.

1635 hrs The S3 calls 4th/9th on the radio, orders them to move by air to an LZ 500 yards north of the LOH's smoke marker, and gives the grid co-ordinates of the area to be searched. He then orders the Light Fire Team back into the area for close fire support. The battalion commander of the 4th/9th now arrives in his command helicopter; he has heard the S3's orders on the radio; the brigade commander drops another smoke marker, for the LOH has again left the scene. To the south the ten 'Slicks' can be seen rising from their pads at Cu Chi.

1650 hrs The LFT arrives and the two *Hueycobras* strafe the area around the selected LZ. Just before the 'Slicks' arrive, an LOH fitted with smoke generators flies along the southern edge of the LZ to mask it from the objective.

1700 hrs The 'Slicks' land, only 25 minutes after the order to take off from Cu Chi. They arrive in three groups with one astern to guard against ambush. The troops, thoroughly drilled, leap from their helicopters and form up on the southern edge of the LZ amidst the smoke.

1705 hrs Two platoons in parallel Indian file move off towards the objective. A third platoon has spread out to guard the flanks. The battalion commander drops another smoke marker.

1715 hrs As the troops start to enter the northern edge of the search area, the CO's gunner spots some movement on the southern edge as a

246

group of Vietcong slip away in order to don civilian clothes and melt into the countryside. As the troops come into the centre of the objective, one Vietcong breaks cover and is shot dead; bunkers and tunnels are taken on with grenades. A few enemy corpses are found – victims of the preliminary barrage and the LFT. Piles of useful documents, ammunition, weapons and rations are picked up.

1800 hrs When it is clear that the enemy have slipped away, the brigade commander decides to end the operation, and orders the company commander to move on through the objective to a pick-up point in the padi fields 500 yards to the south.

1805 hrs The troop begin to leave the objective. This is the most critical stage of the operation; all ranks are aware that only a few days earlier the Vietcong shot down five Air Cavalry pick-up helicopters by anticipating the pick-up point and surrounding it with rocket launchers. On that occasion there had been no suppressive fire – a careless and fatal omission. Now, the withdrawal is carefully executed. The troops file across the padi fields in single file; the last in the line throws a smoke grenade every 100 paces to indicate the tail of the column, and the artillery commander, from the brigade command helicopter, brings down continuous fire support 100 yards north of each smoke puff as it appears.

1845 hrs It is now almost dark as the troops reach the pick-up LZ. Only five 'Slicks' are now available; this means two lifts, so one platoon takes up a defensive position as the other prepares to guide in the 'Hueys', whose rotor blades can be heard slapping the air as they approach from the south. The first platoon commander carries a flashing strobe light to mark his position and the 'Slicks' approach at low level, using their landing lights only at the last possible moment. Within 30 seconds the first platoon is away, and 12 minutes later the empty 'Slicks' are back. The second platoon commander orders his troops to their feet and on his orders the six grenade launchers are volleyed into the jungle edge. Once the troops are aboard, all five side gunners fire sustained bursts to deter any pursuit. By 1915 hrs all troops are safely back in Cu Chi.

An unspectacular small-unit operation this, but it illustrates the high degree of co-ordination between the supporting arms which had now been achieved. If a strong force of enemy had been met, more troops could have been on the scene within minutes to seal off the area, and close air support called in to augment the artillery. The brigade commander, overhead in his command helicopter, was able to use his excellent radios to monitor the Divisional and Battalion command nets in addition to his own Brigade and Air Support nets, and could talk on them all at will. His artillery commander was able to use his own radio on the artillery support net, and could talk freely to the brigade commander whilst airborne on the helicopter intercom system. The battalion commander's helicopter was similarly equipped. All troops taking part knew exactly what to do, acting in accordance with thoroughly rehearsed drills. A few years earlier it would have been unthinkable for a line infantry battalion to operate in this way; but with training and practice, a good unit can turn its hand to anything.

Throughout 1967, 1st Cavalry Division had been operating in Binh Dinh Province, in which it had won its spurs back in 1965. Its ability to cover a huge operational area and react swiftly and effectively to any move by NVA or Vietcong resulted in a remarkable improvement to the political situation in an area which had become inured to Communist domination. The civil government began to return and the Vietcong were progressively rooted out. With elimination of the Vietcong activists the population regained confidence to such a degree that when free local government elections were held for the first time ever, almost 97 per cent of those eligible to vote did so. This, and not the wildly-optimistic 'body counts', was the true measure of American military success at a time when victory seemed to be a reality. Operations ranged from battalion air assaults to small-scale forays such as that already described in this chapter. Despite the enemy's increased fire power, helicopters were managing to avoid a penal casualty rate despite the gloomy predictions of those who maintained that they were hopelessly fragile and therefore were not to be risked in combat. At this stage a helicopter would be hit every 1147 sorties, would be forced down by ground fire every 13,461 sorties and shot down and lost with its crew every 21,194. Despite the unceasing rotation of personnel – about 9000 a year – the Division maintained a high degree of proficiency in all fields. It had now acquired its own special spirit; that of the old horsed US Cavalry. Certain eccentricities of dress were tolerated, the wide-brimmed cavalry Stetson reappeared, and a distinct air of swagger and bravura pervaded all units. 1st Cavalry was an élite formation, and knew it. So did the enemy; there was abundant evidence from the steadily increasing number of prisoners (itself significant – the Vietcong and NVA had formerly fought to the death) that the ARVN and their allies were now in the ascendant.

Early on the morning of 31 January 1968 the Vietnam war abruptly changed direction. It was the festival of Tet, which every Vietnamese household celebrated noisily with fireworks and feasting. Under cover of the preparations for the festival, enemy soldiers slipped into 40 principal towns and cities, including more than half the provincial capitals. Their biggest effort was directed at Saigon itself, where the principal targets were the military airfield and headquarters complex at Tan Son Nhue. General Westmorelands' command post, radio and TV stations, the US Ambassador's residence – all came under heavy fire. For a time, groups of Vietcong, some in ARVN uniforms, raced up and down the streets in stolen vehicles. The American Embassy was assaulted by fanatics who broke in; it was six hours before they were wiped out, and the embassy staff, fighting for their lives, were sustained by helicopters landing on the roof and finally relieved by a party from 101st Airborne Division who were landed in the Embassy grounds.

All over the country, allied troops came under attack; had it not been for the prompt response of 1st Aviation Brigade and 1st Cavalry Division the Vietcong could have brought off a stunning military victory completely against the run of the game. 1st Cavalry had recently started to move further north into the I Corps area and was obliged to spend the next month coping with the demands of the Tet offensive whilst setting up its repair and maintenance bases. The main tasks were to sort out the respective situations at Quang Tri and Hue, two prominent cities where the Vietcong had succeeded in establishing lodgements at the beginning of Tet. Conditions for flying were dismal, with persistent rain and low cloud; many of the roads in the area had been cut, throwing a heavy burden on air supply. Despite this, all ranks rose to the challenge. The Allied forces rallied and turned grimly on their assailants. Hue and Quang Tri were cleared of Vietcong, whose casualties were enormous – more than 30,000 dead and 8000 captured. Huge quantities of weapons had been lost by the enemy. It was also a moral victory, for the civil population, fondly expected to rise in support of the Communist offensive, failed to do so.

Although the NVA and Vietcong had suffered a severe military defeat in the Tet offensive they had not abandoned their long-term aim of seizing the northern provinces of Vietnam where the country was nowhere more than 60 miles wide; the frontier with Laos permitted the enemy to move freely using the Ho Chi Minh trail as a supply line, and to establish sanctuary areas in what was nominally a neutral country. The American high command had long appreciated the vulnerability of this northern salient, which included the so-called 'demilitarized zone', or DMZ, separating North and South Vietnam, and had set up a Marine Corps base at Khe Sanh from which the DMZ and the Laotian border could be watched. By December 1967 the enemy had surrounded Khe Sanh and it was clear that they were aiming to repeat the Viet Minh's success of 1954 against the French at Dien Bien Phu. Apart from eliminating the base, the psychological and propaganda effects of a victory over the US Marines would be enormous.

Even before the Tet offensive broke, Tolson had been ordered to relieve the pressure on Khe Sanh with 1st Cavalry Division, to open Highway 9 – the only east–west land route in that area – and to destroy all enemy forces in the Khe Sanh area. After Tet, the enemy redoubled his efforts against the base, whose garrison was now reinforced by air to a strength of 6000 US Marines and ARVN Rangers. It was a tight perimeter. Surrounded by densely forested hills, it dominated four radiating valleys and overlooked the now deserted Highway 9. The base itself, sited on a low plateau, covered an area about a mile long and half-a-mile wide, with a 1300-yard airstrip whose aluminium-mat runway could accept C130 *Hercules* transport aircraft. By the end of March, however, no C130s were able to land; the garrison was hard pressed by a determined enemy who had sapped his way almost to the perimeter wire, despite pulverizing B52 bombing attacks and heavy artillery support from the American 175mm heavy artillery massed at a fire base further back down Route 9.

Tolson first sent in an air cavalry squadron with the perilous task of pinpointing the besiegers' positions. For five days Lt-Col. Diller's

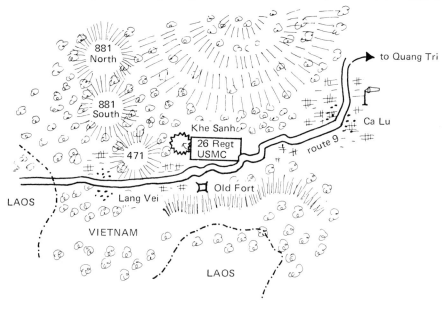

KHE SANH – The Battlefield   Approximate scale

1st Squadron, 9th Cavalry, the unit selected for this mission, scoured the Khe Sanh area under the protection of continuous USAF air strikes. It was clear that the enemy anticipated an attempt to relieve Khe Sanh along Route 9 and Tolson obliged by sending a feint attack up the road. The NVA reacted strongly as American artillery and aerial bombardment of the besiegers around Khe Sanh rose to a crescendo; in 70 days USAF dropped 96,000 tons of bombs on the area, which had now taken on a lunar appearance, for this was twice the tonnage dropped in the whole Pacific theatre in 1942 and 1943. Meanwhile, the hard-pressed defenders, supplied by high- and low-level airdrop, added the fire of their 40 field guns to the cannonade.

On 1 April two Marine Battalions, supported by sappers, opened the main attack up Route 9 towards Khe Sanh as expected by the enemy. At the same time Tolson flew three battalions of his 3rd Brigade into an area some miles ahead of the Marines, together with a field artillery battalion. He now had his 'hand in the enemy's bowels' with a vengeance. The NVA, taken aback, reacted hesitantly and Tolson increased the pressure on 2 April by leap-frogging three more battalions forward on the general axis of Route 9, followed 24 hours later by the whole of his 2nd Brigade; although the enemy shelled and mortared the landing zones his troops were elusive and reluctant to close with the cavalry. The Marines pushed on doggedly against stiff resistance whilst 3rd Brigade found themselves increasingly under attack. By 4 April a full-scale battle was ranging along Route 9 and to its flanks. The Marines in Khe Sanh now struck south to seize higher ground overlooking their positions and on 5 April Tolson lifted two battalions of 3rd Brigade forward to new positions south of Khe Sanh. The NVA, sensing the need to prevent these new arrivals linking up with the Khe Sanh garrison, attacked furiously; but the cavalrymen stood firm. On 6 April the 2nd/7th Cavalry, who had been advancing towards Khe Sanh parallel to Route 9, mopping up NVA units en route, struck towards the road, reaching it at a point only five miles from the fort. Another battalion was sent in by helicopter to augment the Marines to the south and the garrison was reinforced by a battalion of ARVN paratroops who also came in by helicopter. Further back down Route 9 the Marines' column was still meeting with heavy resistance. The enemy only started to break when, on 7 April, Tolson flew in an ARVN airborne task force of three battalions to landing zones west of Khe Sanh, cutting the enemy's shortest line of retreat towards the Laotian border only seven miles away. Small parties of enemy now started to flee for safety, abandoning their kit as they did so. This trickle became a torrent as the remorseless pressure of 1st Cavalry's attack was sustained.

On 8 April, the HQ of 1st Cavalry's 3rd Brigade was flown into the Khe Sanh perimeter where it immediately assumed command of the defence from the exhausted Marines. For three more days the enemy was hunted down in the surrounding hills. By 13 April Route 9 had been repaired and was open all the way to Khe Sanh.

The whole battle was fought in abominable flying conditions of low cloud, rain and poor visibility. It was generally impossible to carry out large-scale air movement of troops before noon. Tolson had anticipated this by building up a launching base near the start point of his drive up Route 9 at Ca Lu. With a 500-yard airstrip suitable for *Caribou* operations, it was provided with well-protected supply and command bunkers, and a network of all-weather tracks. This careful logistic preparation, and the use of the air cavalry to obtain tactical intelligence before battle was joined, ensured success for 1st Cavalry Division in what was arguably its greatest triumph. The NVA were completely unbalanced by Tolson's bold use of leap-frog tactics and were forced out of their well-prepared defensive positions along Route 9 in order to deal with successive threats to their rear. Tolson went on hitting them until he had forced them into rout, driving them into the open where they offered splendid targets for quick-reaction artillery fire and airstrikes controlled by airborne observers of the USAF flying L19 *Bird Dog* light aircraft.

This was a major victory over the regular NVA, which had been brought to battle on the Americans' terms and lost 1300 dead, over 200 field guns, mortars and heavy machine guns (with 12,000 rounds of artillery ammunition), 2 anti-aircraft guns, 6 vehicles including a light tank and 3000 tons of rice. Allied casualties were remarkably low; the relieving force lost 143 killed in action; although 1st Cavalry's helicopters had carried out over 1000 assault landings of platoon size or greater, only 27 helicopters were hit, and of the three shot down only one was a total loss. An extremely high tempo of operations had been sustained for two weeks – a period thought unattainable at the time of the Carolina trials in 1965.

The 1st Cavalry demonstrated its flexibility almost as soon as the Khe Sanh battle was over. Even while it was still raging, Tolson was given a particularly difficult task in conjunction with 101st Airborne Division (soon to become the second Airmobile Division in Vietnam but at this stage still operating in the infantry role). His target was, like Khe Sanh, in the depth of the jungle-clad hills along the Laotian border. Less than seven miles from the frontier lay the 20-mile-long An Shau Valley. It had formerly contained a Special Force base but this had been over-run two years earlier, since when it had been a North Vietnamese base area. The 1st Cavalry was ordered to carry out a direct airmobile assault into the valley to root out and destroy the enemy's supply system.

As Air Cavalry reconnaissance had proved so successful at Khe Sanh, Tolson again sent Diller's squadron in to spy out the land, select flying routes, identify targets and – most important – locate the anti-aircraft defences with which the valley was known to bristle. The weather was so bad that the operation had to be postponed in order to give Diller's pilots three clear days for their dangerous mission. As the result of their reports, Tolson decided to make use of one of the three abandoned airstrips in the valley, seizing it in the early stages so that it could form the hub of his subsequent operations.

A co-ordinated aerial and artillery bombardment preceded the arrival of the leading waves of the assault on 19 April, but a hail of anti-aircraft fire still met every helicopter that showed itself; 23 were hit and 10 of these were destroyed. The enemy was clearly going to fight for every inch of the valley. To make matters worse, low cloud enveloped the hills, and the only way to enter the valley for much of the time was to climb up through the murk and then search for a gap, down which the helicopters would spiral in steep auto-rotation; a disturbing manoeuvre at the best of times but even more frightening when the pilot knew he might emerge at the bottom into clear air to be engaged point-blank by anti-aircraft fire. 'What should have been a simple 20-minute flight,' wrote Tolson, 'was usually an hour and 20 minutes of stark terror . . . the operation was a phenomenal piece of flying, but from a commander's viewpoint it was sheer agony to see what my people had to go through in order to accomplish their mission.'

Despite the weather, the build-up went ahead. The airstrip at A Luoi, commanding the junctions of several roads and tracks much used by the NVA, was firmly in 1st Cavalry's hands by 22 April and the pilots of the C130 *Hercules* now showed their mettle as they flew mission after mission to support the Cavalry with supply drops. The C130 is well equipped with navigational aids including radar; even so, to descend for several thousand feet through dense cloud over mountainous terrain calls for a lot of cold courage. A minor error in navigation would mean crashing into the hills or breaking cloud right over the enemy's anti-aircraft defences; such was the fate of one C130 which on 26 April was shot down in flames before the eyes of the troops it was attempting to succour. By 1 May, sufficient engineer equipment had been flown in to complete the airstrip at A Luoi so that 1st Cavalry's hard-working engineers were able to open it to *Caribou* aircraft, and three days later to C130s.

Scouring around the valley the Americans found abundant evidence that it was indeed a key NVA administrative area. Hundreds of thousands of rounds of ammunition were unearthed, as were 67 wheeled vehicles ranging from captured jeeps to a 2½-ton truck, a PT76 light tank, bulldozers, mines, grenades and food supplies. It was the biggest haul yet made, and brought home to the enemy that none of his sanctuary areas was now safe from attack.

The 101st Airborne Division was converted to the airmobile role in the summer of 1968, having already been partly deployed in Vietnam since the end of 1967. It was a good formation to choose, for its officers and men were attuned to operating on light scales of equipment, well accustomed to movement by air and had the right aggressive mentality for airmobile warfare. Furthermore, they had been given a good taste of their new task in the An Shau Valley and had relished the experience. By early 1969, the 101st were ready to take the field alongside – and in friendly competition with – 1st Cavalry.

By 1969, the United States Government was moving towards disengagement in Vietnam. It had become involved in the war progressively from the early days of 1961–62, when advisory teams had gradually sorted out the chaos of the South Vietnamese military system and overseen its phenomenal growth, to embroilment in a full-scale campaign against the North Vietnamese main army as well as the Vietcong. Casualties had far exeeded those of the Korean war; it was now a most unpopular cause and there were increasing signs of disaffection amongst the civilian population at home. A policy of 'Vietnamization' was therefore pursued with a view to the progressive withdrawal of US Forces. Increased numbers of Vietnamese were trained as helicopter pilots and in the techniques of airmobile warfare. But before the American withdrawal got under way, two Allied operations were mounted against enemy bases across the Laotian and Cambodian borders which raised the tempo of the war to a climax before its unsatisfactory end.

Early in 1969, 1st Cavalry Division had been moved south to operate against enemy supply routes leading across the Cambodian border towards Saigon and the Delta area. It had been anticipated that the Vietcong would attempt a repeat performance of the 1968 Tet offensive and this duly took place, but was easily put down by the thoroughly alerted ARVN. Pressure on the 'Cambodian' trails was sustained throughout the year and a third attempt at a Tet offensive early in 1970 was a total failure. However, it was clear that the repulsed NVA and Vietcong had built up a complex logistic organization on Cambodian territory, and in April the political situation indicated than an operation across the border was feasible. The principal formation assigned with 1st Cavalry Division was the ARVN Airborne Division, and the initial assault was put under the command of Brig.-Gen. Shoemaker the assistant commander of 1st Cavalry, an officer whose wide experience embraced earlier tours in Vietnam as well as the original 11th Air Assault Division trials of 1965. The tactics adopted by 1st Cavalry throughout 1969 reflected his conviction that it was useless to thrash around the countryside by day, returning to safe bases for the night. 1st Cavalry had succeeded in stemming the flow of men and *matériel* from Cambodia by inserting infantry ambush patrols which had operated for days at a time in the heart of territory formerly regarded as Vietcong preserves.

The move into Cambodia started sensationally just after dawn on 1 May 1970 when two 15,000lb bombs, fused to explode a few feet above the ground, were dropped into the jungle to clear two large landing zones and fire bases. Simultaneously, a preplanned B52 bombardment was launched at known targets over the border. By mid-morning, as the ARVN units and the cavalrymen were pouring into the area, dozens of contacts with NVA units were reported. *Hueycobras* pounced on numerous groups of enemy troops who, flushed out of deep cover, were frantically making for safety deeper into Cambodia. It was clear that the enemy had not expected to be attacked across the border, and had not prepared his anti-aircraft defences to meet an airmobile assault. Only two American soldiers were killed on the first day, against hundreds of NVA and Vietcong. Huge stocks of medical supplies were captured, and amongst the few enemy troops taken alive were significant numbers of medical personnel. So confident was the enemy in his supposed immunity that large numbers of vehicles were in open use on roads and tracks in the area. As these emerged, heavily laden with escaping NVA staff officers, they were attacked with gusto by *Hueycobras*. Over 300 vehicles were destroyed or captured.

During the following weeks, until the operation ended on 29 June, the Allies struck out in all directions to continue the search for the enemy's field units and administrative centres. Enemy resistance was ferocious at times, for the NVA infrastructure had received a near-mortal wound; as the fire bases were withdrawn the NVA closed in with the aim of destroying the *Chinooks* as they lifted out the field guns, and some superb feats of airmanship and courage were recorded as the big aircraft, using cloud cover and flying low along sinuous valleys, weaved their way through a curtain of fire to extract the field pieces from bases which were frequently under heavy artillery and mortar fire.

The Cambodian expedition had succeeded beyond expectation; the enemy, taken utterly by surprise and lulled into a false sense of security, was thrown off balance and kept on the run by a succession of quickly mounted heliborne assaults. The troops landed for these operations were able to operate in the jungle for days on end, relying on aerial resupply. 1st Cavalry Division had given an outstanding example of how to conduct aggressive and fast-moving airmobile operations.

Throughout 1970 the Airmobile Divisions were involved in hundreds of small-scale operations. As the NVA's and Vietcong's efforts began to fall off it was no longer necessary to mount battalion, brigade and divisional air-assault operations; it seemed that with the resurgence of South Vietnamese confidence and the vast improvement in the performance of the ARVN, only one more push was required before the Americans pulled out altogether.

The favourable situation at the end of 1970 was due in part to the great efforts made in the development of new weapons and equipment for use by Army Aviation. The *Hueycobra* had been given a formidable 2·75in rocket whose 17lb warhead proved deadly against enemy bunkers and tunnel systems, a 2·75in Flechette rocket with the ability to pierce armoured vehicles, and the new SX35 20mm cannon, mounted in the chin turret and capable of firing ahead and to either flank. Known enemy jungle trails were sown with seismic detectors by UH1 helicopters; when movement was registered by these, ambush patrols were lifted into position, backed by gunship and artillery support. The enemy had now lost the initiative and the hunt was afoot.

The operation which took place in Laos from 8 February to 9 April 1971 was unusual in that no American forces took part in the fighting on the ground. Political constraints dictated that only ARVN troops should be used. The plan was devised by the Commander of the ARVN's I Corps and although the planning of airmobile and aviation support was in American hands, the ground plan dictated the pattern of air operations. There was far less of the spirit of collaboration which had characterized the handling of the Cambodian operation, and this was to result in unprecedented casualties to the helicopter force.

The decision to mount an operation into Laos in February 1971 had been taken as the result of notable ARVN successes in a second Cambodian foray, unassisted by American troops; and the known build-up of NVA supplies in southern Laos, where enemy traffic had been building up for months along the Ho Chi Minh trail. Most of the US Army's helicopters were now based down at the coast; it was decided to reactivate the battered base at Khe Sanh as a forward replenishment and staging post for operations across the Laotian border.

For operation 'Lamson 719', as the assault was code-named, the ARVN allocated a large force: their 1st Infantry Division, 1st Airborne Division, the Marine Division, three battalions of Rangers and an Armoured Brigade. The US Army Aviation effort was provided by a mixture of units from 1st Cavalry Division, 101st Division, 1st Aviation Brigade and the US Marines. The plan was for the ARVN Airborne Division to strike up Route 9, past Khe Sanh and over the border, whilst the Armoured Brigade fought up the road. The 1st Infantry Division was to advance south of the road axis and the Rangers to the north.

The attack got under way on 8 February and was six miles into Laos at last light. There was an immediate reaction from the NVA who poured in reinforcements from all over the theatre. Vigorous attacks were mounted against the firebases which the ARVN insisted on establishing instead of fighting a mobile battle of ambush and counterambush. These firebases were quickly hedged in by NVA anti-aircraft guns and every helicopter that appeared was greeted by intense fire. The enemy now started to use main battle tanks – the elderly but effective T34s – which were launched against an ARVN firebase on 25 February in broad daylight, over-running the defence. The situation was now critical; the attacking force was virtually besieged in a 20-mile salient culminating in the Laotian town of Tchepone. The ARVN's armoured units had failed to keep Route 9 open and the entire expedition was now dependent on aerial resupply.

The withdrawal phase of 'Lamson 719' involved the helicopter crews in the most costly operation of the war; 107 helicopters – mostly UHIs – were lost and hundreds more damaged. The losses would have been much higher had it not been for the heroic work of *Chinook* and *Skycrane* pilots who recovered dozens of downed aircraft and lifted them back to safety. Despite these alarming casualties, which indicate the ferocity of the opposition, 'Lamson 719' inflicted heavy losses on the enemy; among the enemy equipment destroyed or captured were no less than 106 tanks, 406 trucks, 76 field guns; 12,000 tons or rice, 20,000 tons of ammunition, and thousand of personal weapons. Although the notorious 'body counts' of the Vietnam war are to be treated with caution, the claim of 13,914 enemy dead gives some indication of the scale of the battle.

It was unfortunate that the aviation aspects of 'Lamson 719' received so much publicity. The American press, which had been starved of sensational news from the front, pounced on the chance to churn out purple prose on the themes of desperate cavalry charges, famous last stands and Balaklava-like dashes to destruction. A point not made was that the helicopters were being used in conjunction with units unaccustomed to airmobile operations and not trained to the same pitch as 1st Cavalry and 101st Airborne (Airmobile) Divisions or the US Marines, whose troops were less inclined to dig themselves into static firebases, preferring to hunt the enemy, beating him at his own game.

Ten years' experience in Vietnam gave the US Army much to think about. Without doubt, the greatest area of tactical development had been that of Army Aviation, which had expanded from the tentative semi-tactical troop-lifts of South Vietnamese infantry in 1961 to the full-scale divisional air assaults undertaken by 1st Cavalry Division in the latter half of the war. Overnight battalion moves of 100 miles and more were commonplace; the front-line soldier now looked to the air for fire support, transport and his next day's rations. He fought secure in the knowledge that if he was wounded he would be flown rapidly back to a field surgical unit for prompt, life-saving treatment; or that if the tactical situation required, he and his comrades would be retrieved by air and not left to fight hopelessly until killed or captured.

It took some time for US Army aviators to readjust to the changed situation after Vietnam. Tactics and equipment evolved to meet the needs of that campaign were not necessarily well suited to application in central Europe. Despite this, there was every evidence that many aviators imagined that helicopters could range widely around the European battlefield. The dangerous old concept of 'reconnaissance by fire' was far from dead, as indicated by development studies which were in hand during the early 1970s for an 'Advanced Aerial Reconnaissance Vehicle' or AARV, a heavily armoured two-seater helicopter carrying a Gatling gun and rockets, which could survive direct hits by 20mm shells and which was designed to penetrate into the enemy's forward areas. Subsequent studies led to modification of the AARV concept into that of a helicopter operating on the friendly side of the front line, but equipped with advanced sensors capable of obtaining the required 'look over the hill' even in conditions of minimal visibility and even darkness.

The chief differences between Vietnam and central Europe, however, concern the pattern of warfare. In Europe, NATO faces a threat in which the Warsaw Pact's forces, spearheaded by fast-moving armoured formations backed by massive air and artillery support, enjoy the advantages of knowing that NATO will never initiate the offensive, and of being able to choose their own time and place for the attack. They also possess significant numerical advantages and are now on the point of equalling the West in quality of weapons and equipment. The solution clearly lies in NATO's ability to offer, as a deterrent, the clear capability of waging a defensive battle which can inflict such heavy casualties on the Warsaw Pact's armour that an attack would involve unacceptable losses. The means of solving this problem began to be apparent early in the 1960s when first-generation wire-guided missiles were fired successfully from helicopters. Subsequent developments in this field will be discussed in the following chapter.

CHAPTER SIXTEEN

The State of the Game

As the US Army developed its airmobile forces to meet the challenge of Vietnam, other armies turned to the helicopter as a possible answer to their particular problems. The Russians, as the originators of airborne forces on any significant scale, were quick off the mark. Having shown their hand at the Tushino Display of 1956 they began a series of trials which eventually resulted in their adoption of what they termed *desant* tactics.

A *desant* can be described as the insertion of specially trained troops into enemy territory. Although this can be by boat or parachute, the term has come to mean an airlanded operation employing helicopters and fixed-wing aircraft, at any scale from a major strategic operation such as put an end to the Czechoslovakian uprising of 1968 to small-unit tactical operations like the capture or killing of an enemy field commander and his staff. The aims of *desant* operations, whatever their scale, are disruption, demoralization and the infliction of as much damage as possible, forcing the enemy to withhold disproportionately large forces back from the main battle to meet the threat to his rear, thereby weakening the main defence.

A typical *desant* operation, according to Soviet doctrine, will start with the insertion of small groups of up to 20 specially trained men by parachute or helicopter well behind the enemy front line. Their mission is to pinpoint vulnerable targets such as HQs and communications centres, nuclear weapons sites and ammunition dumps, and pass their positions by radio. This task completed, a programme of small-scale sabotage is started; single vehicles and despatch riders are ambushed, and every effort made to unsettle the enemy and deceive him as to the objectives of the main *desant*. The main assault will initially be by helicopter and parachute; helicopter landings are favoured, as ordinary motor rifle units can be used with the minimum amount of preliminary training, and their light vehicles and support weapons can accompany them; the unit, landed simultaneously with its gear in one place, can immediately set about its mission without delay. An outstanding example of a large scale *desant* was revealed after the great Soviet Army exercise *Dnepr* of 1967, colour films of which were distributed world wide for propaganda purposes, much as Hitler impressed the neutrals with films of his Polish and Western Front campaigns of 1939–40. The *Dnepr* film showed an all-helicopter *desant* with a force of over 100 *Hound* and *Hook* helicopters lifting troops, vehicles and guns. Large fixed-wing transport aircraft came in later, once the landing zones had been secured, with armoured personnel carriers, light tanks and self-propelled guns. Not depicted in the film were the unseen weapons employed to neutralize enemy air opposition – the electronic counter measures designed to jam enemy radios and radars and to deceive and confuse the defence with spurious transmissions.

A *desant* operation requires the enemy air force to be neutralized in the area of operations, and the Soviet Air Force is well equipped not only to take on its opponents at high altitude above the combat zone but to attack enemy airfields in order to put them out of commission. In addition, a high percentage of Warsaw Pact airpower is used for close offensive air support of the ground troops; the *Dnepr* film shows waves of ground-attack aircraft using cannon fire, rockets and bombs to clear the way ahead of the vulnerable formations of troop-carrying helicopters.

There is a continuing risk that *desant* operations would spearhead any Warsaw Pact offensive in the NATO theatre. Key airfield and communication centres on the northern and southern flanks would be especially vulnerable, as would the sensitive replenishment system for NATO's nuclear weapons in the Northern and Central Army Group areas. River crossings to the rear of the NATO forces as they deploy forward towards the East German border in the event of a Warsaw Pact invasion would also be particularly susceptible to attack by air-landed troops.

Although *desant* poses a significant threat – there are still at least seven airborne divisions in the Soviet Army's order of battle – the principal menace to NATO stems from the strength of the Warsaw Pact in armour and artillery. The early stages of any aggressive war waged by Russia and its allies would involve massive assaults, generally on narrow frontages, by strong armoured and motor rifle formations under the cover of heavy air and artillery bombardment. It would be essential to destroy as many of the enemy's tanks as possible, and keep on destroying them, whilst yielding as little ground as possible.

It is still true to say that the best weapon to use against a tank is another tank. It is armed with a high-velocity gun, is heavily protected against hostile fire and has a cross-country performance comparable to its opponent. The present and future quality of NATO tanks and their crews is such that despite their being outnumbered by up to five to one, they will hold their own in a defensive battle. The real danger is apparent when the enemy succeeds, by reason of his overwhelming strength and disregard for casualties, in making a breakthrough. Soviet tactical doctrine stresses the importance of capitalizing on such a situation and feeding fresh reinforcements through the gap, ignoring the flanks and brushing light opposition aside. There is also the risk, on a front which cannot be held with uniform density and along which the enemy can choose his own time and place of attack, that NATO formations will frequently be outflanked. In each case conventional armoured and mechanized infantry reserves will not be able to move quickly enough, in the face of the known enemy air threat, to deal with the emergency. They need time to regroup, for reconnaissance, issuing of orders and logistic preparation before a counter-attack can be launched. The speed at which such a battlefield crisis may develop dictates the use of a much faster vehicle as the basis of the counter-attack, one which can move across country without the limitations imposed by terrain or enemy interference.

The value of the helicopter as a battlefield vehicle was only slowly recognized. Its apparent vulnerability, lack of speed and agility, expense, and inability to operate by night or in extreme weather conditions had been noted as the result of trials in Europe and the USA as early as the mid-1950s. With improvements in design and the development of new aids to navigation, however, a quiet revolution took place. By the mid 1960s the US Army was successfully operating large numbers of helicopters in the punishing environment of Vietnam, and examination of statistics from the French campaign in Algeria confirmed what many army aviators had been saying for a long time: that the helicopter's chances of battlefield survival were far better than its critics had been saying. Furthermore, a helicopter fitted with the right sort of weapon could actually play an invaluable role in battle as the provider of three-dimensional mobility for firepower. Until the development of practicable helicopter-mounted guided weapons, it seemed that the helicopter could only take on 'area' targets, with machine guns, cannon and volleys of rockets. The breakthrough came when the French Army mounted wire-guided missiles on *Alouettes* in Algeria for the express purpose of engaging pinpoint targets. The next step was to develop a proper sighting system enabling the helicopter gunner to engage even smaller and moving targets at the extreme range of his weapon, in order to remain out of range of the enemy's guns.

The British Army was intrigued by the anti-tank helicopter. In 1966 and 1967 a number of trials, codenamed *Helltank*, were run in England and Germany in order to find out how vulnerable an anti-tank helicopter might be when pitted against the sort of opposition that the Warsaw Pact could offer. The results were encouraging and development went ahead with an anti-tank weapons system based on the French SS11 missile. Instead of the pencilled 'cross on the windscreen' which had been used in Algeria, it was necessary to fit a complex (and extremely expensive) gyroscopically stabilized optical sight to ensure the high probability of a very precise hit with each of the four missiles carried. The helicopter on which SS11 was carried was the Westland *Scout*, a robust 5–6-seat utility helicopter which proved to be an excellent battlefield vehicle, highly manoeuvrable and fast enough to survive in the sort of situation for which it was now intended.

From the start, the British rejected any suggestion that the anti-tank helicopter should be boldly committed to the battle in a search-and-strike role. There were many old Vietnam hands who advocated this, but they had been conditioned by successive operational tours in a totally different environment. In central Europe there was a constant threat from the enemy air forces and the devastating anti-aircraft firepower at the disposal of the Warsaw Pact's combat troops. The chief menace was – and still is – the ZSU23-4, a quadruple-mounted 23mm automatic cannon on a tracked armoured chassis, carrying its own target acquisition and fire-control radar.

In addition to the threat posed by mobile anti-aircraft guns, the Warsaw Pact's forces are lavishly equipped with anti-aircraft missiles which can be carried into battle on light armoured vehicles. As these can be expected well to the fore in any advancing Warsaw Pact formation, mixed with ZSU23-4 and further augmented by large numbers of heavy anti-aircraft machine guns and cannon, any force of helicopters deployed in the anti-tank role would need to be carefully handled and provided with missiles of great accuracy and considerable range. A head-on 'cavalry charge' against a Soviet tank division would invite disaster; the tactics employed must combine the skills of the stalker and the guile of the assassin. Surprise, ambush and shock action will succeed, providing the intended target can be set up properly.

This brings one back to Gen. Howze's original studies of the late 1950s, but with one significant difference; helicopters are now entering service which offer a high chance of success in the sort of operations Howze envisaged. A combination of anti-tank, reconnaissance and utility helicopters provides the defence with the ability to take on enemy armour with missiles while it is on the move, in mass, and in open ground, or to land parties of troops equipped with portable anti-tank weapons such as *Milan* to flush stationary armoured vehicles out of cover and into the open where the anti-tank helicopter enjoys the advantage.

The Russians have developed armed helicopters to a high degree. Their earlier efforts were on the same lines as those of the French and Americans and consisted of rocket pods and guns mounted on standard cargo and troop-lifting helicopters. By the early 1970s, however, intelligence sources were reporting the appearance of a radically new design. The Mil Mi24 *Hind* has been in service with the Group of Soviet Forces Germany (GSFG) since late 1973 and is a purpose-built attack helicopter designed to provide close fire support for *desant* operations, and for the attack of a wide range of armoured targets. It can also carry a number of assault troops together with their crew-served anti-tank weapons. *Hind* has been seen in several versions, of which the 'A' model was the first to carry anti-tank missiles. The 'B' model carries rocket pods. Both have been seen carrying bombs, and both are fitted with a chin turret in which a 23mm multi-barrel cannon is carried. Such an aircraft, which is heavily protected by armour, poses a far more serious threat to opposing helicopters than high-speed aircraft which are unable to manoeuvre with a helicopter's agility. A *Hind* 'D', even more formidable, is now in service.

Until 1967, experience in the large-scale battlefield use of helicopters had been limited to the conditions of the Algerian and Vietnamese theatres. The war which broke out between Israel and the Arab States in June 1967 was the first occasion in which helicopters were used in something approaching 'conventional' war conditions, and the results were awaited with interest. The area of operations appeared to be highly unsuitable for helicopters; in the south the Sinai offered little natural cover and the dust clouds raised by hovering helicopters betrayed their presence from miles away. Elsewhere, on the Golan Heights from which the Syrians overlooked the fertile agricultural settlements of Israel's northern plain, there was also an absence of natural cover, and pilots would have to rely solely on the agility of their helicopters and their own skill at contour flying.

Israel's success in this 'six-day war' was due to the triumphant use of airpower in a pre-emptive strike early on 5 June against the Egyptian air force, which was effectively destroyed on the ground within three hours. The skies were thus cleared of the first threat to helicopter operations and also allowed Israeli armoured formations to leap at their opponents massed in the Sinai.

During the night of 5–6 June, as three Israeli armoured divisions closed with their enemy, a brilliant helicopter assault was launched against the Egyptian gun areas at Umm Kataff, in which a battalion of paratroops were landed actually amidst the enemy's positions. The Umm Kataff position occupied an area nearly four miles square, sitting squarely astride the main axis of the Israeli advance and flanked by sand dunes and desert ridges which the defenders clearly thought were impassable to Israeli tanks. In well-prepared positions an Egyptian infantry brigade, 6 battalions of field artillery and almost 100 tanks confidently awaited the Israelis.

Before darkness fell, a team of observers with radios was flown unseen into a position from which the Egyptians could be kept under observation. After sunset a shuttle service began to fly parties of troops into forming-up positions in the area of the pathfinder group who had landed earlier. During the night more troops were boldly landed right in the Egyptian gun lines amidst scenes of wild panic on the part of the defence. One pilot, Capt. Tolevano, recalls landing a few yards from a sandbagged tent which turned out to be an artillery battalion command post. The sudden onrush of the helicopters, the downwash of the rotor blades throwing up clouds of choking dust and the dramatic arrival of Tolevano's determined passengers ensured total surprise. As the Egyptians recovered they began to fight tenaciously for every gun, but all was lost. The helicopters got away unscathed in the dark, and the Israeli armour, no longer at risk from the Egyptians' powerful Russian guns, launched a direct assault up the road and sent another column round the flank. By dawn the Umm Kataff defences had been over-run.

This attack had been mounted using elderly Sikorsky S58s with only a limited payload. The Israelis also had a small number of French-built *Super Frelons* which were used to spearhead an imaginative stroke on 8 June. The target was the Egyptian airfield at Ras el Sudr on the Gulf of Suez, about 30 miles south of Suez town. While it was still dark two *Super Frelons* took off from Tel Aviv. As dawn broke they were haring south-west at low level across Sinai, taking care to avoid detection and steering clear of all known enemy units. They had to cover over 180 miles, but reached the objective on time as two *Mirage* fighters strafed the bemused Egyptian garrison to cover the helicopters as they landed. As the first pair of fighters pulled off to refuel and rearm another pair arrived, to keep up a non-stop bombardment as the infantry, now reinforced by eight S58 loads of troops who had made the journey in two hops, worked their way into the Egyptian defences. The battle raged well into the afternoon, when an Israeli armoured column arrived to finish the defenders off.

During the fighting in Sinai, which came to an end with the capture of Ras el Sudr, Israel's other frontier to the north with Syria had been quiet. Here, for 18 years, the Syrians on the Golan Heights had overlooked the thriving *Kibbutzim* in which Jewish settlers had brought up a generation of their children under fire. On 9 June the Syrians intensified their bombardment; the Israelis, using troops hurriedly switched from the southern front to augment their Golani troops, launched a desperate frontal assault into the bald hills. Helicopters were used to land paratroops behind the Syrian front line in order to knock out their artillery. This done, and with the enemy in retreat on the historic road to Damascus, a series of helicopter raids was made to disrupt his line of march. Recoilless guns mounted on jeeps were carried under *Super Frelons* to attack Syrian vehicles which, also harried by Israeli fighter-bombers, lay abandoned by the dozen along the road. Fuel was flown up to advancing Israeli tank units and the returning helicopters brought casualties back for treatment in field surgical units.

The bold use of Israeli helicopters in the 'six-day war' of 1967 can be attributed in part to a visit which had been made by Gen. Moshe Dayan to Vietnam a year earlier. Travelling in partial disguise as a newspaper reporter he was able to watch the 1st Cavalry's airmobile operations. The imaginative handling of meagre aviation resources by the Israelis on this occasion showed how well he had passed on his experience.

In 1969 the Israelis acquired a fleet of modern helicopters in the USA. These were the well-tried UH1 and the large Sikorsky CH53 medium-lift helicopter. A number of selected pilots went to America for quick conversion courses on the new aircraft which were then shipped to Israel and reassembled. Within days the Israelis began to use the CH53s in a series of audacious raids against the Egyptian homeland in retaliation for continuing harassment across the Suez Canal, which now constituted the front line. Power lines deep inside Egypt were cut by heliborne raiding parties flown by night at extreme low level. The most outstanding operation, however, was the capture intact of a brand-new Soviet-built radar station. An air raid was mounted on a near-by military base and the two helicopters, using this to cover the noise of their approach, lifted seven tons of equipment back to Israel. It was a fine example of the bold use of the helicopter and of low-level night navigation and airmanship.

The uneasy truce which followed the 1967 conflict finally broke on 6 October 1973 when the Egyptians burst through the Suez Canal defences and surged into the Sinai while the Syrians attacked in the north. Total surprise was achieved; most Israelis were observing the solemn rituals of *Yom Kippur*, the Day of Atonement, and the border defences were thinly manned. It was clear that both Egyptians and Syrians had learned a lot from their earlier defeats. They now revealed their possession of hundreds of air-defence missiles which were used to great effect against Israeli fighter-bombers. They also used helicopters in the assault roles, the Syrians far more effectively than the Egyptians; for whilst the vital Israeli observation post atop Mount Hermon was surprised and taken by Syrian helicopter commandos in the first hours of the war, Egyptian troop-carrying helicopters attempting to raid the Israeli rear areas were easily shot down.

After initial reverses the Israelis managed to stem the enemy advances, though at grievous cost to those units such as the Golani brigade which had borne the brunt of the attack, buying time for the defenders to regain their balance. At this stage the Israeli helicopter force was used to move ammunition, fuel, supplies and troops forward to the battle zone, and for the evacuation of casualties. Despite frequent incursions by Egyptian and Syrian aircraft, no helicopters were lost. As the war entered its later stages they were used in the assault role; one costly and unsuccessful attempt had been made by the Golani Brigade on 8 October to retake the Mount Hermon position, 'the eyes and ears of the State of Israel', from which the garrison had been ejected 48 hours earlier.

As the war entered its final stages early on the morning of 22 October, with the cease-fire due to come into effect at 1900 hrs that evening, the Syrians were still installed there even though their main forces had been pitched off the Golan uplands and were streaming back once more towards Damascus. The Golani Brigade's weary infantry scaled the slopes yet again and helicopters landed paratroops to recapture the post against desperate resistance. It was in Israeli hands with only eight hours to go before the cease-fire.

In both the 'six day' and 'Yom Kippur' wars the Israelis used paratroops exclusively in the helicopter assault role. They were chosen for this because of their fitness, aggressive qualities and high standard of personal initiative, inculcated by rigorous training at the Centre for Air Mobility at Eqron, the equivalent of an airborne forces depot, airmobility training centre and parachute training school. Parachute training is not confined to male members of airborne units; all Israeli fighter pilots undergo parachute training in order to improve their chances of survival if shot down, when they are expected to walk (and if necessary fight) their way back to base. An increasing proportion of all ranks in armoured, mechanized infantry, artillery and engineer units are parachute trained even though they will never jump into battle. The women soldiers who serve as clerks, orderlies, mess-hall attendants, cooks and cipher operators are encouraged to undergo the parachute course with the men and if assigned to an airborne unit wear the red beret and parachutist badge with evident pride. Yet despite the continued existence of a number of élite parachute battalions the Israelis have not dropped them operationally since 1956. They are used instead as air-landed commandos, never more successfully than in the cutting-out expedition which rescued a planeload of mainly Israeli passengers from Entebbe in 1976.

The Israelis are not alone in retaining a parachute capability. French and Belgian paratroops were used with outstanding success in the 1960s to retrieve European civilians threatened by armed rebellions and political upheavals in ex-colonial territories in Africa. Operation 'Red Bean' was mounted in May 1978 when it was clear that the political situation in Zaire, formerly a province of the Belgian Congo, had deteriorated to the stage where the lives of Europeans were in danger. Belgian and French para-commandos were flown to the scene and although a number of Europeans had already been massacred in the mining town of Kolwezi, the majority were rescued and flown back to Europe. Here was an outstanding example of the flexibility conferred by airmobility: a long-distance strategic airlift into airfields known to be secure; tactical airlandings and parachute assaults within the theatre of operations; and the use of light helicopters, transported to the theatre as airfreight, for invaluable local reconnaissance, casualty evacuation and airborne command posts.

Existing political and economic conditions in most of the emergent states of Africa indicate instability at least to the end of the century and beyond. The old colonial powers are certain to be involved through economic interests and the need to protect expatriates. Contingency plans obviously exist for the rescue of these people in a Kinshasha-type crisis, but the speed with which an African political situation can get out of hand means that strategic and tactical airmobility is essential. The dramatic arrival of a small and determined force, as the Belgians proved in Zaire, is sufficient to defuse the most alarming situation and to bring off the rescue operation. Prompt reinforcement, if requested by the host nation, can follow. The initial step, however, must be taken without delay and requires a firm political will. The first troops to arrive should be on the spot within two or three days and it should be possible to air-land them. If it is impossible to land – either because of a known threat of armed opposition or the unserviceability of the destination airfield – the use of paratroops dropped near by is now feasible even after an approach flight of several thousand miles.

If the retention of a parachute capability is desirable on grounds of flexibility as well as retaining the services of highly motivated and aggressive troops, it is even more important that the talents of such troops are put to good use elsewhere. The threat against NATO in central Europe is clear enough; what is now required is a development of battlefield airmobility by the Western allies to meet it.

★ ★ ★

For 7000 years, since the earliest known records of warfare as described on Sumerian stone tablets, warfare was conducted at the pace of the foot soldier and the horseman, using missile weapons with ranges measured in yards and hand weapons for close-quarter fighting. Armour for the individual was developed at an early stage, but apart from advances in metallurgy the state of the art remained almost static for centuries; there is a marked similarity between the battle-dress of ancient Greece and that of Agincourt, except that iron and steel replaced copper and bronze. The really big changes in the art of warfare have come about with a rush during the past 100 years, with the development of automatic weapons, smokeless propellants, the internal combustion engine and heavier-than-air flying machines. All of these changed the face of military operations; but despite these advances in technique the principles of war remain constant. Mobility and firepower have won battles since man started to fight his rivals. By 1945 it seemed that firepower used defensively was on the verge of regaining the primacy it had held from 1915 to 1918 when the opposing armies in France and Flanders struggled to break the deadlock of barbed wire, machine gun, artillery and unbroken lines of trenches. The tank eventually appeared and, once its potential was properly used, proved to be the key to victory on land.

In the Second World War, mobility overcame firepower with the use of the *Blitzkrieg* techniques so carefully studied and rehearsed by the Germans and belatedly adopted by their opponents. Command of the air enabled the Germans and then the Allies to employ the third dimension, turning the defenders' flanks from above by the use of airborne troops. In 1945, however, the techniques developed for the delivery of troops to the battlefield by air, together with their fighting equipment, were clearly being overtaken by advances in anti-aircraft weapons. As is always the case, an innovation generates the antidote. With the development, after 1950, of improved helicopters, the aerial insertion and redeployment of combat troops became practicable once more. Initially used in counter-insurgency operations where there was little or no threat from anti-aircraft weapons, the costly experience gained by the Americans in Vietnam has led to further developments in design of the helicopter with the object of ensuring that it not only has a good chance of survival on the battlefield but can actually be used offensively. The two most significant American helicopters due to enter service in the 1980's are the Sikorsky S76 *Black Hawk* and the Hughes AH64 Advanced Attack Helicopter (AAH).

Black Hawk embodies the experience of Vietnam but also the knowledge that a utility helicopter designed to operate in the NATO theatre will be performing in an entirely different environment, where it will need to be flown almost entirely behind friendly lines and only rarely employed in a penetration role. It has been designed to replace the well-tried UH1 and will lift the basic tactical unit – the 11-man rifle squad – with its personal and crew-served weapons. Alternatively, it can lift a 105mm field gun, its crew and 50 rounds of ammunition, or a TOW anti-tank missile launcher, its crew of four and a supply of missiles. Great care has been taken in *Black Hawk's* design to ensure its survival under battle conditions. An immensely strong airframe incorporating armour is combined with two powerful engines, giving a high degree of agility and acceleration with a cruising speed in the order of 150 knots. The fuel system is heavily protected against fire, and even if the aircraft is forced down by enemy fire its strength will ensure a high chance of survival for crew and passengers.

If *Black Hawk* is to be the US Army's general-purpose battlefield aerial vehicle, AH64 will be its teeth. Designed to replace the *Hueycobra*, its primary role is to destroy tanks, complementing the more conventional defence offered by existing armoured units. The speed, agility and small size of the Advanced Attack Helicopter, together with careful design, will offer it much of the protection it needs when flown against the Warsaw Pact's known anti-aircraft resources, or when opposed by hostile attack helicopters such as *Hind* 'D'. It will be able to operate by day and night and in bad weather conditions, using electronic aids developed during and since Vietnam. The armament carried enables its crew to engage a wide variety of targets with the most appropriate weapons system: a 30mm cannon, highly effective against 'soft-skinned' and lightly armoured targets out to a range of one and a half miles; TOW anti-tank guided missiles; and up to 76 free-flight rockets for use against area targets. The two-man crew can engage two targets simultaneously, for whilst the gunner in the front seat operates the missiles, the pilot with an ingenious 'slave' gunsight fitted to his helmet, can use the cannon for suppressive fire, the chin turret traversing and elevating with the movements of his head.

Although a complex attack helicopter such as AH64 is beyond the financial resources of the rest of NATO, other nations have realized the potential of the armed helicopter. The British Army will use a two-helicopter family, with the small *Gazelle* for reconnaissance and target acquisition and the larger Westland *Lynx* utility helicopter, equipped with the TOW missile, in the anti-tank role. *Lynx* is much smaller than *Black Hawk*, and is also faster and more agile. Although it cannot lift a ten-man infantry section it can carry the infantry's anti-tank teams with their *Milan* missiles and launcher, as well as freight or underslung loads. The German Army is to fit the small but powerful Messerschmitt-Bolkow BO105M helicopter with six Euromissile HOT anti-tank missiles, and each Army corps will ultimately have a regiment of these *Panzerabwehrhubschrauber-1* (PAH1) helicopters. These will be used in conjunction with regiments of Sikorsky CH53 medium-lift helicopters carrying highly mobile light infantry equipped with crew-served anti-tank weapons. It is no coincidence that the units to be used are parachute battalions, for the Germans consider that these are eminently well suited to the type of airmobile warfare envisaged.

There can be little doubt that the days of the 'conventional' massed parachute assault against a prepared defence are over, and have been since 1945. The target offered by a formation of transport aircraft flying at 130 knots on a steady heading at less than 1000 feet is one which invites slaughter at the hands of even the semi-trained opponent armed with a heat-seeking anti-aircraft missile or multi-barrel cannon. It is also extremely difficult to time an airborne assault, as the Allied staffs found to their cost in 1944. The aircraft required – 21 *Hercules* for a battalion-sized assault – have to be set aside and are therefore not available for use elsewhere; during a period of tension leading to war in Europe, this is just the time when transport aircraft are at a premium. Once war has started, the very pace of operations – far faster than that experienced in 1944 – will make it virtually impossible to mount a parachute assault.

Outside the NATO theatre, however, or on its northern and southern flanks, there will continue to be situations when the use of a parachuted force may be the only way of forestalling a crisis. Although it is always more convenient to air-land troops, thus dispensing with the need for re-forming once on the ground, the need for a parachute landing can arise at any time, as the French and Belgians have discovered. They also found that the moral effect of a parachute delivery is tremendous and can achieve an effect with a few troops which would be unattainable by any other means. In situations calling for the minimum use of force this is an all-important consideration.

271

Periods of change have always brought argument; the over-enthusiasms of progressives clash with the innate prejudices of the con-servatives. Somewhere between lies the commonsense attitude which can make use of both extremes. It was a sad day when the last cavalry regiment trotted past and then exchanged its horses for armoured cars and tanks. At the time, hard words were said, but the spirit of the cavalry lived, to be seen at its best in the Western Desert, where regiments which had charged at Balaklava excelled in the skills of tank warfare, and in Vietnam where the us Cavalry led the way in a new type of combat. It is now the turn of the parachute troops to adapt to changing circumstances; and such is the calibre of the Parachute Regiment and the 82nd us Airborne that it is safe to say that the red beret will be around for many years to come.

Table of Equivalent Ranks

Anglo-American	German Army-Luftwaffe	Waffen-SS
Field Marshal/Marshal	Generalfeldmarschall of the Armies	Reichführer-SS
General	Generaloberst	SS-Oberstgruppenführer und Generaloberst des Waffen-SS
Lieutenant General	General der Infanterie/Flieger/Artillerie, etc.	SS-Obergruppenführer und General der Waffen-SS
Major General	Generalleutnant	SS-Gruppenführer und Generalleutnant der Waffen-SS
Brigadier/Brigadier General	Generalmajor	SS-Brigadeführer/Oberführer/Generalmajor der Waffen-SS
Colonel	Oberst	SS-Standartenführer
Lieutenant-Colonel	Oberstleutnant	SS-Obersturmbannführer
Major	Major	SS-Sturmbannführer
Captain	Hauptmann	SS-Hauptsturmführer
Lieutenant	Oberleutnant	SS-Obersturmführer
2nd Lieutenant	Leutnant	SS-Untersturmführer
Sergeant Major	Stabsfeldwebel	SS-Sturmscharführer
Sergeant	Feldwebel	SS-Oberscharführer
Corporal	Unteroffizier	SS-Unterscharführer
Private	Schutze	SS-Schutze

Select Bibliography

Anon (for Air Ministry), *Airborne Forces (The Second World War, 1939–45)*, London, Air Ministry (Air Historical Branch), 1951

Anon, *By Air To Battle: The Official History of the British 1st and 6th Airborne Divisions*, London, HMSO, 1945

Appleman, Roy E., *US Army in the Korean War: South to the Naktong, North to the Yalu (June–Nov. 1950)*, Washington D.C., Dept. of the Army, 1961

Bauer, C., *The Battle of Arnhem: The Betrayal Myth Refuted*, London, Hodder & Stoughton, 1966

Chatterton, Brig. G., *The Wings of Pegasus*, London, Macdonald, 1955

Edwards, R., *German Airborne Troops 1936–45*, London, Macdonald & Jane's, 1974

Galvin, Lt-Col. J. R., *Air Assault: The Development of Airmobile Warfare*, New York, Hawthorn Books, Inc., 1969

Gavin, Maj.-Gen. J. M., *Airborne Warfare*, Washington D.C., Combat Forces Press Inc., 1947

Gibbs-Smith, C. H., *The Aeroplane. An Historical Survey of its Origins and Development*, London, HMSO, 1960

Jacobsen, H. A. and Rohwer, J. (Editors), *Decisive Battles of World War II. The German View*, London, André Deutsch, 1965

Liddell Hart, Sir B. H., *History of the Second World War*, London, Cassell, 1970

Lorch, N., *One Long War: Arab Versus Jew Since 1920*, Jerusalem, Keter Books, 1976

Molony, C. J. C. (and others), *History of the Second World War: The Mediterranean and Middle East, Volume V*, London, HMSO, 1973

Moulton, Maj.-Gen. J. L., *The Norwegian Campaign of 1940*, London, Eyre and Spottiswoode, 1966

Newnham, Gp-Capt. M., *Prelude to Glory*, London, Sampson Low, 1952

Norton, Maj. G., *The Red Devils*, London, Leo Cooper, 1970

Otway, Lt-Col. T. B. H. (for War Office), *Airborne Forces (The Second World War 1939–45)*, London, The War Office, 1951

Playfair, I. S. O., *History of the Second World War: The Mediterranean and Middle East, Volume II*, London, HMSO, 1956

Rand Corporation, *Symposium on the Role of Airpower in Counter-insurgency and Unconventional Warfare: The Algerian War*, Washington, The Rand Corporation, 1963

Ryan, C., *A Bridge Too Far*, London, Hamish Hamilton, 1974

Saunders, H., St G., *The Red Beret*, London, Michael Joseph, 1950

Seth, R., *Lion With Blue Wings*, London, Gollancz, 1955

Shirer, W. L., *The Rise and Fall of the Third Reich*, London, Secker and Warburg, 1960

Shulman, M., *Defeat in the West*, London, Secker and Warburg, 1947

Tolson, Lt-Gen. John J., *Vietnam Studies: Airmobility 1961–71*, Washington D.C., Dept. of the Army, 1973

Tugwell, Brig. M. A. J., *Airborne to Battle: A History of Airborne Warfare 1918–71*, London, William Kimber, 1971

Tugwell, Brig. M. A. J., *Arnhem: A Case Study*, London, Thornton Cox, 1975

Verney, P., *Anzio 1944: An Unexpected Fury*, London, Batsford, 1978

Von der Heydte, Oberstleutnaut Freiherr, *Daedalus Returned: Crete, 1941*, London, Hutchinson, 1958

Weeks, J., *Airborne Equipment. A History of its Development*, Newton Abbot, London, Vancouver, David and Charles, 1976

Wilmot, C., *The Struggle for Europe*, London, Collins, 1952

Worcester, R., *Roots of British Air Policy*, London, Hodder and Stoughton, 1960

Miscellaneous Sources

OFFICIAL DOCUMENTS

1 UNITED KINGDOM

I have drawn heavily on archival material held by the Public Records Office, formerly at Chancery Lane and now installed in their concrete blockhouse out at Kew. The official reports on all British airborne operations of the Second World War are now available for inspection and are a rich and fascinating mine of information. Apart from consulting these, I found the following files of great value:

SB 15130 – Helicopters; development policy 1938–45

SB 13246 – Troop-carrying gliders and equipment. Trials, 1940–5

CS 6229 – Early parachute training

PM/381 – Training of glider pilots

9/3685 – Army/Air co-operation. Minutes of CIGS/CAS meetings

17/5586 – Formation of Airborne Division

17/5918 – Artillery observation from aircraft

AFEE/MS/19/AIR. Pts. I & II – Provision of an airborne force; Nov. 1940–Dec. 1942

AFEE/S1 38/AIR – Role and use of paratroops

2 UNITED STATES

For the German view of Second World War airborne operations, the best document for anyone lacking a good working knowledge of German is the US Department of the Army's Pamphlet 20-232, published in October 1951, entitled 'Historical Study; Airborne Operations; A German Appraisal'. The US Army (Fort Leavenworth) C & GSC file R 12198 deals at length and in detail with the experiences of the 82nd and 101st Airborne Divisions in the Normandy landing and is characteristically frank. The Report of the Army Ground Forces Board No. 3 on 'Project 1965; The R5 Helicopter', published 15 May 1946, is one of the earliest attempts to evaluate the helicopter as an Army mobility system, concluding that it '. . . has definite possibilities for military use in the realms of command, communications, supply and evacuation'. The report is also interesting as an early examination of the helicopter's vulnerability in the forward combat area.

3 ARTICLES

There is a vast literature on the subjects covered in this book. The following is a select list, drawn up in approximately chronological order, to correspond with the layout of the book:

Broke-Smith, Brig. P. W. L., 'The History of British Military Aeronautics'. The Royal Engineers Institute, Chatham. A highly readable personal account by an officer who flew Cody's man-lifting kites as well as the early observation balloons and aircraft.

Johnstone, John A., 'Remembered with Advantage'. The formation of the 2nd Parachute Battalion. An unpublished document held in File No. 105 at the Airborne Forces Museum, Aldershot.

Leigh-Mallory, Air Chief Marshal, Sir T., 'Air Operations, North West Europe, 15th November, 1943–30th September, 1944'. Published as 4th Supplement, *London Gazette* (HMSO), 31 December 1946.

FitzGerald, Lt-Col. A. D., 'Outline History of the Joint Experimental Helicopter Unit (JEHU)'. The Royal Military College of Science, Shivenham, 1977, for official use only.

Tugwell, Col. M. A., 'Arnhem. The Ten Germs of Failure'. Royal United Services Institute Journal (RUSIJ), London. December 1969.

Beaumont, R. A., 'Airborne: Life cycle of a military sub-culture'. Military Review (USA), June 1971. (Mr Beaumont also contributed an interesting article on Arnhem to this journal in January 1971.)

Rudakov, M. G., 'Thirty years of Soviet Airborne Forces'. Military Herald (USSR), reprinted in Military Review, July 1961.

Gavin, Lt-Gen. James M., 'The Mobility Differential'. *Army*, Volume 13, No. 11, June 1963.

Howze, Lt-Gen. Hamilton, 'The Howze Board'. *Army*, Volume 24, No. 2, February 1974.

Harvey, Maj. Thomas, H. jr, 'Air Cavalry in Battle – a new concept in action'. *Armor*, May–June 1968.

Poe, P., 'How's Air Mobility?'. *Army*, Volume 13, No. 11, June 1963.

Lukens, Col. H. I., 'The Heli-tactic gap'. *Army*, Volume 21, No. 8, August 1971.

Redmond, Col. de Lyle G., 'US Army – Role of helicopters in conventional warfare'. *US Army Aviation Digest*, January 1972.

Williams, Maj.-Gen. Robert R., 'US Army Aviation 1967'. An interview with *Aerospace International*, July–August 1967.

Eley, Wg-Comdr D. L., 'Helicopter Weapons Systems'. *RAF Quarterly*, Volume 7, No. 2, summer, 1962.

Varwell, Lt-Col, P. G. H., 'A helicopter assault operation in South Vietnam'. *British Army Review, 1969*.

Freeman, Gerda L. (transl.), 'Employment of Soviet airborne troops'. *Allgemeine Schweizerische Militärzeitung*, No. 11, November 1961.

Hanson, Lt-Col. Lynn, M., 'Soviet Combat Helicopter Operations'. *International Defense Review*, Volume 81, No. 8/78.

Index

A Luoi airstrip 253
'Aberdeen' 139
Aberdeen Proving Ground 208
Adair, Maj.-Gen. A. 168
Advanced Aerial Reconnaissance Vehicle
    (AARV) 260
Advanced Attack Helicopter (AAH) 208,
    272–3
A.F.E. (Airborne Forces Establishment)
    81
Aga Defile 142–3
Ainsworth, Staff-Sgt 115 et seq.
'Air Assault II' 230
AIRCRAFT:
American
    B24 *Liberator* 182
    B25 *Mitchell* 137
    B52 *Stratobomber* 236, 250, 256
    C46 *Commando* 180
    C47 *Skytrain* (*Dakota*) 89–93, 103–4,
        108, 116, 119, 121, 138–9, 140, 142
        et seq., 165–6, 196
    C82 *Packet* 183
    C119 *Packet* 183
    C123 *Provider* 227
    C130 *Hercules* 214, 249–50, 253, 274
    DHC *Beaver* 227
    DHC *Caribou* 222, 226–8, 242, 252
    DHC *Otter* 227
    L1 133
    L19 *Bird-dog* 252
    OV1 *Mohawk* 226–8
    Piper *Cub* 37, 196, 200, 219
    P51 *Mustang* 137–8
    Stinson *Vigilant* 36
British
    Auster Mk I 37–8
    Auster Mk III 38
    Auster Mk VI/VII 198–9
    Avro *Lancaster* 119
    Avro *Lincoln* 198

Armstrong Whitworth *Albemarle* 89,
    101–2, 120, 166
Armstrong Whitworth *Whitley* 76,
    79–80, 88–91
Bristol *Britannia* 214
Bristol Fighter 31
Cody biplane 26–7
D.H.9a 30
D.H. *Comet* 214
D.H. *Moth* 194
Dunne biplane 26–7
Gloster *Gladiator* 45, 60
Handley Page *Argosy* 214
Handley Page bomber 13
Handley Page *Halifax* 96–7, 101, 116
Handley Page *Hastings* 189, 190, 214
Hawker *Audax* 31, 33
Hawker *Hector* 33
Short *Stirling* 165
Taylorcraft D 35–6, 194
Vickers *Valencia* 135
Vickers *Valetta* 189, 214
Vickers *Vernon* 14
Vickers *Virginia* 31, 75
Westland *Lysander* 33, 36
French
    Mirage 268
German
    Fieseler *Storch* 148–9
    He111 108
    Ju52 19–20, 22, 43, 45–6, 48–51, 63,
        66–7, 68, 69, 81, 174
    Ju87 *Stuka* 59
    Me109 38
    Me323 108
Russian
    Ant6 15
    Bolshoi 193
Airships 27
'A.L.A.T.' 196
Albert Canal 51

278

Aldershot 24
Algerian Campaign 200–1, 212
Allied Airborne Army 152
Andrew, Lt-Col. (VC) 65–7
An Khe 232, 235
An Shau Valley 252–4
Anzio 39–40
'Army' Journal 210
ARMY OF THE REPUBLIC OF VIETNAM (ARVN) 230
    1st Corps 256
    22nd Division 236
    Airborne Division 255
    Rangers 250
Arnhem 153 et seq.
Arnold, Gen. (later Gen. of the USAF) H. H. ('Hap') 136
AUSTRALIAN ARMY
    9th Division 139
    19th Brigade 60
    217th Field Regiment RAA 139–40
    3rd Bn Royal Australian Regt 186

Baden-Powell, Maj. (Later Maj.-Gen. Lord) 25–6
Barlow, Col. 167
Barratt, Air Marshal 77
Bassenge, *Oberstleutnant* 18–19, 22
Bazeley, Capt. (later Lt-Col.) 32, 33, 34–5, 36, 37, 40, 194, 199, 211
Beaumont, Capt. 24
Bellerophon 160
Belov, Gen. 129
Billingham, Capt. 38
Binh Dinh Province 248
'*Biting*' 86–8
Bittrich, *SS Obergruppenführer und Gen. der Waffen SS*, W. 155 et seq., 171
Bols, Maj.-Gen. E. 177, 181
Bone, Staff-Sgt 120
Bong Son 236
Borneo 215
Boscombe Down 85
Bowen, Col. F. 184, 185
Brauer, *Major* (later *Generalleutnant*) 18, 67, 106
Brereton, Maj. (later Lt-Gen.) L. 13, 152, 159, 177
BRITISH ARMY
    21st Army Group 150, 158, 160, 176, 178
    1st Army 93
    2nd Army 122, 153–4, 160–1, 176, 178

8th Army 93
1st (Br) Airborne Corps 152 et seq.
VIII Corps 99
30 Corps 152 et seq.
Guards Armoured Division 153, 162, 168, 171
1st Airborne Division 82, 85, 90, 99, 108, 109, 155 et seq.
6th Airborne Division 109, 113 et seq., 176 et seq.
52nd Lowland Division (Airportable) 170
1st Airlanding Brigade 82, 83, 101, 114, 163 et seq.
1st Parachute Brigade 82, 92, 95, 103, 161, 163–4, 167
6th Airlanding Brigade 114 et seq.
3rd Parachute Brigade Group 114 et seq.
4th Parachute Brigade 164–5, 167
5th Parachute Brigade Group 114 et seq.
16th Parachute Brigade 215
14th Infantry Brigade 60
27th Commonwealth Brigade 186
Royal Artillery *passim*
Royal Engineers *passim*
3rd Hussars 70
4th Hussars 58
Grenadier Guards 167
Irish Guards 162, 167
Royal Scots Fusiliers 103
Border Regiment 102–3
South Staffordshire Regiment 102
Army Air Corps 83, 195, 205
Glider Pilot Regiment 83 et seq., 121, 177, 187, 207
Parachute Regiment 79, 83, 274; 3rd Battalion 189
Royal Army Service Corps 163, 166, 196, 202
Royal Flying Corps 27
5th Bn The Queen's Regiment 84
12th Bn The Devonshire Regiment 181 et seq.
2nd Bn The Leicestershire Regiment 63
2nd Bn Oxford and Bucks Light Infantry (43rd/52nd) 114 et seq.
1st Bn Royal Ulster Rifles 114 et seq., 181
1st Bn The Glider Pilot Regiment 86
2nd Bn The Glider Pilot Regiment 86

British Army (contd)
  1st Parachute Battalion 93, 104–5
  2nd Parachute Battalion 86, 93–5, 104, 163
  3rd Parachute Battalion 92
  7th Parachute Battalion 117
  9th Parachute Battalion 119
  12th Parachute Battalion 182
  No. 2 Commando 74, 79
  No. 11 Special Air Service Battalion 77
  153rd Gurkha Parachute Battalion 136
Brize Norton 81
'Broadway' 138–9
Brooke, Gen. Sir A. (later Field Marshal the Lord) 34
Broke-Smith, Lt (later Brigadier) 26
Browning, Maj.-Gen. (later Lt-Gen. Sir) F. 82, 91, 96, 99, 108, 151–2, 158–9, 160 et seq.
Bruneval 86–7
Bulford 85

Calabria 74, 79
Ca Lu 252
Cambodia 255 et seq.
Cambridge, HRH The Duke of 24–5
CANADIAN ARMY
  1st Canadian Parachute Battalion 181
Canea 62
Cao Lanh 227
Central Landing Establishment 77–8, 80–1
Central Landing School 75–6
Chappel, Brig. 60
Chatterton, Maj. (later Brig.) G. 84, 86, 99–100, 102, 105–6, 109, 158, 166, 177–8
'Chowringhee' 138–9
Churchill, Rt Hon. (later Sir) W. S. C. 74, 87, 88, 118
Chy Pong Mountains 233
Cierva, Juan de la 192
Cochrane, Col. P. 137–8
Cody, S. F. 26–7
'Colossus' 79–80
Corinth 58–9
Corregidor 143 et seq.
Coutelle, Capitaine J-M. J. 9, 24
Coutts, Col. 181
Cox, Flt Sgt 87
Crawford, Maj.-Gen. K. 177

Crete 59, 60–73
Crook, Lt-Col. P. 189–90
Crookenden, Maj.-Gen. (later Lt-Gen. Sir) N. 216
Cu Chi 245–7

Daly, Capt. 79
Dan Nang 218
Danford, Maj.-Gen. Robert M. 37
Dayan, Gen. Moshe 265
Deane-Drummond, Maj. (later Maj.-Gen.) A. 172
Deane, Brig.-Gen. 242
Deelen Airfield 156, 158, 161
'Desant' 260–1
Dien Bien Phu 187
Diersfordter Wald 180–1
Dietrich, *Generaloberst der Waffen SS* ('Sepp') 173–4
Diller, Lt-Col. 250, 253
Doig, Sgt 97
Dordrecht 50
Dnepr 260–1
Dnieper Loop 130–3
Driel 168
Drummond, Air Chief Marshal Sir P. 177
Dunne, Lt J. W. 26–7
DUTCH ARMED FORCES:
  Royal Netherlands Marines 48
  Royal Netherlands Grenadiers 48, 50
Dyball, Maj. (later Maj.-Gen.) A. J. 181

'Eagle Flight' 226
Eben Emael 52–6
Eichelberger, Gen. 141
Eindhoven 153 et seq.
Eisenhowever, Gen. Dwight 106, 150 et seq., 175
Elsdale, Maj. 25
Entebbe 268
Eqron 268

Falaise 41
Falkenhorst, Gen. Nikolaus von 43
'Fall Gelb' 46 et seq.
Flavell, Brig. 92
Fleurus 9, 10, 24
Fliegerzentrale 16 et seq.
Fort Benning 90, 229, 231
Fort Bragg 184, 187, 221, 231
Fort Rucker 235
Fort Sill 37

Franklin, Benjamin 9, 14
FRENCH ARMY:
9th Army 51, 55
2nd Colonial Parachute Regiment 189
'*Freshman*' 96–7
Freyberg, Maj.-Gen. (later Lord) B.
(VC) 59–61, 67–8, 71–2
Frost, Maj. (later Maj.-Gen.) J. 86–7, 93
et seq., 105, 161 et seq.

Gale, Maj.-Gen. (later Gen. Sir) R.
113–14, 151
Galpin, Staff-Sgt 102, 105
Gamil Airfield 189–90, 204
Gavin, Col. (later Lt-Gen.) James
M. 101 et seq., 121, 151, 159, 177,
209–11, 218, 220
Geisler, *Generalleutnant* 43
Gerlach, *Hauptmann* 148
GERMAN ARMY: (for Airborne units
after 1939 see '*Luftwaffe*')
Army Group Centre 130
Army Group South 130
Army Group 'A' 55
Army Group 'B' 52, 111, 113, 155,
173
Army Group 'H' 176
2nd Army 57
4th Panzer Army 127 et seq., 131
5th Panzer Army 127, 172, 174
6th SS Panzer Army 172–3
6th Army 51, 129
7th Army 172, 174
8th Army 131
18th Army 48
Afrika Korps 93
II SS Panzer Corps 155, 168
XXI Corps 43
24th Panzer Corps 133
5th Mountain Division 62, 70, 73
7th Fliegerdivision (to 1939) 19–20
9th SS Panzer Division (*Hohenstaufen*)
155 et seq.
9th Panzer Division 48
10th SS Panzer Division (*Frondsberg*)
41, 155 et seq.
10th Division 131
15th Panzergrenadier Division 98
19th Panzer Division 131, 133
21st Panzer Division 118, 125
22nd Infantry Division 21, 48, 51, 56
34th Division 131
91st Infantry Division 122, 162

112th Division 131
Herman Göring Panzer Division 98,
104
1st Parachute Regiment (to 1939) 18
2nd Infantry Regiment 17
16th Infantry Regiment 20
Graf Yorck von Wartenburg Regi-
ment 17
SS Panzer Grenadier Reserve Battalion
162
Gilles, Col. 89
GLIDERS:
German
DFS230 53–4, 78, 107, 148
Me321 (*Gigant*) 108
British
Hamilcar 78, 109, 114 et seq., 178,
181–2
Hengist 78
Horsa 78, 89, 96–7, 99 et seq., 109–10,
114 et seq., 178, 181–2
Hotspur 78
American
Waco CG4 (*Hadrian*) 89, 99, 102,
137, 178, 181
'Go-Go Bird' 239, 243
Golan Heights 264, 266
Gondrée, M. 115, 117
Göring, *Reichsmarschall*, H. 17–18
Grabner, *SS Hauptsturmfuhrer* 161
Grant, Flt-Lt 102
Grave 156 et seq.
Green, Lt-Col. 186
Greek Army: 2nd Army 58
Grover, Lt 24
Guidoni, Gen. 14
Gurkhas 136
Guzzoni, Gen. 99

Hackett, Brig. (later Gen. Sir) J. 164 et
seq., 171–2
Hafner, Mr Raoul 77
Hamminkeln 180
Hanoi 218
Hargest, Brig. 70
Harmel, *SS Gruppenfuhrer und
Generalmajor der Waffen SS* 155 et
seq.
Harper's Magazine 209
Harris, Air Chief Marshal (later Marshal
of the RAF) Sir A. 15, 88–9
Hartenstein Hotel 167
Harvey, Gp-Capt. 77

Harzer, *SS Obersturmbannfuhrer*, W. 155 et seq.

HELICOPTERS

American

Bell XH40 213
Bell UH1, (*Iroquois*) 213, 222, 229, 242, 269
Bell *Hueycobra* 244–6, 257
Boeing-Vertol CH47 (*Chinook*) 217, 229, 232, 233, 236–8, 241, 255
Hughes AH64 272–3
Piasecki CH21 200, 212, 218, 221–3
Sikorsky VS300 193
Sikorsky R4 (*Hoverfly* I) 137, 193
Sikorsky R5 207
Sikorsky R6 (*Hoverfly* II) 193–4
Sikorsky S51 (*Dragonfly*) 196, 201
Sikorsky S55 196, 201, 203
Sikorsky CH34 200
Sikorsky CH53 269, 271
Sikorsky CH54 (*Skycrane*) 241
Sikorsky S76 (*Blackhawk*) 270

British

Bristol *Sycamore* 201, 203–4
Bristol *Belvedere* 216–17
Saunders-Roe *Skeeter* 213
Westland *Whirlwind* 202–5, 213
Westland *Scout* 216, 263
Westland *Wessex* 216–17
Westland-Aerospatiale *Lynx* 271

French

Alouette 2 212–13, 262
Aerospatiale-Westland *Gazelle* 271
Super Frelon 265

German

BO105M 271
Fa61 193
Fa223 193

Russian

Hind 264
Hook 261
Hound 261

Helicopter armaments 207–8, 222 et seq., 229, 239, 243–4, 258–9, 270
'Helltank' 264
Henderson, Brig.-Gen. 29
Herakleion 62 et seq.
Heydte, *Oberstleutnant* Freiherr von der 62–3, 68 et seq., 149, 173–4
Heveadorp ferry 168
Hicks, Brig. P. 101–2, 163 et seq.
Hill, Lt-Col. (later Brig.) 93, 105, 114

Hitler, Adolf 17–18, 21–3, 73, 129, 131, 146–8, 150 et seq., 172
Ho Chi Minh 187, 218, 249
Hopkinson, Maj.-Gen. 99–100
Horrocks, Lt-Gen. Sir B., 151
Howard, Maj. J. 114 et seq.
Howze, Lt-Gen. Hamilton 219 et seq.
Hue 249
Hurn airfield 115

Independent Air Force 28
Itagaki, Capt. 143–5
Israel 264

'JATE' (Joint Air Transport Establishment) 81
'JEHU' (Joint Experimental Helicopter Unit) 201 et seq., 212
Johnson, Gen. Harold K. 231
Johnson, President Lyndon B. 235
Jones, Col. George M. 140, 143–5
'*Junction City*' 242

Kanev 131–2
Katwijk 50
Kearns, Sqn Ldr D. C. L. 203
Kennedy, President J. F. 218
Kenney, Capt. (later Gen.) George C. 15, 140
Kerr, Staff-Sgt 120
Khe Sanh 249–52
Kimpo Airfield 185
Kim Sonh Valley 236–7
Kindersley, Brig. the Hon H. 114
Kinnaird, Brig.-Gen. (later Maj.-Gen.) H. 228–31, 232 et seq.
Kinsler, Col. 139
Kippenberger, Col. (later Maj.-Gen.) 63–70
Koch, *Hauptmann* 63–4
Kolwezi 270
'*Kondor*' 173–6
Konrad, *Generalmajor* 62
Krafft, *SS Sturmbannführer* 162
Küchler, *Gen.* Georg von 48
Küssin, *Generalmajor* 162

Lackey, Col. J. 144
'*Ladbrooke*' 99 et seq.
Lae 139
Laos 256–7
'*Lamson 719*' 257
Larkhill 32, 35, 84, 194

Lathbury, Brig. (later Gen. Sir) G. 103 et seq., 164
Leigh-Mallory, Air Chief Marshal Sir T. 113
Le May, Gen. Curtis 222
Lentaigne, Brig. J. 139
Leyte 134
Liddell Hart, Capt. (later Sir) B. 31
List, *Feldmarschall* W. 58
Lohr, *Generaloberst* A. 61
Lord, Flt Lt (VC) 166
Los Baños 146–7
Lowe, Thaddeus 24
Lucas, Lt-Gen. 39
LUFTWAFFE (including all German Airborne Forces from 1939–45)
  4 *Luftflotte* 61
  10 *Luftflotte* 43
  1st Parachute Army 149, 154, 159, 162, 176
  VIII *Fliegerkorps* 61
  X *Fliegerkorps* 61
  XI *Fliegerkorps* 55–6, 58, 61, 67, 73, 149
  1st Parachute Division 104
  7 *Fliegerdivision* 19 et seq., 48, 56, 62, 72
  XI *Fliegerkommando* 62
  1st Parachute Regiment 45, 50, 71
  2nd Parachute Regiment 48, 58
  3rd Parachute Regiment 62–3, 70, 72
  4th Parachute Regiment 104
  6th Parachute Regiment 173
  Hermann Göring Battalion 20
  Kampfgruppe von der Heydte 174–5
Lynch, Brig.-Gen. 237

MacArthur, Gen. of the Army D. 139–46, 184, 186
McAuliffe, Brig.-Gen. A. 175
Mackay, Capt. (later Maj.-Gen.) E. 171
McNair, Gen. 107
McNamara, Secretary 220
Maleme 62 et seq.
Malayan Emergency 1948–60 196 et seq., 215
Manila 141–2
Mang Yeng Pass 219
'*Market Garden*' 152–72, 173
Martel, Lt-Col. (later Lt-Gen. Sir) G. 16
Marshall, Gen. 112
Massey, Maj.-Gen. 34

Meindl, *Generalmajor* 62, 65
Mekong Delta 225, 235
Menado 134
Merville Battery 113, 119 et seq.
Milan 263
Mildenhall 31, 80, 84
Miley, Maj.-Gen. W. 177
Mitchell, Col. (later Brig.-Gen.) W. 13–14
Mitla Pass 188
Model, *Generalfeldmarschall* W. 155 et seq., 173
Monsan-Ni 187
Montgomery, Field-Marshal the Viscount 42, 100, 104, 150, 177–8
Moore, Lt-Col. (later Brig.-Gen.) H. 233, 236
Mountbatten, Capt. Lord Louis (later Admiral of the Fleet Earl Mountbatten of Burma) 70–1, 87
Mount Hermon 267

Nadzab 139–40, 141
Nasser, Gamal A. 188
Netheravon 82, 84
New Guinea 139
Newton, Capt. 38
NEW ZEALAND ARMY:
  New Zealand Division 60 et seq.
  5th Brigade 70
  10th Brigade 63, 70
  20th Infantry Battalion 68–9
  21st, 22nd, 23rd Infantry Battalions 65 et seq.
  29th (Maori) Infantry Battalion 68–9
  Divisional Cavalry 63
Nijmegen 156 et seq., 176
Noemfoor 140–1
Norman, Wg-Comdr Sir Nigel, Bt 77, 88, 96
NORTH KOREAN ARMY
  239th Regiment 185–6
NORTH VIETNAMESE ARMY (NVA)
  3rd Division 236, 242
  22nd Division 236
  2nd Regiment 236
  18th Regiment 236
  36th Regiment 236
  66th Regiment 233

Ockenburg 49
Old, Lt-Gen. William 138

Old Sarum 30, 34–5
Oosterbeek 155, 167, 169
Opa-Ri 186–7
Osoaviakhim 15
Otway, Lt-Col. 119 et seq.
Oud Keent airfield 170–1
Overlord 109 et seq.

Palembang 134
Parham, Capt. (later Maj.-Gen.) 31, 193–4
Patterson, 2nd Lt 80
Patton, Gen. George C. 150, 152, 154, 208
Paulus, Gen. (later *Feldmarschall*) F. 129
Pearson, Lt-Col. (later Col.) A. 104–5
Pegasus 160
Pershing, Gen. 13–14
PIAT 117
'Piccadilly' 138–9
Picchi, Signor 80
Pickard, Wg-Comdr 87
Pine-Coffin, Lt-Col. 92
Plei Mei 232
Pleiku 219, 233
'Plunder' 177
Poett, Brig. (later Gen. Sir) N. 118
POLISH ARMY
    1st Parachute Brigade 156, 165, 168–9
Poltava 131
Ponte Grande 102 et seq.
Portal, Marshal of the RAF Lord 88–9
Port Fuad 190
Port Moresby 139
Port Said 188–91, 192, 202–5
Primasole Bridge 103 et seq.
Pritchard, Maj. 79
Puttick, Brig. 60, 68
Pyongyang 185–6

Quang Tri 249
Quilter, Mr R. 76
Qui Nhon 219, 232

Radfan 215–17
Raff, Lt-Col. (later Col.) Edson D. 91–3, 180–1
Ras El Sudr 266
'Red Bean' 268
Reitsch, Hanna 53, 62, 108, 193
Remagen 176
Renkum Heath 162, 169

REPUBLIC OF KOREA ARMY
    (ROKA) – Capitol Division 236
Retimo 62
Richtofen, *General der Flieger* 61
Ridgway, Maj.-Gen. (later Gen.) Matthew B. 114, 121, 151, 176–8, 187
Ringel, *Generalleutnant* 62–3, 70–1
Ringler, Lt 146–7
Ringway 75, 79, 80–1, 83
Roberts, Field-Marshal Earl (VC) 27
Rock, Maj. (later Lt-Col.) J. 75–6, 78, 81, 85–6
Roermond 176
Rogers Board 214
Rommel, *Feldmarschall* E. 98, 111, 113
'Rommelspargel' 113,115–16,118,120,123
Roosevelt, President Franklin D. 88
Rotterdam 47, 50–1
ROYAL AIR FORCE:
    Independent Air Force 13
    2nd Tactical Air Force 158, 178
    Far East Air Force 196
    Bomber Command 15, 88, 119, 178
    Coastal Command 159, 178
    38 Group 109, 152 et seq., 178 et seq.
    46 Group 109, 152 et seq., 178 et seq.
    83 Group 158, 170–1
    38 Wing 88, 101
    1 Parachute Training School 78
    1 Glider Training School 82
    No. 1 Squadron 84
    No. 45 Squadron 15
    No. 651 Air OP Squadron 36
    No. 655 Air OP Squadron 39–40
    No. 656 Air OP Squadron 42, 205
    'D' Flight 34–5, 36
ROYAL MARINES:
    3rd Commando Brigade 203
    45 Commando 202
ROYAL NAVY – HM Ships:
    Barham 70
    Fiji 70
    Formidable 71
    Gloucester 70
    Greyhound 70
    Kashmir 71
    Kelly 70
    Ocean 202
    Theseus 202
    York 71
    848 Helicopter Squadron 203
    Royal Naval Air Service 28

Runstedt, *Feldmarschall* Gerd von 55, 111, 151

RUSSIAN ARMY:
4th Army 133
10th Army 127
33rd Army 127–9
1st Guards Cavalry Corps 129
4th Airborne Corps 128–9
5th Airborne Corps 127
1st Parachute Brigade 131
3rd Parachute Brigade 132
5th Guards Parachute Brigade 131–4

'*Sagebrush*' 208
Saigon 218, 227, 249, 254
Sainte Mère Église 121–2
'*Sally Rand*' 208
Salvatore parachute 14
Sayer, Rear-Adm. 202
Schneider Trophy 34
Scott, Lt-Col. J. F. T. 202–3
'*Seelowe*' 56
Senger und Etterlin, *Generalleutnant* von 99, 102
Seoul 184–5, 187
Sheppard, Col. C. 219–20
Shoemaker, Brig.-Gen. 255
Sikorsky, Igor 193, 195
Skorzeny, Otto 148–9
Slim, Gen. (later Field-Marshal the Viscount) W. 138
Song Re Valley 242–3
Soule, Col. 146
Sosabowski, Maj.-Gen. S. 156, 168–9
South Arabia 215
Speer, A. 151
Sponeck, *General der Flieger* Graf von 48, 50
SS-11 263
Strathdee, Staff-Sgt 97
Student, Hauptmann (later General der Flieger), K. 16 et seq., 56, 58, 61–2, 67–8, 72, 73, 104, 148–9, 154, 159, 162, 172
Sturm, *Oberst* 58–9
Sturmabteilung (SA) 18–20
  Feldhernhalle Regiment 19
Suez Canal 188 et seq., 266
Sukchon 185–6
Sunchon 185
Sussman, *Generalmajor* (later *Generalleutnant*) 43, 62–3, 65

Swing, Maj.-Gen. Joseph W. 106–7, 135, 141–2, 145
Sykes, Maj. (later Maj.-Gen.) 29

Tagaytay 141–2
Tailyour, Lt-Col. (later Lt-Gen.) 204
Tait, Wg-Comdr 79
Taylor, Maj.-Gen. (later Gen.) Maxwell D. 121, 152, 159, 174, 218
Tay Ninh 241
Tchepone 257
Tedder, Air Chief Marshal (later Marshal of the RAF Lord) 121, 178
Tel Aviv 265
Tet Offensive 248–50, 254
'*Thursday*' 136–9
Tidworth 85
Tilshead 84–6
Timor 135
Tolevano, Capt. (later Col.) 265
Tolson, Lt-Col. (later Lt-Gen.) J. 140, 144, 209, 242 et seq., 250 et seq.
'*Torch*' 90 et seq.
Tra My 228
Trenchard, Maj.-Gen. (later Marshal of the RAF Lord) H. 28, 29–30
Trudeau, Lt-Gen. A. 213
Truman, President Harry S. 186
Tukachevsky, Marshal M. 126
Tushino airport 206, 260

Umm Kataff 265

UNITED STATES ARMY:
US 1st Army (1918) 13
US 1st Army (1944) 122, 150, 175
US 3rd Army 150, 154
US 7th Army 150
US 8th Army 141–2
US 9th Army 176–8
'US Army Vietnam' 234
XVIII US Airborne Corps 152, 176 et seq., 221
1st Cavalry Division 142, 209
1st Cavalry Division (Airmobile) 231, 232 et seq.
1st Armored Division 91–2
1st Infantry Division 241
2nd Infantry Division 230
11th Airborne Division 107, 135, 141–6, 228
11th Air Assault Division 228–31, 239, 255

United States Army (contd)
  17th Airborne Division 177 et seq.
  25th Infantry Division 241, 245
  38th Infantry Division 142
  82nd Airborne Division 90, 99, 109, 113 et seq., 155 et seq., 177, 274
  101st Airborne Division 90, 109, 113 et seq., 155 et seq., 175, 214, 218, 229, 249, 252, 254, 257
  101st Airmobile Division 235, 252, 254,
  2nd Air Cavalry Brigade 237, 251 et seq.
  3rd Air Cavalry Brigade 236, 251 et seq.
  1st Aviation Brigade 239, 245
  10th Air Transport Brigade 228
  173rd Airborne Brigade 241
  7th Cavalry Regiment 233, 236, 251
  8th Cavalry Regiment 243
  9th Cavalry Regiment 251
  11th Armored Cavalry Regiment 241
  12th Cavalry Regiment 236
  187th Airborne Regimental Combat Team 184-7
  9th Infantry Regiment 246
  34th Infantry Regiment 143, 145
  187th Glider Infantry Regiment 142
  188th Glider Infantry Regiment 142, 146
  187th Parachute Infantry Regiment 135
  501st Parachute Infantry Regiment 159
  502nd Parachute Infantry Regiment 159
  503rd Parachute Infantry Regiment 90-2, 139, 141-5, 241
  504th Parachute Infantry Regiment 103, 167
  505th Parachute Infantry Regiment 101-2
  506th Parachute Infantry Regiment 159
  513th Parachute Infantry Regiment 181
  501st Parachute Battalion 90
  509th Parachute Battalion 92
  101st Combat Aviation Battalion 214
United States Army Aviation School (see also Fort Rucker) 211, 235
United States Army Air Force (USAAF):
  8th USAAF 178
  IX Troop Carrier Command 109, 152, 178
  317th Troop Carrier Group 144
  52nd Troop Carrier Wing 101, 104
  No. 1 Air Commando 136, 193

United States Air Force (USAF) 195, 197, 207, 222
United States Marine Corps 195, 207, 218, 235, 249 et seq., 257
Upavon 84
Urquhart, Maj.-Gen. F. 158 et seq.

Valkenburg 49-50
Vance, Cyrus 222
Vanderpool, Col. J. 211-12
'*Varsity*' 178-82
Vasey, Brig. 60
Vickers Machine Gun 212-13
Vietcong 218 et seq.
Vietnam Campaign 218 et seq.
Vo Nguyen Giap, Gen. 187
'Vortex Ring' 194
Vught 154, 162
Vyazma 127 et seq.

'*Waffenhalter*' 81
Wagner, *Hauptmann* 45-6
Wallwork, Staff-Sgt 115 et seq.
Walker, Gen. Sir Walter 215
Warminster 213
Warrack, Col. 172
Warren, Gen. Sir Charles 25
Wavell, Maj.-Gen. (later Field-Marshal Lord) A. 16, 23, 61, 66-7
Weichs, *Generaloberst* Maximilian von 57
Wells, Lt-Col. Tom 83
Wesel 176, 178-9, 180
'*Weserübung*' 43 et seq.
Western Aden Protectorate 215
Westmoreland, Gen. 239, 249
Weston, Maj.-Gen. 60
Wilson, Capt. 194
Wingate, Maj.-Gen. Orde 136-9
Winkelman, *Luitenant-Generaal* H. G. 48
Withers, Lt 102-3
Witzig, *Leutnant* (later *Major*) 54, 147
Woods, Gen. Sir Evelyn 25
Woolwich 24
Wright Field 14

Ypenburg 49-50

Zaire 268
Zitadelle 129
ZSU23-4 263